# DREADNOUGHT GUNNERY
# AND THE BATTLE OF JUTLAND

In 1913, the Admiralty rejected Arthur Pollen's Argo system for the Dreyer fire control tables. Many naval historians now believe that, consequently, British dreadnoughts were fitted with a system that, despite being partly plagiarised from Pollen's, was inferior, and that the Dreyer Tables were a contributory cause in the sinking of *Indefatigable* and *Queen Mary* at Jutland. This book provides new and revisionist accounts of the Dreyer/ Pollen controversy, and of gunnery at Jutland. In fire control, as with other technologies, the Royal Navy had been open, though not uncritically, to innovations. The Dreyer Tables were better suited to action conditions (particularly those at Jutland). Beatty's losses were the result mainly of deficient tactics and training; his battlecruisers would have been even more disadvantaged had they been equipped by Argo. After a foreword by Professor Andrew Lambert, the book reviews critically recent studies of fire control, and describes the essentials of naval gunnery in the dreadnought era. It follows the development of the Pollen and Dreyer systems, refutes the charges of plagiarism and explains Argo's rejection. It outlines the German fire control system, and uses contemporary sources in a critical reassessment of Beatty's tactics throughout the Battle of Jutland.

**John Brooks** read Natural and Electrical Sciences at St John's College, Cambridge before working in computing and telecommunications. He has published historical articles on circular dividing engines and, particularly, on naval fire control. Now retired from industry, he received his doctorate in 2001 from King's College London; this book was developed from his thesis.

# CASS SERIES:
# NAVAL POLICY AND HISTORY
## Series Editor: Geoffrey Till

This series consists primarily of original manuscripts by research scholars in the general area of naval policy and history, without national or chronological limitations. It will from time to time also include collections of important articles as well as reprints of classic works.

# DREADNOUGHT GUNNERY AND THE BATTLE OF JUTLAND

## The question of fire control

### *John Brooks*

with a foreword by
*Professor Andrew Lambert*

Routledge
Taylor & Francis Group

LONDON AND NEW YORK

First published 2005
by Routledge
2 Park Square, Milton Park, Abingdon, Oxon OX14 4RN

Simultaneously published in the USA and Canada
by Routledge
270 Madison Ave, New York, NY 10016

*Routledge is an imprint of the Taylor & Francis Group*

Transferred to Digital Printing 2006

© 2005 John Brooks

Typeset in Times by
Book Now Ltd

The publisher makes no representation, express or implied, with regard to
the accuracy of the information contained in this book and cannot accept any
legal responsibility or liability for any errors or omissions that may be made.

*British Library Cataloguing in Publication Data*
A catalogue record for this book is available from the British Library

*Library of Congress Cataloging in Publication Data*
A catalog record for this book has been requested

ISBN10: 0–714–65702–6 (hbk)
ISBN10: 0–415–40788–5 (pbk)

ISBN13: 978–0–714–65702–8 (hbk)
ISBN13: 978–0–415–40788–5 (pbk)

*This book is for Anne,*
*with my love and thanks*

# CONTENTS

# ILLUSTRATIONS

## Figures

Figures 2.2, 4.1, 4.2, 4.3 and 5.3 are reproduced with the permission of the Admiralty Historical Library, Figures 5.1 and 5.2 with the permission of The National Archive (Public Record Office).

## Tables

# FOREWORD

For much of the twentieth century there was an unquestioned acceptance of the argument that navies in general, and the Royal Navy in particular, were hostile to new technologies and opposed successive innovations in weapons, propulsion systems and other aspects of naval affairs. Such assumptions had their origins in the mid-Victorian deification of the engineer as hero, a trend reinforced by dissatisfaction with the Royal Navy's performance in the First World War. The connection between these ideas was easily made; the Royal Navy had failed because it had resisted new technology.

After the Second World War historians sought to explain Britain's loss of empire and naval mastery. Economic explanations based on the relative decline of industrial production, lack of innovation and the failings of educational and social systems were developed. By the mid-1970s a clear 'declinist' line had emerged, which used aspects of the technological obscurantism line to sustain the argument. Britain lost power because she failed to innovate, and her main strategic instrument, the Royal Navy, was as guilty in this regard as the rest of the state.

However, this argument had serious problems, and with the shift in the perception of British fortunes from the late 1970s new questions were being asked. The most significant school of thought on these issues emerged in the Department of War Studies, at King's College London, where Professor Bryan Ranft worked with a group of talented students, including the editor of this series, to challenge these assumptions. In the key text of 1977 *Technical Change and British Naval Policy, 1860–1939* Ranft and some of his students demonstrated how closer study of the issues revealed that the Royal Navy had taken a much more intelligent approach to the question of new technology. In 1989 Professor Jon T. Sumida opened a major new line of argument with his book *In Defence of Naval Supremacy: Finance, Technology and British Naval Policy 1889–1914*. In the process of demonstrating how Admiral Fisher had adopted a radical new strategy to square the circle of rising naval costs and limited national budgets, Sumida examined the new fire control system pioneered by Arthur Pollen, extensively tested by the pre-1914 Royal Navy, and ultimately rejected. Not only did Sumida's book employ new questions and new evidence, but also it opened a new issue for naval history, the technology of the mechanical computer.

Among those to be intrigued by this new subject was computer engineer John Brooks, who decided to pursue the subject further. His understanding of computing and mathematics provided a critical base from which to re-examine the Admiralty's handling of the fire control question, and reconsider Sumida's judgement on the relative merits of the systems developed by Pollen and his naval rival Captain Frederic Dreyer. The scope of his research, which initially led to a successful doctoral dissertation at King's College London, has been broadened for this book. While the core of the book concerns the competitive development of these two fire control systems, the conclusions add a new dimension to the debate on British technological and industrial innovation in the early twentieth century. If Britain was in decline, and her industries backward, there is no evidence to support conclusions in the naval sector.

By placing the fire control question in the wider context of contemporary naval gunnery developments, John Brooks has been able to assess the relative merits of the Pollen and Dreyer systems, both as mechanisms and as solutions to the problem of long-range fire control. The proof of the pudding lies, as ever, in the eating, and here a fresh examination of Jutland, the most contentious naval action of all, shows how the failure to integrate tactics with the capabilities of the new systems led to catastrophic failures in the opening battlecruiser action. The examination of gunnery records opens a new and very revealing window onto the performance of Admiral Beatty during the climactic afternoon of his career.

Ultimately this book demonstrates how a thorough technical analysis of specific equipment can illuminate both the wider field of naval history, and the history of technology and industry. Historians of navies need to understand the technologies that they use, and the complex agendas that underlay innovation and industry before reaching judgements of the competence of those making the decisions. If John Brooks' book causes readers to take a more favourable view of the pre-1914 Admiralty policy-makers, and question old assumptions, he has placed us all in his debt. History is a debate without end; this important book has added a new voice, and new arguments to a subject of critical importance for all naval historians.

Andrew Lambert
Laughton Professor of Naval History
King's College London

# PREFACE

It is a great pleasure to begin by thanking the many naval historians who, since 1992, have so generously shared their knowledge and expertise with me, a relative latecomer to the field. Also, with sincere apologies to anyone whom I have inadvertently omitted, I must express my gratitude to all who have provided me with comments and advice, and with references and copies, including their own published and unpublished works; they are John Abbatiello, Keith Allen, John Bradley, David Brown, Chris Carlson, John Covington, Kent Crawford, Iain McCallum, Anita McConnell, Steve McLaughlin, Fred Milford, Philip Pugh, John Roberts, Bill Schleihauf, Michael Simpson, Andrew Smith and Sebastien Soubiran. Particular contributions to this book are further acknowledged in the Notes.

My thanks are also due to Ron Bristow for guiding me through the archive of Elliott Brothers (now in the care of the Museum of the History of Science, Oxford); to Gloria Clifton for showing me the Compass Collection of the National Maritime Museum; to Jenny Wraight of the Admiralty Historical Library and to Lt. Com. Brian Witts of the *Excellent* Museum for their help during my visits to their libraries; and to Malcolm Llewellyn-Jones and Peter Greatrex for their assistance with my illustrations.

I remain very grateful to the late Commander Michael Craig Waller for the opportunity to study his father's papers, and to the late Commander Christopher Dreyer for his comments on my thesis chapter on the Dreyer Tables, and for his help with biographical details of his uncle's naval career.

It has been my good fortune to receive advice on line-of-bearing manoeuvres (see Chapter 8) from Captain Peter Grindal, and on many aspects of naval engineering from Captain David Garstin; the latter also commented most helpfully on the draft of Chapter 2, as did Andrew Waldrum. Ruddock Mackay kindly provided a valued critique of the draft of Chapter 1, as well as the suggestion that led to my title. John Horne showed me how to interpret the Argo Company accounts. I alone am to blame for any errors that remain in this book, which found its publisher thanks to the good advice of Andrew Gordon.

I must also gratefully acknowledge three historians whose influence on my work has been especially strong. The first is Jon Sumida, whose seminal publications inspired my own interest in naval fire control. When I began my research, Professor Sumida, with true scholarly generosity, provided me with copies of many vital sources (as will be apparent from the individual citations), with good advice and with valued criticism of my early papers. I am particularly grateful for the reference and comments which put my attempt to analyse slippage errors in Vickers clocks and similar mechanisms on the right track – see Chapter 3.

Second, Andrew Lambert showed me that, to reach a judgement on developments in fire control, it was necessary to appreciate how successfully the Royal Navy had exploited much new technology in the period from the introduction of steam propulsion to construction of the Grand Fleet. Third, David Edgerton made me aware of the importance of armaments to the wider histories of industry and technology in Britain after 1870.

Lastly, I must also thank Andrew Lambert for his patience and forbearance while supervising my long-running thesis, and for kindly providing the Foreword to this book.

Harpenden, Hertfordshire

## On the notes

All sources are cited in the Notes. After their first, full citation, the most frequently used sources are referred to by the abbreviations listed at the start of the Selected Bibliography. The bibliography also lists important manuscript collections and published sources.

Within the Notes for a single chapter, repeated references to the same source are by a short title. The *first* appearance of a short title is followed, in square brackets, by the number of the earlier note in that chapter that contains the fuller reference. In some cases, this fuller reference may itself be the shortened title of a published source listed in the bibliography; these references are identified by [B] after the title.

# 1

# OLD CONTROVERSIES, NEW HISTORIES

On 2 October 1905, Portsmouth Dockyard laid the keel of the first all-big-gun battleship, HMS *Dreadnought*. She was completed in an astonishingly short time and, on 5 January 1907, sailed on her first, experimental cruise. Her construction marked the beginning of the era named after her, in which the world's navies, those of Britain and Germany in particular, vied to re-equip themselves with capital ships armed with many heavy guns of a single calibre. *Dreadnought* herself had ten 12-inch guns; she was also the first large warship to be fitted with turbine propulsion, which gave her a speed of 21 knots, three knots faster than most battleships in the British Fleet.[1]

Between 1906 and 1908, the Royal Navy also constructed (though at a less frenetic pace) three large armoured cruisers that were even more radical. The eight 12-inch guns mounted on each of the *Invincible* class were of battleship calibre and their speed, again obtained from turbines, was an unprecedented 25 knots; yet their armour protection (a 6-inch belt and 7-inch barbettes) was no better than previous armoured cruisers. These ships, the first of the type later called battlecruisers, were built at the insistence of Admiral Sir John Fisher, First Sea Lord from October 1904, whose belief (if not always consistently expressed) was that they could combine in one hull the qualities needed to fight both armoured cruisers and battleships.[2] His brief to the 1905 Committee on Designs declared that the new type would render all other armoured cruisers obsolete, and that:

Indeed, the Armoured Cruisers are Battleships in disguise.

The committee itself concluded that their strong broadside fire '*makes the Armoured Cruisers all the more qualified to lie in the line of battle if required to do so*' [original italics].[3]

Whether or not this claim was justified, even in 1905, it was certain that, until other countries also built dreadnoughts, any opponents of the new British ships would have fewer heavy guns, but more of lesser calibre that were capable of higher maximum rates of fire. However, the greater speeds of the dreadnought battleships and battlecruisers allowed them to dictate

1

the range of battle; thus they could choose the long range at which their heavy guns were more accurate and at which lighter guns were less able to develop their full firing rate. But this tactic depended on their being provided with fire control that enabled them to hit frequently at long range. *Dreadnought* herself was equipped with a basic set of instruments; subsequently, two more elaborate fire control systems were developed in Britain, one by a civilian inventor called Arthur Pollen, the other from proposals put forward by a serving gunnery officer, Frederic Dreyer. Eventually, the Admiralty chose the Dreyer Tables rather than Pollen's Argo system, though the decision was disputed, both in public and within the naval establishment. This book is a new study of these old controversies, of the consequences of the Admiralty's choice in the battles of the First World War, and of the interpretations of these matters in recent naval histories.[4]

The development of long-range fire control at sea took place in the period of growing naval rivalry between Britain and Imperial Germany. Since her first Naval Law of 1898 Imperial Germany had been steadily building up her own battlefleet; from 1900 onwards, she laid down in each year two battleships and one armoured cruiser. Once details of *Dreadnought* became known, the start of construction of the battleships of the 1906 programme was delayed while they were redesigned to mount twelve 11-inch guns. Despite the late start, the tempo of completions was maintained, *Nassau* and *Westfalen* being commissioned in the autumn of 1909. In the first half of that year, the three ships of the *Bellerophon* class had joined the British Fleet; thus, albeit temporarily, the British lead in dreadnought battleships had been cut to two. In 1908, Germany had laid down her first dreadnought battlecruiser, the *Von der Tann* of the 1907 programme – though it was to be some years before it was learned that her armour protection was, to within a fraction of an inch, equal to that of contemporary British battleships. Furthermore, in the same year, Germany resolved to lay down annually three battleships and one battlecruiser under the programmes for 1908 to 1911.[5] Thus, by forcing the technological pace, Fisher had started a new shipbuilding race; whereas Britain's lead in pre-dreadnoughts was unassailable, Germany could hope to build a fleet of dreadnoughts that in size was not much smaller than Britain's, and in quality might even be better. By the end of 1908, the strength of the German challenge was clearly apparent in Britain, further aggravating the tensions and rivalries between the two powers. The response, goaded by the agitation that 'We want eight, and we won't wait', was dramatic. Powers were taken to build no fewer than eight ships (six battleships and two battlecruisers) under the estimates for 1909–10. Furthermore, all but the first two battleships were to have 13.5-inch guns, while the two *Lion*-class battlecruisers were given improved protection and a yet higher speed of 28 knots. Though falling behind, Germany stayed in the race until 1911 but, by 1912, was obliged to allocate ever more of her increasing military expenditure to the Army. In contrast, Britain's rate of construction increased further.[6] At the outbreak of the First World War, the dreadnoughts in service with the German Navy numbered thirteen battleships and four battlecruisers; the Royal Navy had twenty battleships and nine battlecruisers. But even these numbers understate the extent to which Britain outbuilt Germany. A better indication is obtained from the situation on the eve of the Battle of Jutland. British yards had then supplied the Royal Navy with no fewer than forty-three dreadnought battleships and ten battlecruisers. Germany had completed only seventeen battleships and six battlecruisers.[7]

Despite its superiority in numbers, the Royal Navy recognised the Imperial German Navy as a worthy and dangerous opponent. Britain's wartime strategy was to enforce a distant blockade of Germany, by means of the Battle Cruiser Fleet based at Rosyth, and the Grand Fleet in Scapa Flow and the Moray Firth. With Germany's High Seas Fleet secure in its bases in the Heligoland Bight, the North Sea became a 'no-man's ocean', though one in which the Germans hoped to reduce British numerical superiority by torpedo attacks and mining, and by attempting to lure isolated British squadrons within reach of their full battlefleet.[8] Eventually, on 31 May 1916, off Jutland, an initial action between the opposing battlecruisers developed into a confused and indecisive encounter between the two fleets. The outcome was a profound disappointment for the Royal Navy, which lost many more ships and men. But, despite its tactical successes, it was the High Seas Fleet that, at dawn on 1 June, withdrew to its bases. Strategically, nothing had changed. In terms of cold numbers, the loss of three battlecruisers barely dented Britain's numerical predominance, whereas Germany could ill afford to lose her latest battlecruiser.[9]

The opening action at Jutland, between the German battlecruisers and a British force of battlecruisers and fast battleships under the command of Vice Admiral Sir David Beatty, is now known as the Run to the South. Despite its restrained language, the initial assessment of the British Commander-in-Chief (C.-in-C.), Admiral Sir John Jellicoe, was gravely critical.

> The disturbing feature of the battle-cruiser action is the fact that five German battle-cruisers engaging six British vessels of this class, supported after the first twenty minutes, although at great range, by the fire of four battle ships of the 'Queen Elizabeth' class, were yet able to sink the 'Queen Mary' and 'Indefatigable' . . . the result cannot be other than unpalatable.

The anonymous author of an article in *Brassey's Annual* for 1924, who was clearly not one of Beatty's supporters in the Jutland controversy then raging, was a great deal blunter:

there is no precedent at all for a British squadron superior to its opponents in speed and gun-power being outfought and defeated in fifty-three minutes.[10]

In reality, probably only *Tiger* had a clear speed advantage.[11] It must be recognised that, even after the loss of *Queen Mary*, Beatty barely flinched; it was the German commander, Vice Admiral Franz von Hipper, who turned away from the fire of the battleships and the threat of a destroyer attack. Nonetheless, there can be no doubt that the Run to the South was a disaster for British arms. The losses can be partly explained by the inferior armour protection and the exposed and inflammable propellant charges in the British ships, and the effective armour-piercing German shell.[12] But these factors were important only because the British battlecruisers were decisively beaten in the gunnery duel; in the whole action they made no more than eleven hits compared with at least thirty-four scored by their opponents.[13]

There is now something of a broad consensus on the main cause of this failure of British gunnery and how it had arisen.

The British undoubtedly paid a severe penalty for the failure to adopt before the war the system devised by Arthur Hungerford Pollen . . . The Pollen system would undoubtedly have enabled the British battlecruisers to hit before they were hit in return, thus offsetting their deficiencies in armour protection and unsuitable propellant.[14]

Instead of [Pollen's] effective Argo Clock, Dreyer had persuaded the Admiralty to adopt a plagiarized and inferior instrument co-designed by himself and . . . Keith Elphinstone.[15]

In taking observed and estimated data, and adding both manual delays and mechanical errors, Dreyer's system deprived the guns of the responsiveness of direct observation, and yet failed to produce accurate results in conditions of fast-changing rates of change of range and bearing.[16]

By the eve of World War I, fire control devices had become so complex that the admirals who had to decide what to approve and what to reject no longer understood what was at issue . . . Decisions were therefore made in ignorance, often for financial or personal or political reasons.[17]

What the effects on Jutland might have been if most of the British heavy ships had been fitted with the Argo Clock is of course largely conjectural; but its obvious superiority to the system actually installed, together with the fact that the *Queen Mary*, which did the

4

best shooting of Beatty's ships, was fitted with the Argo Clock Mark IV leaves one in little doubt that they would have been substantial.[18]

Had all British capital ships been equipped with Pollen's 'Argo Clock' at Jutland . . . the outcome . . . might after all have been the destruction of the High Seas Fleet by sheer weight of numbers for which the Royal Navy pined.
    Yet defective technology, reflecting the scientific and technical backwardness of British industry, was not the only ingredient in the failure to annihilate at Jutland.[19]

All these conclusions are based on the research and publications of Professor Jon Tetsuro Sumida. After his first paper in 1979, he edited the papers of Arthur Pollen (published in 1984) and, in 1989, brought out *In Defence of Naval Supremacy*, now recognised as a classic of naval history.[20] Among other notable studies of many aspects of naval history, Sumida has returned to the subject of gunnery in two more recent papers. 'The Quest for Reach' of 1996 proposes that the Admiralty abandoned their efforts to increase the effective range (and, at the same time, their relationship with Pollen) because they believed in, and welcomed, a German intention to fight at medium ranges. He expanded on this theme in 2003 in 'A Matter of Timing', which suggests that British commanders intended to close quickly, smash their opponents with rapid fire and then turn away before torpedoes fired from the German line could reach them.[21]

Sons of both protagonists have also contributed accounts of the original fire control rivalry. In 1980, Anthony Pollen published a loyal defence of his father's work. In 1986, Admiral Sir Desmond Dreyer responded to the many criticisms that had already been levelled at his father in a carefully balanced review of the affair,[22] but this has subsequently been largely overlooked.

*In Defence of Naval Supremacy* itself has three principal themes. It shows how Britain financed the construction of her great pre-dreadnought battle-fleet, how financial constraints were imposed at the start of the dreadnought era, and how they were overcome to pay for the construction of the Grand Fleet. It emphasises Fisher's strong preference for battlecruisers over battleships, and suggests that he was influenced by developments in fire control which promised to make fire effective at long range. Lastly, it describes Arthur Pollen's campaign from 1901 to 1913 to persuade the Royal Navy to adopt his fire control system, and its eventual rejection in favour of the Dreyer fire control tables. As the above quotations imply, it furthermore concludes that, although the Dreyer Tables were functionally inferior to Argo designs, they were in part plagiarised from them, and that, at Jutland, Beatty would not have lost gunnery superiority if his battle-cruisers had been equipped by Pollen's company. My own fascination with the subject of fire control was inspired by Professor Sumida's works and, like all naval historians studying the dreadnought era, I am greatly in his debt. However, notwithstanding the evidently wide acceptance of his conclusions, I now believe that there is more to be said on the matter.

To begin with a brief summary of the principal events in Pollen's protracted dealings with the Admiralty:[23] the inventor made his first approach in 1901, but it was not until 1905 that Pollen received his first order. In the following winter, a two-observer rangefinder and a manually operated table for plotting enemy course were tried, though unsuccessfully, in *Jupiter*. During 1906, Pollen made new proposals for a gyroscopically stabilised mounting for the new 9-foot Barr & Stroud rangefinder, and for an automatic course plotter. The Admiralty ordered new instruments for trial and accepted that, if a production order were placed, Pollen would receive £100,000 in royalties. In January 1908, the formal trial in *Ariadne* was conducted by Admiral of the Fleet Sir Arthur Wilson, assisted by the newly promoted Commander Frederic Dreyer. But Wilson had already decided that the tests must demonstrate that cheaper, hand-worked devices could be equally effective. Pollen's instruments performed well, but no production order was placed; however, after some questionable dealings with Pollen, the Admiralty did make a further payment to enable him to continue development. New designs of rangefinder mounting and plotter were ready for trial in *Natal* in September 1909 and they were followed in early 1910 by the Argo Clock Mark I. In April 1910, Pollen's Argo Company received a production order for forty-five gyro-stabilised rangefinder mountings. However, the prototype instruments proved unreliable, especially the plotter, which had been hastily modified in an unsuccessful attempt to create a true-course plotter i.e. one that could plot the enemy course even when its own ship was under helm.

Meanwhile Dreyer had been developing his own fire control scheme, in which enemy range and bearing were plotted separately against time to obtain their rates of change – hence the term 'rate-plotting'. In September 1910, he patented a complete fire control system, his ideas then being developed into working designs by the firm of Elliott Brothers under the direction of Keith Elphinstone. This first Dreyer Table was tried in *Prince of Wales* in late 1911, by which time Elphinstone was working on the design of a more elaborate version. At the same moment, the Argo Company was finishing off an entirely new design of range-and-bearing clock, which became the Argo Clock Mark IV. Argo had also designed its own rate-plotter, which, with the new clock, was going to be tried in the battleship *Orion*.

In the spring of 1912, the Director of Naval Ordnance (the DNO), Captain Archibald Moore, asked Pollen to quote for the supply of further clocks and rate-plotters, but no agreement on prices could be reached. In August (after his appointment as Controller) Moore recommended that Argo's secrecy and monopoly supply agreement with the Admiralty should not be renewed at the end of the year, although an order for five (later six) clocks was placed in October, before the successful trial in *Orion* a month later. However, no further orders were placed, relationships deteriorated further and, after the controversy became public, the Admiralty severed all connections with Argo in the summer of 1913. By then, Argo had completed the prototype of a new true-course plotter, but it was never tried by the Royal Navy. Of the six Argo clocks, one was fitted in the battlecruiser *Queen Mary* and the remainder in battleships, including *Orion* – but other British dreadnoughts received various marks of Dreyer Table.

This outline provides the time-frame within which to examine Professor Sumida's conclusions and to explain why they may be worth reconsidering. To begin with the question of plagiarism:

> a tribunal of the Royal Commission on Awards to Inventors . . . ordered that Pollen be paid the sum of £30,000 compensation for the plagiarization of the Argo Clock that had occurred in 1911, the fact of which had been exposed in hearings that had taken place in August 1925.

From evidence to the Royal Commission, it is concluded that, in mid-1911, thanks to information passed on by one of the DNO's assistants, Dreyer and Elphinstone were fully informed about the design of the new Argo clock, and that, in October 1911, Elphinstone was even shown the clock under construction, and all its drawings, during a visit to Argo. Yet, according to Sumida, Dreyer and Pollen had been rivals since the end of 1906;[24] why, then, would Pollen have allowed Elphinstone, the designer of the competing system based on Dreyer's ideas, to see the new Argo clock and any, let alone all, of the drawings? And what, exactly, had been plagiarised? The new Dreyer-Elphinstone clock is described as 'an imperfect development' of two Service instruments – the Dumaresq and the Vickers clock – that had nothing to do with Pollen. But Sumida also states that:

> The clock mechanism bore an unmistakable resemblance to the disc-ball-roller arrangement of the Argo clock.

This Argo mechanism was a special instance of a type called a variable-speed drive; as finally developed, four of them were used in the completed Argo clock. In contrast, the Dreyer-Elphinstone had only two variable-speed drives of different and inferior design based on a simple disc-and-roller arrangement.[25] The Argo mechanism was evidently better, but since neither the numbers nor the designs of the drives were the same, where lay the 'unmistakable resemblance'? Furthermore, the Argo clock was also 'equipped with a virtual-course-and-speed calculating mechanism – in essence a dumaresq'.[26] There seems to be a need for a better understanding of the functional and mechanical details of the rival clock designs, in order to determine how closely the Dreyer-Elphinstone really resembled the Argo, and, indeed, whether Argo, for its part, owed any debts to Service antecedents.

Many historians have now accepted Sumida's view that, functionally and mechanically, the Dreyer Tables were inferior to the Argo system. His particular criticism is that the tables were unable to cope with enemy ranges and bearings that changed rapidly, at rates that themselves were changing.

> Dreyer's method could not have produced satisfactory results . . . if forced to contend with the high and changing change of range and bearing rates, and interruptions in visibility that Pollen and others believed were likely to occur in battle.

One reason given by Sumida is that changing rates could be measured only inaccurately from the Dreyer rate-plots, because they were then curved. Another is that, because of the manual, discontinuous transfer of range-rate to the Vickers clock, the instrument did not keep the range accurately.[27] However, it seems that this criticism can be directed only at one mark of Dreyer table; the tables in Beatty's ships at Jutland are characterised thus:

> *Indefatigable* and *New Zealand* were fitted with the Dreyer Table Mark I whose dumaresq/Vickers clock arrangement was incapable of taking account of a changing change of range rate with any degree of precision . . . *Lion* and *Princess Royal* . . . were fitted with the Dreyer Table Mark III . . . *Tiger* . . . with the . . . Mark IV, both of whose dumaresq/Dreyer-Elphinstone Clock combinations were probably much superior . . . but still not entirely satisfactory. Only the *Queen Mary* was equipped with the Dreyer Table Mark II, which incorporated an Argo Clock Mark IV . . . designed to deal with high and changing change of range rates, and interruptions in the observations of the target.

However, Sumida states elsewhere that, in the Dreyer Table Mark I, the 'dumaresq and clock were connected by a mechanical linkage which automatically set the rate of the former to match the indications of rate on the latter instrument', and that, in the Dreyer Table Mark III, the rates were also 'transmitted automatically via a mechanical linkage to the clock'. The later Mark IV had a 'new model "electric dumaresq"' which, although not described, does not sound any less automatic than its mechanical predecessors. Also, the Argo Clock Mark IV could not always contend with interruptions in visibility.

> If the firing ship turned the automatic setting of calculated bearings was superseded by hand set bearings obtained by observation.

Sumida suggests that, in the Dreyer-Elphinstone clocks, 'translation of the roller along the diameter of the disc probably resulted in slippage that introduced errors in the generation of ranges and bearings', but he also acknowledges a valuable feature of the Dreyer Tables:

> to compensate for inaccuracies . . . that were the result of rate plotting – if not for the inherent defective operation of the clock mechanism, which may not have been appreciated – the Dreyer-Elphinstone Clock was made to drive a marking pencil that plotted generated ranges alongside the plot of observed ranges. By this means, ranges . . . could be quickly compared . . . and the clock settings adjusted whenever the plots diverged. This ingenious method of 'feed-back' correction did much to enable the various production marks of the Dreyer Table . . . to produce acceptable results under the unrealistic and easy conditions of Battle Practice, and this was a major factor in the rejection of the far superior Argo system.[28]

It appears, therefore, that at least some of the Dreyer Tables may not have been prone to the errors arising from discontinuous rate transfer, and that the advantages did not all lie with the Argo system. These questions of accuracy and functionality must be resolved before judgements can be made on whether the Admiralty did in fact reject a 'far superior . . . system', and whether the Dreyer Tables were chosen because 'state-of-the-art sight-setting equipment would not be required to deliver overwhelming firepower in the first few minutes of the close-range naval battle that it [the Admiralty] believed would be fought against the Germans'.[29]

Only then will it be possible to determine the true consequences of the Admiralty's choice during the Run to the South. *In Defence of Naval Supremacy* states that, due to the convergence and divergence of courses, in both phases of the battlecruiser action, range-rates were high (nearly 600 yards per minute at one point) and changing rapidly. These conditions were critical since 'the rate-plotting mechanisms of the Dreyer tables were incapable of producing estimates of the . . . rates'. However, in the second phase, the Fifth Battle Squadron were also engaged, but for them:

> speeds were nearly equal and the angle of convergence moderate, the change of range rate was well under 200 yards per minute and probably nearly constant.

Yet they were required to contend with the same changes of German courses as the battlecruisers, while, after 4.19 p. m., all Beatty's big ships were on similar courses. The German fire control system itself is described as having 'nothing better than the German equivalent of the dumaresq . . . and Vickers clock'; the ranges from their stereoscopic rangefinders were not plotted, but their average was calculated by a special machine. It is suggested, though without explanation, that:

> The absence of a [range] plot ... may have enabled the German fire control team to respond more quickly, if not precisely, to changes in the change of range rate.[30]

All this seems to raise yet more questions. What were the courses and speeds, and hence ranges, rates and changes-of-rate, throughout the engagement? Were the values too high for the different marks of Dreyer Table in Beatty's ships? What advantage did *Queen Mary* obtain from her Argo Clock Mark IV? How accurate were the ranges taken by the two sides? And why did Hipper's ships shoot so much better, even though, apparently, they were equipped with fire control systems no more elaborate than those in *New Zealand* and *Indefatigable*? All these issues require a detailed, quantified analysis if the true causes of Beatty's gunnery defeat are to be determined.

In relating Pollen's long commercial relationship with the Admiralty, *In Defence of Naval Supremacy* shows that, in 1906, both the order for new instruments (those tried in *Ariadne*) and the scale of Pollen's production royalties were approved by the then DNO, Captain John Jellicoe, with the backing of the First Sea Lord, Fisher. But, in August 1907, Jellicoe was superseded by Captain Reginald Bacon, who is described as:

> opposed to the employment of complicated machinery for fire control purposes ... There is good reason to believe, therefore, that Bacon was determined from the start to prevent the adoption of Pollen's mechanised system of fire control.
>
> Bacon's objectives were undoubtedly also those of Lieutenant Frederic C. Dreyer.

The book adds that 'It was while serving under Wilson that Dreyer's rivalry with Pollen as an inventor of fire control instruments had begun', and that Bacon's nomination of Admiral Wilson, assisted by Dreyer, 'to umpire the official trials insured that Dreyer's desire to play a major role in the blocking of Pollen would be fulfilled'.[31] It shows conclusively that Wilson became adamantly opposed to the scale of Pollen's royalty payments and that the Admiral's hostile recommendations were accepted by the Board of Admiralty, although his report was apparently most difficult to follow.

> Fisher and Jackson had little technical understanding of the latest advances in gunnery, which meant that they were incapable of exposing subtle prevarication when it came to the arcana of fire control.

However, the same Board also agreed in 1908 that Pollen should receive additional development funds. And, before both Fisher and Bacon left the Admiralty at the end of 1909, the *Natal* instruments had been ordered, while Bacon was in favour of a comprehensive agreement between Pollen and the Admiralty.[32]

Moore replaced Bacon as DNO, while Wilson took over as First Sea Lord. Sumida describes Moore as 'an inveterate opponent of Pollen's approach to fire control' and Wilson as 'adamantly opposed to any monopoly agreement'. Yet it was in 1910, albeit after some tough negotiations, that the Admiralty placed a production order with Argo for forty-five rangefinder mountings and agreed that monopoly and secrecy should be maintained until the end of 1912.[33] Five months after Wilson's departure:

> On 10 April 1912, Moore . . . informed Pollen that he would recommend the adoption of the [Argo] clock for the five [*sic*] battleships of the King George V class pending the outcome of sea trials and an agreement over prices.

However, by this time the Original Dreyer Table had been tried and Elphinstone's new design was taking shape, while Pollen persisted in holding out for much larger orders. In August, Moore advised the Board:

> I do not see any reason for continuing the privileged position of this inventor . . . it is full time that he was placed in the same position as all other inventors.

Nonetheless, Moore still went ahead with the purchase of the Argo clocks. However, subsequent negotiations became increasingly acrimonious until, in mid-1913, Argo was removed from the list of Admiralty suppliers.[34]

There seems to have been much more to Admiralty policy on fire control than inveterate opposition to Pollen. But to explain that policy and how it changed, we need some understanding of the many considerations that shaped it within the hierarchy of the Service. Personal relationships and prejudices were doubtless a factor. But so also were operational requirements, technical comparisons, commercial and contractual concerns, and financial and political influences. In 1912, Moore had remarked that, until then, Pollen's position had been unusually privileged. This prompts an important question: how were inventions (from within and outside the Navy) normally developed into serviceable instruments, and what were the roles played by Admiralty and industry in this process? A study of the evolution of the Royal Navy's complete fire control system – of which clocks and plotters were but a part – will, it is hoped, provide a technical and commercial context for the Admiralty's decisions concerning fire control.

In his concluding chapter, Professor Sumida declares:

It cannot be doubted . . . that full Admiralty cooperation with Pollen's efforts would have resulted in the putting into service of a fire control system that was far superior to that . . . actually adopted [and which] almost certainly would have enabled British ships to hit more often – perhaps even much more often – when range and bearing rates were high and changing.

While he accepts that Pollen 'was probably ill-suited by nature to work easily with naval officers', he also suggests that:

Most naval officers, by education and experience were not equipped to deal with technical issues, and this was especially true of fire control, which involved both mathematical and mechanical matters that were novel, difficult and complicated. . . .

The negative effects of Pollen's background and personal short-comings . . . were much exacerbated by what appears to have been the obstinacy and technical ignorance of Wilson and Bacon, and the zeal and ambition of Dreyer. Fisher, when properly advised in 1906, had supported Pollen with decisive results [but] Fisher . . . lacked the technical knowledge to make informed decisions on his own.[35]

The imputation of technical ignorance among senior officers is an unexpected criticism of a naval elite which is usually said to have been much too concerned with material and technical matters.[36] In fact, Fisher had an aptitude for mathematics, had been responsible for early experiments in the electrical firing of guns and mines and had been Captain of *Excellent* and DNO.[37] Both Wilson and Bacon were torpedo specialists and so were familiar with some of the most advanced technology of their time, including gyroscopes and applications of electricity, while, in the passage quoted earlier, Sumida allows Wilson a sufficient understanding of 'the arcana of fire control' to accuse him of 'subtle prevarication'. Jackson qualified as a torpedo lieutenant and was Assistant DNO (with responsibilities for torpedoes) before becoming Captain of *Vernon* in 1904; most notably, his pioneering work on wireless earned him a Fellowship of the Royal Society. Only Moore is omitted from these strictures, but he was a gunnery officer who had specialised in mathematical theory and had a reputation for clever-ness.[38] None of these officers would have had difficulty in understanding either the principles or the functionality of fire control instruments.

Almost at the end of his book, Professor Sumida suggests that:

Aspects of the fire control story may throw light on the question of lagging British technical development during the late industrial period.

However, his more recent fire control paper at least excludes British naval technology from the country's industrial and technical failings:

> the problems of British gunnery equipment and method exposed at Jutland were the product of ... mistaken decisions by naval officers about complex and difficult technical and tactical issues, not manifestations of industrial failure or cultural conservatism. Britain may have been generally backward in technical development, social organization, and cultural attitudes, but evidence for such indictments must be found elsewhere than through criticism of Royal Navy engineering and doctrine.[39]

This newer interpretation is in sympathy with those naval historians who, for some time, have been systematically questioning what Andrew Gordon has described as the Admiralty's 'matchless reputation as an opponent of innovation'.[40] It does not, however, recognise that the specific case of naval technology in the nineteenth and early twentieth centuries also provides yet further reason for doubting the reality of the supposed general industrial decline of Britian after 1870.[41]

In rejecting one of the sources of this older view of the Navy and technology, Professor Andrew Lambert has written:

> The self-serving, politically naïve and technologically determinist accounts left by nineteenth-century engineers, who wished to portray themselves as high-minded servants of humanity, have been taken at face value for too long. By contrast the Admiralty was technologically dynamic, and adopted a professional approach to the management of change, which it handled with great skill between 1815 and 1914.[42]

Technological determinism is also found in naval memoirs (for example, those of Fisher and Scott)[43] and in older historical works.[44] In contrast, Professor John Beeler concluded in his reassessment of what Oscar Parkes called 'the Dark Ages of the Victorian Navy' that:

> With the exceptions of ordnance and the substitution of steel for iron, neither of which was wholly in the Admiralty's power to influence, the allegation that the British Navy suffered from a technological lag, either *vis a vis* other powers, or in absolute terms, is difficult to sustain.[45]

Even the two exceptions deserve further qualification. Until the mid-1870s, the power and safety of British muzzle-loaders (with steel barrels and wrought-iron hoops) compared well with foreign breech-loaders.[46] But the future lay with long, breech-loading, all-steel guns like those exhibited by Krupp at Meppen in 1879.[47] It would take a decade before British guns (of wire-wound construction) were once more as good as any. Yet, even so, there were only two British battleships (*Ajax* and *Agamemnon*) that might have been completed with breech-loaders, but were not.[48]

The technological lag in steel shipbuilding was of even shorter duration. Steel of sufficient quality for shipbuilding was first produced by the French-developed Siemens-Martin process and used, with wrought-iron, in the *Redoubtable*, laid down in 1873; the French then continued with mixed construction into the 1880s. As soon as suitable steel (from the Siemens-Martin and improved Bessemer processes) became available, Britain rapidly made the transition to all-steel construction, commencing with two despatch vessels in 1875–6.[49] This was but one more manifestation of the Admiralty's general policy in the second half of the nineteenth century, as described approvingly in 1877 by the Chief Engineer of the US Navy.

> The British Navy, charged with the administration of by far the largest and most powerful navy in the world, [is] always cautious in the application of new inventions, rarely adopting any untried plans, but surely accepting the most successful in practical operation.[50]

Much the same approach was still taken at the dawn of the twentieth century. Once practicable (though still primitive) submarines had been developed in France and the United States, the Royal Navy licensed the technology of the American Holland boats and provided the resources for further rapid development and construction. By 1914, the British submarine fleet, even if it did contain too high a proportion of coastal boats, was the largest in the world.[51] Even where the Royal Navy was more technically conservative than others (for example, in its reluctance to adopt small-tube boilers), an explanation can be found in the demands placed on equipment by a navy with global responsibilities.[52]

Although Admiralty policy was often more reactive than innovative, this was not always the case. As well as Jackson's pioneering work on wireless, the Royal Navy funded the development of Parson's turbines and, under Fisher, was prepared to adopt them for capital ships even though such large installations were unproven.[53] However, Fisher went further, by creating ships that were not only faster but also more heavily armed than anything seen before. This introduced a new measure of naval power in which Britain no longer had a considerable numerical advantage. Of course, the idea of what became the dreadnought-battleship was already in the air, but no other country would, or could, have commissioned one as early as the end of 1906.[54] Nor would the naval rivalry between Britain and Germany have been heightened so soon if the ships of the 1905–6 programme had been (or at least had been presented as) evolutionary developments of the preceding classes of battleship and armoured cruiser. And the actual dreadnought building programmes of Britain and Germany suggest that, if Britain had held to her earlier reactive policy, she could still have comfortably outbuilt Germany, at less cost, if her lead had been challenged. Professor Marder asked:

> Was the dreadnought policy Fisher's greatest blunder, or was it a stroke of genius? The writer feels that it was the latter.[55]

Since, in formulating his dreadnought policy, Fisher did not even regard Germany as Britain's principal rival,[56] he cannot have anticipated its subsequent destabilising effects. But, if not an outright blunder, it does appear in retrospect more of an unnecessary, technology-led provocation than a stroke of genius.

Whatever its eventual political impact, Fisher's dreadnought policy provides yet one more reason for rejecting any general notion of Britain's 'scientific and technical backwardness'. Nonetheless, in the particular case of naval fire control, the present consensus is that the Admiralty chose a system that, if not backward in comparison with its German equivalent, was inferior to that offered by Pollen. Yet, as we have seen, there are many reasons for questioning whether the decisions taken on these 'complex and difficult technical and tactical questions' were indeed mistaken. In retelling the history of fire control in Britain in the dreadnought era, this book will address:

- the fundamental principles that govern long-range gunnery at sea;
- the development of the Royal Navy's first, manually worked system of fire control;
- the evolution of the Argo system and of the Dreyer Tables;
- the influences (possibly mutual) between Argo's designs and both Service systems;
- the choices – not only technical but also commercial – that faced the responsible Admiralty officers as the rival Pollen and Dreyer systems were being developed, and the factors that shaped their decisions;
- the assumptions about battle conditions and tactics when those choices were made;
- the realities of battle gunnery in the First World War;
- lastly, the actual consequences, especially for Beatty's battlecruisers at Jutland, of the Admiralty's choice of the Dreyer Tables in preference to Pollen's Argo system.

# Notes

1 John Roberts, *The Battleship Dreadnought* (London: Conway Maritime Press, 1992) pp. 13–17 (copy gratefully acknowledged). Oscar Parkes, *British Battleships* (London: Leo Cooper, reprinted 1990) pp. 380–483.

2 Ruddock Mackay, *Fisher of Kilverstone* (Oxford: Clarendon Press, 1973) pp. 269–70 and 322–5.

3 *Report of the Committee on Designs* (London, 1905) pp. 33 and 41, FISR 8/4, Fisher Papers, Churchill College, Cambridge [CC].

4 The most influential being Jon Sumida's *In Defence of Naval Supremacy* (London: Unwin Hyman, 1989) [*IDNS*].

5 David Stevenson, *Armaments and the Coming of War. Europe, 1904–1914* (Oxford: Clarendon Press, 2000) pp. 98–102. Arthur Marder, *From the Dreadnought to Scapa Flow* [*FDSF*], *Volume I* (London: Oxford University Press, 1961) pp. 105–10 and 439–42. Erich Gröner (revised Dieter Jung and Martin Maass), *German Warships 1815–1945, Volume I* (London: Conway Maritime Press, 1990) pp. 16–24. Parkes [1] pp. 497–502 and 515.

6 Stevenson [5] pp. 1–9 and 165–70. *FDSF I*, pp. 151–70.

7 Completion dates from Parkes and Gröner [5]. The second British battleship total includes the three foreign ships taken over in 1914.

8 Paul Halpern, *A Naval History of World War I* (London: UCL Press, 1994) Chapter 2.

9 Sources for Jutland are given in Chapter 8.

10 'Commander-in-Chief's Despatch' 18 June 1916 in *Battle of Jutland . . . Official Despatches with Appendices*, Cmd 1068 (London; HMSO, 1920) [*OD*] p. 2. 'The Jutland Controversy: An Historical Appreciation', in Sir Alexander Richardson and Archibald Hurd (eds) *Brassey's Naval and Shipping Annual 1924* (London: William Clowes, 1924) p. 95.

11 John Roberts, *Battlecruisers* (London: Chatham, 1997) pp. 40 and 80–1 (copy gratefully acknowledged).

12 *FDSF III*, pp. 204–15. N. J. M. Campbell, *Jutland, an Analysis of the Fighting* (London: Conway Maritime Press, 1986) pp. 369–87. Stephen Roskill, *Admiral of the Fleet Earl Beatty* (New York: Atheneum, 1981) p. 130.

13 Campbell [12] pp. 55, 78 and 94; as explained in Chapter 8, Campbell's total of forty-two hits on the British battlecruisers appears overgenerous.

14 Halpern [8] p. 328.

15 Eric Grove, *Fleet to Fleet Encounters* (London: Arms and Armour Press, 1991) p. 72. Keith Elphinstone was director of the firm that made the Dreyer Tables.

16 Andrew Gordon, *The Rules of the Game* (London: John Murray, 1996) p. 12.

17 William H. McNeill, *The Pursuit of Power. Technology, Armed Force and Society since A.D. 1000* (Oxford: Blackwell, 1982) p. 294.

18 Roskill [12] p. 192.

19 Corelli Barnett, *Engage the Enemy More Closely* (New York: Norton, 1991) pp. 6–7.

20 Jon Sumida, 'British Capital Ship Design and Fire Control in the Dreadnought Era: Sir John Fisher, Arthur Hungerford Pollen, and the Battle Cruiser', *Journal of Modern History*, 51 (June 1979) pp. 205–30. Jon Sumida (ed.) *The Pollen Papers* (London: NRS, 1984) [*PP*].

21 Jon Sumida, 'The Quest for Reach' ['QfR'], in Stephen Chiabotti (ed.) *Tooling for War. Military Transformation in the Industrial Age* (Chicago: Imprint Publications, 1996) pp. 49–96 (advance copy gratefully acknowledged) and 'A Matter of Timing' ['MoT'] *Journal of Military History*, 67 (January 2003) pp. 85–137.

22 Anthony Pollen, *The Great Gunnery Scandal* (London: Collins, 1980). Admiral Sir Desmond Dreyer, 'Early Developments in Naval Fire Control', *The Naval Review*, July 1986, pp. 238–41.

23 Based on *IDNS*, Chapters 3–6.

24 *IDNS*, pp. 316, 219 and 121–2.

25 *IDNS*, pp. 219 and 210–14 and Plate 5. The function of the roller was quite different from the rollers (there were actually two) in the Argo design.

26 *IDNS*, p. 211.

27 *IDNS*, pp. 217–8. 'QfR', pp. 60 and 87.

28 *IDNS*, pp. 213, 219–20, 284 and 300.

29 'QfR', p. 80.

30 *IDNS*, pp. 300–3. For courses, see *FDSF III*, Charts 4 and 5.

31 *IDNS*, pp. 98–100 and 121–3.

32 *IDNS*, pp. 124–38, 164–5, 170–1 and 174. The Controller, Rear-Admiral Sir Henry Jackson, was Bacon's superior.

33 *IDNS*, pp. 262 and 196–201.

34 *IDNS*, pp. 219–29 and 235–47.

35 *IDNS*, pp. 331–3.

36 K. G. B. Dewar, *The Navy from Within* (London: Gollancz, 1939) pp. 58–64. Lord Chatfield, *The Navy and Defence* (London: Heinemann, 1942) pp. 25 and 191. Gordon [16] p. 381. *FDSF I*, p. 401.

37 Mackay [2] pp. 22–3, 44–6, 100, 173, 187, 193 and 231. Nicholas Lambert, *Sir John Fisher's Naval Revolution* (Columbia, SC: University of South Carolina Press, 1999) pp. 74 and 145–6. Sumida (*IDNS*, p. 333) acknowledges Fisher's 'past experience with the introduction of new technology' but suggests that it 'caused him to underestimate the difficulty of the fire control problem'.

38 *IDNS*, pp. 91 and 121. Gordon, pp. 167,369 and 383: Beatty thought Moore 'too clever'. Moore's Service Record, ADM 196/42, p. 64, Admiralty Papers, Public Record Office [PRO]. Adrian Blond, 'The Papers of Sir Henry Jackson 1855–1929', in *New Researchers in Maritime History, Papers presented at the Third Annual Conference 18 March 1995*, Royal Naval Museum, Portsmouth. *Dictionary of National Biography* [DNB] *1922–1930*, pp. 448–50.

39 *IDNS*, p. 337. 'MoT', p. 122.

40 Gordon, p. 165.

41 For a comprehensive study and the sources for an anti-declinist account, see David Edgerton, *Science, Technology and the British Industrial 'Decline' 1870–1970* (Cambridge: Cambridge University Press, 1996).

42 Andrew Lambert, 'Responding to the Nineteenth Century: The Royal Navy and the Introduction of the Screw Propeller', in Graham Hollister-Short (ed.) *History of Technology, Volume 21, 1999* (London: Continuum, 2000) pp. 24–5.

43 Technological determinism is the assumption that, from its first appearance, an eventually triumphant technology was practicable, immediately the right choice and assured of success.

44 Mackay pp. 66–7 for Fisher and early torpedoes. John Brooks, 'Percy Scott and the Director', in David McLean and Antony Preston (eds) *Warship 1996* (London: Conway Maritime Press, 1996) pp. 150–70. J. D. Scott, *Vickers. A History* (London: Weidenfeld & Nicolson, 1962) p. 29 for the breech-loader.

45 John Beeler, *Birth of the Battleship. British Capital Ship Design, 1870–1881* (London: Chatham, 2001) p. 87.

46 *Treatise on the Construction and Manufacture of Ordnance in the British Service* (London: HMSO, 1879 reprinted 1881) pp. 76 and 80–8. Beeler [45] pp. 73–4 and 79.

47 Parkes, p. 287. William Manchester, *The Arms of Krupp 1587–1968* (London: Michael Joseph, 1964) pp. 205–8.

48 Beeler, pp. 79–84. Parkes, pp. 287–8, 302, 321–2 and 382–4. Ian Hogg and John Batchelor, *Naval Gun* (Poole: Blandford Press, 1978) p. 98. John Roberts, 'The Pre-dreadnought Age' (pp. 112–13), and John Campbell, 'Naval Armaments and Armour' (pp. 161–3), in Andrew Lambert (ed.) *Steam, Steel and Shellfire* (London: Conway Maritime Press, 1992); this important book provides many examples of the Royal Navy's forward-looking acceptance of new technologies.

49 W. K. V. Gale, *The British Iron and Steel Industry. A Technical History* (Newton Abbot: David & Charles, 1967) pp. 96 and 101–2. Beeler, p. 38. David K. Brown, 'The Era of Uncertainty, 1863–1878' (p. 90), and John Roberts, 'Warships of Steel, 1879–188' (p. 96), in *Steam, Steel and Shellfire* [48]. Paul Quinn, 'Wrought Iron's Suitability for Shipbuilding', *The Mariner's Mirror*, 89, 4 (November 2003) pp. 456–8.

50 James W. King cited by Beeler, p. 208.

51 N. Lambert [37] particularly Chapters 2 and 7. Norman Friedman, *Submarine Design and Development* (London: Conway Maritime Press, 1984) pp. 27–9.

52 David K. Brown, *The Grand Fleet. Warship Design and Development 1906–1922* (London: Chatham, 1999) p. 25. Roberts, *Battlecruisers* [11] pp. 72–3.

53 Hugh Lyon, 'The Admiralty and Private Industry', in Bryan Ranft (ed.) *Technical Change and British Naval Policy 1860–1939* (London: Hodder & Stoughton, 1977) pp. 46–7.

54 Parkes, pp. 466–7. N. Lambert (p.345) shows that the US Navy did not decide on an all-big-gun armament for *Michigan* and *South Carolina* until 1906.

55 *FDSF I*, p. 69.

56 Mackay, p. 321.

# 2

# LONG-RANGE
# NAVAL GUNNERY

You must hit first, you must hit hard, and you must keep on hitting.[1]

At the start of the Run to the South, firing began when the range between the opposing battlecruisers was 16,000 yards (about eight sea-miles or nine land-miles). At that distance, the waterline of an enemy ship was pretty well on the distant horizon,[2] while even a battlecruiser almost 700 feet long could be entirely obscured behind a little finger held vertically at arm's length. It was no easy matter to hit such an apparently tiny target from a ship that, except in a flat calm, would be rolling, yawing and pitching, and when both ships were steaming on different courses at speeds that might exceed 25 knots. This chapter describes the essential principles of long-range shooting at sea, and a few key instruments that embody those principles. It also introduces those unavoidable 'terms-of-art' (in italics on their first appearance) which are indispensable in describing the technical evolution of the rival systems of fire control.

Especially at long range, hits cannot be made simply by pointing the gun along the *line-of-sight* to the target. First, as soon as a shell leaves the barrel, it is pulled downwards by the force of gravity. Thus the barrel must be elevated i.e. inclined upwards from the line-of-sight; the shell then follows a curved trajectory that should end on the enemy ship. However, the *elevation* can be set correctly only if the distance or *range* of the enemy is known. Second, when viewed from above, the shell does not fly straight. Due to the stabilising spin imparted to the shell by the barrel's rifling, it drifts sideways (to the right with British guns), by several hundred yards at long range. Thus, to correct for *drift*, it is necessary to apply a suitable *deflection* i.e. to 'aim off' horizontally from the line-of-sight

Thus a gun was properly aimed if, at the moment of firing, the elevation and deflection were correct relative to the line-of-sight. Heavy guns were mounted in turrets; each gun was aimed by a *layer*, who controlled the elevation: and by the *trainer*, who determined the training of the whole turret. In British turrets, both elevation and training relied on hydraulic machinery and controls.[3] Each layer or trainer aimed through a telescope or periscope that was part of the *gun-sight*. Each sight had a pair of scales, one graduated for ranges, the other for deflections. When the scale pointers indicated the correct enemy range and deflection, the two telescopes were set relative to the gun axis at exactly equal but opposite angles to the required angles of elevation and deflection. Thus, if the guns were fired only when the target lay under the cross-wires of both telescopes, the aim was correct and hits could be expected. Once sufficiently responsive hydraulic controls had been developed, the layer and trainer tried to maintain *continuous aim* i.e. by counteracting the ship's roll and yaw, to keep their cross-wires on the target. Then, when the firing gong was sounded, only small, quick adjustments to the aim were needed before firing.

In the simplest case of gunnery at sea, two opposing ships are on parallel courses at equal speeds. Looking from our own ship, the relative position of the enemy does not change; thus the enemy range and bearing remain constant. Hitting, however, still depends on an accurate knowledge of the range. Thus the first necessity for long-range gunnery is a rangefinder. At Jutland, all the British battlecruisers depended on the 9-foot Barr & Stroud FQ2 coincidence rangefinder. Unfortunately, only a few sources have been found that give some indication of its accuracy in use. In theory, the 'uncertainty of observation' was 85 yards at 10,000 yards, increasing to 190 yards at 15,000 yards,[4] but in practice it was greater. In 1913, *Thunderer*, taking eight ranges per minute with three of these rangefinders, observed an 'average spread' of 700 yards at 9,800 yards,[5] while, at Jutland, *Iron Duke* noted: 'Error reported by Rangefinder Plot was 500 yards. Range 11,000 yards'.[6] In post-war trials on a destroyer, a 'consistency' of 185–330 yards was obtained when taking about 3½ ranges per minute between 12,500 and 14,000 yards.[7] Now, if many ranges were taken with one rangefinder and plotted on a graph, they would appear as a scatter of points around a mean (or average) value. Although these four sources are not unambiguous,[8] in service, it is likely that, at 15,000–16,000 yards, the ranges from a 9-foot rangefinder could be randomly scattered by *at least* 400 yards on either side of the correct value i.e. the total spread was 800 yards or more. However, every observation in a series could also be skewed from the true value by an error that was common to all. Thus both random and common errors may be included in the warning that 'a single range observation may [be] at 16,000 yards easily as much as 600, 700 or even 800 yards from the truth'.[9] Later in the First World War, common (also called systematic) errors of up to 1,000 yards or more, high and low, were sometimes obtained; fortunately, the relative changes of range within a single series were normally less seriously affected. These phenomena were investigated during and after the war; the rather tentative conclusion was that they were due to a combination of the effects of atmospheric refraction and temperature, aggravated by uneven heating of the rangefinder tube if the instrument was in direct sunlight.[10]

Inaccurate though they were, before firing began only rangefinders could measure the actual or *true-range* of the enemy. However, even if this was unchanging, the *gun-range* on the sights was rarely the same as the true-range. The sights were calibrated for windless conditions at a specific atmospheric density. If, as was usually the case, the conditions were different, allowances were made by applying *ballistic corrections* to the best estimate of the true-range; the resulting gun-range, when put on the sights, then gave an elevation closer to that required to hit. The range correction for wind allowed for the effect of wind blowing along the line-of-sight; likewise, a deflection correction was usually needed for wind across the range. However, wind corrections were only approximate; wind could be measured only at sea level, but this was not always the same as the wind experienced throughout the shell's trajectory.[11] Errors in gun-range, due to inaccuracies in rangefinder range and ballistic corrections, affected all shots equally. But other errors were individual to each gun and its crew. A gun's muzzle velocity changed as the barrel became worn; shells and cordite charges were not identical, while cordite temperatures could also vary.[12] And not all layers and trainers were equally skilled at firing only when their cross-wires were exactly on the designated point-of-aim.

When fire was opened, even if the true-range was unchanging, the opening range on the gun-sights was unlikely to find the enemy with the first shots.

We know that, broadly speaking, the initial range is <u>never</u> right.[13]

It was then necessary to correct the unknown (and unknowable) errors in range and deflection by observing the large splashes thrown up by the shells falling near the enemy: and correcting the next shots accordingly. This process was called *spotting*. However, corrections derived from the fall of an individual shot could be seriously misleading, because of the variations from shot to shot. Especially at long range, it was necessary to fire in *salvoes*, usually consisting of one gun from each turret, that is, four or five rounds per salvo. The splashes from the individual rounds could then be judged as a group, in which the inevitable variations due to aiming and ballistic factors could be averaged by eye, and any wild shots could be ignored altogether. At 12,000 yards, the typical salvo spreads for range were 200 yards for 15-inch guns, 300 yards for 13.5-inch and 400 yards for 12-inch.[14]

Spotting was regarded as a necessary evil.

In all fire-control systems, good spotting is the first essential of hitting. This, however, does not alter the fact that the less a system is dependent on spotting the better, since spotting in its turn is dependent on a clear view of the object fired at.

First, the deflection was corrected by spotting for deflection until the salvoes were falling on the line-of-sight, though probably over or short of the enemy. Then the range was corrected in order to obtain a *straddle* i.e. a fall of shot such that one or two splashes were short of the enemy. This was the best indication that other shells in the salvo were hitting (actual hits, especially with armour-piercing shell, were difficult to see). Prior to straddling, little could be made out except whether a salvo had fallen *over* or *short*. Hence, until after Jutland, the Royal Navy used the system called *bracketing*. Essentially, firing began with bold corrections – typically 800 yards – until the target was crossed (i.e. two successive salvoes fell on opposite sides of the target); each subsequent correction was then half the preceding one in magnitude and in the direction that would find the target. For example, after crossing the target with 'DOWN 800', the next correction would be 'UP 400'; the bracket was completed by the next correction of 200 yards, UP or DOWN as necessary. If the initial range error was 1,000 yards, as many as five salvoes might be required to find the target.[15] Since the interval between spotted salvoes could exceed 50 seconds at battle ranges,[16] this might take 3½ minutes; the disadvantage of an inaccurate opening range is clear.

## STEADY UNEQUAL COURSES

Normally, two opposing ships are on different courses at different speeds. Therefore, as seen from our own ship, the enemy appears to be moving. While the two ships hold their courses and speeds, the enemy appears to move relative to own ship on a fixed heading, the *virtual-course*, at a constant speed, the *virtual-speed*.[17] In other words, to observers on own ship, the enemy appears to move as though we were stopped and he was steaming past on the virtual-course at the virtual-speed. Both depend on the values of own and enemy speeds, and on the angle between the two courses. If the speeds and courses of both ships are similar, the virtual-speed is low; it is zero when courses and speeds are identical. But, as the angle between courses increases, the virtual-speed rises; if courses are opposite, it reaches its maximum, the sum of the speeds of both ships.

If one ship steams on a steady course past another that is stopped, she passes through a point at which the line-of-sight is perpendicular to the course and the range reaches a minimum value. Before reaching that point, the range was decreasing; after it, the range will increase. Assume that the *bearing* of the moving ship from the stopped one is expressed as a *compass-bearing*, which is positive when measured clockwise from True North; then if the first ship is moving from left to right, his bearing always increases, though it does so most rapidly at the point of minimum range. Range and bearing change in exactly the same way when both ships are on steady courses i.e. when their relative movement is expressible as a virtual-course-and-speed. While enemy bearing can still be expressed as a compass-bearing from own ship, it can also be measured as a *course-bearing* i.e. the angle from own ship's nominal or *mean-course* to the line-of-sight. Moreover, while own course is steady, the changes in both these bearings are the same.

Now consider any typical moment when the line-of-sight is not perpendicular to the virtual-course. In a brief interval of time, the enemy appears to move a short distance along the virtual-course at the virtual speed. But the same total movement would be obtained by two movements, one along the line-of-sight, the other at right angles to (that is, across) the line-of-sight. In other words, the single movement due to the virtual-speed is equivalent to two separate movements due to speeds along and across the line-of-sight. The *speed-along* describes how rapidly the enemy is moving towards or away from us; it is, therefore, a direct measure of the *rate-of-change-of-range*. Though often used, this term is rather long-winded; in this book, the shorter *range-rate* is preferred. Range-rate was expressed not in knots of speed-along but in yards-per-minute (yds/min.). In action, it could sometimes exceed 700 yds/min. At the long range of 18,500 yards, the *time-of-flight* of each salvo was over 31 seconds,[18] so, in that time, the range could change by 360 yards or more. Consequently, hits could be made only if each salvo was fired not at the range at the moment of firing, but at the moment of striking. Thus a knowledge of range-rate was essential, so that the change-of-range in time-of-flight could be calculated and the gun-range adjusted accordingly. Furthermore, range-rate was equally important in predicting the change-of-range between one salvo and the next; when the salvo interval was 50 seconds, this change exceeded 580 yards at the same range-rate.

The movement of the enemy across the line-of-sight was expressed as a *speed-across* in knots. In some tactical situations (for example, when two ships are steaming at right angles) the speed-across may exceed 20 knots. An enemy at 18,500 yards then appears to travel some 350 yards to left or right from his position at the moment of firing; to hit, we must apply an additional deflection to allow for the change-of-bearing in time-of-flight. At short ranges the time-of-flight increases in proportion to range; consequently, this angular deflection does not alter appreciably with range and is directly proportional to speed-across. For this reason, before the end of the nineteenth century, when ranges were still short, the Royal Navy adopted the convention of calibrating its gun-sights for deflection not in angular units like degrees, but in knots of speed-across.[19] Even as ranges increased, this convention was retained. However, because at longer ranges the time-of-flight increases more rapidly, it became necessary to apply a correction to the actual speed-across;[20] this corrected value was then added to the other components of deflection (like that for wind across the line-of-sight) to obtain the *gun-deflection* that was set on the sights.

The change-of-bearing due to speed-across is expressible as a *bearing-rate* in degrees-per-minute (°/min.). When own course is steady, both compass-bearing and course-bearing have the same rate, which is proportional to the speed-across divided by the range.

If the speed-across is high, the enemy bearing changes significantly from salvo to salvo. These changes can be followed directly by the turret trainers – as long as the enemy remains visible. But, if the bearing changes, so too does the angle between the line-of-sight and the virtual-course. As a result, although the virtual-speed remains constant (we are still assuming that courses are steady), the range-rate and the speed-across do change. These changes can be disregarded over short periods of time like the time-of-flight of one salvo,[21] but they must be taken into account when firing a whole series of salvoes.

## THE DUMARESQ

Range- and bearing-rates and speed-across can be concisely expressed by the quite simple equations in the Appendix. But the last thing that gunnery control officers should be expected to do in action is to solve mathematical equations. An instrument was needed that could calculate and keep the range-rate and the speed-across, even as they changed with enemy bearing. This was devised, probably as early as 1902, by Lieutenant (later Rear Admiral) John Dumaresq; in the Royal Navy, his original design and its more elaborate successors were named *Dumaresqs* after him. It provided a precise mechanical model of the rate equations,[22] and it had an important influence on later inventions. The instrument had a circular base, spanned by a bar; when fixed in the ship, the bar lay fore-and-aft (Figure 2.1). A slide on this fore-and-aft bar carried, on its underside, a pivot for a rotating block. An enemy bar, its pointed end representing the enemy's bow, was arranged to slide in the block; it also rotated with it. The other main component was the circular, rotatable dial-plate. Its large arrow was always pointed at the enemy. The dial-plate was engraved with two sets of lines at right angles. Each line running parallel to the arrow represented a value of speed-across, either to left or to right; the values read off were often referred to as knots of *Dumaresq-deflection*. The lines at right angles represented range-rates in yds/min., either *opening* (increasing, positive) or *closing* (decreasing, negative).

When it first entered service, the Dumaresq was set using visual estimates of the enemy course and speed. To begin, position the slide so that its distance from the centre is proportional to own ship's speed. Then adjust the enemy bar, by rotating it to lie parallel to the enemy's course, and by sliding it in the block so that the distance from point to pivot is proportional to enemy speed. (Use the speed scales engraved on the two bars.) Lastly, point the dial-plate arrow at the enemy. The enemy bow pointer now lies at or

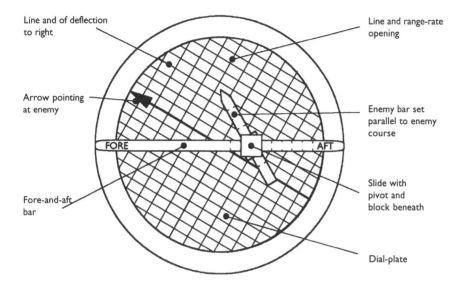

*Figure 2.1* Dumaresq schematic.

close to the intersection of a line of range-rate and a line of speed-across. Thus the current values of range-rate and speed-across are read directly from the dial. Furthermore, if the operator follows the movement of the enemy with the arrow, the Dumaresq keeps track of the range-rate and speed-across, even as they change with enemy bearing.

## THE RANGE CLOCK

It might seem that long-range gunnery needed only a rangefinder to give the range and a Dumaresq to keep the range-rate and the speed-across. But, at long ranges, rangefinders were not accurate, and ranges could be taken only discontinuously, about four ranges per minute even in good conditions. What was needed was a range-keeper – a device that continuously indicated the best current estimate of the changing range, and did so even if the supply of rangefinder ranges was interrupted due to smoke, poor visibility or the effects of enemy fire. The range-keeper also needed a means to apply corrections to the predicted range, especially those obtained from spotting.

In the Royal Navy, this need was met in 1906 with the first large order for the Vickers range clock (Figure 2.2). The large range hand rotated at a rate set by the handle to the right; thus the hand indicated the changing range on the circular scale. The range scale could itself be rotated by a second handle; thus it was easy to alter the range until the hand pointed to the corrected value. The range-rate set on the clock was obtained from the Dumaresq. If

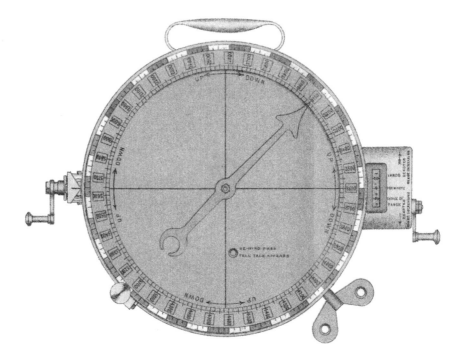

*Figure 2.2* Vickers clock.

The scale numbers could be chosen for ranges of 2,000–6,000, 6,000–10,000 or 10,000–14,000 yards. The left-hand handle rotated the scale and numbers relative to the dial and hand. The right-hand handle set the range-rate.

Source: Admiralty, Gunnery Branch, *Addenda (1909) to Gunnery Manual Vols I (Part I) and III*, November 1909, Plate XXXVII (detail), AL.

the clock rate could have been adjusted continuously to follow that indicated by the Dumaresq, the *clock-range* would have changed at exactly the correct rate. In mathematical terms, the clock would have perfectly *integrated* range-rate to generate *change-of-range*. But, in practice, the range-rate could be transferred from the Dumaresq to the clock only at intervals, in steps. Thus, to an extent depending on how frequently the clock-rate was adjusted, the clock-range lagged behind the correct value. The magnitude of these lagging errors will be examined later: but, for now, it will be assumed that they did not compromise range prediction unduly.

With the Dumaresq and the Vickers clock to keep the range, spotting for range became almost as straightforward as when the range was constant. Assume first that the Dumaresq had been set with the correct enemy course and speed. Just before opening fire, the range scale of the clock was rotated so that the hand indicated the opening gun-range, which was calculated as the true-range (estimated from the rangefinders), plus or minus the ballistic corrections. The first salvo that was correct for line probably did not straddle. But, throughout the firing, the clock itself took care of the change in range due to the relative motion. Thus the same spotting rules could be used as when the range was unchanging. Applying each spotting correction to the clock was easy, since one turn of the handle rotated the range scale by 100 yards.

In reality the initial range-rate might well be wrong. But the best thing to do was still to work a range bracket. Normally, the bracket still obtained a straddle, but the clock could not then correctly predict the subsequent change of range and the salvoes drifted off the target. The same happened if the enemy, in taking avoiding action to avoid further straddles and probable hits, altered course. Another possibility was that, if the error in the range-rate was excessive, the bracket might be completed without obtaining a straddle at all.[23] But, in all these cases, once a bracket had been completed, any subsequent corrections for range were accompanied by a change of range-rate in the same sense. Thus, if a salvo fell SHORT, the correction was 'UP 200, OPEN 100', which meant 'increase the range by 200 yards and the range-rate by 100 yds/min.'. This was called *rate-spotting*. After some years of experiment, rate-spotting was simplified to a few easily applied rules-of-thumb – as in the example, where the range-rate correction is, in magnitude, half the range correction.[24]

The need to correct deflection or range-rate by spotting was an indication that the enemy settings on the Dumaresq were wrong; the corrections to speed-across (Dumaresq deflection) and range-rate also suggested how to adjust the enemy bar. The Dumaresq and Vickers clock should then keep the deflection and range more accurately and the firing ship could keep on hitting. Thus it had a real chance of inflicting serious damage before, inevitably, the enemy altered course to throw out the *rates* (a convenient term embracing both range-rate and speed-across) and avoid further hits.

## RATES IN ACTION

A short episode from the Run to the South provides values of the ranges, rates and changes of rate that were typical of actions in which two lines of dreadnoughts engaged on not greatly differing courses (Table 2.1). After the loss of *Indefatigable*, the two forces drew apart for a time. Then, at 4.12 p. m., while *Lützow* steered SbyW at 23 knots, *Lion* began a steep SE'ly approach, speed 24 knots (Chapter 8). By 4.20, both had turned away to courses of S and SSE, respectively. (In this book, as in most documents, signals, etc. from the First World War, courses and bearings are normally expressed in terms of the thirty-two points of the compass. A one-point change corresponds to an angular change of 11¼°.)

*Table 2.1* Rates and change of rates during the Run to the South

| Time | Lion's course | Lützow's course | Lion's enemy bearing | Range yards | Range-rate yds/min. | Rate-of-change of range-rate yds/min/min. | Speed-across knots | Rate-of-change of speed-across knots/min. | Bearing-rate °/min. |
|---|---|---|---|---|---|---|---|---|---|
| 4.15 | SE | SbyW | −80° | 18,500 | −702 | 3.69 | −7.73 | −0.29 | −0.81 |
| 4.22 | SSE | S | −109° | 15,300 | −251 | 2.23 | −5.47 | −0.09 | −0.69 |

Both before and after 4.20, while courses were steady and converging, the speed-across was quite low, though not insignificant. As a result, the bearing-rate was also low, as were the rates-of-change of range-rate and speed-across. Indeed, the rates were almost constant. In contrast, during the turns by both sides, there was a very large change in the range-rate. Thus, in this typical tactical sequence of an approach followed by turns onto courses that closed the range less quickly, the only causes of rapid change of range-rate were the turns themselves. The turns also resulted in changes in speed-across, but, proportionately, they were much less dramatic.

## CHANGING COURSES

When own ship changed course, the large arrow on the dial-plate of the Dumaresq could still be kept pointing at the enemy; this maintained the setting for the enemy's course-bearing, represented by the angle between the fore-and-aft bar and the arrow. The angle between courses was represented by the angle between the fore-and-aft bar and the enemy bar; during a turn, this also changed, by an equal but opposite amount to the change of course (though only if the enemy held his course). The early versions of the Dumaresq provided no more assistance for making this adjustment than for setting the enemy bar in the first place; both had to be done by eye alone. But later versions added bearing scales and gears to help in manipulating the enemy bar. These later Dumaresqs could keep the rates, at least approximately, through a turn by own ship.[25] If the range-rate was transferred to the Vickers clock in sufficiently small steps, the range could also be kept – if not exactly, then at least well enough so that, once the turn was completed, it could be corrected by rangefinding or spotting.

During a turn by own ship, the course-bearing changed rapidly, mainly due to the turn itself. But, even in turns, the compass-bearing-rate remained proportional to the speed-across divided by the range.

Small course changes (normally two points but one point at high speed) could be made by the firing ship without interfering seriously with aiming and firing.[26] But larger and faster turns were much more generally disruptive. In the first place, it was more difficult to adjust the Dumaresq, because own speed fell substantially:

> at speeds from 12 to 16 knots the loss of speed is from 5 to 8 knots for turns over 4 points. When steadied . . . speed . . . is gradually increased by about one knot per minute until the original speed is attained.[27]

Second, under more severe helm, the ship tended to slip sideways appreciably, so the course line no longer corresponded with the fore-and-aft line; this could result in range errors of one to two hundred yards. Third, heel and vibration could cause other difficulties, notably in taking ranges and bearings from positions aloft; in the battleship *Bellerophon* at full speed, 'our mast-head shook like an aspen each time the helm was used'. Aiming and judging the moment to fire were also more difficult during a turn.[28] Thus there were many reasons for, whenever possible, maintaining 'that steady course which is so important for gunnery'.[29]

## PLOTTING

So far, the only method described for setting the Dumaresq for enemy speed and course is by estimation. In the period before the First World War, neither of these vital factors could be measured directly, so a means was needed to deduce them from what could be measured, namely enemy range and bearing. But rangefinder ranges, especially when long, were liable to substantial spreads. As for enemy bearing, a simple telescope and angular scale could be used to measure *relative-bearing* (relative, that is, to the fore-and-aft line), but this bearing fluctuated even when on a nominally steady course; in bad weather, yaws could be as much as 6° in two or three seconds.[30] In contrast, if course-bearing or compass-bearing could be measured relative to a fixed directional reference – defining, respectively, mean-course or North – they would be unaffected by yaw. Such a reference could be provided by a suitable gyroscope, but, even after the adoption of the first gyrocompasses, accuracy was limited. Despite extensive design changes after it entered service with the Royal Navy, the Anschütz model still tended to wander slowly by 5–10° in anything except smooth water.[31] Furthermore, the virtual meridian of any gyrocompass (the direction in which it settled) was influenced by own course and speed; in the North Sea, it could change by as much as 2° following a course alteration of four points by a 25-knot ship.[32] During the First World War, Sperry replaced Anschütz as the Royal Navy's supplier of gyrocompasses, though, even in 1918, the gyrocompass still did not 'enable own ship's motion to be accurately dealt with'.[33] Yet another source of uncertainty in observed bearings was that, until late in the war, they could be transmitted electromechanically between fire control stations only in rather coarse steps of ¼°.[34]

Could these less than precise ranges and bearings be processed to yield values of enemy course and speed that were, at the least, more accurate than those estimated by eye? To this end, both Pollen and Dreyer advocated different forms of plotting. On all types of plot, observed ranges and bearings were recorded as plotted points. Because of the errors in individual values, at first the points appeared scattered at random. But, as plotting proceeded, their general trend became increasingly apparent and it was possible to make out the *mean line* about which the points were scattered. Depending on the nature of the plot, this line could be straight or curved: though it was always easier to make out (or, put another way, it could be made out earlier) if it was straight. This mean line gave an approximate indication of the *true line* that would have been plotted if the data had been error-free. A particular advantage of plotting was that each point could be assessed visually against the general trend and given less weight, or even ignored altogether, if it appeared anomalous.

Pollen always preferred *course plotting*, in which own and enemy courses were plotted as though on a chart. All course plots relied on range-bearing pairs, each pair being taken simultaneously and used to plot a position of the enemy relative to own ship. The easiest variant to describe, though the hardest to implement, was *true-course* plotting. On a single sheet, which represented the sea's surface, the plotter drew own ship's course as a continuous line, which reproduced all changes of heading, whether due to yaw or actual course alterations. A range-bearing pair was taken when own ship was at a certain position on the own-course line; relative to this position, an enemy point was plotted at the observed range and bearing. While the enemy held his course, it appeared as a scatter of points about a straight mean line; if he turned, the new course would be perceptible after a time as a new straight line. If own ship alone altered course, in theory the enemy course plot continued as before, though this depended on the meridian of the gyro reference remaining undisturbed (Figure 2.3).

A course plotter was much simpler in design and construction if own course was plotted as a straight line; this line represented the mean of own course, and, when plotting began, enemy bearings were measured relative to a gyroscopic reference set parallel to this mean course. Any subsequent alterations by the enemy could be registered as on the true-course plot. However, if own ship altered course, the plotter, by design, could only continue to draw a straight line, advancing the plotting point relative to the paper at a speed proportional to own-speed. In one variant of this *straight-course* plotting, the bearings continued to be measured with respect to the old course line; thus the technique required a gyroscopic reference which remained undisturbed by the turn. The figure at b shows how the true courses illustrated previously would appear on this type of straight-course

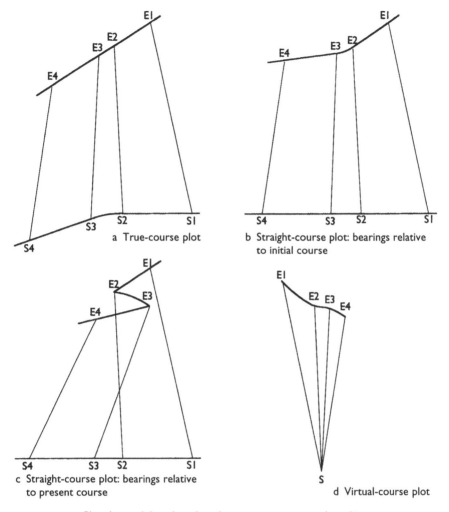

a True-course plot

b Straight-course plot: bearings relative to initial course

c Straight-course plot: bearings relative to present course

d Virtual-course plot

Plots b, c and d are based on the same true-courses plotted in a.

*Figure 2.3* Course plots.

plot. The enemy course plotted after own ship's turn was clearly not the actual course; however, it can be shown that, if a Dumaresq was set with the apparent enemy course, speed and bearing from the plot, the instrument showed the correct virtual course and speed: and so the correct range-rate and speed-across.[33] In a second variant of straight-course plotting (c in Figure 2.3), the gyroscopic reference was reset to the new course once it had steadied. Through the turn, the plot could trace approximately the resulting large change in the enemy's relative bearing; however, no useful information could be extracted from this portion of the plot; in effect, plotting began again after the turn was completed.

The simplest version of course plotting was of *virtual-course*, in which the plotting ship was represented by a single point. Enemy bearings could be taken relative to any convenient fixed directional reference, in practice a compass meridian. The plot gave the virtual course and speed, which could then be used to set the Dumaresq. (On the Dumaresq, the notional line joining the centre of the instrument to the enemy bow pointer represented virtual course and speed.) Any change in course *or* speed by *either* ship resulted, in general, in a change in virtual course *and* speed. Furthermore, unlike real ship speeds, virtual speed could in some situations be small; it was then difficult to make out the virtual enemy movement among the scatter of plotted points.

While courses and speeds were steady, the true lines of all course plots were straight. Once sufficient points had been plotted, the enemy course could be estimated as the direction of the mean line. In contrast, enemy speed could not be obtained as a graphically determined mean based on all the points. A simple method was, by means of dividers or some sort of ruler incorporated in the plotter, to measure the distance between two well-separated points; a speed could then be calculated by dividing the distance by the time interval between the two points. However, in practice the times of the individual points were not printed on the plot; instead, regular minute-marks were made so that the times of individual points could be inferred. But, even if these times were available, the positions of the two points were displaced from their true positions by the errors in their ranges and bearings. If, respectively, errors of ±400 yards and ±½° are assumed, and if the errors all combined to maximise the speed error, then, at the long range of 16,000 yards, the speed calculated from two points plotted two minutes apart could be as much as 12 knots out. Thus a speed derived from only a single pair of points could not be relied on. The worst case error could be reduced by increasing the interval between each pair of points. But it was also necessary to obtain speeds from sufficient pairs until the mean of all the speeds settled down to a consistent value. All these measurements and calculations required time; even four minutes may have been barely sufficient.[36]

An alternative method was to use the timing marks directly to infer how far the enemy moved along the mean course line in some interval of time. We shall return to this possibility when describing Argo's true-course plotters in Chapter 4.

The fire control tables named after Frederic Dreyer relied on *rate-plotting*. Separate plots were made of enemy ranges and bearings against time; thus there was no need for the ranges and bearings to be taken simultaneously. Each plot was drawn on a broad paper band wound at a steady speed between a pair of rollers; thus the time axis for the plot ran up the paper in its direction of motion, and the range (or bearing) axis was horizontal. A plot consisted of a zone of plotted points that could be straight or curved (Figure 2.4).

When own-course was steady, the bearing plot could use either course-bearings or compass-bearings. First, if both courses and speeds were equal,

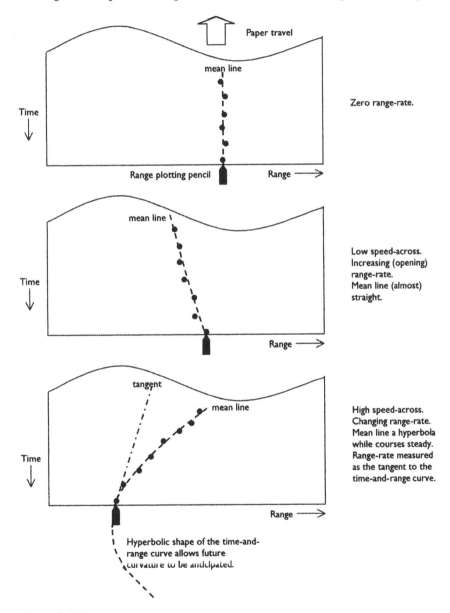

*Figure 2.4* Time-and-range plots.

the plots ran vertically up the paper; the mean line through the *time-and-range plot* then gave a good estimate of the constant range. Second, if the speed-across was low, both rate plots were straight (or almost) and they sloped away from the vertical time axis. The slope of each mean line through all the more recently plotted points was a direct measure of the mean rate. The slope of the *time-and-bearing* plot was only slight. But the time-and-range slope was considerable if the range-rate was high. The mean-line through the most recent part of the plot gave a value for the *mean-rangefinder-range-of-the-moment*.

Third, if the speed-across was high, the bearing, and hence the range-rate, the speed-across and the bearing-rate all changed with time. Thus both rate plots were curved. The most extreme case was when two ships on opposite courses were passing beam-to-beam; for example, as two 25-knot ships passed at 16,000 yards, the range-rate changed at the rate of 178 yds/min/min. Therefore, it was necessary to obtain the current values of bearing-rate and range-rate not from the whole plot, but from only the most recently plotted parts of each curve. This could be done by measuring the slope of the *tangent* to the most recently plotted part of each curve. The time-and-range plot was the more sharply curved. But, when courses were steady, the operators, in judging the slopes of the tangents, could rely on all time-and-range plots having the same characteristic shape. They are all instances of a type of curve called a *hyperbola*, which has two almost straight outer segments separated by a curving middle part.[37] Thus the change of slope was predictable. For example, if the range was falling, then the operator of the plot knew that the slope of the tangent to the most recent part of the curve must be less steep than any earlier tangent. Nonetheless, it was harder to judge this slope accurately in the sharply curved middle part, near the point where the range reached its minimum.

A course plot gave enemy course and speed directly. These could then be set on a Dumaresq (or similar calculating mechanism) to obtain the range-rate and speed-across. In contrast, rate-plotting gave the range-rate directly, while deflection could be calculated once the bearing-rate had been converted into speed-across. But, to reduce dependence on plotted values, it was still necessary to set the Dumaresq with enemy speed and course, so that any changing rates could be predicted. This was done by making a *cross-cut*. As usual, the Dumaresq was set for own-speed and enemy bearing. Then it was, in effect, worked 'in reverse'. The operator obtained from the plotters the latest values of range-rate and bearing-rate and converted the latter to speed-across. Then he found on the dial-plate the point of intersection of the two lines that corresponded to the values from the plot. Finally, by pulling out the enemy bar until its bow pointer lay at the intersection, the enemy course and speed were determined automatically. Thereafter, the Dumaresq worked as usual, keeping range-rate and speed-across even as they changed.

The examples from the Run to the South demonstrate well that, when courses changed, large changes, particularly in range-rate, were likely. This resulted in rate-plots that were sharply curved. Also, if the bearing plot were based on course-bearings, there would be a large discontinuity in the plot with every change of course. It was much better to plot compass-bearings, not least because the momentary speed-across could always be calculated from the bearing-rate measured from the plot. During course changes, the curvatures of the rate plots were much more complex than when courses were steady.[38] Even so, the general direction of curvature of the time-and-range plot could be anticipated to some extent; for example, a turn towards by either ship would make the range-rate close more rapidly, or open less rapidly. Also, the later types of Dumaresq could predict, at least approximately, the changes in rates due to own ship's turns. In any case, it was still worthwhile continuing the rate plots during turns. In many cases, the segments before and after a turn were fairly straight. Thus it was possible to see when an enemy had steadied on a new course and, as soon as new slopes could be measured, to make a new cross-cut.

As already touched on in the introduction, it was possible to record on a time-and-range plot not only the observed rangefinder ranges, but also the range as predicted by the clock. Thus, from moment to moment, the clock-range could be compared with the mean-rangefinder-range-of-the-moment. And, if the actual rangefinder range-rate differed from that predicted by the Dumaresq, the difference in the slopes gave an indication of how to correct the cross-cut. However, since this 'method of "feed-back" correction' was so much a part of the Dreyer Tables, a more detailed discussion can wait until later.

## HIT OR MISS

At the long range of 16,000 yards, the angle of impact of a 13.5-inch shell from *Lion* was 15°. If she was firing at a 30-foot tall battle practice target (a typical superstructure height), any shell holing the target above the waterline would strike the water somewhere beyond it. Thus hitting ranges lay somewhere between the range of the target itself and the range for a shell that just grazed its top. This span of ranges was known as the *danger space*; at 16,000 yards, it was 35 yards for a 30-foot target.[39] Unlike a target, a ship, even broadside on, had considerable width: in the case of *Derfflinger*, almost 32 yards. Consequently, in action she would be hit by any shell falling in the 67-yard-wide zone covered by her waterline extended on the non-engaged side by the danger-space. The shots in a 13.5-inch salvo were spread randomly over at least 300 yards at long range; thus, even if the centre of every salvo were exactly in the middle of this zone, no more than 29 per cent of shells (averaged over many salvoes) would actually hit. This percentage was reduced slightly, to 25 per cent, when the centres of the salvoes and the zone were displaced by 50 yards, but a 100-yard displacement reduced the hit probability to 16 per cent.[40] In other words, changes of range of at least 100 yards were needed for a significant effect on hitting. This, not the danger space alone, provides an indication of the accuracy to which the range had to be determined.[41] In any case, there was no point in striving for accuracies better than the errors detectable by spotting. Wartime experience established that the minimum spotting correction for range should normally be 200 yards (though 100 yards was allowed if the target had already been straddled) and, for rate, 100 yds/min.[42] It should be emphasised that, proportionately, range had to be determined much more accurately than range-rate; in percentage terms, the acceptable range error was 1 per cent or less, whereas the rate error could exceed 10 per cent.

The uncertainties in ranges and bearings, and the additional errors arising from the use of some form of plotting to obtain rates, meant that the initial errors were likely to exceed these minimum corrections. Success in battle then had to rely on the skill of the control officer and spotter in reconciling the imperfectly predicted ranges and rates with what they could see of the enemy and the fall of their salvoes. Long-range gunnery in the dreadnought era was, literally, a hit and miss affair.

## Notes

1 Admiral Sir John Fisher, quoted in Mackay, *Fisher of Kilverstone* [B] p. 385.
2 As seen from *Queen Mary*'s Argo Tower, 54 feet above the waterline: plan in Roberts, *Battlecruisers* [B].
3 Roberts, *Dreadnought* [B] pp. 216–29.
4 *The Barr and Stroud Rangefinders* issued by Barr & Stroud . . . Glasgow, 1906, p. 19, Ja 190, Admiralty Historical Library [AL].
5 'Summary of Results' and *Thunderer*, 'Report on Firings carried out at "Empress of India" 8 November 1913', in 'Gunnery Practice at Sea: Sinking of HMS Empress of India 4/11/13', in ADM 1/8346, PRO.
6 *Iron Duke*, 'Notes made in the . . . Gun Control Tower', in ADM 137/302.
7 Admiralty, Gunnery Branch, *Progress in Gunnery Material 1922 and 1923*, p. 38, ADM 186/259; the higher values were probably due to vibration induced by high speed; *idem, Handbook for Naval Range-Finders and Mountings, Book I, 1921*, p. 24, ADM 186/253.
8 It appears that the second and third refer to the total spread of the scatter: the first to half the spread, and the last, if it is derived from the mean error, may even be only about a quarter of the spread.
9 F. C. Dreyer and C. V. Usborne, *Pollen Aim Correction System. Part I. Technical History and Technical Comparison with Commander F.C. Dreyer's Fire Control System*, printed May 1913, p. 19, P. 1024, AL.
10 *Grand Fleet Gunnery and Torpedo Orders*, 312. 'Rangefinder Errors', 29 December 1917 and 106, 'Rangefinder Errors', 5 October 1918, ADM 137/293 (new numbering sequence from May 1918). Admiralty, Technical History Section, 'Fire Control in H.M. Ships' (TH23), pp. 33–4 in *The Technical History and Index, A Serial History of Technical Problems Dealt with by Admiralty*

*Departments, 1919*, AL. Admiralty, Gunnery Branch, *Progress in Gunnery Material 1921*, p. 9, ADM 186/251 and *PGM 1922–3* [7] p. 53.

11 For a range of 16,000 yards, a 13.5-inch shell reached an altitude of 2,664 feet: Admiralty, Gunnery Branch, *Range Tables for His Majesty's Fleet, 1918, Volume I*, p. 150, ADM 186/236.

12 All sights corrected automatically (though not always exactly) for drift; the more modern also had their own correctors for muzzle velocity and cordite temperature. Admiralty, *The Gunnery Pocket Book 1932*, pp. 60–3.

13 Reginald Plunkett, 'Notes on "Rate"', March 1911, in DRAX 3/4, Drax Papers, CC.

14 Admiralty, Gunnery Branch, *Spotting Rules 1916*, p. 4 in Ja 011, AL. See also ADM 137/2028.

15 Admiralty, Gunnery Branch, *Manual of Gunnery (Volume III) for His Majesty's Fleet 1915*, p. 14, Ja 254, AL. John Brooks, 'Fire Control for British Dreadnoughts: Choices in Technology and Supply' (University of London: PhD thesis, 2001) p. 25 ['FCBD'].

16 Chapter 8.

17 'FCBD', pp. 25–6.

18 *Range Tables 1918* [11] p. 150.

19 Peter Padfield, *Guns at Sea* (London: Hugh Evelyn, 1974) p. 199.

20 Admiralty, Gunnery Branch, *Addenda (1909) to Gunnery Manual Vols I (Part I) and III*, November 1909, p. 13, Ja 254, AL.

21 Even in the worst case, the error resulting from the assumption that range-rate is constant throughout the time-of-flight does not exceed 20 yards.

22 'FCBD', p. 32. In this book, 'Dumaresq' refers to the different marks of instrument used in the Royal Navy, 'dumaresq' to other instruments and mechanisms based on the same principles. (The stress is on the middle syllable.)

23 'FCBD', Appendix I.

24 *Manual of Gunnery 1915* [15] p. 15.

25 'FCBD', Appendix VII.

26 '80. Further remarks on action of 24 January 1915' in 'Secret Packs of the C.-in-C. Grand Fleet. Operations', ADM 137/1943.

27 *Manual of Gunnery 1915*, p. 173.

28 *Technical Comparison*, 1913 [9] pp. 18, 20 and 36. C. V. Usborne, *Blast and Counterblast* (London: John Murray, 1935) p. 9 (for *Bellerophon*).

29 Chatfield, *Navy and Defence* [B] p. 142; also pp. 109 and 134.

30 *PP*, '*Jupiter* Letter III', January 1906, p. 83. 'Fire Control. An Essay by Captain C Hughes-Onslow, completed August 1909, Section IV, p. 5, PLLN 1/5, Pollen Papers, CC.

31 A. E. Fanning, *Steady As She Goes* (London: HMSO, 1986) pp. 177–8.

32 *The Anschütz Gyro Compass* (London: Elliott Brothers, 1910) pp. 69–70 and 91–2, Elliott Archive. Automatic course correction was available, but only from some makers, by the early 1930s: Fanning [31] p. 232 and *The Gyro-Compass and Gyro-Pilot* (London: Sperry Gyroscope, *c.* 1931), p. 14, author's collection.

33 Fanning, pp. 180 and 196–7. Phillpotts committee, 'Report of Inspection at York of Pollen Fire Control System', n.d. but 1918 in DRYR 2/1, Dreyer Papers, CC.

34 *Technical History*, 1919 [10] p. 27.

35 'FCBD', Appendix IV.

36 *Ibid.* Appendix V.

37 The two straight lines to which the outer segments approach ever more closely are called the asymptotes of the hyperbola; their slope is proportional to the virtual speed: 'FCBD', pp. 28–30.

38 'FCBD', Appendix III gives the relevant equations.

39 *Range Tables 1918*, p. 150.

40 The probabilities were calculated assuming that the striking ranges of the shells were distributed normally about the mean salvo range and that 90 per cent of the shells fell within ±150 yards of the mean range.

41 Danger space was defined as the distance *beyond* a 30 ft. high target (a typical superstructure height): *Range Tables 1918*, p. 7. However, in 'The Quest for Reach' Sumida states: 'For the purposes of this paper, the plus-or-minus margin for [range] error was considered to be half the danger space' and concludes that the range tolerance at 15,000 yards was only 13 yards: 'QfR', pp. 50 and 82.

42 *Spotting Rules 1916* [14] pp. 8 and 14. See also '14. Fire Control Organisation', Home Fleet General Orders, 5 November 1913, p. 3, DRAX 1/9.

# 3

# PROGRESS IN GUNNERY

I suppose the years from 1904 to 1914 covered more real
material progress in naval weapons and equipment than any
other ten year period, before or since.[1]

At the start of this decade of progress in gunnery,[2] few ships had more than a
short-base rangefinder and some sight telescopes to use in their long-range
firings; by its close, the latest dreadnoughts were being fitted with Dreyer
Tables and Directors. However, in 1914, most of the battlefleet still
depended on a simpler, manually worked system comprising instruments
which, in several cases, had been invented even before 1904. This chapter
examines the origins of these devices, how they were developed by the
Royal Navy and its suppliers, and how they were used in this, the first British
system of long range fire control.

Under the Controller, the Director of Naval Ordnance and Torpedoes
(the DNO) 'is generally responsible to the Board of Admiralty in regard to
... the armament of the Fleet [and] all matters connected with the Ordnance
and Torpedo material of the Navy'. His deputy, the Assistant Director of
Torpedoes, had his own staff to deal with torpedo matters; the DNO also
had a large staff concerned with the inspection of guns and mountings, and
he was aided by an Assistant DNO. However, only a few officers within the
Naval Ordnance Department (NOD) – they appear in the *Navy List* as
'Assistants to the DNO' – were assigned to the development of new
material; for example, under Captain H. D. Barry, DNO from October 1903
to February 1905, Commander Lynes had sole responsibility for experimental work on non-transferable mountings, sighting gear, rangefinders,
firing gear and communications. The DNO and his assistants could,
however, call on the resources of the gunnery and torpedo schools at
Portsmouth, *Excellent* and *Vernon*. *Vernon* and the torpedo branch
provided special expertise in all electrical matters. Gun trials were
conducted by *Excellent*.[3] Her Captain was also regarded as 'the principal
Admiralty Experimental Officer', a role in which he was assisted by his

Experimental Commander. One of their duties was to examine and report on the 'innumerable inventions' submitted to the Admiralty.[4]

The first attempts at long-range firing (up to 6,000 yards) were made in the Mediterranean Fleet soon after Fisher assumed command in September 1899. An annual long-range gunnery practice at 6,000 yards had been introduced in 1901,[5] but, without proper instruments or training of gun crews, Percy Scott was probably justified in describing it as 'trying to run before we can walk'.[6] In April 1903, Scott was appointed Captain of *Excellent*.[7] In September, the Admiralty agreed to trials of 'the various methods of Controlling, Directing and Ranging Gun Fire in Action' then in use afloat,[8] the ships selected being *Victorious* (Channel Squadron) and *Venerable* (Mediterranean Fleet). Their *Joint Report*, with some qualifications submitted by Scott,[9] established the requirements which led to the first set of instruments for long range gunnery: and, with one exception, these were ready for the first, experimental cruise of HMS *Dreadnought* in early 1907.

*ARETHUSA* TO *DREADNOUGHT*

## Rangefinders

Following the developments in gun materials, construction, propellants and mountings made in the later 1880s, the Admiralty took the first step towards increasing the range at sea by issuing a requirement for a rangefinder accurate to 3 per cent at 3,000 yards. The need had already been anticipated by Professors Archibald Barr and William Stroud, who had designed their first coincidence rangefinder in 1888. Their 4½-foot model proved superior during comparative trials in HMS *Arethusa* in April 1892.[10] With orders in hand from the British and foreign navies, Barr and Stroud were able to establish their company in Glasgow; 'by March 1898 the firm had sold over 150 of their rangefinders around the world'.[11]

By 1901, Barr & Stroud instruments, mainly the improved Mark II, otherwise FA2, were in full service, though they were inadequate at long range,[12] and, since 1899, the Admiralty had been attempting to procure a more accurate rangefinder.[13] In 1903, Barr & Stroud introduced a new 4½-foot model, the FA3, with nearly twice the previous accuracy; the *Joint Reports* of both committees recommended that it could 'be usefully employed up to even 8,000 yards', particularly if given finer graduations, 'but for the longer ranges . . . an even better one should be obtained'.[14] In 1904, the Admiralty decided to advertise again; the products of several suppliers, including Barr & Stroud, were being considered in 1905,[15] and by July 1906 'satisfactory trials have been carried out with a rangefinder produced by Barr and Stroud having a 9-foot base'.[16] Sufficient were ordered to fit two of these instruments (designated FQ2) in the latest all-big-gun ships.[17] The new instrument further secured Barr & Stroud's position as, in effect, the monopoly supplier; at £325, the FQ2 was not inexpensive, but the firm refused to compromise on quality or price.[18]

## Gun sights

Naval memoirs credit Percy Scott with the invention of the telescopic sight and even with having forced it upon the Navy.[19] Yet, in May 1898 (just over a year before the famous prize-firing by *Scylla*),[20] the Ordnance Committee decided to seek the advice of Dr A. A. Common FRS, a past president of the Royal Astronomical Society and an eminent optician, on the best form of telescope for use with automatic sights. From 1900 onwards, telescopes were purchased in quantity, either through Common or direct from manufacturers, including Barr & Stroud.[21] Initially, priority was given to fitting the more mobile hand-worked guns over turret guns but, by the end of 1903, the supply of 'one [telescopic sight] per gun, 12-pr. and above, is now nearly complete' while 'Money has been provided in the 1904–05 Estimates for . . . the supply, to all existing 6-inch guns, of a second telescope (the variable power [by Ross])'.[22]

Unfortunately, fitting telescopes to old sights served only to emphasise their mechanical imperfections.[23] After some improvements were introduced for the *King Edward VII* class, a new direct-action sight was designed for the paired 9.2-inch and 12-inch turrets of the *Lord Nelson* class; since it was mounted directly on the trunnions, backlash due to mechanical linkages was eliminated. In fact, the first five B.VIII mountings with these sights were installed in *Dreadnought*.[24]

More accurate sights warranted precise calibration for the individual characteristics of each gun. An allowance of ammunition for calibration had been authorised in October 1904 but, once again, Scott considered this premature. In 1905, as soon as a ship with accurate sights was available (*Commonwealth* of the *King Edward VII* class), a Calibration Committee was appointed, with Scott, now Inspector of Target Practice (ITP) as President. In August 1905, their recommendations were promulgated to the Fleet and, by 1907, six calibration ranges had been established world-wide.[25]

## Electrical fire control instruments

While the Royal Navy still relied on voice-pipes for the communication of ranges and orders, in 1894 Barr & Stroud began the development of electrical instruments for this purpose. The company's first customer was the Imperial Japanese Navy in 1898, the Royal Navy ordering its first set a year later. Further sets were purchased for the experiments in *Venerable* and *Victorious*,[26] but the *Joint Report* described them as 'somewhat complicated and cumbersome'; it also recommended that the instruments of other manufacturers should be tried and that, in future, ranges should be displayed 'as on a cyclometer', rather than on circular dials.[27] Barr & Stroud had already submitted proposals for a double-dial instrument that could transmit ranges in 25-yard steps up to 12,000 yards. For the moment, this improvement was enough to retain the Admiralty's custom; in February 1905, the outgoing DNO reported that Barr & Stroud range and order instruments were being bought as quickly as possible and, eventually, fifteen ships were fitted.[28] However, they were judged 'clumsy and not all we would wish',[29] probably because, although on the step-by-step principle (which required only a few wires between transmitter and receiver), the instruments relied on spring-powered clockwork and an electrically-operated escapement.

Barr & Stroud were not, however, without rivals. Even in 1902, the Admiralty were considering fire control instruments from Messrs Cory of New York (as fitted in the *Illinois*), Eversheds and a design by Captain Grenfell.[30] By February 1905, *Vernon* had tried types by Elliott Brothers, Watkin, Thorp, Chatham E.E. and others, though none had proved satisfactory. The British Siemens Brothers company were offering three direct-working (synchronous) instruments,[31] as well as a step-by-step instrument that may have originated with the German firm of Siemens & Halske; subsequently, the latest direct-working design was selected for use in nineteen pre-dreadnoughts.[32] Meanwhile, in early 1905, trials were beginning of new step-by-step instruments submitted by Vickers; the design was strongly influenced by Percy Scott and tried out by *Excellent*. The electric pulses from the transmitter alone powered the receiver motor, while its rotor could take up only four stable positions.[33] This technical advance enabled Vickers to supplant Barr & Stroud and, eventually, forty-two ships had complete Vickers installations; an installation for HMS *Illustrious* (*Majestic* class) cost £1,242. The list was headed by *Dreadnought* herself.[34]

## The Dumaresq

Lieutenant John Dumaresq may have invented his instrument in 1902 but he was still developing it in May 1904, after it had been tried by the fire control committee in his own ship, the *Victorious*. Although two other 'Rate of Change' instruments were mentioned by the Mediterranean Committee,[35] the *Joint Report* recommended the adoption only of the Dumaresq, for control tops, turrets and 6-inch groups, noting specifically that it 'combines rate of change and deflection'.[36] The first Service model Dumaresq (subsequently known as the Mark I) and later models were manufactured by Elliott Brothers, who paid the fees when the device was patented (though in Dumaresq's name) in August 1904.[37] These orders were an early success for a firm which was later to supply many more of the Royal Navy's fire control instruments.[38] The Mark I was graduated for deflection in knots, but the range-rate was expressed in seconds to change 50 yards. The range could then be kept with a stopwatch; the watch was run for the number of seconds indicated, then the range transmitters were altered up or down by 50 yards as the watch was reset.[39]

By mid-1906, it had been decided to add small sights to the dial-plate while 'a design is also being got out of an instrument of greater size',[40] although this was not, apparently, ready in time for *Dreadnought*'s first experimental cruise. By mid-1907, 'from two to six of these instruments are supplied to electrical fire control ships ... half being of the large Mark II size and half small Mark I'.[41]

## Scott/Vickers clock

In a lecture delivered in December 1903, Percy Scott first described a 'range indicator' with the characteristic features of the range clock i.e. a hand rotating at a continuously adjustable rate over a circular range scale that could itself be rotated.[42] In April 1904, Scott's associates at Vickers applied for a patent which described a number of alternative designs, all based on variable-speed drives, including the disc-and-roller eventually adopted. Despite Scott's hopes, no clock had been completed for trial by the committees on fire control, though the Channel Committee still recommended his proposal rather than an earlier design by Lieutenant Fawcet Wray.[43] Some Scott/Vickers clocks were available for the 1905 Battle Practice; by mid-1906, delivery was awaited of the first production order of 246.[44] On her experimental cruise, *Dreadnought* had several (probably three) Vickers clocks in her transmitting station, sufficient to allow some of her turrets to be controlled independently if required.[45]

Of the Dumaresq, Scott remarked:

> I do not think that machines to calculate the rate of change in distance will be of much use, their working must depend upon what you estimate the relative speeds and courses to be.

Instead, he proposed that the range-rate should be 'obtained by Range Finding and timing, or guessed';[46] by 1906, finding the rate by timing was accepted as one 'of the two principal methods of ascertaining and keeping the rate',[47] though, at longer range with 4½-foot rangefinders, it was considered no more accurate than using a Dumaresq with estimated enemy speed and course. Scott also suggested that: 'If the fall of shot shows that too much or too little change in range is being applied, the rate can be altered';[48] this is the first mention of what was later called rate-spotting, but Scott did not say how the rate might be altered, any more than he explained how to obtain an opening deflection without a Dumaresq. Scott agreed with the

Mediterranean Committee that the contemporary 4½-foot rangefinders could give an approximate indication of the opening range, but that the target could be found only by spotting.[49]

## *Dreadnought*

By 1906, the supply of almost all the fire control instruments for *Dreadnought* had been arranged. However, after successful experiments aboard *Duke of Edinburgh*, it was decided that, in future, the clocks and the range and deflection transmitters to the individual turrets should be moved below to a transmitting station (TS), protected by armour, near the base of each mast. The TS would be connected by a large diameter voice-pipe to its top, where the rangefinder and Dumaresq remained, 'the initial range and spotting corrections and deflection being passed by voice-pipes and the "rate" by special electrical transmitters'.[50] On her experimental cruise *Dreadnought* was fitted with an improvised TS above the armoured deck; also, she had to rely only on voice-pipe communication from the top, the new range-rate instruments not being yet available. But *Dreadnought* was fitted with all the other new fire control instruments that had been developed in the preceding years.

Despite her many novelties, in one respect *Dreadnought* was no different from her predecessors. In October 1906, the report on *Dreadnought*'s gun trials noted that 'it is extremely difficult to readily obtain a slow movement of the guns in elevation which is required to follow the small roll or to keep the sights on at the bottom or top of a larger roll', while the training gear was 'not good enough to keep the sights continuously on for fire at a moving object when the ship is under way'.[51] Thus the continuous aim necessary for salvo firing was impossible with any motion on the ship. Even in the calm conditions of the Experimental Cruise, on two runs *Dreadnought* ranged with a single gun and fired a single salvo, but then, presumably due to induced roll, followed after more than a minute with a four-gun ripple. The mean range was no more than 5,000 yards but only three-quarter charges were used against a small (15 ft by 20 ft) target;[52] these firings were, therefore, no more than the first test of a still imperfect weapons system.

## Battle Practice 1904–6

By 1904, the annual long-range practice had been renamed Battle Practice and, for the following year, uniform rules were laid down (by Scott as ITP) for the first time; 17.2 per cent of hits were made on the moored target, 90-ft long and 30-ft high. In 1906 (as in 1905) each ship was led by the umpire on an unknown course; firing began at just over 6,000 yards and, when the range had fallen to about 5,000 yards, a course alteration of two points or so changed the range-rate from closing 200 yds/min. to much the same opening.[53] Trainee gunnery officers in *Excellent* had to cope with even more demanding conditions.

> Fire was opened at ranges between 7,000 and 8,500 yards, with the target bearing 45 degrees to 60 degrees before the beam, the minimum range being about 6,000 yards. The speed was 8 to 11 knots, *the exact amount being unknown at the control position* and a turn of two to three points was made during the run [my italics].[54]

Arthur Pollen was very critical of what he called 'the kindergarten conditions of battle practice'. However, he acknowledged 'the astounding variation that the present tests . . . exhibit', and he admitted that, with a moored target, 'change of range is far more rapid than in many cases where the target will be moving'.[55] Until a towed target was introduced, Battle Practice may have been somewhat artificial, but, in view of the elaborate provisions to ensure that the changing rates could be obtained, as in action, only from observations of the target, it was not as childishly simple as Pollen alleged.

## Laying and training

Even before *Dreadnought* had been laid down, Captain John Jellicoe, DNO since February 1905, recognised that effective shooting required salvo firing, and he initiated a programme to improve the hydraulic elevating and training gear, so that turret guns could be aimed continuously.[56] While the *Manual of Gunnery 1907* (written, of course, for a pre-dreadnought fleet) admitted that 'no facilities exist at present for keeping "continuous aim" with turret guns',[57] in July 1907 Jellicoe was able to report to his successor, Captain Reginald Bacon, that experiments by *Excellent* had established that:

> with suitably shaped elevating [valve] ports, worked by wheel elevation gear, it is possible to 'hunt the roll' with hydraulically controlled mountings to the same extent as is at present possible with hand-worked mountings.[58]

Fisher was able to claim 'a tremendous improvement . . . in the controlling apparatus for power-worked guns' and to announce that 'Provision has been made in the 1908–09 Estimates to fit this gear to all the hydraulic turrets in the Service'.[59] At the end of 1909, Bacon handed over to Captain Archibald Moore, informing him that 'the speed of elevating has been increased up to 3° per second', though this was obtained only by three full turns of the controlling handwheel; this speed was even 'slightly increased' when the heavier 13.5-inch guns were introduced in the *Orion* and *Lion* classes. By May 1912, Moore could report that 'it is arranged for 1911–12 ships [*Iron Dukes* and *Tiger*] to have a speed of elevating of 5° per second with one turn of handwheel'.[60]

Continuous aim also depended on continuous training. *Dreadnought*'s turrets were trained by a pair of three-cylinder hydraulic engines.[61] These engines were controlled by a lever-operated reversing valve and a separate 'creep-valve', worked by a wheel, which proved 'very awkward' in use.[62] Eventually, Portsmouth Dockyard designed a satisfactory training control in which a single wheel operated both the reversing and creep valves; by November 1909, both *Dreadnought* and *Inflexible* (the latter having the same training arrangements) had been refitted on these lines.[63]

To obtain more even training torque, in 1906 Elswick (EOC) developed a six-cylinder rotary engine, which was first installed in HIJMS *Kashima*. For British ships, Portsmouth again worked out a design for a control valve operated by a single wheel. The new control and engine, the latter rotating the turrets through a worm drive, were adopted for the battlecruiser *Indomitable*, the *Bellerophon* class and later ships. During *Indomitable*'s gun trials in 1908, the new gear showed a marked reduction in throw-off and good control of starting, stopping and creep with little effort on the handwheel, whereas, with *Inflexible*'s Vickers turrets, which retained the older three-cylinder training engines: 'a marked feature . . . was the poor training control. The creep . . . is jerky: the turrets do not start or stop with precision [and] the reversal of direction is erratic'.[64] A further improvement in '"sweetness" of control' of training was obtained with the introduction (again by Elswick) of the swash-plate engine, seven-cylinder engines of this type being adopted for the turrets of *Hercules*, *Colossus* and later classes.[65] Thus, by 1912, the guns mobility was transformed, so that:

> in 'Orion' all gunlayers [are] able to follow a roll of 12 degrees out to out without difficulty and some a roll of 16 degrees to 18 degrees out to out.[66]

Thus continuous aim, and hence salvo firing, was possible in all but heavy weather.

### Fire control instruments and gunsights

By mid-1907, Barr & Stroud had recaptured the lead in fire control instruments; compared with the Vickers, its Mark II instruments were judged to be better electrically – they used only one-third the current and the receiver had no commutator – and generally very satisfactory. They were chosen for the *Invincible* class and a later variant, the Mark II*, for the *Bellerophon* and *St. Vincent* classes and *Neptune*, while, by the end of 1909, the unsatisfactory Mark I range and order instruments were being replaced by Mark IIs, a process which had been completed by 1912.[67]

In the transmitting stations of the first dreadnoughts, a clock operator would 'call the 25s and also call the range every time a full hundred yards is reached', while the transmitter men (one per turret) would rotate the transmitter handles at each 25-yard step. At the guns, the sight-setters then had to read the ranges and deflections off the receivers and set the sights accordingly: although, by 1909, they had been provided with telephone headsets, through which they could hear the range steps being called in the TS. Nonetheless, it must have been difficult to keep up when the range-rate was high – at 600 yds/min., the range changed by 25 yards every 2½ seconds.[68] Some help could be provided in the TS by connecting the multiple transmitters mechanically; first tried in 1908, this 'cross-connecting gear' was widely fitted in pre-dreadnoughts and in dreadnoughts up to *Neptune*.[69] However, sight-setting was the greater problem. Even in 1904, two proposals were under consideration for setting sights automatically with ranges and deflections transmitted from the control. The first was due to Lieutenant A. V. Vyvyan and Mr L. Newitt, Electrical Engineer at Chatham Dockyard; the second was initially from Siemens Brothers, though, encouraged by the Admiralty, they soon reached a collaborative agreement with Vickers. Unfortunately, despite several years' effort, neither group was successful; by mid-1907, a Siemens-Vickers electrically set sight had been tried but rejected and the Vyvyan-Newitt sight was also about to be abandoned.[70] However, Vickers had already submitted a simpler alternative in conjunction with the new cam-sights on the Vickers 4-inch mountings for the light cruiser *Boadicea*. This was the follow-the-pointer sight, which still used the sight-setter's muscle power to set the sight, but required him only to keep a pointer (driven by a new brushless step-by-step receiver motor connected to a transmitter in the TS) aligned with an index-marker.[71]

In turrets, the sights for the *St. Vincent* class introduced two important changes. They used a cam and roller (rather than the previous curved rack with pinion) to determine elevation. And the straight telescope was dropped in favour of a magnifying periscope.[72] Then, for *Hercules*, *Colossus* and *Indefatigable*, the sights were fitted with Vickers follow-the-pointer gear, an arrangement which became the standard thereafter; by 1916, it was considered that:

> The outstanding improvements of the whole [pre-war] period are the introduction of the cam system and its adaptation to 'follow-the-pointer'.[73]

However, while Vickers now monopolised the supply of instruments on the circuits to the guns, Barr & Stroud continued to provide the instruments for communicating all other ranges, as well as rates, bearings and orders.[74]

The Obry/Petravic gyro-stabilised gun firing apparatus must also be mentioned.[75] It was offered to the Admiralty by its Austrian inventors in 1908 and, after a visit to their Vienna works, Frederic Dreyer (from mid-1907 to the end of 1909, the assistant to the DNO for fire control) recommended a trial. This was held in September 1908 at HMS *Excellent* but was not a success, the gyro being deranged by the shocks of firing and by changes of course and speed.[76] Obry and von Petravic persisted with development, but were unable to persuade the German Navy to adopt their apparatus until after the Battle of Jutland, when the similar Henderson gyro firing gear was also added to the British Director.[77]

## The Director

Vickers' follow-the-pointer technology was an important element in the production Director system. This enabled the aim of the guns to be controlled from a master gun-sight positioned aloft. This Director sight – which itself incorporated follow-the-pointer receivers for gun-range and deflection from the TS – transmitted its elevation and training angles to the guns. In the turrets, the layers and trainers watched follow-the-pointer receivers; by working their hydraulic controls, they kept the receiver pointers that indicated gun elevation and turret training in line with the pointers showing the angles received from the Director sight.[78]

The first director proposal was put forward by Percy Scott in February 1905 as a means of elevating all turret guns at a fixed angle of elevation; the guns could then be fired together from the director sight as the ship's roll brought its telescope 'on'. His idea was welcomed by Jellicoe as a means of firing salvoes from *Dreadnought* even if continuous aim proved unattainable. Scott's design was constructed by Vickers and tried in the battleship *Africa* in early 1907. Before handing over to Bacon, Jellicoe recommended further trials and also arranged for materials to enable Scott to fit an extempore director once he joined his flagship, the *Good Hope* – though Scott probably also borrowed components from Vickers. In 1909, the equipment performed fairly well in Battle Practice and in subsequent trials. Bacon also initiated work by Portsmouth Dockyard on yet another fixed-elevation director. However, its design and construction suffered many delays; it was first installed in *Dreadnought* but, to avoid its trials interfering with the work of the flagship, it was moved to *Bellerophon*. Trials were eventually held in May 1910 but Captain Hugh Evan-Thomas recommended against adoption.

However, well before Bacon left the NOD at the end of 1909, he had become sceptical of the utility of fixed-elevation directors. When Moore took over as DNO, the Admiralty had already arranged for Scott to work with Vickers on the development of a full elevation-and-training director, and approval had been given to fit *Neptune* with the new system. Trials held in the first quarter of 1911 were sufficiently successful for Moore to recommend that, beginning with the *Orions* and *Lions*, all ships should be wired for director firing. However, he was not satisfied that the *Neptune* gear was yet sufficiently accurate or reliable. A second prototype, with many improvements, was fitted in *Thunderer* and proved itself in the famous competitive shoot with *Orion* in November 1912. In 1913, after Moore had been promoted to Controller, two large orders, for twenty-nine ships in all, were placed with Vickers, while the first production model was installed in *Ajax*. By August 1914, another six ships had been fitted,[79] while, on the eve of Jutland, only *Erin* and *Agincourt* were without Directors.

Apart from Scott's own unreliable memoirs, there are no grounds for Sumida's suggestions that:

> The replacement of Jellicoe by Bacon . . . appears to have ended Ordnance Department support for director firing

or that the trials of the *Neptune* director:

> were successful enough to convince Jellicoe to advise its adoption, but his recommendations were not followed, which may have been the result of the opposition of Moore.[80]

Bacon probably did cease supporting further development of fixed-elevation directors, but it was during his time as DNO that Scott and Vickers began their collaboration on the full elevation-and-training director. Moore, rightly, was opposed to adopting the still imperfect *Neptune* design, but, after two further design iterations, he, as Controller, was ultimately responsible for placing the production order.

> The finished Scott/Vickers director system was one of infinite refinement which would have been impossible some years earlier.

It was also in advance of the German system, which controlled only training, and even further ahead of other navies.[81] Scott deserves due credit for his inventiveness and drive, but so too does the Admiralty for putting him to work with Vickers, and for supporting director firing from its simple beginnings in 1905 to the massive wartime production programme.

## Target bearings

Following tactical exercises by the Home Fleet in early 1910, the C.-in-C., Admiral Sir William May, requested action on the 'very general desire . . . for some accurate and reliable means of pointing out at the gun positions the ship to be attacked'.[82] As a result of Wilson's recommendations after the

*Ariadne* trials, instruments for the transmission of target compass bearings (designated Mark I) had been obtained from Barr & Stroud. These were soon superseded by the Mark II, which indicated relative-bearings to port or starboard. Both designs, of the usual step-by-step cyclometer type, indicated in steps of ¼°.[83]

A new type of bearing instrument was under consideration even in 1908. In 1907, the firm of Evershed & Vignolles had submitted range, order and deflection instruments working on the balanced-bridge principle that the firm had used previously in helm indicators. Although judged too large and expensive as first proposed, the technology proved adaptable to target bearing indication; the first prototype Evershed installation was ready in January 1910 for trials aboard *Superb*, though supply of the more elaborate production version did not commence until December 1912, with *Bellerophon*.[84]

The Evershed transmitter was coupled to an optical target indicator, which could be a telescope, periscope or an Argo rangefinder mounting. One form of receiver was mounted on the telescope of a trainer's sight; its needle indicated the direction of training to bring the designated target into the field of view of the sight telescopes. By the outbreak of war, all the 12-inch battleships and battlecruisers had been supplied, except for *Neptune*, *Australia* and *New Zealand*; of the 13.5-inch ships, only *Lion* and *Princess Royal*, *Orion*, *King George V* and *Centurion* had been fitted. After the start of the war, priority was given to 15-inch ships as they were completed, so (with the exception of *Conqueror* in February 1915) no more installations were made in the earlier ships until after Jutland. Ships without Eversheds or Directors had to rely on Barr & Stroud Mark II bearing receivers to keep all turrets on the same target.[85]

## Rangefinders and mountings

As first mounted in *Dreadnought*, the 9-foot rangefinder was elevated and trained by the one operator who also took the ranges. By the end of 1909, improved mountings with separate training gear – the rangetaker remained responsible for elevation – were on order for the *St. Vincent* and later classes, together with conversion kits for existing ships. By early 1912, deliveries had begun of Argo's gyro-stabilised rangefinder mounting. In the *Lion* and *King George V* classes and later, this was placed beneath a revolving armoured hood (the Argo Tower) atop the conning tower. In earlier classes (except *Hercules*), the Argo mounting was located aloft, where necessary in an enlarged (fore) top.[86]

In 1908, the DNO's department under Bacon began investigating how a rangefinder could be fitted in a turret; by 1909, Bacon also recognised that such a turret could be further equipped as an alternative control position. In 1910, work had begun on installing a 9-foot rangefinder beneath an armoured hood in one turret of all ships from *Dreadnought* to the *Orion* class, while two turrets were to be equipped in *Lion* and *Princess Royal*. However, consideration was then being given to the local control of fire, which would require a rangefinder for every turret. By mid-1912, this had already been approved for *King George V*, *Queen Mary* and later ships; by the next year, it had been extended to the turrets of all dreadnoughts, though the rangefinders were fitted, in haste, only after the outbreak of war.[87]

While he was DNO, Jellicoe had encouraged Barr & Stroud to persevere with the development of a longer and more accurate rangefinder, and his successor had ordered a trial 15-foot FR instrument by January 1908. Bacon reported that it 'has given good results. It is being returned to the makers to remedy certain [unspecified] defects before further trials take place'.[88] Unfortunately, under Moore, progress seems to have stalled. One apparent cause was the hope that the Argo mounting would enable the 9-foot instrument to 'to get accurate R.F. [rangefinder] readings up to 12,000 or 13,000 yards'.[89] Second, Barr & Stroud was slow to remedy the defects in the FR. In May 1912, Moore advised his successor as DNO, Captain F. C. T. Tudor:

Some two years ago Barr and Stroud submitted a 15-foot range-finder for trial ... but the gain in accuracy was not as great as might be expected.

A second 15-foot, much improved, has been purchased for the B turret of the 'Ajax'.[90]

This second instrument was probably of the recent FT design, which was put into production in 1913 as the Glasgow firm's standard 15-foot instrument, the FT24. From that year, Barr & Stroud routinely supplied 12- and 15-foot rangefinders to foreign navies and had even delivered one turret rangefinder 33 feet in length. Yet, while Moore was Controller – from May 1912 to August 1914 – the Admiralty did little to fit these more accurate instruments. Apart from the single trial rangefinder (later moved to *Orion*), the 15-foot FT24 was ordered in quantity only for the *Queen Elizabeth* class.[91]

Jellicoe and his two successors all invited Thomas Cooke and Sons of York to submit rangefinders for trial. A principal motivation is made clear by Bacon.

The trials of the Cooke 10-foot range-finder showed this to be an excellent instrument, but the price was found to be prohibitive. This is regrettable, as the introduction of this range-finder would have started competition with Barr and Stroud's.[92]

After comparisons between 12-foot instruments from the two firms, Moore concluding that:

> the Cooke appears to have better light-gathering capacity, and possibly, owing to this cause, greater accuracy.[93]

There is no reason to doubt that the Cooke-Pollen rangefinder was an excellent if expensive instrument; the Russian Navy preferred it to the Barr & Stroud even though it cost three times as much. However, the Admiralty's policy of fitting many rangefinders in each ship, and Cooke's close association with Pollen, made it doubly difficult to secure orders. Eventually, in March 1918, thirty Cooke rangefinders were ordered but, overburdened with other work, the firm was able to deliver only ten by the time hostilities ended,[94] so Barr & Stroud's monopoly position still remained unassailed.

Rangefinders could give accurate ranges only if worked by trained and experienced rangetakers. In early 1910, the Inspector of Target Practice (Rear Admiral Richard Peirse) insisted on the need for proper training and regular courses of instruction, while the DNO urged the Board, unsuccessfully, to introduce the non-substantive rating of rangetaker.[95] The conference convened after the unsatisfactory 1911 Battle Practice concluded that: 'The supply of a properly qualified Seaman or Marine Rangetaker for every 9-ft. rangefinder . . . is urgently required' and again proposed the introduction of the rating of rangetaker.[96] This cannot have been accepted since the DNO made the same submission in April 1913 and repeated it yet again in December after the *Empress of India* firing had shown that 'the Range-takers . . . are at present the weak spot in our fire Control personnel'. Even then, another six months was to pass before, at last, the Board gave its approval on 19 July 1914.[97] Thus as the war began, it is doubtful whether, for rangefinding, the Royal Navy was as well trained – or, indeed, as well equipped – as it could have been.

## Dumaresqs

The Dumaresq evolved through cooperation between naval officers and designers from industry. In February 1908, Frederic Dreyer suggested how, by adding gears to the Dumaresq, the enemy bar could rotate with the dial-plate during a turn. Hence the inclination – the angle between the line-of-sight and the enemy course – would remain constant. This was not exact, but it was a good approximation when (as in the examples from the Run to the South) the speed-across was low. A mechanical implementation was worked out by Elliott Brothers after consultation with Dreyer; although no instrument was then constructed, the principles would be taken up again later.[98]

In 1909, two compass rings had been added experimentally to the Dumaresq Mark II so that it could indicate own and enemy compass courses;

the second ring, centred on the pivot of the enemy bar, was in the form of a spoked wheel suggested by Elphinstone. While the design did not depend on any approximations, making the necessary adjustments through a turn must have been tricky. Nonetheless, the design became the prototype for the Dumaresqs Mark II* (modified Mark IIs) and the new Mark III.[99] On the dial-plate, range-rates were now expressed in yards-per-minute. Also, new graduation lines, for bearing-rate and for range, permitted rapid conversion between bearing-rate and speed-across.

The Dumaresq Mark IV was developed during 1910 for use in turrets under local control. After conferences in June with Commander R. Backhouse (Experimental Commander at Whale Island),[100] and with Commander J. Henley at the Admiralty, the design 'was worked out into practical form by Elliott Brothers' and, by the October, was ready for supply, subject only to some final modifications. The Mark IV used a simplification of Dreyer's original idea from 1908. The Dumaresq Mark VI was a complete realisation, based on a model developed at *Excellent* by Lieutenant Prickett, which was shown to Elphinstone in December 1910. During a turn, the operator, using a special handwheel, followed the target by rotating the dial-plate, and, with it, the enemy bar. In most tactical situations, the error in enemy course after the turn was only a few degrees.[101] These instruments were intended not to be exact in all circumstances, but to be easy to use in the most likely ones.

Up to 6 January 1913, Elliotts had supplied a total of 1,042 Dumaresqs at the modest cost of £9,539; simple models like the Mark IV turret instrument cost only £4 10s 0d. Even after the Mark VI, the Dumaresq continued to evolve,[102] and variants of the instrument became vital components in the Dreyer fire control tables.

### The Vickers clock

By mid-1907, two or more clocks had been supplied to ships with electrical fire control 'according to the description of guns on board', a policy reiterated by Bacon in 1909. The clock was later fitted with a second red gun-range pointer mounted frictionally on the same axis as the original black pointer, the latter then indicating rangefinder range; this dual-pointer clock had already been introduced by 1913.[103] Even the first production models provided for firing at long ranges. The graduated rim 'is divided into 4,000 yards but the graduations are numbered through windows in the face so that 3 ranges are available, 2,000–6,000 6,000–10,000 and 10,000 to 14,000 yards'. The numbers were in 100-yard steps, with scale divisions every 25 yards. Originally, the rim was revolved by hand but, in 1908, a handle was added, one turn changing the indicated range by 100 yards.[104] In the first models, the rate drum was calibrated in knots but also, like the contemporary Dumaresq, in seconds-per-50-yards 'so that, in case of breakdown of the clock a stop-watch can be used'.[105] However, in 1909 the rate scales on the clocks were changed to yards-per-minute; these units were also adopted for the Barr & Stroud Mark II rate transmitters and receivers,[106] and for Dumaresqs.

*In Defence of Naval Supremacy* states categorically that the 'motor [of the Vickers clock] could not be made to vary in speed continuously ... the speed ... was altered in steps'.[107] In fact, the clock was based on a conventional disc-and-roller variable-speed drive (Figure 3.1) with springs driving the 'rotating disc at a constant speed controlled by a governor'.[108] The variable speed was obtained by moving the roller along the diameter of the disc, and it is clear from the clock's mechanism that the roller could be moved continuously by means of threaded rods coupled to the rate handle. 'The Quest for Reach' attributes the earlier interpretation to some misleading statements by Arthur Pollen, but it also states:

> Changes in the indication of the rate by the dumaresq had to be transferred manually to the Vickers clock, and because the transfers could not be carried out continuously, continuous change in the range rate was imperfectly represented by the clock to a greater or lesser extent depending on the rapidity of change and the time intervals between resettings.[109]

When necessary, the rate was read from the Dumaresq and applied to the clock as frequently as every quarter-minute. Nonetheless, the clock-rate and, therefore, the clock-range lagged behind the true rate and range: but by how much?

While in some cases the rates may have been transferred at fixed intervals, it must have been much easier to transmit the rates in fixed steps. If, to take an extreme case, two 25-knot ships were passing beam-to-beam on opposite courses at 8,000 yards, the range-rate changed by over 350 yds/min. in each minute; thus the only practicable method was to alter the rate each

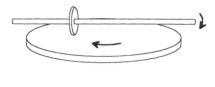

Disc-and-roller

Speed of rotation of the roller (clockwise or anticlockwise) proportional to the distance of the roller from the centre of the disc.

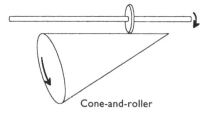

Cone-and-roller

Speed of rotation of the roller (in one direction) proportional to the distance of the roller from the apex of the cone.

*Figure 3.1* Variable speed drives.

time the Dumaresq pointer crossed a major rate division on the dial i.e. in steps of 100 yds/min.,[110] at intervals of about 17 seconds. Mathematical analysis shows that, whenever the rate changes frequently in equal steps, the lagging error of the clock-range behind the true-range can be expressed very simply. It is the same error that would arise if the range-rate were incorrect by half the size of each rate-step.[111] Thus, if the rate-step was 100 yds/min., the effective rate-error was 50 yds/min., i.e. in each minute, the clock-range lagged a further 50 yards behind the true-range. However, normally (again, see the figures from the Run to the South) the range-rate changed much more slowly and there would have been plenty of time for rate transfers in steps of 50 or even 25 yds/min., thus halving or quartering the worst case lagging errors.

Sumida also states that 'the disc-roller drive of the early production Vickers clocks is known to have been mechanically unsatisfactory' and refers to 'the weakness of the drive, which meant that it could not be connected to a transmitter'.[112] However, since the clock had been designed as a self-contained instrument powered by springs, it had never been intended to drive step-by-step transmitters directly. On the other hand, when in 1925 the Vickers clock was examined by the Royal Commission on Awards to Inventors, it was seen to 'check' or even, briefly, 'stop altogether' when the range-rate was altered.[113] While the rate changed, the roller moved sideways across the disc, so, at their point of contact, there was sliding rather than rolling friction. Hence, to some extent, the roller could slip relative to the disc: and so the indicated range would fall behind the correct value. But it has been possible to calculate the extent of this slippage error, and it turns out to have been barely significant; a change in rate of 100 yds/min. induced a range lag of only 5.4 yards.

Nonetheless, the early history of the Vickers clock shows that, initially, it had a number of mechanical problems, particularly with the governor; by 1909, it had been necessary to fit both a compensating brake and a second driving spring.[114] These seem to have been satisfactory when the rate was constant, but they evidently did not prevent a drop in the disc speed when (as calculation shows) the load on the spring drive doubled while the rate was being changed. Fortunately, the resulting checks were only brief; they caused range errors that were usually negligible and always less than those due to the stepwise setting of rate.[115] The Vickers clock was by no means a perfect mechanism – but its accuracy was sufficient for its purpose, which was to keep the *change of range* in the intervals between corrections to the clock-range derived either from the mean rangefinder range or from spotting.

## Other fire control instruments

In 1908, Frederic's brother, Captain John Dreyer RA, submitted a design for a Direct Reading Range Corrector. Once set for true-range, air density, wind speed along the line of fire and range-rate, the instrument calculated the difference between true- and gun-range – what was later called the straddle correction. Further, the correction scale could then be re-zeroed so that any subsequent changes, due (say) to change of range or rate, could be read off as further spotting corrections. Simple cardboard circular calculators had been supplied by 1909 which indicated the deflection corrections for wind and speed – across.[116] In that same year, Macnamara time-of-flight watches were first mentioned, though they had not yet been issued. By 1913, they were considered 'indispensable' for concentration firing and were recommended for use in main and local control positions.[117]

Three more instruments show the firm of Elliott Brothers further expanding its business as a supplier to the Admiralty. In 1909, the firm was making the Robinson anemometer (which gave a direct reading of apparent wind speed and direction and of the wind-you-feel along and across the line of fire),[118] and the first examples of the Forbes speed log; by 1912, speed logs were available in all dreadnoughts for keeping the Dumaresqs set for own speed.[119] Third, in 1910, Elliotts signed an agreement to manufacture and sell the Anschütz gyrocompass in Britain and the colonies. (Technology transfer was not only one way, Elliott's granting Anschütz a licence for the Forbes log in 1911.)[120] However, the Anschütz gyrocompass was not sufficiently accurate for all gunnery purposes and, in comparative trials with a Sperry compass conducted in 1913, even the improved three-rotor model showed both a larger error and rate of change of error.[121] Once the First World War had severed Elliott's connection with its licensor, Sperry replaced it as the established supplier and even Anschütz compasses already in service were replaced.[122]

## Manual plotting

A towed target was introduced for the 1908 Battle Practice. In May 1908, after the rejection of Pollen's automatic plotter, the pamphlet *Fire Control* gave the first recommendations to the Fleet on the use of manual plotting to determine target course and speed; its promulgation marked the beginning of what was later called the 'experimental plotting period'.[123] Wilson himself described the manual virtual-course plot that had been tried in *Vengeance* (*Ariadne*'s target during the trials). Bearings were taken simultaneously with ranges by means of a Chetwynd liquid compass mounted on the rangefinder mounting. This type of compass was 'constructed so that the card might be affected as little as possible by the motion of the bowl'; it was, therefore, not unpromising as a cheaper alternative to Pollen's gear. However, Wilson had to admit that, in the *Vengeance* experiments, the bearing errors had been too great to make a useful virtual-course plot when the bearing-rate was low; in such circumstances, he recommended the use of a supplementary time-and-range plot.[124] Dreyer contributed a separate section on rate-plotting; his 'Hints on Battle Firing' included a description of a time-and-range plot, and also a time-and-range-rate plot from which he hoped to obtain a mean range-rate. He also explained the setting of the Dumaresq by a cross-cut; however, bearing-rate was to be obtained from timed bearings, not a plot.[125]

Their separate recommendations do not give the impression of 'a complete manual scheme of obtaining sight-setting data'.[126] Wilson advocated his own scheme only as 'a guide for officers carrying out further experiments' and for further trial in 'not less than six ships with different descriptions of armament'. Similarly, Dreyer's 'Hints' began:

> It is not advisable to lay down any exact rules [which] would probably tend to fetter initiative and delay improvement.[127]

The DNO, Reginald Bacon, while agreeing that six ships should be completely fitted for virtual-course plotting, hoped that 'in a very short time the time curve method will be in general use and good practical results in firing at moving objects should be obtained'. By May 1908, the Board had approved the purchase of training gear for rangefinders and of 142 roller boards, T-squares and squared paper for time-and-range plotting.[128] However, neither these nor any other special Service plotters were ready for that year's practice, although fifteen to twenty gunnery lieutenants obtained manual straight-course plotters from Pollen, which were also copied by others.[129] Thus, for 1908: 'makeshift arrangements were necessarily practised this year i.e. Plotting Boards were often employed aloft etc., and the bearing arm kept actually trained on the target'.[130] The outcome was summarised as shown in Table 3.1.[131]

*Indomitable* and *Dreadnought*, which were ranked first and fourth in the Home Fleet, may have used virtual-course, since they were among the six ships nominated by the DNO to be fitted according to Wilson's recommendations.[132] Yet an essay on fire control for the War College declared that 'no instance has come to light of any Ship making successful use of the Virtual Plot combined with Time and Range diagram' and that 'experience ... in 1908 shows this system to be difficult and un-natural'.[133] ·As Dreyer

*Table 3.1* Plotting methods used in Battle Practice, 1908

| Plotting method | Numbers of ships | | |
| --- | --- | --- | --- |
| | using | giving insufficient information | obtaining satisfactory results |
| Enemy course | 33 | 4 | 18 |
| Virtual course | 8 | 3 | 4 |
| Range and time | 13 | 5 | 4 |

later recalled, in 1908 rate-plotting was 'badly received afloat, as "straight-line" plotting, with the power to forecast the range for some minutes ahead was . . . considered far superior by the majority'.[134]

Before the 1909 Battle Practice, the Admiralty issued a new pamphlet which listed equipment on order or about to be issued; the list included the time-and-range boards, 121 Chetwynd compasses, the fittings to modify the rangefinder mountings and the gear to adapt rate instruments to the transmission of ranges from aloft. The Admiralty had also ordered 121 manually worked course plotters of its own design; this used a cone-and-roller variable-speed drive (see Figure 3.1) to rotate the lead screw which advanced the pencil plotting own ship's course. The screw was positioned along one edge of the paper, so the pencil could be moved in both directions.[135] Pollen also supplied thirteen more 'slightly improved' manual plotters; assuming that these resembled his patents of 1908–9, the lead screw ran down the centre of the plot, but its speed could be changed only in steps, by means of interchangeable discs of different diameters. With their long, straight lead screws, both instruments were essentially straight-course plotters. However, the Admiralty pamphlet and the Argo patent each proposed similar methods to plot while own ship was turning; these depended on knowing the diameter of ships' turning circles at different speeds and angles of helm, and on pivoting the paper on the plotting boards about appropriate centres of rotation.[136] Both proposals seem equally impractical, but they remain important as marking the emerging concern with plotting that could continue irrespective of helm.[137]

Lectures by the staff of the Inspector of Target Practice on the 1909 practices, prepared at the end of the year, stated that all but one of the ships inspected 'plotted the true course and speed of the enemy', though these must actually have been straight-course plots. Thus virtual course seems already to have been abandoned. Of thirty-nine ships, eleven obtained the course to within half a point and sixteen to within one point, although the average time to complete the plot was 5.2 minutes. Taking simultaneous ranges and bearings proved especially difficult in a seaway, while results were also noticeably inaccurate if plotting was continued after opening fire. The ITP's staff concluded that:

> Plotting is not yet sufficiently developed to be of practical use under general service conditions . . .
>     The future of plotting depends upon the development of the rangefinder mounting, a more accurate method of obtaining bearings and measuring the observing ship's speed.[138]

They also described the difficulties with continuous aim experienced by *Inflexible* and some pre-dreadnoughts, with range transmission and sight-setting when the rate was high, and with target indication.

Sumida cites these lectures as evidence that 'the entire Inspectorate had been transformed into a bastion of opposition to the policy of the Ordnance Department'. Yet the second lecture begins:

The opinions expressed must not be taken as fundamental, but contingent to the progress in materiel.

The ITP's staff also found that 'a large number of ships' achieved 'considerable success' more quickly with the help of the range-rate plotting preferred by Bacon.

The Dumaresq is first adjusted to the estimated course and speed of the target, the range-finder observations are plotted with the times on squared paper, and the clock is started with the meaned range and rough rate. The amount the clock gains or losses [sic] on the meaned range is the error in rate; the clock and Dumaresq are then corrected accordingly.[139]

Further, by the time the lectures were delivered, all the Inspectorate's concerns were being addressed. The production order for Argo mountings was being negotiated and would be placed in the following spring. Laying and training gear was being improved in both new and old ships (though only so much could be achieved with the outmoded training engines in *Inflexible* and earlier ships). *Neptune*, laid down in January 1909, was the last dreadnought without Vickers follow-the-pointer sights. Forbes logs were already under trial and the first Evershed installation imminent. To represent the departments of the DNO and ITP as fundamentally opposed is an exaggeration which obscures their true relationship.[140] The position of ITP had been created to ensure 'that improvements are quickly carried out and new ideas promptly taken up'.[141] Thus he and his staff were expected to criticise systems and equipment provided by the Admiralty, and they were uniquely placed to report on experimental techniques like manual course plotting. These lectures are, therefore, evidence only of the expected tensions within the naval hierarchy between the supply department and a department established to assess the shooting of the Fleet and to improve its material and technique.[142]

The limitations of manual course plotting were further exposed in early 1910 during tactical exercises conducted by Admiral Sir William May with the Home Fleet. It was found that, with practice, enemy course could be estimated to within a compass point (11¼°) by eye, which error was equivalent to only about 100 yds/min. in range-rate. This was as accurate as all but the best course plotting, yet incurred no delay. Admiral May concluded that, in poor visibility, fire could not be withheld to give time to plot, while, in good visibility, tactical manoeuvring largely negated the results from plotting before they could be used. He also confirmed that the system described by the ITP's staff, in which the clock range and rate were 'tuned' to follow the mean rangefinder ranges, was 'used very generally now' and the 'rate . . . has almost invariably been arrived at some time before any "plotting" results'.[143] All manual course plotting (including virtual-course) was also rejected by the Colville Committee in July 1910: though they still hoped that Pollen's automatic true-course plotter, despite its failings in the *Natal* trials, could be made to work.[144] After the conclusion of the *Natal* trials:

> the Admiralty ordered a further comparative trial between 'Africa' using virtual plotting and 'Superb' using Time and Range plotting assisted by clock tuning. From this trial, 'Superb' emerged victorious.[145]

Meanwhile, no new recommendations had been promulgated for the 1910 Battle Practice, which was already in progress. Of sixty-one ships witnessed by the ITP, forty-three still used course-and-speed plotting,[146] while ten preferred time-and-range. The important change was that eight ships employed dual-rate plotting.[147] Even Dreyer acknowledged that the first dual rate plots of ranges and bearings were made by Lieutenant (N.) A. H. Norman of *Arrogant* in 1908 and that the technique was used in her delayed 1908 battle practise on 24 February 1909, and also in her 1909 practice. Norman plotted bearings from a Chetwynd compass,[148] but, by August 1910, it was expected that:

> The plotting of ranges and bearings will be greatly facilitated when Pollen's rangefinder is supplied as the two [plotting] operators will have the ranges and bearings automatically transmitted to receivers in front of them.[149]

With accurate bearings in prospect, by early 1911:

> The system now recommended is Time and Range and continually tuning up the Range Clock with the Range Finder, in addition the Rate on the Range Clock being manipulated as necessary in order to make the Range Clock run in agreement with the Range Finder thus obtaining the rate . . .
>
> When a reliable bearing instrument has been obtained, the system . . . which most commends itself is . . . to plot –
>
> Time and Range and Time and Bearing on two diagrams and from these data setting the Dumaresq to the Course and Speed of enemy.

The most convenient method of plotting the Time and Range diagram is to utilise the Admiralty Plotting instrument . . .

The Admiralty Time and Range Board is also suitable for Time and Range or Time and Bearing Plotting.[150]

Another factor encouraging the adoption of a fire control system based on rate was a wider use of rate spotting. This was not new,[151] but the *Manual of Gunnery* for 1911 provided the first official guidance on the method. However, it was another two years before the rules were simplified so that the rate was altered in fixed steps of 100 yds/min. for targets abeam.[152]

## The manual fire control system

At the outbreak of the war, of the dreadnoughts with 12-inch guns, only *Neptune* had the prototype Director and *Hercules* the Original Dreyer Table (Chapter 5). All the others still relied on the simpler fire control system in which, at many points, gunnery data was transferred manually between its components. Notwithstanding variations in equipment, this manual system was much the same in all these ships, and its working will now be described for a typical ship, like *St. Vincent* or *Indefatigable*.

### *Communications*

Gunnery was controlled from the fore-top (the only top in the final 12-inch battleships). However, the main-top (in two-masted ships) and two turrets (A and Y in *St. Vincent*) were also equipped with the instruments needed to take over control if necessary.[153] Each control position had a 9-foot rangefinder, with that in the fore-top on an Argo mounting. It also had a Dumaresq (Mark IV or VI) and transmitters for sending ranges, target bearings and range-rate to either the forward or after transmitting stations. The control positions could also communicate with the TSs through voice-pipes and telephones. Each TS was equipped with a Vickers clock, its own Dumaresq and a set of transmitters for each turret. By means of change-over-switches, each turret could receive gun-range, deflection and orders from either TS, both by fire control instruments (Barr & Stroud or Vickers follow-the-pointer) and by telephone; furthermore, for local control, the sight receivers could be switched to transmitters in the turret itself. Once ships had been given an Evershed installation, a selected control position could transmit the target bearing directly to the Evershed receiver on the sight used by each turret trainer. The whole scheme was resilient to damage and permitted divided control should it be necessary. However, normally, as the following description assumes, the whole main armament was under the control of one fire control top through one transmitting station.

## *The approach*[154]

In the TS, own ship's speed was indicated on the receiver of the Forbes log; any changes in speed were called up to the top so that the setting of the Dumaresq could be maintained correctly. The Robinson anemometer was installed in the top.[155]

As soon as the enemy was sighted from the top, the Evershed transmitter, the rangefinder and the vanes of the Dumaresq and anemometer were all trained on the target. The Evershed gave the enemy bearing to the turrets, while the enemy bearing was also read off the control's Dumaresq and transmitted; then, in the TS, its own Dumaresq could be set likewise for bearing. Initially, the rate-keeper in the top estimated the enemy course and speed; set on the Dumaresqs, they gave the first values of range-rate and speed-across. At the same time, the first enemy range was obtained, preferably by rangefinding but if necessary by estimation. In the top, the speed-across, wind-across and the initial range were put on the circular deflection calculators; the opening deflection was then called down to the TS and transmitted onwards to the guns. The range, and the range-rate read off the Dumaresq, were also transmitted to the TS, while the wind-along was called down. In the TS, all the data were now available to set the Dreyer range corrector and thereby estimate the difference between rangefinder- and gun-range. The Vickers clock could be set and started, after which the gun-range, changing at the estimated range-rate, was transmitted to the turrets. Thus, if necessary, the guns could open fire. If the enemy bearing was changing, the range-rate and the speed-across indicated by the Dumaresqs also changed. The rate on the Vickers clock was adjusted to follow the changing rate, while any changes in deflection were transmitted to the guns.

As ranges were received in the TS from rangefinders in the tops and turrets, they were used to make a time-and-range plot. As soon as a mean range could be discerned, the true-range hand of the Vickers clock could be tuned as necessary to the mean range from the plot. A little later, the slope of the plot would become apparent, perhaps suggesting a different range-rate from that in use. Additionally, the Argo rangefinder mounting transmitted yaw-corrected bearings that were suitable for making a time-and-bearing plot; this plot could suggest a correction to the bearing-rate and speed-across in use. Plotted rates were not applied immediately by the TS but were called up to the rate-keeper aloft, with an indication of their reliability, e.g.:

"A *very good* range rate is 'opening 250.'" "An *unreliable* range rate is 'closing 200.'"

The rate-keeper in the control top was responsible for deciding, on the basis of these suggestions from the plots and what he could see of the enemy, how to alter the enemy settings on the Dumaresq; sometimes, this could be done using a cross-cut of range-rate and speed-across from the plots. Any change in range-rate was transmitted to the TS and set on the clock, while any change in deflection was called down.

Particularly if both ships maintained steady courses, the longer plotting continued, the more accurate the gun-ranges and deflection transmitted to the guns. If own ship altered course, the Forbes log showed the loss in speed to be called up to the top, where the Dumaresq Mark VI kept the rates, at least approximately; clock tuning could correct for any range errors accumulated in the turn. If the enemy changed course, the alteration might be seen from the control top, when the Dumaresq could be adjusted immediately by eye. Alternatively, the turn might first become perceptible as a change in the slopes of the rate plots; in this case, the TS could, as normal, propose a Dumaresq adjustment in terms of different rates.

### *Firing*

Although, due mainly to the restrictions on ammunition available for practice, ranging with single shots persisted, the *Manual of Gunnery* for 1911 required that, if conditions permitted, fire should be opened with ranging salvoes of not less than three guns.[156] The Macnamara time-of-flight watch indicated when each salvo was expected to fall. Spotting orders were called down from the control top to the TS. Opening salvoes were corrected first for deflection, with corresponding adjustments to the Dumaresq's speed-across. Then the bracket system was used to straddle the target, starting with an initial range-step of not less than 400 yards. Each range correction was set on the clock, and transmitted onwards to the guns. If possible, ranging and plotting continued between salvoes as a check on the clock's indicated true-range. If the clock-range deviated from the mean rangefinder range, the clock officer ordered a correction. This was also called up to the control position; if it conflicted with the observations of the fall of shot, it could be countermanded, in whole or in part, by calling down an opposite spotting correction.

> The maximum rapidity of fire should be developed after the range
> has been found, the object in view being to envelop the enemy in
> fire so as to render it very difficult for him to reply.

However, the question of the best firing method to achieve this objective, which also inflicted the greatest damage as quickly as possible, remained open. The highest firing rate was obtained by allowing the turrets to fire independently at the transmitted gun-range as often as possible, but smoke and concussion interfered with aiming and ranging and made spotting very difficult. In 1915, the recognised alternative (no more) to independent was to fire '"double gun salvos" or "rapid salvos," not waiting for fall of shot'. In any case, independent was unavoidable, even before straddling, in bad weather or during smoke interference.[157]

If the opening rate was incorrect, though not excessively, the target could still be straddled but then lost. The same result would be observed if the enemy, on being straddled or after receiving a number of hits, altered course to throw out the rate. The quickest method of regaining the target was to spot for rate, that is, to accompany each range spotting order by a rate correction.

> After straddling, a simple rule of thumb for keeping the rate is to accompany every spotting order required by a similar rate correction of half the amount of the range order

for example UP 200, OPEN 100. Both corrections were put on the clock, while the enemy bars of the Dumaresqs were adjusted to produce the required change in range-rate, without altering the (presumably correct) speed-across.[158]

Finally, if own ship altered course while firing, the Dumaresq Mark VI in conjunction with the Forbes log could keep the rate reasonably well through the turn. The salvoes might stray off the target, but the errors in deflection, range and rate would not be too great to correct by spotting (in that order) once the course had steadied.

## INNOVATION AND PROCUREMENT

Although many new fire control instruments had been introduced, the progress in material had been accomplished with largely unchanged resources. In 1912, just one of the DNO's assistants, Lieutenant C. V. Usborne, remained responsible for:

1. Fire control and communications.
2. Range-finders and plotting.
3. Sights.
4. Calibration.
5. Ballistic questions and range tables.
6. Alterations and additions, including estimates.
7. Attends gun trials.

as well as for handbooks on fire control and other matters. He did at least now share the assistance of one warrant officer, while one of the torpedo assistants dealt with 'experimental and new designs of electrical fittings [including] fire control'. By 1914, the DNO's gunnery assistants remained at five, one attending to fire control, another to the Director. In a post-war report, the DNO was described as 'heavily and consistently overworked', which must also have applied to his assistants; with considerable understatement, Reginald Bacon recalled that:

> The whole of the DNO's staff was none too large to deal with the work in hand.

With such limited manpower, the procurement of the new components could not have been accomplished had not much of the research, design and development been done by the Admiralty's industrial suppliers, both established and new.[159] Though with some delays, Barr & Stroud introduced more accurate rangefinders as they were needed. While the firm enjoyed an effective monopoly in rangefinders, both Siemens and Vickers provided effective competition in fire control instruments, Vickers eventually establishing itself as the sole source of follow-the-pointer and director gear. Eversheds brought new technology to the problem of target indication.

The vital advances in sighting and aiming were accomplished by several means. A scientific consultant developed the first purpose-designed sight telescopes. Captain J. T. Dreyer RA (Frederic's brother) invented the auto-correcting cam sight; this was considered such as important advance that, whereas previous sights seem to have been supplied largely with the mountings, by 1909 the cam sights were being manufactured at Woolwich to protect the service designs.[160] Better turret training engines were largely due to the mounting manufacturers, but the improvements to the hydraulic elevating and training controls were mainly achieved by *Excellent* and Portmouth Dockyard. Unfortunately, other attempts at development within the Navy, like the Vyvyan-Newitt automatic sight and the *Dreadnought/Bellerophon* director, were not successful. The record was much better when the inventions of naval officers (including the DNO's assistants)[161] were developed by industry. Percy Scott's special relationship with Vickers may have been anomalous,[162] and his financial rewards uniquely generous, but it was certainly productive; even before the development of the production Director, he had played an important part in the development of the Vickers range clock and the firm's step-by-step transmitters and receivers.[163] Elliott Brothers under Keith Elphinstone were particularly successful as a manufacturer of instruments invented by others.[164] Above all, the firm participated from the start in the evolution of the Dumaresq, not only developing the ideas of naval officers (like Dreyer, Prickett and others) but also incorporating its own improvements into the fully developed production versions.

The history of the Royal Navy's first, manually worked fire control system has now shown what were the normal sources of technical innovation and the usual processes by which ideas were turned into instruments for supply to the Royal Navy at acceptable levels of profit. By 1913, the commercial and contractual conventions between the Admiralty and industry were also well understood by both sides.

> Usually inventions of importance . . . are brought to the Admiralty in a more or less complete state . . . ready for trial . . .
>
> If the inventor, or the firm which has taken up the invention, are bearing all the preliminary cost and risk . . . they are naturally entitled to substantial profits . . .
>
> Nevertheless, it is not uncommonly found that . . . firms . . . are content with . . . quite reasonable rates of profit . . . merely stipulating that they shall have the orders for any gear required by the Admiralty.[165]

This, then, was the technical, organisational and commercial context in which the rivalry between Pollen and Dreyer developed.

## PRACTICES AND RANGES 1907–13

To complete this account of the Royal Navy's first system of fire control, two remaining questions must be addressed: what progress in actual hitting had been made since the practice of 1906, and what would be expected of any newer system?

Battle Practice continued to be held in the second half of each year.[166] At first, the conditions and results suggest a steady improvement in shooting. In 1907, the last practice in which the target was moored, the range was still about 6,000 yards but the rate was increased to some 400 yds/min. *Dreadnought* came top and, on average, the 12-inch guns made 29.1 per cent of hits.[167] A manageable towed target, 90 feet by 30 feet, already under development as a matter of 'supreme importance' in 1907, was ready for the 1908 Battle Practice.[168] This also introduced two more new difficulties: a large turn (for example, *Indomitable* turned eighteen points) to bring both broadsides to bear, and simulation of damage to the primary fire control system. According to Pollen, the average hitting rate fell to 17–20 per cent. But *Indomitable*, at ranges from 8,300 to 9,600 yards, made a remarkable eighteen hits from thirty-one rounds fired (58 per cent), five of her hits being scored after the turn.[169] Conditions were similar in 1909. The target was still towed at 8 knots at a range of 'about 8,000 yards', while the firing ship worked up from 8 to 15 knots before firing began. Transmitters were disabled to test alternative methods of communication and casualties were simulated; *Bellerophon* (which tied in second place with *Dreadnought*) made 45 per cent of hits.[170]

Information on conditions and results after 1909 becomes more scarce. In 1910 and 1911, the effects of damage and casualties were still being imposed.

In 1910, 'the conditions . . . differed considerably from those of former years', but the best ships were still making almost 50 per cent of hits at ranges 'far longer' than 7,500 yards.[171] In 1911, the conditions again 'differed widely' from previous years, though the only known change was an increase in range to more than 9,000 yards. Yet the average percentage of hits was only about 13 per cent (no figures have been found for the best ships); furthermore, even though the number of dreadnoughts taking part had increased since the previous year from eight to fourteen, only four appeared among the top twenty ships.[172] The year 1911 was the first one in which the new recommendations on rate-plotting and clock tuning were generally in force. Perhaps, therefore, these results do give 'an indication that rate-finding and rate-keeping difficulties were posing serious problems',[173] though why were the all-big-gun ships affected more than the others? Certainly, the results of the 1911 Battle Practice caused serious concern at the time, but were blamed mainly on the increased (though unspecified) difficulty of the conditions year-by-year, a reduction in the points allowed for ricochets, and inadequate training (including of rangetakers); however, no criticisms of fire control gear or of rate-plotting have been discovered.[174]

In 1912, the average range was reduced somewhat, to 8,600 yards. However, the course imposed on the firing ship required only one small turn, of two points, on opening fire. Dreadnoughts obtained thirteen of the top twenty places, but the percentage of hits, even by the best ships, only recovered to about 25 per cent.[175] In 1913, the range was not increased, though the test somehow introduced 'new elements of actuality'. The results were again better than the year before and the best ships may once more have attained percentages of hits similar to those from the period 1908–10.[176]

These fleeting glimpses of Battle Practice could suggest that the Royal Navy's gunnery suffered a severe setback in 1911 and that, even if hitting rates had recovered by 1913, course changes may have been less demanding than in 1908–9. The problem is that so little is known at present about the true severity of the tests. It is clear, however, that the Battle Practice was intended not only as a test of gunnery but also to 'resemble actual conditions of battle as far as can be done under peace circumstances';[177] it included simulations of damage and casualties, and it was made 'more difficult year by year'.[178] It was also conducted as a competition for the whole Fleet, large cruisers as well as capital ships, and for the crews of the secondary (6-inch) armament as well as the turret guns. This imposed restrictions on maximum range and appears to have influenced the conditions in other ways. After the 1909 practice, there was concern about the very high proportion of hits being made by the dreadnoughts.[179] Yet, in 1911, pre-dreadnought battleships still outnumbered the all-big-gun ships by twenty-two to fourteen; perhaps the rules for that year unduly handicapped the heavy guns.[180]

Further, the new orders for the 1910 Battle Practice laid down, for the first time, that Battle Practice should be supplemented by additional firings for which:

> Conditions and scheme of practice to be as ordered by the Commander-in-Chief.

Thus, while Battle Practice continued to be a competition for the whole Fleet, the C.-in-C. of each fleet had been given the discretion to devise more demanding tests if his ships were appropriately equipped. It is, therefore, to these 'Commander-in-Chief's Special Firings' that we must look for measures of the later advances in gunnery. During the appointment of Admiral Sir George Callaghan as C.-in-C. Home Fleets (from December 1911), opportunities were taken to conduct firings at unprecedented ranges. In November 1912:

> the 'COLOSSUS' carried out practice at a towed target (150ft. by 30ft.) at ranges between 14,000 and 15,000 yards spotting from her own top ... seven rounds out of 40 [17½ per cent] being direct hits on the target.[181]

During the firings against the moored *Empress of India* in November 1913, it had been intended that *Neptune* and *Hercules* should carry out long-range runs at up to 15,000 yards. However, squadron firings were held first and the old ship was so damaged that she sank. Callaghan could only report that:

> It was most unfortunate that it was not possible to carry out the long-range runs . . . as although everyone is agreed as to the great desirability of hitting first we have little to guide us as to the range at which we can open fire with good prospect of hitting.[182]

And, in the spring of 1914, the C.-in-C. authorised (reluctantly, according to Chatfield) the Battle Cruiser Squadron to:

> fire at two large towed targets at ranges of 16,000 yards and steaming at not less than twenty-three knots. All five ships [two, *Indomitable* and *Indefatigable*, had 12-inch guns and manual fire control] fired simultaneously at the two targets, the firing was not too good, nor altogether bad. Our rangefinders could only just measure such ranges and were very inaccurate at them.[183]

These few recorded instances remain as the best indications of the capabilities of the manual fire control system at long ranges. However, it seems unlikely that they were the only such firings by the Home Fleet; when Jellicoe was the Second-in-Command in 1912, his War Orders specified:

RANGE FOR ENGAGING

A slow fire will be opened by guns of 9.2" and above at 15,000 yards providing weather conditions and the motion of the ships permit. The fire will be quickened as the range and rate of change are found and decrease, and at 13,000 yards to 12,000 yards the maximum rate of fire should be established if hits are being obtained.[184]

Callaghan held the same view on the opening range in favourable conditions, but he assumed a lower effective range: similar, in fact, to the range of Battle Practice.

> For ships of the all big gun type in fine clear weather, deliberate fire may well be opened at about 16,000 yards; 8,000 to 10,000 yards should suffice for effective range at which superiority of fire may be established.[185]

Opinion in the Admiralty was similar. In 1913, the DNO, Captain Tudor, insisted:

> I am very strongly of the opinion that the probability that the modern battleships and battlecruisers can knock themselves out . . . at say 9,000 yards will merely lead . . . to ships opening at much greater range than 9,000 yards.

And, in 1914, the Admiralty issued specific orders that:

> Certain ships of each class should open fire at the extreme range of their guns.[186]

These came too late, and the Royal Navy entered the First World War with insufficient experience of firing at the longest ranges.

Professor Sumida proposes that, rather than being pursued with insufficient vigour, 'The Quest for Reach' was abandoned in 1912. He attributes this chiefly to the Admiralty's belief, not shared by the commanders of the Fleet, 'that a battle against the German fleet could be won by rapid fire at relatively close range'.

> The adoption of medium-calibre quick-firers . . . suggested that the Germans would seek to engage at shorter ranges than were being contemplated by the Royal Navy . . . A knowledgeable British naval officer later recalled that 'so firm was the conviction' that the Germans would fight at close range that 'our whole tactics were based upon it'.[187]

This quotation is taken from a lecture delivered by Captain H. G. Thursfield in 1922: but it is incomplete, the passage concluding:

therefore we should endeavour to avoid it [a close range action]: we must develop and practice the game of long bowls.[188]

This does seem a more rational response; why should the Royal Navy, with less well armoured ships, elect to fight at ranges at which the German 5.9-inch guns (and, indeed, the latest torpedoes) were more likely to be effective?[189] Neither 'The Quest for Reach' nor 'A Matter of Timing' provide any other strong primary evidence of an intention, held only by the Admiralty, to engage at short ranges even if the visibility was good.[190] However, since Bacon had been DNO and May commanded the Home Fleet, there had been agreement that poor visibility in the North Sea could force encounters at short range, when fire would have to be opened immediately:[191]

in the North Sea . . . on 7 or 8 days out of every 10, the visibility does not exceed 8,000 yards.[192]

Thus, both at sea and in the Admiralty, it was recognised that a fire control system had to meet two requirements. When visibility was good, fire must be opened at long range (up to 16,000 yards), but, if visibility was poor, at 8,000 yards or even less. These expectations had influenced the choice of rate plotting for manual fire control; would they be equally important in the choices made by the Admiralty between the Pollen and Dreyer systems?

## Notes

1   Hugh Clausen, 'Design and the Conditions which Influence It', lectures to the NOD, March 1947, p. 1, CLSN 3/1, Clausen Papers, CC. From 1936, Clausen was Chief Technical Adviser to the Director of Naval Ordnance. See also Chatfield, *Navy and Defence* [B] pp. 30–1.
2   From July 1903, the Admiralty, Gunnery Branch, *Half Yearly Summaries of Progress in Gunnery* [*SPG*] reported on the latest developments. The earliest issue in the Admiralty Library (Ja 238) is no. 7 of July 1906. See also 'Institution of Half Yearly Summary of Gunnery Progress' in ADM 1/7685.
3   C. I. Thomas, *Instructions for the Director of Naval Ordnance and Torpedoes and Assistant Director of Torpedoes*, 24 September, 1907. *Paper prepared by the Director of Naval Ordnance and Torpedoes for the Information of his Successor* [*DNOfS*] February 1905, pp. 25–6, AL (author's copies courtesy Professor Sumida). Frederic Dreyer, *The Sea Heritage* (London: Museum Press, 1955), p. 57.
4   Lord Selborne to Senior Naval Lord, 12 May 1904, MS. Selborne 41, f.158, Bodleian Library. R Travers Young, *The House that Jack Built* (Aldershot: Gale & Polden, 1955) Chapter 10 and p. 166. Reginald Tupper, *Reminiscences* (London: Jarrolds, 1929) p. 183.
5   Admiralty, Naval Staff, Gunnery Division, *Extract of Gunnery Practice in Grand Fleet 1914–18. Battleships and Battlecruisers*, March 1922. Mackay, *Fisher of Kilverstone* [B] pp. 225 and 229. *Manual of Gunnery (Volume I) for His Majesty's Fleet 1901* (London, 1901) p. 382, Ja 254, AL.

6   Percy Scott, 'Remarks on . . . Straight Shooting . . . ' 28 February 1902 in *Gunnery* (lectures privately printed 1905), p. 11, Craig Waller papers.

7   Peter Padfield, *Aim Straight* (London: Hodder & Stoughton, 1966) pp. 95–107.

8   Admiralty letter 5 September 1903 in 'Communication and Control of Gunfire in Action' in ADM 1/7756. DNO's submission 7 June 1902 in '3116: Systems of Communication to Guns' in *Principal Questions Dealt with by Director of Naval Ordnance, January to December 1905*, p. 418, PQ16, Hampshire Record Office [HRO] [*PQ/DNO*].

9   *Joint Report of the Mediterranean and Channel Committees on Methods of controlling Gun Fire in Action*, 16 May 1904, p. 12 and Percy Scott, *Remarks of the Captain of 'Excellent' on the Joint Report of the Mediterranean and Channel Committees on the Control of Fire*, 2 July 1904, both in ADM 1/7758.

10  Padfield, *Guns at Sea* [B] pp. 194–7 and 221. Ian Hogg and John Batchelor, *Naval Guns* (Poole: Blandford Press, 1978) pp. 93–101. *IDNS*, p. 72.

11  Michael Moss and Iain Russell, *Range and Vision* (Edinburgh: Mainstream, 1988) pp. 24–32.

12  *Manual of Gunnery 1901* [5] p. 138. 'Schemes of Communication', n.d. but 1903, f.10 in 'Communication and Control' [8]. Admiralty, Gunnery Branch, *Interim Report of the Mediterranean Committee on the Control of Fire, &c*, forwarded 18 February 1904, pp. 20 and 21 in ADM 1/7756.

13  Admiral A. H. May (Controller), 13 July 1904 in 'Report of Committees on Control of Fire', in ADM 1/7758.

14  *Joint Report of the Mediterranean and Channel Committees Relative to the System of Firing and Allocation of Ammunition*, 30 May 1904, p. 2 in ADM 1/7759. *Joint Report . . . Controlling Gun Fire* [9] p. 12.

15  F. C. Dreyer and C. V. Usborne, *Pollen Aim Corrector System. Part I: Technical History and Technical Comparison with Commander F. C. Dreyer's Fire Control System*, February 1913, p. 4, P. 1024, AL. *DNOfS*, February 1905, p. 14. The other suppliers were Dunlop & Grubb, Stevenson and Lawrence & Capper.

16  *SPG, July 1906*, p. 15.

17  *SPG, January 1907*, p. 23. *DNOfS*, July 1907, p. 26.

18  *Range and Vision* [11] pp. 39, 44 and 54–6.

19  Chatfield [1] p. 33. Usborne, *Blast and Counterblast* [B] p. 1.

20  Percy Scott, *Fifty Years in the Royal Navy* (London: John Murray, 1919) p. 88. These memoirs must be treated sceptically: Brooks, 'Scott and the Director' [B] pp. 151–2 and 167–70.

21  Report by Lt. Craig and DNO to Captain of *Excellent*, 30 November 1900 in 'New Pattern Telescopic Sight for Barbette and Turret Guns', in ADM 1/7686. 'Proceedings of the Ordnance Council . . . 26th February 1903' in *Ordnance Council Cases 1901–1902–1903* in ADM 1/8222.

22  Admiralty, Gunnery Branch, *Manual of Gunnery for His Majesty's Ships Vol. I, 1901, Addenda (1902)*, December 1902, p. 26, Ja 254, AL. *DNOfS*, December 1903, p. 14. 'QfR', p. 56 and footnote 24 for expenditure on sights.

23  *Joint Report . . . Allocation of Ammunition* and Scott, *Fifty Years* [20] pp. 182–5. For delays to resighting older ships caused by Scott's interference, see Brooks, 'Scott' [20] p. 152.

24  *DNOfS*, February 1905. p. 15. Peter Hodges, *The Big Gun* (London: Conway Maritime Press, 1981) p. 51. Roberts, *Dreadnought* [B] p. 28.

25  Captain of *Excellent* to DNO, 7 March 1903 and Scott to DNO, 17 October 1904, etc. in 'Calibration of Guns. Report of Committee &c' in ADM 1/7835. Scott, *Fifty Years*, pp. 180–1. *DNOfS*, July 1907, p. 26.

26  *Range and Vision*, pp. 34–5. 'Schemes of Communication' [12] p. 10. Controller

to Admiral Superintendent, Chatham, 25 October 1903 in 'Communications and Control'. *Mediterranean Interim Report* [12] p. 5.

27 *Joint Report... Controlling Gunfire*, pp. 11–12.

28 Correspondence in 'Barr and Stroud Electrical Transmitters and Receivers ... 1903–04' in ADM 1/7760. Admiralty, Gunnery Branch, *Handbook for Fire Control Instruments 1906*, pp. 8–10 in PLLN 1/8, CC. *DNOfS*, July 1907, p. 18.

29 *DNOfS*, February 1905, p. 19.

30 Minutes by the Controller 1 August and DNO 18 September 1902 in *PQ/DNO 1905*, pp. 418–19. For Grenfell's instruments, see also 'Schemes of Communication', p. 9.

31 Direct-working instruments, unlike the step-by-step type, could not get out of step but they required many more wires between transmitter and receiver.

32 W. H. May, 13 July 1904 [13]. 'Report on Range and Order Telegraphs and on Sight Moving Gear', 12 August 1904 in 'Barr and Stroud's Transmitters and Receivers' [28]. *Annual Reports of Torpedo School [ART] 1904* (pp. 93–4) and *1905* (p. 77) in ART2, HRO. *DNOfS*, February 1905 p. 19, July 1907 p. 18 and November 1909 pp. 14 and 19. Admiralty, Gunnery Branch, *Handbook of Fire Control Instruments, 1914*, pp. 11–13, National Maritime Museum [NMM] and ADM 186/191. Guy Hartcup, *The War of Invention* (London: Brassey's Defence, 1988) p. 14.

33 Scott, 'Gunnery Lecture No. IV', 28 February 1905 in *Gunnery* [6] p. 53. *PQ/DNO 1905*, p. 460. *Fire Control Instruments 1906* [28] p. 19. For Scott's royalties on these instruments, see Brooks, 'Scott', p. 152.

34 *PQ/DNO January to December 1906*, p. 749. *DNOfS*, November 1909, pp. 14 and 17. The Vickers installation comprised range, order and deflection instruments. Captain R. H. Bacon, *Report on Experimental Cruise*, March 1907, pp. 27, 83, 85, 101, 103 and App. HG V, ADM 116/1059.

35 'Recommendation of the Royal Commission on Awards to Inventors', 30 October 1925 in Anthony Pollen, *Great Gunnery Scandal* [B] p. 252. 'Draft Report of the Channel Fleet Fire Control Committee', 21 April 1904, p. 4 in 'Report of Committees' [13]. *Mediterranean Interim Report*, p. 16.

36 *Joint Report... Controlling Gunfire*, p. 11.

37 G. K. B. Elphinstone, 'Dumaresq Designs & Patents. Notes as to History', January 1916 in 'Fire Control Apparatus, Various Patents', ADM 1/8464/181. Patent 17,719 of 1904, applied for 15 August 1904.

38 For Elliott's early history, see Gloria Clifton, 'An Introduction to the History of Elliott Brothers up to 1900' and H. R. Bristow, 'Elliott, Instrument Makers of London: Products, Customers and Development in the 19th Century', *Bulletin of the Scientific Instrument Society*, 36 (March 1993), pp. 2–11, copy courtesy of Mr R. Bristow.

39 *Joint Report... Controlling Gun Fire*, p. 11. Admiralty, Gunnery Branch, *Fire Control. A Summary of the Present Position of the Subject*, October 1904, p. 8, in ADM 1/7760.

40 *SPG, July 1906*, p. 23.

41 *Experimental Cruise* [34] pp. 28 and 95. *DNOfS*, July 1907, p. 20.

42 Scott, 'Remarks on Long Range Hitting', 15 December 1903, in *Gunnery*, p. 27 and Plate II.

43 Patent 9461 of 1904 applied for 25 April 1904, complete 24 February 1905 though without any details of the clockwork drive. Scott to Jellicoe (Captain of *Drake*) 2 January 1904 in 'Report of Committees'. 'Channel Draft Report' [35] p. 6. Report by Lieut. A. V. Vyvyan in R. A. Burt, *British Battleships 1889–1904* (London: Arms and Armour Press, 1988) pp. 45–51, reference courtesy Professor Sumida.

44 Scott, 'Gunnery Lecture No. 5', 24 February 1906, pp. 93–4, *Excellent* Historical Library. *SPG, July 1906*, p. 22. The clock is not mentioned in *DNOfS*, February 1905. 'QfR', p. 11 states that the first clocks had been tested by the end of 1903.

45 *SPG, January 1907*, p. 31. *Experimental Cruise*, pp. 83 and 101.

46 Scott, 'Long Range Hitting' [42] pp. 27–8.

47 *SPG, July 1906*, pp. 39 and 42. See also 'Memorandum by Director of Naval Ordnance on Towing Targets' in *Navy Estimates Committee. Report upon Navy Estimates for 1908–9*, Admiralty, November 1907, FISR 8/11.

48 Scott, 'Long Range Hitting', p. 27.

49 *Mediterranean Interim Report*, p. 22. Scott, *Remarks on Joint Report* [9] pp. 2 and 12. For the necessity to spot shorts, see Scott, 'Lecture IV' [33] p. 51. Scott's reservations about contemporary rangefinders and the Dumaresq seem insufficient grounds for Sumida's view ('QfR', pp. 10–11) that opinion was polarised into 'spotting and instrument factions'.

50 *SPG, January 1907*, pp. 26–8.

51 'Report of Gun Trials', 23 October 1906, Ship's Cover 213A/82, *Dreadnought*, NMM.

52 *Experimental Cruise*, pp. 96–100. The intervals between the salvoes and the first rounds of the subsequent ripples were 65 and 63 seconds, respectively. The duration of the ripples were 16 and 12 seconds. Dreyer [3] p. 57 claimed that the guns could be reloaded every 30 seconds (the reported average was 33 seconds) and that salvoes could be fired every 15 seconds, but the latter figure is not substantiated by the report on the cruise or any other known source.

53 'Revised Rules for carrying out Battle Practice', 6 May 1905 in *PQ/DNO 1905*, p. 476. Scott, 'Lecture 5' [44] 1905, p. 78. Rules of 1 February 1906 in 'Revised Rules for Battle Practice 1906', in ADM 1/7896

54 'Instructions to Officers in Battle Practice in HMS "Revenge"' in *SPG, January 1907*, p. 48; in the best run, 50 per cent of 13.5-inch made hits. *Revenge* was the gunnery ship attached to *Excellent*: Young [4] p. 160.

55 *PP*, 'Jupiter Letter II', January 1906, p. 77 and 'An Apology for the A.C. Battle System', printed December 1907, p. 151. Pollen to Admiral Wilson, 17 December 1907 in 'Royal Commission on Awards to Inventors, Claims Files for Argo Co . . . ', T. 173/91 Part VII, PRO.

56 'Admiral Scott's proposals for "Dreadnought"', 17 August 1905 in 'Director for Turret Firing' in ADM 1/7955. Brooks, 'Scott', p. 155. 'Dreadnought and Lord Nelson & Minotaur Class. Fitting of Single Lever gear and Creep valves to 12" and 9.2" Mountings' in ADM 1/7896.

57 *Manual of Gunnery Vol. III for His Majesty's Fleet 1907*, p. 37, Ja 254, AL.

58 *DNOfS*, July 1907, p. 15. *SPG July 1907*, p. 10 and *January 1908*, p. 6.

59 *The One Calibre Big Gun Armament for Ships*, printed June 1908, pp. 11–12, ADM 1/7898 and FISR 8/31. *DNOfS*, November 1909, p. 7. John Brooks, 'All-Big-Guns: Fire Control and Capital Ship Design 1903–1909', *War Studies Journal*, 1, 2 (1996), pp. 36–52.

60 *DNOfS*, November 1909, p. 11. *SPG 1910*, p. 5 and *1911*, p. 6. *DNOfS*, May 1912, p. 8 (experimental servomotor valves intended to give the same performance in earlier ships were also under trial).

61 Roberts, *Dreadnought* [24] pp. 218–21 and 225.

62 Commander A. W. Craig, 'Hydraulic Training Gear', H.M.S. 'Excellent', 23 December 1907, para. 20, Craig Waller Papers the principal source for this section.

63 *SPG, January 1909*, p. 11 and *DNOfS*, November 1909, pp. 7–8.

64 DNO's Minute 13 March 1906 in Ships' Cover 222, *Bellerophon* Class. 'Reports

of Gun Trials of HMS *Indomitable* 23 April 1908 and HMS *Inflexible* 18 June 1908' in Ships' Cover 215A/51 and 52, *Invincible* class.

65 *SPG, July 1909*, pp. 27–9 for the experimental ten-cylinder engine in *Superb*. *DNOfS*, November 1909, p. 11. Hodges [24] pp. 54 and 62.

66 Captain A. Craig, 'Rough Weather Test Firing, HMS Orion', 15 November 1912 in Craig Waller Papers. 'The term "continuous laying" is used in the sense that the sights are kept approximately laid and can be brought exactly on by a small movement when about to fire.'

67 Patent 4422/1906. *DNOfS*, July 1907, p. 21, November 1909, pp. 14 and 17 and May 1912, p. 14. Admiralty, Gunnery Branch, *Handbook of Fire Control Instruments 1909*, p. 23, Ja 345a, AL.

68 Admiralty, Gunnery Branch, *Fire Control*, 1908, p. 49 in ADM 1/8010 and 'Royal Commission on Awards to Inventors. Claims Files for Argo Co . . . ' [T.173/91] Part I, PRO. Staff of Inspector of Target Practice, 'Battle Practice 1909', ff. 7, 8 and 16 (copy courtesy Professor Sumida); errors in sight ranges of 50 yards were common.

69 *Fire Control*, 1908 [68] pp. 32–3, 45, 49 and Enclosure XV. *Fire Control Instruments, 1909* [67] p. 34 and Plates 46 and 47. Cross connection gear was supplied by both Barr & Stroud and Vickers for use with their respective instruments.

70 DNC's minute 'Report on Range and Order Telegraphs and on Sight Moving Gear', 12 August 1904 in 'Barr and Stroud's Transmitters and Receivers'. 'Vyvyan-Newitt, Siemens & Vickers Electrically Controlled Gun Sights', in ADM 1/7832. *SPG, January 1907*, p. 17. *DNOfS*, February 1905, p. 19 and July 1907, p. 22. See also *Fire Control*, 1908, p. 5 and Viscount Hyde (ed.) *The Naval Annual 1913* (reprinted Newton Abbot: David & Charles, 1970) pp. 322–3.

71 *DNOfS*, July 1907 pp. 22 and 24. Vickers, Sons and Maxim Ltd, *Fire Control System 1910. The Vickers Mark III Follow-the-Pointer Instruments*, p. 3, Ja 391, AL.

72 Admiralty, Gunnery Branch, *Addenda (1909) to Gunnery Manual Vols I (Part I) and Part III*, November 1909, p. 30 and Plate XXV, AL. *DNOfS*, November 1909, pp. 9, 14 and 18.

73 *DNOfS*, May 1912, p. 14. *Fire Control Instruments 1914* [32] pp. 18 and 72, ADM 186/191. Admiralty, Gunnery Branch, *The Sight Manual 1916*, pp. 4 and 6–7, ADM 186/216.

74 *Fire Control Instruments 1914*, p. 72 and Plates 65 and 66 (*St. Vincent*), 68 (*Orion*) and 69 (*Iron Duke*).

75 *IDNS*, p. 153 and 'QfR', p. 66.

76 'Trial and Report on Obry (Petravic) Gunfiring Apparatus', in ADM 1/8011.

77 Georg von Hase, *Kiel and Jutland* (London: Skeffington & Son, 1921) p. 84. Padfield, *Guns at Sea*, pp. 253–4.

78 This short history of the Director summarises Brooks, 'Scott'.

79 Including *Audacious*: 'Practices of Ships Fitted with Director Firing', May 1914 in 'Important Questions dealt with by DNO', Copies, precis, &c ['IQ/DNO'] Volume III, 1914, p. 131, AL.

80 *IDNS*, pp. 154 and 207.

81 Padfield, *Guns at Sea*, pp. 250, 252 and 254. Norman Friedman, *US Naval Weapons* (Annapolis, MD: Naval Institute Press, 1982) pp. 31–2 and 35 (reference courtesy Steve McLaughlin).

82 May to Admiralty Secretary, 25 April 1910 (H.F. No. 802/071) in 'Gunnery: Effects on . . . Plotting . . . etc. of New Developments in Fleet Tactics' in ADM 1/8051.

83 *Fire Control*, 1908, p. 4. DNO's minute, 27 May 1908 in 'Change of Range

Experiments in . . . "Vengeance". Report of Admiral . . . Wilson', in ADM 1/ 8010. *Fire Control Instruments 1909*, p. 32.
84 Dreyer to Hughes-Onslow, 19 October 1908 in T.173/91 Part VII. Hugh Clausen, 'Invention and the Navy – the Progress from Ideas to Ironmongery', *The Inventor*, 10, 1 (March 1970), CLSN 3/7. *DNOfS*, July 1907, p. 21 and November 1909, p. 16; in 1909, the trial installation was intended for *Dreadnought*. Minute from DNO received 4 May 1910, in 'Gunnery: Effects of New Developments' [82].
85 *Fire Control Instruments 1914*, pp. 30–42. 'Bearing Plates . . . in Night Control Positions', 25 June 1914 in 'IQ/DNO III', p. 633. 'Details of Bearing Indicators, Main Armament' in 'Gunnery Information Derived from or Confirmed by the action of 31st May 1916, Report of Dreadnought Battlefleet Committee', June 1916, ADM 1/8460/149. *Fire Control Instruments 1914*, pp. 25–6 and Plates 65–6, 68–9. *ART 1912*, pp. 64–5 [32].
86 *DNOfS*, July 1907, p. 26 and November 1909, p. 19. *IDNS*, pp. 196–201 and 214. John Brooks, 'The Mast and Funnel Question', in John Roberts (ed.) *Warship 1995* (London: Conway Maritime Press, 1995) pp. 44–50 (in *Hercules*, the Argo mounting was on the compass platform). Roberts, *Battlecruisers* [B] p. 28.
87 *Fire Control*, 1908, p. 6. *DNOfS*, November 1909, pp. 5 and 19 and May 1912, p. 7. Minutes on 'Local Control of Turret Gunfire', Oct.–Nov. 1910 in 'Local Control of Turret Guns' in ADM 1/8147. *Home Fleet General Orders*, '39. Local Control', 15 September, 1913, p. 2, in DRAX 1/9. Admiralty, Technical History Section, *The Technical History and Index* (TH23) 'Fire Control in H.M. Ships', 1919, p. 32.
88 *Range and Vision*, p. 79. *SPG, January 1908*, p. 17. *DNOfS*, November 1909, p. 19. See also Admiralty, Gunnery Branch, *Progress in Gunnery Material 1922 and 1923*, p. 40, ADM 186/259.
89 May to Admiralty Secretary, 25 April 1910 (H.F. No. 803/0194) and minute by DNO received 4 May 1910 in 'Gunnery: Effects of New Developments'.
90 *DNOfS*, May 1912, pp. 7 and 15.
91 *Range and Vision*, pp. 78–9. *Naval Annual 1913* [70] pp. 315–17. *Technical History*, 1919 [87] pp. 32–3.
92 H. Dennis Taylor to DNO, 4 June 1907, in 'Invention of 15' Range Finder, Sea going tests of', in ADM 1/8051. *DNOfS*, November 1909, p. 19.
93 *DNOfS, May 1912*, p. 15. *PGM, 1922–3* [88] p. 41.
94 Patent 30,090 applied for 31 December 1912. E. Wilfred Taylor, 'The New Cooke-Pollen Range-Finder', *Journal of the American Society of Naval Engineers*, XXVI, 3 (August 1914), pp. 813–31 (copy courtesy Chris Carlson); mirror assemblies rather than pentaprisms permitted an aperture area 2½ times that of the Barr & Stroud. Correspondence between Pollen and A. J. Balfour 29 February – 3 March 1916 in T.173/91 Part VII. *Technical History*, 1919, p. 33.
95 Minute ITP to DNO, 18 May 1910 in 'Gunnery: Effects of New Developments'. DNO's minute, 18 October 1910 in 'Local Control of Turret Guns' [87].
96 'Report of Conference on Gunnery', para. 38 in 'Gunnery in the Royal Navy, Conference at Admiralty, Dec. 1911/Jan. 1912, Report and Action', in ADM 1/8328.
97 Admiral Callaghan to Admiralty Secretary, 8 December 1913, para.12 and DNO's remarks and actions thereon in 'Gunnery Practice at Sea: Sinking of HMS Empress of India 4/11/13' in ADM 1/8346. 'Increase to G & T Complement of Battleships and D'Cruisers, 23 July 1914 in 'IQ/DNO III', pp. 39–60.
98 Elphinstone, 'Dumaresq History' [37], the principal source for the remainder of this section. Elliott's drawing E.S. 1165 of 6 February 1908 is in T.173/91 Part III (with a quote of £19–20 for manufacture).

99 Admiralty, Gunnery Branch, *Information regarding Fire Control, Range Finding and Plotting*, 1909, pp. 14–17, in 'Miscellaneous Gunnery Experiments 1901–1913', Ja 010, AL. The Mark III and later Dumaresqs are illustrated in William Schleihauf, 'The Dumaresq and the Dreyer', *Warship International*, 38, 1 (2001), pp. 11–15 (advance copy gratefully acknowledged).

100 Young, p. 166.

101 'FCBD', Appendix VII.

102 DNO's minute, 18 October 1910 in 'Local Control of Turret Guns'. Admiralty, Gunnery Branch, *Manual of Gunnery (Volume III) for His Majesty's Fleet 1915*, pp. 172–3 in Ja 254, AL. Claim Form by Major R. G. F. Dumaresq in T.173/91 Part XII. Up to 1925, an additional 1533 instruments had been supplied. Schleihauf [99] for Marks V, VII, VII* and VIII.

103 *DNOfS*, July 1907, p. 20 and November 1909, p. 16. *Fire Control*, 1908, pp. 50–2. *Home Fleet General Orders*, '14. Fire Control Organisation', 5 November 1913, p. 4 and 'Local Control', 1913 [87] p. 3.

104 *Addenda (1909) to Gunnery Manual* [72] p. 54 and Plate XXVII. *SPG, July 1908*, p. 8.

105 *SPG, July 1906*, p. 24.

106 *Fire Control*, 1908, p. 5. *Fire Control and Plotting*, 1909 [99] pp. 17 and 31. *Fire Control Instruments 1909*, pp. 10 and 28 and *1914*, p. 27.

107 *IDNS*, p. 75 and also pp. 217–18.

108 *Addenda (1909) to Gunnery Manual*, p. 54.

109 'QfR', pp. 12 and 39.

110 *Technical Comparison*, 1913 [15] Chapter V, Figure 6 shows the dial graduations.

111 'FCBD', Appendices VIII and XXII.

112 'QfR', pp. 87 and 60.

113 Examination of Mr R. H. Ballantyne in 'Royal Commission on Awards to Inventors. Minutes of Proceedings, Claims of Argo Co . . . ', [T.173/547] Part 12, pp. 54–5 and 92–3.

114 *SPG, July 1908*, pp. 8–9. *Fire Control*, 1908, p. 5. *Addenda (1909) to Gunnery Manual*, p. 54.

115 'FCBD', Appendix IX. The analysis of slippage was developed from A. B. Clymer, 'Mechanical Integrators' (Ohio State University: Master of Science thesis, 1946) – copy courtesy of Professor Sumida. It benefited greatly from comments on my initial unsatisfactory attempts at calculating slippage error from Professor Sumida, Mr Clymer and Mr William Newell (the last two having worked for the Ford Instrument Company, Mr Newell as chief designer and president).

116 *DNOfS*, July 1907, p. 22 and November 1909, p. 18. *Fire Control*, 1908, p. 44 and Enclosure XIVa. *Addenda (1909) to Gunnery Manual*, p. 19.

117 Admiralty, Gunnery Branch, *Fleet Fire Control and Concentration of Fire Experiments*, 1910, p. 7, AL, copy courtesy John Roberts. Captain, *King George V* to VAC Second Battle Squadron, 7 November 1913 in 'Empress of India, 1913' [97]. *Home Fleet*, 'Control Organisation', 1913 [103] p. 4. See also Dreyer, p. 75 and *Manual of Gunnery 1915* [102] p. 21.

118 *Addenda (1909) to Gunnery Manual*, p. 19.

119 *DNOfS*, November 1909, p. 16 and May 1912, p. 13. Elliott Brothers (London) Ltd, *Forbes' Ships' Log and Speed Indicator*, London, n.d., 2.61 in the Elliott Archive.

120 Fred T. Jane (ed.) *Fighting Ships 1911* (London) pp. 519–21. G. K. B. Elphinstone, *The Anschütz Gyro-Compass* (London: Elliott Brothers, 1910) 2.23, Elliott Archive, with agreements between Anschütz and Elliotts.

121 'Very severe rolling and pitching was imparted to the compass[es] . . . both . . . indicated a rapid "yaw effect" of over a degree'. Longer-term meaned fluctuations for the Sperry were 1° for error while the time for the error to change by 1° was 20 minutes; the corresponding figures for the Anschütz were 5.7° and 4 minutes: *ART 1913*, p. 121. Also *ART 1912*, p. 69.

122 Fanning, *Steady As She Goes* [B] pp. 175–80, 195–9. *Technical History*, 1919, p. 20; in 1916, the Anschütz gyros were reused in the first seventeen sets of Henderson gyro firing gear for Director sights.

123 Captain Tower before RCAI, T.173/547 Part 11, p. 8.

124 'Report of Admiral of the Fleet Sir A. K. Wilson', in *Fire Control*, 1908, pp. 26–7. *Chetwynd's Patent Liquid Compass*, pamphlet, n.d. and compasses ACO 163, 164, 168 and 168A, NMM, courtesy of Dr Gloria Clifton. The card diameter in this type of compass is about three-quarters that of the bowl.

125 'Hints on Battle Firing', in *Fire Control*, 1908, pp. 50–4. For Dreyer's authorship, see *Technical Comparison*, 1913, p. 10.

126 *IDNS*, p. 127.

127 *Fire Control*, 1908, pp. 26, 35 and 47.

128 DNO's minutes of 18 March and 27 May 1908 in 'Change of Range Experiments' [83].

129 *Fire Control and Plotting*, 1909, p. 31. *IDNS*, p. 149.

130 'Fire Control', An Essay by Captain C. Hughes-Onslow, n.d. but 1909, Section II, p. 21, PLLN 1/5.

131 *Fire Control and Plotting*, 1909, p. 30.

132 Admiralty, Gunnery Branch, *Results of Battle Practice in His Majesty's Fleet 1908* bound with results to 1913 in Ja 156, AL. DNO's minute 27 May 1908 [128].

133 Hughes-Onslow [130] 'General Remarks . . . on Plotting', p. 1 and Section III, p. 1.

134 'A Short History of Range Plotting in the Royal Navy' appended to 'Some Comparisons made between the Argo Clock and the Fire Control Table in "Monarch"', n.d. but 1912 in T.173/91 Part VII. The style, with its frequent underlinings, is unmistakably Dreyer's.

135 *Fire Control and Plotting*, 1909, pp. 10–12, 31. *Technical Comparison*, 1913, p. 7.

136 *IDNS*, p. 150. Patent 5031 of 1909 (applied for 2 March 1909) references 25,654 of 27 November 1908, which describes the drive with interchangeable discs. *Fire Control and Plotting*, 1909, p. 9.

137 Pollen to Hughes-Onslow, 1 November 1909 in *IDNS*, p. 172.

138 'Battle Practice 1909' [68] ff. 2–3, 7–8 and 17–18.

139 *IDNS*, pp. 154–5. 'Battle Practice 1909', ff. 2–3, 7–9, 11 and 17–18.

140 K. G. B. Dewar was one of the ITP's staff and, while criticising the 'most favourable conditions' of Battle Practice (pp. 112–14), he does not mention any rift between ITP and DNO: *The Navy from Within* (London: Gollancz, 1939).

141 Padfield, *Aim Straight* [7] p. 146.

142 Peirse's successor as ITP, Captain Montague Browning, used the position to oppose the adoption of the Director and, in 1913, the post was abolished. *FDSF*, p. 415. *IDNS*, p. 246. Padfield, *Aim Straight*, p. 221.

143 Captain Richmond (*Dreadnought*) to C. in C. Home Fleet, recvd. 21 March 1910 and May to Admiralty Secretary (H.F. No. 803/0194) 25 April 1910 in 'Gunnery: Effects of New Developments'.

144 Enclosure I, p. 2 with Colville Committee to C.-in-C. Home Fleet, 1 July 1910 in DRAX 3/3.

145 *Technical Comparison*, 1913, p. 8.
146 Despite widespread dissatisfaction: see *PP*, pp. 260–2 for letters to Pollen from gunnery officers.
147 'Summary', p. 11 in DRYR 2/1.
148 *Technical Comparison*, p. 10. Dreyer and Tower before RCAI, T.173/547 Part 11 p. 8, Part 17 pp. 43 and 68 and Part 18 p. 20. 'Battle Practice 1909' f.12 mentions Norman but not dual-rate plotting; it also describes a dual-rate scheme due to Lieutenant Burke of *Suffolk*, in which two clocks were tuned to the ranges and bearings without the aid of plots.
149 May to Admiralty Secretary, 1 August 1910 in 'Invention by Commander Dreyer – improved method of obtaining the range . . . ' in ADM 1/8147.
150 The Secretary of the Admiralty to Commanders-in-Chief and Officer Commanding, 15 February 1911: copy in DRYR 2/1, and reproduced in *Technical Comparison*, 1913, p. 9.
151 'Previous to the introduction of Rate Plotting early in 1908 . . . in a few ships spotting corrections for Rate were also made': 'Remarks by Commander F. C. Dreyer R.N. on the question of how to best obtain and maintain the gun range in action', 22 July 1910 in T.173/91 Part III.
152 *Manual of Gunnery for His Majesty's Fleet 1911*, pp. 11–12, Ja 254, AL. 'Long Course Lecture Notes, 1910–11', 4 March 1911 in Papers of Commander D. T. Graham Brown, *Excellent* Historical Library. *Home Fleet*, 'Control Organisation', 1913, p. 4.
153 Brooks, 'Mast and Funnel Question' [86] pp. 40–4. *Fire Control Instruments 1914*, pp. 6–11 and Plates 65–6.
154 The principal source for this and the next section, including uncited quotations, is *Home Fleet*, 'Control Organisation', 1913.
155 *Fire Control Instruments 1914*, p. 9. *Addenda (1909) to Gunnery Manual*, p. 19.
156 Usborne [19] p. 9. *Manuals of Gunnery 1911* [152] p. 16 and *1915*, p. 9.
157 *Manual of Gunnery 1915*, pp. 10–11.
158 *Ibid.* pp. 15 and 17.
159 *DNOfS*, May 1912, pp. 28–9. DNO's minute 28 November 1918 and 'Naval Ordnance Department: Proposed Post-War Complement' p. 4 in 'Naval Ordnance Department 1918–1920', ADM 116/1849. Reginald Bacon, *From 1900 Onwards* (London: Hutchinson, 1940) p. 162. Jon Sumida, 'British Naval Administration and Policy in the Age of Fisher', *Journal of Military History*, 54 (January 1990) pp. 20 and 22.
160 *DNOfS*, December 1903, pp. 13–14; February 1905, pp. 15–16; July 1907, pp. 13 and 22–5; and, for cam sights, November 1909, pp. 2, 9 and 11; May 1912, pp. 6 and 9–10.
161 For Usborne's pointer accelerator for 6-inch gun-sights, see *Fire Control Instruments 1914*, p. 21
162 As was long recognised: Captain H. D. Barry to Lord Walter Kerr, 13 May 1904, MS. Selborne 41[4] f.146. Usborne, p. 15.
163 Brooks, 'Scott', p. 152; Scott also received royalties for 'a "blow-out" for guns'.
164 For Elphinstone's involvement in 1910 with an unsuccessful design for a plotting and range-keeping instrument, see 'Fire Control Instrument devised by Asst. Paymaster Noyes RN, Reports, &c.', in ADM 1/8145.
165 Admiralty, *Pollen Aim Correction System. General Grounds of Admiralty Policy and Historical Record of Business Negotiations*, February 1913, p. 2, P. 1024, AL.
166 *Manual of Gunnery 1911*, p. 121.
167 *Results of Battle Practice* [132] *1907*. Jellicoe to Fisher, 17 November 1907, in FISR 8/27.

168 'Memorandum by Director of Naval Ordnance on Towing Targets' in Navy Estimates Committee, *Report upon Navy Estimates for 1908–9*, p. 114, FISR 8/11. *DNOfS*, July 1907 p. 31 and November 1909 p. 20. Pollen himself acknowledged the difficulties of handling towed targets: *PP*, 'Reflections on an Error of the Day', 1908, p. 182.

169 *PP*, pp. 239, 280 and 329. 'Memorandum by Director of Naval Ordnance on Gunnery of the Fleet', in *Navy Estimates 1908–9* [168] pp. 111–12. *Fire Control*, 1908, p. 4. *Results of Battle Practice 1908*. Rear Admiral Inglefield to Admiral Fisher, 18 January 1909 in *IDNS*, p. 160.

170 *Results of Battle Practice 1909*. Letters from Vice Admiral Berkeley Milne 28 October 1909 and Admiral May 31 October 1909 and minute by Rear Admiral Peirse (ITP) 23 November 1909 in 'Revised Instructions for the Expenditure of Heavy and Light Gun Ammunition', in ADM 1/8065. 'Battle Practice, 1909', f.18. Usborne, pp. 8–12.

171 'Remarks on Local Control by Commander F.C. Dreyer RN of HMS "Vanguard"', 5 September 1910 in 'Local Control of Turret Guns. Special Firing by HMS "Vanguard" . . . ', in ADM 1/8147. *Results of Battle Practice 1910*. Minute by ITP, 23 November 1909 [170].

172 *Results of Battle Practice 1911*. Admiralty, Naval Staff, Gunnery Division, *Progress in Naval Gunnery 1926*, Plate 1, ADM 186/271. Captain Hopwood (*Prince of Wales*) to VAC Atlantic Fleet, 20 November 1911 in T. 173/91 Part III. 'Recent Gunnery Practises [sic]. (Capt. C. Fuller 6.6.12)' in DRAX 1/9. 'Final Report of the Committee on Director Firing', 15 November 1912, MB1/T22/161, Battenberg Papers, University of Southampton.

173 *IDNS*, p. 283.

174 Correspondence and report in 'Gunnery 1911/1912.' [96].

175 *PNG 1926* [172] Plate 1. Battle Practice Chart, HMS Orion 1912 and Table 'Class 1 Ships', Craig Waller Papers. *Results of Battle Practice 1912*.

176 *The Times*, 27 June 1913, p. 77. *PNG 1926*, Plate 1. *Results of Battle Practice 1913*.

177 *DNOfS*, July 1907, p. 30.

178 VAC Atlantic Fleet to Admiralty Secretary, 18 December 1911 in 'Gunnery 1911/1912'.

179 Letter from Admiral May and minute by ITP, 1909 in 'Revised Expenditure of Ammunition' [170].

180 '[It] is desirable not to discourage the training of the Officers and Men concerned with the secondary armament if it considered that they will be of value in Action'. Jellicoe to Admiralty Secretary, 18 December 1911, in 'Gunnery 1911/1912'.

181 DNO's Minute 13 February 1913, in 'IQ/DNO I', 1912, p. 337–8. See also *IDNS*, p. 250.

182 Admiral Callaghan, memorandum 'Firings to be carried out at "Empress of India"', and letter to Admiralty Secretary 8 December 1913, in 'Empress of India, 1913'.

183 Chatfield, pp. 105 and 113. *IDNS*, pp. 251–2 and 284–5, citing descriptions of high speed exercises in DRAX 4/1, states that these firings 'actually took place in 1913 and not in 1914' at ranges of 12,000 yards. In fact, the 1913 exercises were of rate and range keeping between ships of the BCS, without firing.

184 A. Temple Patterson (ed.) *The Jellicoe Papers, Volume I* (London: NRS, 1966) p. 24.

185 Memorandum 'Conduct of a Fleet in Action. Commander in Chief's Instructions (Supplementary to the Instruction issued by the Admiralty . . . October 1913)' attached to Captain H. G. Thursfield, 'Development of Tactics in the Grand Fleet', Lecture I, 2 February 1922, THU 107, Thursfield Papers, NMM.

186 DNO's minute, 18 November 1913, in 'IQ/DNO II', 1913. 'Instructions for Annual Gunnery Practice', 1914 and draft of 5 April 1914, referencing Board decision of 1913, in 'IQ/DNO III', 1914, pp. 1–5 and 324.
187 'QfR', pp. 70–1.
188 Thursfield, 'Development of Tactics', Lecture I [185].
189 Also, the maximum range of the German 5.9-inch secondary armament was a long 13,500 metres (about 14,700 yards). Erich Gröner, revised Dieter Jung and Martin Maass, *German Warships 1815–1945, Volume I* (London: Conway Maritime Press, 1990) pp. 23–8 and 53–7.
190 'QfR' p. 93 cites the firings at *Empress of India* at 9,800 yards as evidence that in 1913 this was regarded as 'very long range'. The footnote mentions neither that 13.5-inch ships fired shell from the old *Royal Sovereigns* with reduced charges, nor the intention for *Neptune* and *Hercules* to fire at up to 15,000 yards with full charges.
191 *IDNS*, pp. 151–2. May to Admiralty Secretary, 25 April 1910, in 'Gunnery: Effects of new developments', ff.51–2.
192 Hughes-Onslow, 'General Remarks and Conclusions on Plotting', p. 1.

# 4

# A.C. AND ARGO

In February 1900, Arthur Pollen was invited by his cousin, Lieutenant William Goodenough, to watch a gunnery practice off Malta from the cruiser *Dido*. Thus began what Pollen described in 1913 as 'a fourteen year's sentence to the hard labour of producing the A.C. [Aim Correction] system'.[1] During this time, Pollen's system changed considerably; thus the first section of this chapter will identify each phase of its long development: the constituent instruments (both proposed and actually completed): and their technical characteristics, particularly their claims to be described as 'helm-free'.[2] The second section then follows the unusual and often difficult commercial relationship between the Admiralty and Pollen and (latterly) his Argo Company, and the personal, financial and political factors that shaped it. Both themes are explored against the time-frame fixed by the four trials of Pollen's gear aboard HM ships *Jupiter* (1905–6), *Ariadne* (1907–8), *Natal* (1909–10) and *Orion* (late 1912).

## TECHNICAL

The range of *Dido*'s practice was 1,400 yards, so it must have been a gunlayer's test. Pollen also recalled that: 'I was told that no practice was carried out at any much greater range' due to 'the absence of an accurate range-finder'. In 1898, Pollen had become the managing director of the British Linotype Corporation, in the same year that he had married the daughter of the chairman, Joseph Lawrence.[3] Pollen was now able to use the resources of the firm to develop a rangefinder on the two-observer principle, in which simultaneous bearings of the target were taken from two, well-separated positions and transmitted to a range-calculating machine. In early 1901, he made his first approach to the Admiralty, submitting only drawings of the calculating machine.[4] He also claimed that 'observing to within eight seconds . . . with telescopic sights . . . should not be a difficult feat' and that 'important inventions have been made . . . for combining the telescope with one or more gyrostats'; he also recognised that 'Simultaneity of observation is of course absolutely vital'.[5] His letters were followed by a pamphlet which acknowledged that, with 150 feet between observers, the claimed bearing accuracy could still lead to range errors of 621 yards at 20,000 yards. The pamphlet made no mention of gyrostats,[6] but repeated the proposal that the enemy's position should be plotted manually on a navigation chart, thereby obtaining his speed and course.

> The primary use of this device . . . would be for tactical and strategic purposes . . . The secondary use . . . would be as a range-finder for guns . . . at ranges hitherto considered impractical at sea.[7]

The Admiralty rejected Pollen's proposal but work continued, principally on the calculating machine; it was probably completed before the end of 1902.[8] He and his engineers then turned to the much more difficult problem of taking and transmitting simultaneous bearings. In 1904, two pamphlets, produced in July and December, described not just the rangefinder and calculator, but a charting table and clock. The second pamphlet explained that each observer had to judge the position of the same target feature relative to seven lines subdividing a narrow vertical band. Yet this band took up only one-sixtieth of the width of his telescope's field of view, while, at best, only the two outer lines and the central line were visible; the rest had to be imagined. To transmit a bearing, an observer pressed one of seven keys, that which corresponded to the line closest to the target feature. The calculating machine was supposed to use only pairs of bearings that were transmitted simultaneously.[9] The chart or plot was to be made on a broad paper ribbon moved by clockwork at a speed proportional to the speed of the firing ship, enemy position being plotted manually with the pin sliding on the plotting arm. Own course was traced by a second 'pricker' beneath the pivot of the plotting arm. Since own course could be represented *only* by the straight line at the edge, this was a straight-course plotter. Yet its patent seems to imply some notion of plotting while altering course:

> the ribbon carrier may be, and preferably is, mounted to turn on a suitable pivot so that it can be swung according to a change of course.[10]

A figure from the second pamphlet suggests that the plot would then rely on a gyroscopic directional reference that was undisturbed by change of course. However, this type of plotting did not require a pivoting ribbon-carrier, while no gyroscopic reference was mentioned.

Even by July, Pollen was clear that an enemy course plot could average out the errors in individual observations, although, by December, he claimed, extravagantly, that the range could be 'accurate probably to 1-10th of 1 per cent'.[11] In July, he also described for the first time a 'clock' which forecast ranges and transmitted them to the guns. However, it was only an incomplete concept, since it had dials for setting speeds and enemy course but not for enemy bearing. Nor does the pamphlet contain a single reference to deflection. At about the time of its publication, Pollen was given permission by Vice Admiral Lord Charles Beresford to seek advice from gunnery experts in the Channel Fleet,[12] after which the December pamphlet shows a greater appreciation of all the factors affecting hitting at long range. It also displays a knowledge of the latest Service instruments, notably the Dumaresq, the Scott/Vickers clock and an appliance by which the 'range may be put upon the sights with great rapidity'; this was probably the Vyvyan-Newitt direct sight-setting gear, which was under trial in the Channel Fleet in the last quarter of 1904.[13]

Pollen now proposed a 'change of range and bearing machine', though no hints are given of its mechanism. Having been 'set to own and enemy's course and speed', this would keep both enemy range and bearing and transmit them to dials in the gun positions '[s]o long . . . as the courses and speeds remain unaltered'. The difference between true and gun range was to be determined by using the two-position rangefinder to measure the distance of the fall of ranging shot from the target. The final element of the system was a separate deflection machine which was 'in the course of design'. In mid-1905, Pollen produced a further pamphlet in which he first named his system 'Aim Correction'. He dropped any idea of 'ranging the splash', proposing instead that the range and deflection machines would calculate the known ballistic corrections, and that bracketing (with single shots) be used to correct for unknowable factors.[14]

### *Jupiter*

Only the rangefinding system and plotter were ready for trials in *Jupiter* from November 1905 to January 1906. Conditions were sometimes severe, but Pollen acknowledged that:

> It has, however, to be stated without any reservation that the instruments have failed to carry out the requirements of the system under weigh.

He blamed the means for training the telescopes and confusion between the transmitted bearings.[15] In fact, quite apart from the difficulties of observation, it can be calculated that the range accuracy promised so confidently required synchronisation within milliseconds between bearing observations, impossible demands on the observers and the electromagnetic transmission.[16] Manual plotting also proved too slow and prone to error. Pollen later admitted: 'Our first experiment was a complete failure', but he also claimed that lack of time and money before the trials prevented the development of '[g]yroscopic correction, a plotting table adjustable for the turn and the change of range and bearing machine'. He blamed the Admiralty for advising that gyroscope control 'was not indispensable' and for being unwilling to fund 'prolonged and . . . costly experiments'. In fact, after the brief reference to gyrostats in 1901, they are not heard of again until improvised experiments in *Jupiter* with a torpedo gyroscope for yaw correction. Furthermore, Pollen had no settled scheme for a plotter 'adjustable for the turn':[17] and, while the Admiralty was prepared to purchase a 'change of range and bearing machine', Pollen had been unable to develop it in time.

Undaunted, in February 1906 Pollen suggested:

> that as the final development of the two-observer system must take some little time, the Aim Corrector System should be tried with one-observer range finders in the meantime[18]

by which he meant the new Barr & Stroud 9-foot instrument. The two-observer system was soon dropped and, with the help of Harold Isherwood,[19] the A.C. system was transformed into a gyroscopically controlled range-finder mounting and an automatic plotting table. The description of the 'One Observer System of Charting' submitted in June 1906 also included a 'change of range' machine which could be set for 'yaw correction' and transmit elevation and deflection angles, preferably direct to the gun sights; however, no range clock of any description was made at this time,[20] nor was one included in the agreement (concluded in October) for the supply of a prototype mounting, transmission system and plotter. In the same month, Pollen and Isherwood applied for a patent for the dual-gyroscope directional reference, on which the whole system depended. In a remarkably short time, by November 1907, the equipment was ready for installation aboard *Ariadne* in readiness for trials under the supervision of Sir Arthur Wilson.[21]

### *Ariadne*

On 3 August 1907, Pollen wrote to the new DNO, Captain Reginald Bacon, with an explanation of his work. He regretted that, 'as a matter of deliberate policy last year', the forthcoming trials did not include a clock or automatic sights.

> In such a clock . . . it would not be difficult . . . to make it calculate and transmit the deflection as well as the range; and . . . automatically set the sights to the elevation and deflection indicated by the clock.[22]

In the same month, Pollen also prepared a set of lecture notes in which he criticised the Service system (with which he was evidently thoroughly familiar) and also described the complete A.C. system as it might be installed in *Invincible*. The rangefinder was trained by 'a gyroscopically-controlled electric drive, which . . . consequently neutralises . . . changes of course due to the yawing of the ship'. Ranges and bearings were transmitted to the 'charting table' and plotted automatically. Enemy speed and course from the plot were set on the change-of-range machine (this also kept the target bearing) and on a separate deflection machine. Range and deflection were then transmitted from the machines to the automatically set sights; the two machines worked 'on the assumption that both ships are maintaining a steady course and a level speed'.[23]

After the *Ariadne* trials, Pollen printed a detailed description of the rangefinder mounting, the complex, synchronous transmission system and the plotter.[24] The mounting consisted of a pedestal carrying inner and outer vertical tubes, with the rangefinder and a seat for the operator carried on the outer tube. (This basic layout was retained for all the mountings supplied by Pollen to the Royal Navy.) When the ship was on a steady course, the inner tube was gyro-stabilised; although the ship might yaw, the tube should not rotate relative to the direction of the mean course as defined by the dual gyroscopes. The operator was provided with a handle to train the outer tube (and hence both the rangefinder and himself) relative to the inner; with the rangefinder trained on the enemy, the angle between the inner and outer tubes, which was transmitted to the plotter, gave the enemy bearing relative to mean course.

While the course was steady, each of the twin gyroscopes was coupled in turn to the contact arm that controlled the rotation of the inner tube. When uncoupled, each gyro was clamped to the fore-and-aft line and driven up to speed with an air blast. The result was to keep the contact arm parallel with the mean course, even if the ship yawed. However, the stabilising action was limited to 12½° on either side of mean course; in larger turns, both gyros were clamped until a new course was established.

The inner tube was rotated by a clutch plate that was sandwiched between two electromagnetic clutches driven continuously in opposite directions. If the inner tube was not correctly aligned with the controlling contact arm, the arm completed an electric circuit that energised one of the clutches; this then rotated the clutch in the appropriate direction to drive the inner tube back into alignment. However, in behaviour characteristic of this type of simple servo-mechanism, the inertia of the load – in this case, mainly that of the 9-foot rangefinder and its operator – tended to carry it past the desired position; the other clutch was then energised, after which the mounting 'hunted' around the correct angle. It appears that the mounting tended to hunt continuously rather than to settle down, Pollen himself stating that the observer was 'relieved . . . of everything except a rhythmical motion for the training by the gyro correction'.[25]

As in *Jupiter*, the straight-course plotter drew own ship's mean course as a straight line down one side of the plot. The plotting arm and the pencil for plotting enemy course were now positioned automatically by means of two more clutch servos; these were controlled by the enemy bearings and ranges transmitted from the rangefinder. While the course was steady, the bearings were relative to mean course and, while altering course, to the fore-and-aft line. Normally, plotting was suspended in a turn since,[26] as explained in Chapter 2, no useful results could be obtained. The *Ariadne* rangefinder mounting and plotter may be characterised as 'yaw-free', but they were not 'helm-free'.

The criterion for success in the trials (agreed in October 1906) was that, two minutes after the target range had fallen to 8,000 yards, the range should be predicted to within 80 yards for a further three minutes. In the absence of an A.C. clock, the enemy speed and course from the plot were to be set on a Dumaresq, the rate then being applied to a Vickers clock. These demanding requirements were tested on 11 and 13 January 1907 in Torbay, where the courses could be accurately surveyed.[27] Pollen declared that his gear had come 'successfully through the Torbay tests for exactness in results'.[28] Out of five runs, four obtained the enemy course to within 70 yards of the surveyed courses. However, in only two were ranges obtained to this accuracy, while these were extrapolated from the plot rather than predicted with the Dumaresq and clock. Pollen insisted:

> It was no part of the plan of the designers to consider chiefly facilities for getting the data off the chart with rapidity; it appeared that this was a matter in which only experience could indicate the best method.[29]

Yet the complete A.C. system itself depended on setting the clock from the plotted results.

In the Torbay trials, the maximum rate was 'not 500 yards a minute' but on 15 January, in 'the only experiment made at sea, there was no change of range at all'.[30] In such conditions, the A.C. gear must have given accurate results but, although Wilson's report has not been found, he undoubtedly recommended rejection in favour of manually worked alternatives. From Pollen's subsequent riposte, it is clear that Wilson also criticised the performance of the A.C. equipment. Most seriously:

> (a) A change of course throws the instruments out of gear. An operator has to stop the gyroscopes ... and release them again when the ship is on her new course.
> (b) The gyroscopes creep ...
> ...
> (e) The instruments were shown to be unreliable.

The first point was valid, despite being rejected by Pollen because 'the gyroscopes, after . . . a change of course, automatically select and keep the new course'. Pollen unwisely asserted that 'the gyroscopes do not and cannot creep', particularly since he had already admitted that

in the experiment carried out by Admiral Wilson on the 12th [December] with the ship anchored . . . it was found that the creep of the gyros was . . . some 2 or 3 degrees in 4 or five minutes.

Whatever the extent of the creep at sea, the dual-gyroscope design was superseded within the year. As for general unreliability, Pollen claimed that 'the gear . . . never once broke down, or failed in a single particular'.[31] Yet, only one year later, he implied that the *Ariadne* gear was not 'in all respects fitted for its purpose' and admitted to defects in the plotting devices.[32] While Wilson's report probably exaggerated the gravity of the defects, it is unlikely that the A.C. gear was yet fit for service. And, as Pollen admitted in private correspondence:

The Ariadne thing . . . is . . . of course . . . exceedingly incomplete as a fire control system . . . and I reckon it will take me a full year to get the other instruments . . . running to my satisfaction.[33]

After the *Ariadne* trials, Pollen received further funds to continue development. In January 1909, he announced

the completion of the drawings of the entire system . . . The mechanical devices we shall employ . . . have all, during the last twelve months been exhaustively tried and proved to be reliable . . . The system is now no longer in a tentative stage.

The principal instruments of the 'Pollen A.C. Battle System' were as before. In the rangefinder mounting, the dual gyroscopes had been replaced by a single, continuously running, air-driven gyroscope with small air jets correcting for precession. However, the gyroscope was still clamped during any substantial course change, so the mounting remained only yaw-free.

Pollen's description indicates that the charting table was being completely redesigned to plot on both broadsides; it was also intended to place marks at one minute intervals along the enemy's course as an aid to measuring his speed. However, at least one fundamental design issue remained undecided, since plotting on moving paper is mentioned as well as the preferred arrangement in which:

Our position on the Charting Table will be driven instead of the paper.

> ... The Chart will be rotatable about an adjustable centre at the moment of change of course [by own ship]. The extent of the turn can be controlled by the rangefinder or by hand.[34]

Just such an adjustable centre (a pin sliding in a carrier pivoting about own-ship's pencil) was described in the contemporary patent for the manual course plotter, but, before a turn even commenced, the pin had to be positioned according to the *expected* radius of the turn. This scheme evidently proved unworkable, since Pollen stated subsequently that the table as originally designed could represent own course only as rectilinear.

> To plot a turn, or to plot during a turn, was consequently impossible. We had long been of opinion that this was a grave omission.

To justify the latter claim, he harked back to his 1904 patent, even though he had to admit that it 'would certainly not have given us the results we wanted'.[35] He blamed 'the cry, that the gear was too complicated already' for the original *Natal* plotter being on the straight-course principle,[36] but in fact there is nothing to show that, prior to the 1909 trials, Argo had any worked-out scheme for helm-free, true-course plotting.

The 'change of range and bearing machine' as described in January 1909 was set with own speed, enemy's speed, course (as the angle between courses), range and bearing, and the time of flight. It generated and transmitted gun range and deflection to automatic sights. Its settings could be corrected if they differed from the plotted values, but spotting corrections were transmitted directly from the spotters to the sights.[37] No specific mention is made of change of own course. However, a contemporary description of Argo's 'range and deflection clock' stated:

> Any dial can be altered while the Clock is running including own speed. If own Course is changed it has the effect of altering the angle between Target Course and Own Course so the alteration due to the change of Own Course is made on the Target Course Dial.[38]

Clearly, Pollen had given the impression that the clock could keep the range and bearing through a turn.

### *Natal*

No detailed description has been found of the plotting table which, with the rangefinder mounting and transmission equipment, were delivered to *Natal* on 25 September 1909.[39] However, Pollen stated that it 'was originally designed so that the paper on which the chart was to be made should be pinned upon the plotting table, and the plotting pen traversed over it',[40] which confirms that the general arrangement was similar to the patented manual plotter. The carrier for the own-course pen was advanced down the centre of the table by a long screw turning at a rate proportional to own speed. The arm plotting the enemy course was pivoted about this pen, the angle of the arm and the position of its sliding pen carrier being controlled automatically from the enemy bearings and ranges, the former relative to own mean course, transmitted from the rangefinder mounting. In the first trials, the equipment impressed the Captain of *Natal*, although there may have been a 'few minor mechanical difficulties'. However:

> Captain Ogilvy, almost as soon as the gear was installed . . . pointed out to us that the military importance of plotting during a turn seemed to him to be overwhelmingly critical . . . He urged us therefore to ignore all the complication objections and adapt the table forthwith.[41]

Pollen and Isherwood were already working on the necessary alterations to the *Natal* table when, on 15 January 1910, they submitted a provisional patent specification for true-course plotters, in which they claimed widely for various outline designs. In the complete patent specification, the only remaining scheme resembled the *Natal* table after it had been modified. The plotting point was now fixed at the centre of the table, while the paper was driven from below, both linearly and rotationally, by a pair of wheels, one on either side of the pencil plotting own course. In the patented design, the paper was held in direct contact with the wheels below by pressure wheels above, all wheels having rubber rims. In the *Natal* table (possibly because there was no room for the pressure wheels) the driving wheels were provided with short spikes, while the paper was pinned to a wooden board of a weight sufficient (it was hoped) to give these 'prickers' enough purchase. When the table was returned to *Natal* in early May 1910, it had also been fitted with its own gyroscope; by following its directional indication, an operator set course changes manually.[42] The mounting must have been modified at the same time to transmit enemy bearings relative to ship's head, as required to position the enemy plotting arm correctly. The mounting's own gyroscope continued to stabilise it against yaw while the course was steady, but, when it was changing, the plotting accuracy depended on the rangetaker's unaided skill in keeping on the target. Because of this and the manual setting of course changes at the table, the mounting and plotter hardly deserve to be called helm-free, even though they were a first attempt at a true-course plotting system.

Meanwhile, the long-delayed Argo clock had finally been completed and delivered to *Natal* in February 1910.[43] Two early clock patents from 1906 and 1908 had described mechanisms employing linkages which, by forming a triangle of velocities, obtained virtual course and speed;[44] in the second, the virtual speed was generated not by a variable-speed drive, but by an adjustable inclined link. Some clock drawings were seen by a naval delegation to the Linotype works in June 1907, but the 'manufacture was not begun at this time of the finished clock'.[45] Yet, just as he was taking out the second patent, which still described mechanisms only in principle, Pollen declared:

> My change of range clock was designed before we left the *Jupiter*, and the sight setting mechanism, to be run straight from the range clock, very shortly after.[46]

By July 1909, work was well advanced on what was later called the Argo Clock Mark I,[47] which also relied on a 'simulacrum' of virtual course and speed. An internal cross-piece, which represented the enemy ship, was moved by the combined actions of two pairs of drive screws, one pair vertical, the other horizontal. Their rotational speeds were proportional, respectively, to the components of virtual speed perpendicular and parallel to own course. These rotations were generated by variable-speed drives, their discs being driven by a speed-regulated electric motor.[48] A variable-speed drive of very similar design was also shown in the patent for the true-course plotter.[49] These mechanisms are significant as the first Argo drives based on a disc, a ball and a pair of rollers. However, at this stage of development, the rollers were stationary so, to change the rate, the ball had to be forced sideways against sliding friction at its points of contact with disc and rollers.

On 29 April 1910, the Argo Company accepted the Admiralty's terms for the supply of forty-five rangefinder mountings. After preliminary experiments from 24 May and 9 June 1910, the actual 'Aim Corrector Trials', conducted by a committee presided over by Rear Admiral S. C. J. Colville, followed between 16 and 29 June.[50] They were intended to compare *Natal's* automatic plotting with manual plotting of true and virtual course by, respectively, *Lord Nelson* and *Africa*, and to verify 'the general suitability and reliability of "NATAL'S" installation for use in action'.[51] Unfortunately, even the preliminaries established that:

> in their present form, [*Natal's*] instruments are neither reliable without more skilled attention than they can get in a newly commissioned ship nor in many of their unessential details suited to ship or sea conditions . . .
>
> That many elements . . . need radical alteration has already been recognised . . . in the case of the rangefinder mountings . . . The case . . . is more obvious and stronger in the case of the other instruments.[52]

Electrical terminals came loose and, more seriously, 'rubbing contacts' (on which the relays throughout the system depended) failed due to sparking and becoming dirty. Pollen had to accept that the rangefinder mounting was still 'seriously defective', both the gyro and its relay (that is, the clutch servo and its control gear) proving unreliable. The worst problems were with the hastily modified plotter. The pricker wheels lost their hold on the wooden board; both board and table-top had warped, but also the weight of the board caused it to 'take charge' if there was any motion on the ship. These sudden movements also broke the already temperamental plotting pens. The table's gyroscope, which indicated changes of course, wandered. And the minute marks along the enemy course were little help in estimating enemy speed, because they were made automatically, whether or not the rangefinder had a good 'cut'.[53]

Except for an adjusting nut working loose, the clock was reliable, though Pollen himself admitted that 'the backlash is excessive' and, functionally, it was far from satisfactory. If wrongly set, its range and bearing could not be altered without stopping it and disconnecting the drive screws. For the same reason, there were no means during a turn of applying the large change in the target bearing relative to own course.[54] In any case, the variable speed drives were 'not capable of [driving] while the speed was being altered'.[55] Thus:

> The principal defect in the working theory of the clock is that it runs, like the original plotting table, on the 'straight-line' principle.[56]

It was in no sense helm-free.

Admiral Colville's committee concluded that:

> The installation <u>as at present fitted in 'NATAL', and as tested in these trials</u> is unsuitable and unreliable for use in action.

Yet they concurred with the adoption of the rangefinder mounting and recommended the 'improved model [clock] as proposed by the makers'. They decisively rejected both forms of manual course plotting but proposed new trials of the A.C. automatic plotter when 'further developed'. The Admiralty, however, decided to reject the plotter outright: but they also invited Pollen to submit 'detailed designs of an improved and reliable clock' which could 'transmit to Follow-the-Pointer sights with unequal graduations'. They also informed him that the drum-type indicators in *Natal*'s turrets had failed to maintain synchronism. In reply, Pollen confirmed that.

> We are already engaged in re-designing the gear, and our present intention is to rebuild it in its entirety . . . we shall, so soon as the

range finder mounting and indicator drawings are complete, put the clock in hand before any other devices.[57]

Meanwhile, by 2 August, Lieutenant Reginald Plunkett[58] of *Natal* was already experimenting with time-and-range plotting using the Argo plotter; the method was used successfully in her Battle Practice on 16–18 August. Isherwood wrote to Plunkett: 'I am interested to hear that you are trying "Time and Range" plotting',[59] while Argo personnel may have plotted range-rates (though not dual rates) while aboard *Natal*.[60] By November, Pollen conceded that, when used with the Argo mounting, dual-rate plotting was 'a good alternative means of getting and keeping rate – alternative, that is, to straight line plotting'.[61]

## *Orion*

Pollen and Plunkett continued to correspond privately while *Natal's* table was modified so that it could also plot bearings manually. Although unsuccessful,[62] the experience must have been useful for the automatic dual-rate plotter that Argo supplied as part of the system for trial in *Orion*. It was delivered in early 1912 and patented in the following October.[63] On this table, the ranges and bearings transmitted from the Argo rangefinder mounting were plotted in tandem on one broad band of paper moving at a steady speed. The complex synchronous transmission system was replaced by much simpler step-by-step gear. However, the receivers still used counter-rotating electromagnetic clutches to position the plotter's pencils, and were never entirely satisfactory.[64] The *Orion* trials found that:

> If the working head [of the rangefinder] is moved too fast . . . the receiver will get out of step. To prevent this the working head is geared down [but] this is . . . very inconvenient for the range taker who likes to move the working head quickly to and fro before obtaining the 'cut'.[65]

while the Phillpotts committee, which re-examined the Argo system in 1918, reported that the 'magnetic clutches . . . fitted in the plotting table, in H.M.S. "ORION" have given considerable trouble at times'.[66]

Before the end of 1910 (perhaps for the *Natal* trials) the Argo mounting had been fitted with a variable-speed power training drive for rotating the outer tube relative to the inner; thus, provided that the gyro stabilisation took care entirely of the ship's yaw, the controlling lever gave a direct indication of the rate of change of enemy bearing relative to mean course. Pollen then proposed that, if a similar drive were attached to the rangefinder adjustment head, range-rate could be obtained directly.[67] This required a continuous 'cut', but, as the *Orion* report states, this was the very opposite of the normal method of working a coincidence rangefinder. Lieutenant J. C. W. Henley, now the DNO's assistant responsible for fire control, wrote privately to his predecessor, Frederic Dreyer:

> Mr. P. has tried to push this forward into the 45 sets several times but we have opposed it as absolutely impractical.

Even so, Pollen persisted and the power-cut device was included in the *Orion* trials, but it did not prove satisfactory.[68]

The forty-five production rangefinder mountings were ordered only with receivers that displayed ranges and bearings digitally. Argo was able to adapt their original synchronous transmission switches to control arrays of lamps, each lamp projecting one digit onto a ground-glass screen.[69] In July 1911 (two months before the contracted date) Henley inspected the prototype of the improved design.

> The Training Control is excellent and the Air Gyro is satisfactory but his [Pollen's] mechanical Clutch relay between Gyro and Mounting gives a jerky motion of about ¼° each way. An electrical relay which we tried however improved this enormously.[70]

The handbook establishes that, in the production models, the clutches were finally abandoned in favour of a sophisticated electric relay; the inner tube was driven directly by a reversible electric motor, to which the electrical power was switched in three increasing steps as the mounting deviated further from its correct bearing. By February 1912, Argo had 'delivered ten out of the 45 sets and the others are now coming forward at the rate of about 3 sets a month'.[71] These first units retained the air-driven gyroscope, which could stabilise the mounting against yaw and small course alterations only up to 15°. In the last twenty sets, it was replaced by an Anschütz gyrocompass receiver which could maintain the directional reference even during large course changes.[72] Thus for the first time these final models were helm-free (Figure 4.1).

In principle, the rangefinder operator had only to set the power training lever to keep on the enemy, and to use his other (right) hand both to elevate the rangefinder and adjust the cut. Especially after the failure of the power-cut device, all this proved too much for one man and the mounting was modified for a separate trainer, who would also have been better able to correct for wander by the gyros and any residual hunting by the electric relay. Nevertheless, the conclusion after the *Orion* trials was that:

> The arrangements for training are very good and are universally liked ... With these alterations [for a separate trainer], the instrument is suitable for service use and is a decided improvement on the Barr and Stroud Mounting.[73]

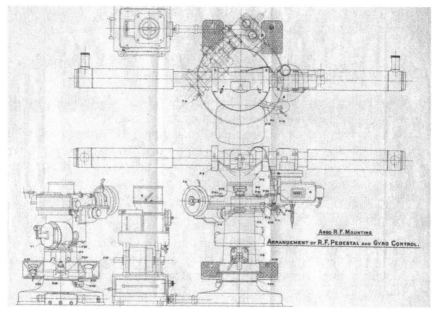

*Figure 4.1* Argo rangefinder mounting.

The whole mounting above the pedestal was stabilised by the gyro-control to the left – note the air gyro and its limited deviation from mean course. The power training control is on the operator's left hand. He used his right hand to elevate the rangefinder and to control the 'cut'. The 'equal-step' range transmitter is also to the right.

Source: Dreyer and Usborne, *Technical History and ... Comparison*, February 1913, Plate I, AL.

However, this level of satisfaction appears to have been short-lived.

> The 45 sets . . . ordered had the Argo Gyro fitting in them, but except when first installed were never used as they proved unsatisfactory and were never incorporated in the Admiralty Fire Control System.[74]

Perhaps this refers only to the mountings with the air-driven gyros. While, as late as 1921, most ships with 13.5-inch guns still retained their Argo mountings,[75] the Anschütz gyrocompass installations had long since been replaced. However, even if gyro stabilisation had been disabled in the surviving mountings, the efficient power training gear was almost certainly still in use.

Once the rangefinder mounting and indicators had been redesigned, Isherwood turned next to the new clock. Starting from the earlier type of variable-speed drive, his inspired innovation was to mount the rollers in a sliding carriage; thus the rate could be changed by rolling the ball diametrically across the disc; this required minimal force and did not disrupt the rolling friction between the ball and the disc and rollers.[76] On 15 May 1911, Argo submitted to the Admiralty a proposal for 'the A.C. Range and Bearing Clock Mark II', although it actually described in detail a design with one of the new drives, for the generation of ranges only. To set its rate, the roller carriage was coupled directly to the rate-generating mechanism. The latter changed considerably as the design developed, but from the start it embodied the essential Dumaresq principles: a sliding pivot displaced in the opposite direction to own ship's course by a distance proportional to own speed: and a pin or pointer (representing the enemy bow) displaced from the pivot in the direction of enemy course by a distance proportional to enemy speed.[77] To simplify the automatic transfer of range-rate to the variable-speed drive – which is conveniently called the 'range clock' – the line-of-sight was fixed.

In the Mark II design, enemy-bearings – as course-bearings – were set by hand on its large bearing-dial; the slots or slides representing own and enemy courses were mounted beneath this dial. When courses were steady, the mechanism held constant the angle between own and enemy course. If own ship altered course, it was necessary to throw over a lever until the turn was completed; the lever's action clamped the angle between enemy-course and line-of-sight i.e. the inclination was held constant through the turn. This approximation, the same as that used in the Dumaresq Mark VI 'neglects the change of bearing due to alteration of position during [a] turn but at long ranges the error introduced is very small'. The Mark II proposal introduced the spiral range scale characteristic of all later Argo clocks.[78] And it declared that:

> By the addition of a simple linkage and another variable speed drive, 'Bearings' can be operated automatically . . . the Mark II Clock will [then] do all that the A.C. Mark I Clock will do . . . but will also indicate deflection due to speeds.

Although not described, this linkage must have been some form of proportional lever that divided speed-across by range to obtain bearing-rate; this rate could then be set on the variable-speed drive that generated change-of-bearing. The proposal also admitted that:

> subsidiary portions such as 'transmitter drive', 'spotting corrections', 'motor speed control' etc. are but vaguely indicated, as the problems introduced by them are the ordinary problems incidental and usual in Engineering design.[79]

The importance of the new design was recognised immediately in the Admiralty. On 22 May, Pollen wrote to Isherwood:

> While it is fresh in my mind, I had a talk with Henley today and explained to him the proposed additions and alterations to the Clock. He suggested we should send a sketch – which need not be in any kind of detail – showing a clock with automatic bearing generating and that could be set either by speed and course or by rates of change.

The sketch was sent to Henley, probably on the 27th. On 26 June, Argo sent the Admiralty its provisional patent specification, though this contained nothing about bearing generation; the application was lodged on 4 September, after the patent had been assigned as secret.[80] Then:

> On 11th October 1911 ... Henley inspected the working drawings of the Argo Clock at York and the Clock itself which was then under construction.[81]

The finished instrument was ready for inspection by the end of January 1912,[82] while a complete patent specification was left on 4 April.[83] On 17 April, Pollen informed the DNO of a four to six weeks' delay if the clock were to be fitted with a spotting pointer. Since such a pointer and its associated scales were illustrated in the patent but not mentioned in the text, they were probably not fitted to the prototype. This was still in the factory in the third week in July, and it was not installed in *Orion* until September,[84] the delay being in part caused 'by alterations necessitated to the clock as a result of suggestions by various Naval Officers'.[85] After satisfactory pre-trial experiments with the clock, *Orion* participated in the director trials that culminated in the firing with *Thunderer* on 13 November. The successful trials of the Argo clock followed on 19 and 20 November.[86]

> The Clock [was] thoroughly tested in ... 'Orion' ... and has worked well ... On the whole ... it solves in an efficient and reliable manner the problem which it undertakes.[87]

Meanwhile, on 27 September, the Admiralty had accepted Argo's tender for a further five clocks. These production models were designated Argo Clocks Mark IV.[88] However, there were significant differences between the patented design and that described in the Mark IV handbook of January 1914, particularly in the means of applying spotting corrections and transmitting gun ranges to follow-the-pointer sights. Since the method of working the transmission dial during the trials resembled that described in the handbook,[89] it appears that the prototype had already been modified to something like Mark IV standard even before it was installed in *Orion.* Thus the following description is based on the 1914 handbook (Figure 4.2).

The clock's mechanisms were entirely enclosed. On top of the case, the

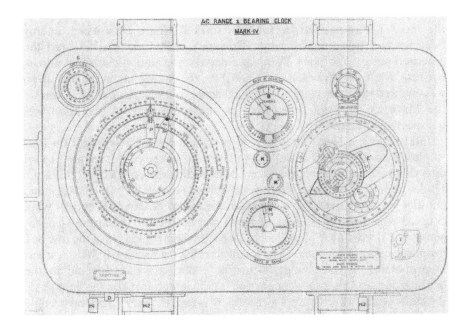

*Figure 4.2* Argo Clock Mark IV: top view.

Handle H1 set each spotting correction on the scale S; button D then reset the scale. Handles H2 and H3, when pushed in, tuned the indicated ranges and enemy bearings, respectively.

Source: Gunnery Branch, *The Argo Range and Bearing Clock Mark IV*, January 1914, OU 5180, AL.

large spiral range dial had pointers for gun and predicted rangefinder ranges; the difference between them was set using the spotting scale and handle H1 (the button D reset this scale to zero after each spotting correction was applied). The dumaresq-type linkages lay beneath the second large dial; the scale around its circumference was of course-bearings of the enemy. The bearing-dial carried smaller scales for setting own and enemy speeds, and enemy course relative to our own. The small pointer above the bearing-dial represented the enemy and indicated the enemy's inclination. The two central dials were for rates. The range-rate pointer was coupled directly to the dumaresq-linkage; the bearing-rate pointer was connected through a special mechanism that converted between the graduated bearing-rate and dumaresq speed-across. The adjacent knobs could be used to adjust the rates. Thus, the clock could be set either directly for enemy speed and course, or by a cross-cut of rates.[90]

When courses were steady, the clock generated ranges and bearings automatically, although, if the predicted values deviated from those obtained by observation, they could be 'tuned' using the handles H2 and H3.

But, if own course changed, the 'Angle of Courses' clamp was released and the lever T thrown from STEADY to TURNING, after which enemy bearings had to be set by hand. However, unlike the Mark II and the patented design, the Mark IV maintained the inclination exactly in a turn, because, while the lever was at TURNING, the enemy link in the dumaresq was coupled in the theoretically correct sense to the bearing clock. Even so, the Mark IV was not 'helm-free' in the sense that its operation was irrespective of helm.

Internally, the Mark IV (like the patented design) was based on four 'slipless' variable-speed drives. Drive I was the 'range clock'; its rate was set directly from the dumaresq, and one of its rollers was coupled to the Range Finder hand. For bearings, Isherwood did not employ 'a simple linkage and another variable speed drive'. Instead, the rollers of Drives II and III were coupled together; the rate of Drive II was set by the dumaresq's speed-across and the distance of the ball of Drive III from the centre of the disc was proportional to clock-range. The result was that the rotation of III's disc was in proportion to the change-of-bearing;[91] thus it was connected to the bearing-dial. By this 'cross-connection' of the integrators and the dumaresq, the clock could, while courses were steady, solve 'the ever-changing triangle of velocities' continuously and automatically; with good reason, Professor C. V. Boys saluted Isherwood's 'genius'.[92]

On the other hand, the arrangements for transmitting ranges to the follow-the-pointer (FP) gunsights were much less elegant. The range scales of these sights were not uniform i.e. at different ranges, one step change by the step-by-step transmitters and receivers equated to a different change of range. The patent described Drive IV as coupled to a FP transmitter, so that ranges could be transmitted automatically. Drive IV was set for rate from the dumaresq, but indirectly through a centrally pivoted lever and spiral cam; this mechanism was arranged so that, at different ranges, the same range-rate produced transmitter steps at different rates. Yet, in an extra-ordinary oversight, no means were provided to incorporate spotting or other range corrections in the transmitted ranges. This omission was circumvented in the similar Mark IV, though only by abandoning automatic transmission. A FP receiver with two hands was mounted on the side of the clock. The red hand (which was coupled to the clock through appropriately shaped cams) showed the same range as that indicated by the clock's gun range pointer. The black hand indicated the range being transmitted to the guns. The two hands moved together, but only until the clock-range was corrected; an operator then had to work a handle to realign the black hand with the red.[93] After the earlier airy dismissal of transmitter drive and spotting arrangements as no more than incidental problems, they seem to have been given insufficient attention until it was too late to devise a really satisfactory solution.

## A.C. completed

Design work on an entirely new Argo true-course plotter did not restart until the turn of 1911–12. Detailed drawings were ready by the following September but the prototype plotter itself was not completed until April 1913, after significant amendments to the design.[94] The Mark IV plotter plotted both own and enemy courses on a sheet of stiff card which was free to slide and rotate on the flat top. A long fixed arm extended over the top; the pencil plotting the enemy course was at the far end. The own-course pencil was mounted in a carriage that could be positioned at any point along the arm, at a distance from the enemy pencil proportional to the range received from the Argo rangefinder mounting – to a maximum of 16,000 yards. At one-minute intervals, both pencils automatically marked the plot with small circles. A lower carriage, sliding in a wide slot in the table top, was always positioned exactly beneath the carriage on the arm. The card was gripped between two pairs of pressure wheels in these carriages. The wheels could rotate in the same or opposite directions, while the carriages could also rotate bodily as a pair. These rotations were derived from changes in own compass course received from the gyrocompass, and in enemy relative-bearing received from the Argo mounting; the mounting also depended on the directional reference provided by a gyrocompass receiver. The correct representation of own ship's movements depended on the speed from the Forbes log.

The Mark IV plotter (Figure 4.3) was, without a doubt, another mechanical *tour de force* by Isherwood. However, while the design was theoretically correct, there are many reasons for doubting its accuracy and utility. First, bearings were transmitted from the Argo mounting in rather coarse steps of ¼°, and the plotter used the same magnetic-clutch receivers which were troublesome in the *Orion* rate-plotter. Second, the Phillpotts committee of 1918 concluded:

> The Gyro compass and Forbes log [are] not . . . even yet . . . sufficiently reliable . . . to enable own ship's motion to be accurately dealt with. Hence a confused plot results.[95]

Third, the complex rotations of the wheels moving the chart relative to the plotting pencils depended on the actions of long trains of differential gears; no provisions can be seen to minimise the backlash that, especially at long range, could have resulted in errors in the position of the chart under the enemy pencil.

Fourth, the plotter was always connected to a single Argo rangefinder mounting; since the power-cut had not worked, the transmitted ranges fluctuated between cuts, which must have scattered the majority of minute marks at varying ranges from the mean enemy course line. The scatter of the

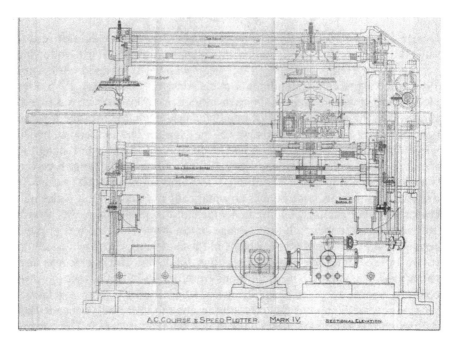

*Figure 4.3* Argo True-course Plotter Mark IV.

The fixed pencil to the left plotted enemy course and the pencil in the upper sliding carriage plotted own course; the distance between them was proportional to the range transmitted from the rangefinder. The two carriages together moved laterally and rotated. The chart was plotted on thin card gripped between the upper and lower wheels. The differentials in the lower carriage generated and added together rotations of the wheels in the same and opposite directions.

Source: Dreyer and Usborne, *Technical History . . . and Comparison*, February 1913, Plate VII, AL.

minute marks would have added to the difficulty of making out the mean enemy course from the actual plotted points, and they would have been little help in any attempt to infer the position of the enemy at each minute along that course. Thus:

> The enemy's speed can only be obtained by measuring on the plot the distance between any two dots or minute circles [which] is bound to be inaccurate.[96]

Argo proposed a multi-pointer range receiver for meaning the ranges from several rangefinders before transmitting the mean to the plotter; it might, perhaps, have been workable with continuous ranges from a power-cut, but not otherwise, and it never progressed beyond a cardboard model.[97] Fifth, there was no convenient means of measuring the mean range from the plot, while enemy range, course and speed could only be transferred to the clock manually. Finally, the Argo plotter could not compare observed enemy positions with the predictions of the clock.[98]

Relations between Argo and the Admiralty were in terminal decline by the time the Mark IV plotter was completed, and it was never tried by the Royal Navy. Pollen claimed complete success for the whole Argo system, including the new plotter, in trials by the Russian Navy in June 1914. Although the firm then received an order for five complete installations, in October Argo shipped to Russia only three rangefinders and mountings and two Mark V clocks with gyroscopes.[99] The cancellation of the plotters does nothing to dispel the many doubts about the Mark IV as a practicable true-course, helm-free plotter. In contrast, evidence from Russian sources indicates that all five clocks were eventually delivered, while the Russian preference for Cooke-Pollen rangefinders has already been noted.[100]

The Cooke-Pollen rangefinders for Russia were probably on a new naval mounting designed after the break with the Royal Navy. The rangefinder was carried on two pillars, each with a seat, the left for the trainer, the right for the rangetaker. All were carried on a circular platform, trained by hand, or by power with an variable-speed control. The rangetaker was also provided with both hand and power control of the cut.[101]

The final Argo clock, the Mark V, was at last truly helm-free. The prototype was probably complete by mid-October 1913, though the Admiralty declined an offer for a demonstration.[102] A new feature was the compass ring, a rotating circular scale around the main bearing-dial. By means of a coupling to a relay motor controlled by a gyrocompass receiver, own compass course and enemy compass bearing were indicated on the compass ring, and the dumaresq links were kept at the correct angles;[103] thus the clock 'automatically eliminates yaw and applies alterations of own ship's course'.[104]

In July 1913, Pollen and Isherwood applied for a patent that, the Admiralty believed in August 1914, 'describes the mechanism of the latest type of Argo clock . . . already . . . on the open market'.[105] To generate change of enemy compass bearing, the Mark V reverted to the Mark II scheme of a single variable-speed drive, set for bearing-rate by a linkage. The linkage, in the form of a lever pivoted at one end, actually multiplied speed-across by the reciprocal of range, the latter being obtained from a suitably cut spiral cam coupled to the range clock. The new design was less liable to slipping at low ranges than that used previously. However, no complaints of such slippage in the Mark IV clocks have come to light; when re-examining the Argo system in 1918, the Phillpotts Committee had nothing but praise for the clock as a mechanism. Their main criticism was of its lack of integration with the plotter.

There is no record on paper of what the clock is doing in comparison with the information given by the plot.[106]

By 1914, Argo had at last developed a fully helm-free fire control system. Yet, in the middle of 1913, Argo had been removed form the list of Admiralty suppliers and its final system was never even tried by the Royal Navy. It is now necessary to return to 1901 and to trace the often troubled commercial relationship between Pollen and the Admiralty that ended in this final rupture.

## COMMERCIAL

Even Pollen's earliest approach to the Admiralty went straight to the top. In putting forward his two-position rangefinder in 1901, he wrote directly to the First Naval Lord, Lord Walter Kerr, a family friend and fellow Roman Catholic. Presumably following Kerr's advice, Pollen then approached Lord Selborne, the First Lord, but insisted that:

> Before submitting . . . drawings . . . we shall have to ask that a binding pledge of secrecy shall be given and an undertaking in no way to imitate or use the entirely novel mechanical and mathematical principles incorporated in the machine.[107]

Since both Watkin and Fiske two-position rangefinders had been found wanting during the *Arethusa* trials,[108] Pollen's claims for both novelty and accuracy were probably treated sceptically and, on 7 February, he was informed that his invention 'does not seem to the Admiralty to offer them advantages sufficiently good to warrant their buying the secret'.

On 9 May 1904, Pollen's father-in-law, now knighted and a Member of Parliament,[109] wrote to Selborne announcing that the calculating machine had been perfected, but also with an implied threat:

> People who have heard . . . of the invention have made approaches with a view to acquiring the Patents, possibly for foreign navies.

The accompanying Memorandum described the rangefinder, calculating machine and plotter and emphasised, as in 1901, that knowledge of enemy course and speed:

> would enormously simplify all cruiser tactics . . . The secondary use which this device could be put to would be as a rangefinder for guns.

By 27 May, after Pollen had seen the DNO, Captain H. D. Barry, Lawrence again wrote to the First Lord, urging:

> Is it not worth some experimenting with, or must it be dealt with on purely commercial lines, which would necessarily deprive the

Admiralty of any opportunity of getting a monopoly of the system when it is evolved.

However, Barry considered that Pollen's instrument 'is in no sense a rangefinder' for shipboard use:

> I explained the whole case clearly to Mr. Pollen . . . & said it was not the instrument that the Admiralty wanted. He replied that he wanted – 'the Admiralty to take what they didn't want'.
>
> . . .
>
> I may say I know the Pollen family personally and they are all pushing and persistent.[110]

Barry's opinion was confirmed when Pollen went over his head to meet with Lord Walter Kerr and Admiral May, the Controller. Because of problems with procuring more accurate one-observer rangefinders, May was prepared to consider a 'double-observer instruments with good communications at all events for trial', but Pollen was told that any experimental installation must wait on the completion of the other instruments.[111] In November, Pollen claimed in two letters to the Admiralty that 'it may be confidently said that [the system] has passed the experimental stage' and the 'system has now been completed'.[112] Barry preferred to leave a decision to his successor, Captain John Jellicoe, DNO from February 1905. On 3 April, Captain Edward Harding RMA (one of the DNO's assistants) wrote a highly favourable report on preliminary experiments in *Narcissus* with the observation units.[113] A month later, Pollen was informed that his terms had been accepted for the supply by 1 October at latest, or earlier if possible, of two observation units with bearing transmitters, the machines for computing range from the bearings, and a charting table. The 'Rate of Change' machine was:

> To be put in hand as soon as the final designs are decided upon and delivered as part of the order at probably a later date.[114]

Pollen was paid £2,000 on 3 May towards expenses incurred in the preceding five years, plus a further £2,000 in November for the instruments delivered to *Jupiter*, although £500 was retained against the completion of the rate-of-change machine.[115] This term proved conveniently imprecise; on 18 June 1906, Pollen declared:

> I have also completed designs for an improved tactical change of range machine similar in principle, but very different in design to that already supplied to the Admiralty in fulfilment of my contract of May 1905.[116]

The key word here is 'tactical'; the machine already delivered was 'not a machine for shooting' but a tactical aid for predicting future relative positions.[117] Nonetheless, the Admiralty seem to have accepted this contractual sleight-of-hand, since at some point Pollen received the outstanding £500.[118]

## *Jupiter* to *Ariadne*

Shortly after the *Jupiter* trials, Pollen wrote to Jellicoe proposing the use of the 'best one observer rangefinder that the market can supply'; the letter was also copied to the First Lord, now Lord Tweedmouth. Despite the inevitably unfavourable report on the trials, Pollen was encouraged to submit his new ideas and, by 18 June, had completed the proposal entitled the 'One Observer System of Charting'. In late June, at a conference of experts, Harding (supported by Percy Scott) argued successfully in favour of secrecy; subsequently, Harding wrote describing the discussions, so he was now serving Pollen inside the Admiralty as both advocate and informant. After the conference, at the insistence of the Controller, Captain Henry B. Jackson, Jellicoe raised the possibility of plotting by non-automatic methods but Pollen was able to persuade him against such an attempt.[119]

On 9 August, following a decision of the Board, negotiations began on a new agreement to purchase equipment for trial and, in the event of success, for supply in quantity. Pollen initially demanded £8,000 for the trial system, although this figure included £3,600 towards his earlier development costs; the Admiralty side was reluctant 'to make good his losses on a trial that was unsuccessful' and offered £4,500. Pollen was also told that his hope for a guarantee to equip twelve ships a year for fifteen years, worth, it was estimated, some £300,000, was out of the question. This sum was intended as a consideration for giving up his foreign markets, but, when it was pointed out that 'inventors usually have to perfect their inventions at their own expense', Pollen declared that he would be seeking much more for a completed system and that 'he had had offers from a Foreign Government and from large firms to take it up'.

> It was also explained to him that if the trial took place, he could not fail to acquire further knowledge of range-finding in general and of British Naval methods in particular, in addition to that which he already owes to us . . . if we then decided to let him go abroad with that knowledge we might in fact be almost obliged to accept his terms so as to keep the knowledge from others. This being so, he ought to be prepared to offer terms . . . which the Admiralty would accept.

These concerns explain why the Admiralty had insisted that Pollen was:

to attend preliminary trials to see any necessary adjustments carried out . . . and to demonstrate the utility of his invention . . . but not to be present at the final trials.[120]

On the following day, Pollen informed the Admiralty that 'The smallest sum which would enable me to carry on is £6,500'. He also proposed conditions which, after the *Ariadne* trials, were to prove much more to the Admiralty's advantage than his own.

The Admiralty to decide, after two months working of the instruments . . . whether or not they wish to acquire a monopoly of my system.

On 21 August, the Admiralty agreed to £6,500 for the trial instruments, while Pollen was also paid an additional £802 10s towards 'expenses which he had not anticipated' for the earlier trials;[121] thus in total he would receive over 90 per cent of the sum he had first asked for. However, the Admiralty refused to entertain more than £90,000 for monopoly; by this time, a clock no longer figured in the negotiations, the agreement relating only to the supply of the rangefinder mounting and plotting table. On 27 August, Pollen again wrote directly to the First Lord, still asking for a total payment of £255,000, on the grounds that:

what I have to sell is not instruments but a system, the embodiment of certain laws of gunnery which I was the first to codify . . . The monopoly of instruments is only incidental.

Yet Pollen was clearly aware that his position was exceptional:

perhaps the fact that there is no parallel to the present negotiation may explain some of the difficulties that have arisen in dealing with it.[122]

Meanwhile, Captain Harding had been preparing a 'Memorandum upon the Professional and Financial Value of the A.C. System'. This he submitted to Jellicoe on 4 September, while informing Pollen that:

I have got out a regular snorter for the D.N.O., if it doesn't convince him nothing will.[123]

As might be expected, his arguments were often similar to Pollen's.

Throughout the negotiations he [Pollen] has laid more stress on the principles involved . . . on the <u>idea</u>, that is to say, than on the details of the mechanism.

105

His technical assessment relied on the false assumption that, by course plotting, the 'errors of individual readings of the Range Finder [may be] eliminated' rather than just reduced; he then concluded that the geometric range could be found without observation of fire and, consequently, that concentration would be more effective. Concerning the originality of the system, Harding affirmed that 'the necessity for some form of gyroscopic control is probably totally unrecognised' elsewhere, but he acknowledged that:

> the solution of plotting only occurred incidentally to Mr. Pollen and it was not immediately that he recognised its technical application and importance.

and that:

> Probably every Coast Artillery Control system in the World employs some form of chart, but it may be said with safety that not one of them uses it exactly in this way.[124]

Harding here gives some credence to Dreyer's later accusation that Pollen's plotter was no more than a *rechauffé* of the Watkin system used in British coastal defences and tried unsuccessfully aboard *Arethusa*.[125] Pollen mentioned coastal defence systems or their depression rangefinders in four proposals from 1901 to 1904.[126] Thus his claim that he had never heard of the Watkin 'inventions . . . until 1906 . . . and could not now [1909] give an intelligent account of his system' must be discounted.[127] Harding, who was well acquainted with the Watkin gear, recognised that the originality in Pollen's proposals lay not in course plotting *per se*, but in his conviction that this type of plot could be made from a ship at sea.[128]

There were no qualifications in Harding's support to the inventor's negotiating stance:

> IN CONCLUSION the system will be of immense national value as a monopoly . . . the sum thus spent must be looked upon as an insurance against the possible acquisition of the invention by other powers or as money spent on research, and not as relieving the inventor of financial risk.[129]

To the Royal Commission on Awards to Inventors (RCAI), Harding acknowledged that, at this time:

> I saw a good deal of Mr. Pollen. I was very enthusiastic . . . possibly over enthusiastic.[130]

Nevertheless, his recommendations were accepted. Sumida makes a convincing case that his memorandum (or a *précis* by Jellicoe) was instrumental in persuading Fisher that a monopoly of Pollen's gear must be obtained.[131] Thus, on 21 September, the Admiralty renewed its offer of £6,500.

> My Lords will agree . . . to decide after 2 month's working of the instruments . . . whether or not they wish to acquire the monopoly of your system.

If they so decided, Pollen would receive £100,000 for the monopoly rights to the system and its installation in forty ships: £1,000 for each additional ship up to eighty ships: after which no further royalty payments would be made.

> The instruments required by the Admiralty from you to be supplied at a cost of 25% above that paid by you to the manufacturers.

Provisional agreement reached by 29 October enabled the Admiralty to pay the £6,500 for the trial instruments on 8 November.[132] In correspondence with the Treasury, the Admiralty stated that the full £100,000 would be paid as an initial instalment of £50,000, followed by two annual payments of £25,000, also that the contractual terms:

> are so arranged that unless the invention is completely successful and gives an accuracy of fire at a moving ship at long ranges immensely in advance of that which is now possible, the price to be paid will not be that named but will be some lesser sum which will be arrived at by arbitration . . . a partial success only will be of great value.

Nonetheless, the report of the Naval Estimates Committee of 26 November included in the 1907–8 estimates a provision of £62,500 for 'Pollen's aim-correcting apparatus', despite the adverse effect on attempts to reduce expenditure.[133]

With the immediate urgency removed, the Admiralty did not send Pollen a draft contract until 11 March 1907, but this only initiated another protracted round of negotiations. At one point, Pollen seems to have been accused of sharp practice, while, on 31 July, he declared that 'the whole purpose . . . of the Admiralty has been . . . to leave us in the position of an expropriated patentee'. Thus the temper of the discussions had deteriorated even while Jellicoe was still at the Admiralty. Pollen later admitted to Bacon:

> Your predecessor took the line (which undoubtedly was right) that, until the Service had made up its mind about the A.C. gear, I had to be regarded as a person who might at any moment be making his knowledge and experience of gunnery available to the world.[134]

Although the formal contract was still unsigned, the cruiser *Ariadne* had been nominated as the trial ship and, by 20 November, the instruments had been installed aboard and were inspected by Admiral Wilson. Initially, his relations with Pollen were cordial.[135] Furthermore, in November the Admiralty still anticipated a favourable outcome, since the Navy Estimates Committee assumed that, for the year 1908–9:

> 50,000l. [£50,000] has to be re-provided . . . to meet the liability in respect of the Pollen Aim Corrector which will not mature during the current year.[136]

However, on 8 December, Wilson asked Pollen for 'a written statement showing exactly what are the advantages you claim for your system'. Pollen responded with a copy of 'An Apology for the A.C. Battle System', but this only helped Wilson to appreciate both that the system was incomplete and that the Admiralty's rights were limited to only a part of it. Shortly afterwards, at the end of a second inspection, Wilson turned on Pollen demanding:

> You will have to explain to me sometime or other why on earth the Admiralty should pay you £100,000 more than to Barr and Stroud or any other maker of Fire Control instruments that have got to be used for your system.[137]

Having decided that Pollen's exceptional treatment was unjustified, Wilson was now determined to demonstrate that, when tried in *Vengeance*, his own manual virtual-course plotting could produce equal results. In Torbay, the A.C. plotter produced a chart of the required accuracy. By the luck of the draw, the conditions at sea on 15 January 1908 were so easy that neither ship had any difficulty in keeping the range; Wilson peremptorily halted the trial and ordered *Ariadne*'s return to port. It is hardly surprising that, ever afterwards, Pollen was convinced that he had been cheated of the opportunity to demonstrate the superiority of his gear in more demanding circumstances.

### *Ariadne* to *Natal*

Wilson's official report on the trials was submitted on 31 January 1908, but we do not know whether it contradicted Pollen's assertion on the 24th that the 'complete success' conditions had been met in full.

> The sum the Lords Commissioners have agreed to pay for mono-poly . . . can now neither be increased by my system being shown to be better than has already been proved, nor diminished, as partial

failure might have caused it to be . . . If I had such attractive offers from foreign navies when nothing was proved, is it likely that they will not materialise when everything is established?[138]

The formal contract with Argo was not actually signed until 18 February; it stipulated that:

If complete success can be obtained at the trials *and* if the Commissioners thereupon decide to acquire the sole and exclusive rights to use the Pollen Aim Correction System . . . *and* shall give to the Inventor within one calendar month from the . . . completion of the . . . trials notice in writing . . . the Inventor shall forthwith grant [said] rights [my italics].[139]

Thus Pollen could still hope for a decision in his favour. Unfortunately for him, the Admiralty's 'right of refusal had been carefully safeguarded in the agreement',[140] so that they could reject exclusive rights *even though* complete success had been attained. In fact, other pressures had already made this the most likely outcome. On 26 November 1907, the Cabinet had refused to accept the proposed Navy Estimates for 1908–9, which represented an increase over the previous year of £2,150,000. After spirited discussions, by the beginning of February the increase had been reduced to only £900,000 and Pollen's £50,000 (not to mention similar large sums in subsequent financial years) had become a tempting candidate for the inevitable cuts.[141]

Even so, no decision had been taken by 2 March, when Pollen wrote to Tweedmouth asking to see the parts of Wilson's report dealing with 'matters of fact' and directly criticising the Admiral.

On certain mechanical questions, he [Wilson] seemed not to have given himself time to understand either the principles or actual working of the instruments.

Pollen also risked causing further serious offence by comparing his present situation with 'the straightforward and honourable way in which their Lordships treated me on the occasion of the *Jupiter* trials'. Nonetheless, on 6 March, presumably at Tweedmouth's instigation, the Admiralty offered further trials. In his reply of 9 March, Pollen only 'noted' the proposal, regretted that other business would prevent his continuous attendance, and also questioned why the Admiralty assumed that the contract of 18 February provided for additional trials.[142] However, he undertook to make Isherwood and his engineers available 'at a moment's notice'; he was therefore dumbfounded to receive the letter of 10 March in which the Admiralty inferred that:

> By your letter of the 9th March, you do not appear to wish these further trials to take place. In the absence of such further trials, the Agreement between yourself and the Admiralty will expire on the 14th instant.
>
> . . .
>
> . . . My Lords have . . . decided not to exercise the option . . . of acquiring the sole rights of the 'Aim Corrector System'.
>
> . . . as from your letter to Sir A. Wilson of the 24th January they understand you wish to enter into negotiations with certain Foreign Powers, they would be glad to know if you are desirous of re-purchasing the [*Ariadne*] instruments.[143]

At just this moment, the First Lord's position had been fatally weakened after, on 9 March in the House of Lords, he had failed to defend his correspondence with the Kaiser about the British Navy Estimates;[144] Tweedmouth, not unnaturally, refused to see Pollen on the 10th. Further, if the new trials were indeed outside the Agreement, the expiry date was now very close. And, Pollen's imputations against the present Board and particularly his attack on Wilson probably undermined any remaining support, since he found it necessary to declare:

> I am most anxious that no member of the Board should think that I wish in any way to reflect on Sir Arthur Wilson.[145]

Even Pollen admitted:

> I have felt from the beginning, and the contract makes it clear, that . . . the Admiralty were perfectly free to take it or leave it as they please.[146]

However, while Pollen's £100,000 was lost for good, the Board were agreed that he should receive an award to cover his expenses and his contributions to the development of fire control, though they were still divided on the question of secrecy.[147] After new negotiations, by 18 June it had been accepted that secrecy would be maintained for a further eighteen months, that the *Ariadne* instruments (including the rangefinder) would be returned, and that Pollen would receive a payment of £11,500. At least at first, he took a remarkably sanguine view of this outcome.

> In binding myself . . . not to approach any foreign power for a year, I am not in the slightest degree hurting the commercial development of the thing, and . . . I am getting the working capital necessary to carry on with it without the necessity of making it public. This is virtually understood, I think, at the Admiralty . . . by Jackie & Co. that the thing will be reopened.[148]

With funding secured, Pollen and Isherwood were free to tackle the defects in the *Ariadne* gear and to begin work on the clock. Pollen also found time to write *Reflections on an Error of the Day*. In the later sections, he argued at length against manual methods, but the pamphlet began with a critique of rate-plotting. Nevertheless, Pollen still claimed to have been the first to think of time-and-range plotting, though we 'did not proceed . . . for the reason that it seemed to us both unscientific and impracticable'; however, no mention was made of plotting bearings against time.[149]

On 5 January 1909, Pollen announced the formation of the Argo Company, although, in fact, the company had been registered on 31 December 1907, with Pollen as the only major shareholder.[150] He declared:

Unlike the devices tried in the Jupiter and Ariadne, which were experimental sections of the system, the gear we are now building will be in all respects fitted to its purpose as integral parts of a fighting ship's equipment . . .

. . . the A.C. system owed its complete development largely to the £22,000 of public money voted to Mr. Pollen . . . and the exceptional opportunities for study and investigation that the experiments in H.M.S. Jupiter and H.M.S. Ariadne afforded.[151]

Pollen had submitted his Argo prospectus just as the Navy Scare of early 1909 was coming to the boil.[152] Despite this not inconsiderable distraction, on 12 February his proposal for further trials was discussed by the Admiralty Board, on which Jackson had been replaced as Controller by Jellicoe.

A circular letter to the Fleet to be prepared informing the Service that Mr. Pollen having formed a commercial company was now in the position of an ordinary manufacturer.

At a meeting with Bacon on 15 February:

The DNO informed me [Pollen] that it was desired to make further investigation into the value of the Gyroscopic Control of the Range finder . . . I am not to quote for the Automatic Charting devices . . . it had been decided not to re-open the question of monopoly or a possible extension of the period of secrecy.

However, having obtained Pollen's acceptance that the agreement of February 1908 had expired, on 4 March the Board overruled the DNO.

The First Sea Lord to see the Director of Naval Ordnance who is to arrange for the purchase of a complete set of apparatus.[153]

It is curious that Fisher was deputed to convey this decision, since Jellicoe, Bacon's direct superior, was present at the meeting. Pollen had heard nothing further by 22 March. By this time, the demands that 'We want eight, and we won't wait' were at their loudest and a vote of censure on the Government's dreadnought programme was to be held on the 29th. Pollen seized his opportunity for a piece of blatant political arm-twisting, writing to the First Lord, now Reginald McKenna, of his fears that:

> . . . those who succeeded in turning the Ariadne trials into a mockery last year may do their best to prevent my getting a prompt and fair trial now.
> . . .
> . . . for the last three days, I have been doing my utmost to prevent this matter being brought up in the Unionist Press and the House of Commons . . . the Front Bench Unionists, who were formally members of the Board, are perfectly familiar with . . . my inventions . . . it is believed a very strong polemical value would attach to bringing the matter out in the forthcoming vote of censure.
> . . . I hope . . . that I have prevented this matter being publicly discussed. But naturally I should like to hear from you whether this assurance I have given has any foundation.

At a brief meeting with Jellicoe on 24 March, Pollen was given to understand that he might be asked to tender for a trial of his complete Battle System and Argo was sent a formal request to tender on 2 April.[154]

Fisher probably assented only reluctantly to this invitation. Pollen's relations with Beresford and Custance were cordial and of long standing, while, in 1908, Beresford had unsuccessfully sought permission for Pollen to attend a Battle Practice and had declared that 'Pollen's manual true-course plotting scheme was superior to the methods recommended by the Ordnance Department'. The letter to Tweedmouth of 22 March then revealed that Pollen was in touch with the Conservative opposition. Fisher's antipathy must have been quickly reinforced when, also on 2 April, the First Sea Lord was criticised both in an anonymous *Times* article, and in a speech by Sir George Armstrong, who claimed that in 1906 Bacon had been sent out to the Mediterranean by Fisher to spy on Beresford.[155] Fisher believed Pollen was involved in both attacks.

> I have been told that Pollen's ramifications are extraordinary and his newspaper influence very considerable and his being a Roman Catholic of immense support to him. I have consistently refused to have anything to do with him or see him.[156]

It seems likely that Fisher, with Bacon's connivance, had been responsible for the delay in Argo's invitation to tender, but that Pollen had been able to overcome their obstruction by his letter to the First Lord.

Pollen had previously estimated that the trial instruments would cost about £6,800. Now, apparently forgetting the prospectus claim that the instruments were 'no longer in a tentative stage', he declared that a complete set could not be delivered until well after secrecy expired in November 1909. He demanded £4,150 for additional gear plus £6,540 to extend secrecy for another year, while blaming the increases on the Admiralty for delaying a decision and demanding more extensive trials than he anticipated. The Admiralty would not entertain such an increase and asked for new prices with and without automatic sights. On 21 April, they accepted Argo's delivery dates (in June and July) and a price of £6,400 for:

1 Gyro-controlled Rangefinder
1 Charting Table . . .
1 Change of Range Machine with transmitting and Observer's
   correction attachments
1 Set of Observer's Correcting mechanisms.

In place of sights (which almost certainly were never constructed), they asked the company to quote for the supply of two range and two deflection indicators; a formal order was placed on 8 June and eventually Argo would receive about £9,800 for the *Natal* gear and for prolonging secrecy. On 21 June, even though the delivery dates had already slipped, the Admiralty invited Argo to tender for a production order of at least 30 rangefinder mountings.[157]

Just before the Admiralty accepted his tender, on 20 April Pollen wrote to McKenna blaming Bacon for the present delays and, with Wilson and Dreyer, for 'the farce' of the *Ariadne* trials. He repeated his allegations at even greater length in the pamphlet 'Notes, Etc., on the *Ariadne* Trials' and, although it may not have been widely circulated, its violent language offended Jellicoe. In any case, Bacon refused to be drawn into a quarrel. Indeed, by July there had been a remarkable improvement in relationships, when 'the D.N.O. went arm in arm with Pollen to Manchester [probably on the 8th] and came back much impressed'.[158] The Assistant DNO, Captain Arthur Craig, and Dreyer (then responsible to the DNO for fire control) also visited the Linotype works on 12 July. Dreyer's technical report on the A.C. instruments was favourable; his recommendations were endorsed by the Assistant DNO, though he hoped 'the prices can be made more reasonable', and he was not very impressed by the clutch-operated training gear of the rangefinder mounting.[159] On 16 July, Bacon wrote to Pollen:

I sincerely wish you every success with your apparatus . . . My definition of success may be too flavoured with a hatred of complications but this will do no harm as an antidote.

Yet Sumida proposes that, in June, 'the Ordnance Department retained both the means and the will to prevent a fair trial', his main ground being that, on 4 June, Pollen protested to the Admiralty because 'the trials would again take the form of a competition with service equipment, that he and his employees would be excluded from the ship during trials and that he would not be allowed to test his gear at sea or train officers in their use before the trials'. In fact, in the Admiralty letter of 21 June he was assured that thorough training would be arranged for.[160] Moreover, since Pollen had declared that the gear was no longer experimental, the Navy was entitled to insist that it be worked only by Service personnel, while the secrecy agreement was due to expire in only five months, unless extended temporarily month-by-month. Thus exclusion was no more than a continuation of the cautious policy first laid down by Jackson and Jellicoe in August 1906 and expressed most recently in the February letter to the Fleet, which emphasised the 'importance of observing strictly the regulations as to the secrecy of fire control apparatus'.[161]

The rangefinder mounting, transmission equipment and straight-course plotter were eventually delivered to *Natal* at the end of September. Plotting exercises were conducted during October and, by the end of the month, Captain Frederick Ogilvy was impressed by what Pollen had already achieved and urged him to make the plotter helm-free.[162] Pollen later alleged that:

> Save on the first day [our gear] was put together, I have not been permitted to see it running.

This must be an exaggeration, even if, during tests, the equipment was worked only by Service personnel. Sumida provides several instances of Pollen writing from *Natal*, and it was not until 10 November that Pollen and Isherwood were ordered off the ship before the start of gunnery exercises. Further successful tests were then made until, apparently as a results of mishandling, the gear broke down. An Argo engineer was then allowed back on board 'to make repairs and to supervise subsequent operations'.[163]

Once ashore, Pollen was able to resume negotiations on a contract to supply his instruments in quantity. On 23 June, he had responded to the Admiralty's invitation to tender with a price of £1,915 for each rangefinder with indicators, though he also proposed a royalty of £250 per ship per annum. In November, Bacon advised his successor, Captain Moore:

> The really useful portion of Mr. Pollen's apparatus appears to be the gyroscopically controlled range-finder . . . but there is no reason

why he should be paid any large royalties on the instrument . . . If Mr. Pollen can be put on the same basis as all other Admiralty contractors a difficulty which has existed for the last two years would be successfully removed.[164]

On 10 December, at a meeting with the Assistant DNO, Pollen was invited to quote for seventy-five rangefinder mountings with indicators and for fifty plotters; he asked for a fixed royalty of £1,000 on each mounting or table. He stated that 'it cost about £5,000 to £6,000 a year to run the Argo Co.', and revealed that the Linotype Company had quoted only £275 for the manufacture of each mounting with transmitters – though he asked that a cost to him of £380 should be assumed to allow for contingencies and tooling. He also proposed that:

> if the Admiralty saw its way to paying £20,000 in advance, it would enable Mr. Pollen to obtain a Controlling interest in the firm of Cooke & Son [sic] of York, where the apparatus could . . . be manufactured under Mr. Pollen's direct control.[165]

This meeting was held six days before Moore took up his position as DNO,[166] while Wilson was about to supersede Fisher as First Sea Lord. In October 1909, apropos the latest Battle Practice, Fisher had gloated that 'the new system of Fire Control is quite excellent and knocks Pollen into smithereens', yet Pollen seems to have been unaware that he was in Fisher's black books and feared that Wilson would be hostile. However, in the following March, 'Pollen appears to have been told [probably by Jellicoe] that Wilson's opinions were not the obstacle that he had supposed'.[167]

Moore followed Bacon's advice, further negotiations focusing solely on the mounting, with transmitters and range and bearing indicators, and on a single inclusive price for each set. On 22 January 1910, Pollen proposed £1,750 each for seventy-five sets supplied over five years with monopoly,[168] a price to which he then held through most of the following negotiations. Even after allowances for contingencies, the very large difference between the manufacturing and selling costs may explain the 'fraudulent contractor theory' apparently held by some in the Admiralty. In January, the Admiralty had warned Pollen that no decision could be expected before the start of the next financial year but their opening counter-offer, of 11 April, was for only fifteen sets at £1,000 each, without secrecy. Following the advice of Jellicoe, who had returned to the Admiralty as Controller, Pollen's formal rejection was temperately worded: but in a private letter to the First Lord, also dated 13 April, he declared, not for the first time, that.

> We have never contemplated giving foreign – and perhaps hostile – governments the benefits of the experience and skill we have

acquired at the cost of the British Admiralty . . . unless . . . we were driven to do so by compulsion.

He also sought an advance of £25,000 since:

> owing to my having understood before Xmas, that an order for 75 units was virtually decided, I entered . . . into an obligation to acquire a share in an important factory . . . and have consequently to find £15,000 before June 15th.[169]

Even before writing to McKenna, Pollen had expressed his disappointment in a letter to J. A. Spender, the editor of the Liberal *Westminster Gazette*, which ended with much the same implied threat which he had used a year earlier.

> P.S.
> You know the grounds I have for being quite certain that the giving up of the monopoly will be raised by the Front Opposition Bench in Parliament, and in the Press.

Since this letter is now in the McKenna Papers, it evidently reached the person for whom it was really intended. However, it did not produce the desired effect and, after a meeting on the 19th, McKenna received another letter leaving him in no doubt of the consequences if Pollen did not get his way.

> As the responsibility for the Board's decision to abandon secrecy and its defence in public will fall on you alone . . . you ought to know why this interest [in secrecy] is so great.

However, Pollen also offered some reduction in price, proposing £1,600 each for forty-five sets.[170] Meanwhile, Jellicoe had asked the Director of Navy Contracts (DofC), F. W. Black, to recommend what would be a fair price. Black concluded that, without secrecy, a price of £1,200 each for fifteen mountings plus indicators would be necessary to yield a 'substantial and liberal' profit. By 27 April, the parties were close enough for the Admiralty Board to give its general approval.[171] On the 29th, Argo were sent the Admiralty's offer to purchase forty-five sets over the next three years at £1,350 each, while secrecy was to be maintained until the end of 1912; the first £15,000 of the value of the contract was to be paid in advance. The price covered payment by the Admiralty of all the Argo Company's charges of £6,000 per annum for the three years; consequently, any other parts of the A.C. system would be supplied at the cost to Argo plus 'a fair commercial rate of profit only'. Argo were also required to acknowledge that the agreement of 18 February 1908 was 'a dead letter' and that the Admiralty manual plotting table did not infringe their patents.[172]

Although the 'Argo Company accepted the conditions "without qualification" on the day they were offered', Sumida proposes that:

> Pollen's acceptance of the Admiralty's unfavorable terms of purchase for only a portion of his fire control system . . . provided a margin of profit that was too small to enable the Argo Company to carry on experimental work on the remaining instruments.[173]

In fact, of the total contract value of £60,750, £18,000 covered Argo's company charges, leaving £42,750 for the mountings and indicators. Black had assumed that the manufacturing costs for thirty sets would be about £700 each, so the Admiralty allowed Argo a manufacturing profit of almost 36 per cent – more than the 33 per cent which Black regarded as a good 'ordinary trading profit'.[174] And, in addition, the Admiralty was prepared to pay Argo's running costs, at the rate of expenditure declared by Pollen, while the remainder of the A.C. system was developed. Pollen acknowledged after the trials had ended that:

> I have been treated for years with unparalleled generosity, and I can well imagine a Government Department wearying of being dragged for ever in the wake of a light-hearted optimist.[175]

With the production order settled, Pollen and his colleagues were able to prepare for the trials aboard *Natal*. Once again, after the preliminary tests, the Argo representatives were ordered off the ship. Pollen made a formal protest, but, apparently forgetting earlier boasts that the system would be 'ready for war', admitted that the instruments could be run reliably only by his own engineers.[176] However, the trials were to make comparisons with Service methods and the Admiralty, presumably mindful of Pollen's recent threats to take his system and experience to 'foreign – and perhaps hostile – governments', insisted on the instruments being worked by naval personnel.

## *Natal* to *Orion*

Pollen, like Isherwood, was quick to appreciate the significance of the rate plotting experiments being made by Plunkett in *Natal*. To the concern of Lieutenant Joseph Henley, by 13 August Pollen had declared that he was preparing 'a scheme for Automatic Time and Ranges Plotting'.[177] By November, he was also describing a time-and-bearing curve and the use of a dumaresq-like linkage by which 'the two rates could be resolved into speed and course of the enemy'.[178] Since discussions were still proceeding on modifying the *Natal* table for dual-rate plotting, on 20 December, the

Admiralty informed Argo of 'an instrument for automatically plotting Time and Range and Time and Bearing, devised by another inventor . . . and protected by secret patent'. The company was also asked whether its receivers could be adapted to work rate plots. In his reply, Pollen displayed an over-eager interest in Dreyer's rate-plotter:

> we shall be very glad to be informed of what his means of plotting are, so that we can give you finished designs for experimenting with it . . . it is a matter of entire indifference to us . . . whether we use the inventions of others or our own.

This uncharacteristic declaration could not in a moment reverse the Admiralty's wary attitude to Pollen.

> You have asked for certain particulars of the . . . invention . . . but my Lords . . . do not see their way to complying . . . as the secret invention goes a good deal further than the plain Time and Range and Time and Bearing which your Company propose to fit in HMS 'Natal' and their Lordships prefer that the two methods should be developed independently and then tried in comparison with each other.[179]

The modified *Natal* plotter was not a success but, on 2 May 1910, Argo was invited to quote for a rate-plotter, though the company was also reminded that it would be covered by Admiralty secret patents; its price for the plotter that was subsequently tried in *Orion* was £550.[180]

Immediately after the *Natal* trials, Pollen had undertaken to design a new clock;[181] by the end of 1911, the new prototype was nearing completion.[182] On 7 December, while the DNO submitted that five ships should be equipped with Dreyer instruments, he also noted that it had already been decided to fit *Orion* with the Argo rate-plotter and clock, even though the rough estimates of costs were £1,200 for a complete Argo installation compared with £300 for the Dreyer.[183] On 11 December, the Controller (now Rear Admiral C. J. Briggs) minuted:

> Before committing ourselves to one type of instrument I think it would be desirable to carry out comparative trials with the two systems and I suggest Argo Co. should be requested to quote a price.

This prompted the drafting of a letter to Argo requesting a quotation for one trial clock and for a further five sets; this draft was concurred in by Moore on 18 January 1912.[184] However, as soon as the clock had been demonstrated at the Argo London offices, on 18 March Pollen offered to loan it for trials, so the question of purchase of the prototype did not then arise. On 10 April, he was informed that Moore would recommend the adoption of the Argo clock for the next five capital ships to be completed, subject to the outcome of the trials and an agreement on prices.[185] However, the subsequent negotiations were to be dominated by an apparent crisis in the company's finances.

In evidence to the RCAI, Pollen and Argo presented a set of company accounts for the six years ending 31 December 1913. It shows investments of £12,650 at the end of 1910, increasing to £15,650 a year later. Pollen had, as intended, acquired a major holding in Thomas Cooke and Sons of York, thereby gaining an interest in the manufacturers of his instruments as well as access to Cooke's rangefinder expertise. However, this investment also tied up funds which could otherwise have been used to meet some of the large commitments, to design and manufacture, which lay ahead. The accounts confirm that Argo's expenses in 1909 were indeed close to the £6,000 estimated by Pollen, but, thereafter, they increased each year to a maximum of £12,807 in 1913. At first, Pollen was able to raise sufficient funds by means of bank loans (which reached £13,730 by 1911) and, in 1911, by the issue of Preference shares, which made £11,700.[186] The share offer had been backed by letters from a number of prominent naval officers, including Vice Admiral Prince Louis of Battenberg and Rear Admiral Peirse; Peirse admitted to the RCAI:

> I told him [Pollen] I should be only too pleased to give him my opinion in writing if it would help matters in the way of raising capital . . . I may say I very much regret if my opinion misled any money [sic].[187]

Despite these cash injections, by December 1911 there were clear signs that Argo was short of working funds.

> Argo company appealed to the Admiralty to pay for the first 15 sets in full, as delivered, instead of deducting from the price of each a proportion of the 15000l. advanced.

In February 1912, having concluded that 'The Argo Co. now find themselves very seriously handicapped by lack of capital',[188] the Admiralty agreed, but, when Moore attempted to obtain a price for five clocks in April, Pollen's response suggests that Argo was still in difficulties. Having declined 'to quote because it is impossible to make so small a number at commercial prices', he suggested three alternatives.

> The first is for the Admiralty to acquire the monopoly of our system, the second is to tell us at once that we are free to supply our devices elsewhere and the third is to give us a sufficiently large order for

plotting tables, rangefinders [presumably he meant the Cooke-Pollen model] and mountings to enable us to raise the capital requisite for manufacturing the clocks on a commercial basis.

On 20 April, Moore assured Pollen that he intended to place an order for five clocks 'without waiting for results of the trial one', but, on the 22nd, Pollen proposed an order for some 170–80 clocks. This might seem an excessive expectation, except that discussions were probably already taking place on ways to improve local control in turrets. A month later, an Admiralty conference attended by Moore recommended that both the Argo clock and 'somewhat modified' Dreyer apparatus could be suitable, while, as late as 7 August, the Fleet was advised that both instruments were to be included in comparative trials of local control arrangements.[189] Thus, on 7 June, Argo was asked to quote for clocks and range-rate plotters in numbers up to ninety-six each. Separate figures were requested with and without the maintenance of secrecy. Without secrecy, for five clocks and five plotters, they quoted £2,400 and £500 each, respectively, the prices falling to £1,350 and £400 for quantities of ninety-six each. However, the company refused to quote for the maintenance of secrecy either for a limited period, or for only a part of the system, which 'must be regarded in its entirety'.[190]

Meanwhile, Argo's financial crisis appeared to deepen further, since, on 13 May:

> They . . . asked the Admiralty to pay them an additional 26,000l. or else to release them from secrecy obligations in advance of the agreed date so as to enable them to raise capital outside.[191]

This request led to an examination of Argo's books. Expenses were considerably heavier than those assumed in 1910, due to the 'high salaries to directors and skilled designers &c [while] a large part of their work was upon other features of the A.C. system not included in the 45 sets', and also to high spending on experimental and prototype gear and on offices. The company also claimed that it 'was about 8000l. to the bad at the time when the order for the 45 sets was given', yet Pollen himself admitted to being at least £5,700 to the good in May 1908. Argo also represented the purchase of the shares in Cooke's as an expense rather than an asset.[192] By 23 July, Pollen was able to announce that his financial embarrassments had, somehow, been resolved, while by the end of the year, with the mountings delivered, Argo was once more in profit.[193] Thus, in attempting to justify additional payments, Argo seems to have exaggerated its problems. The outcome was the opposite of that intended, since the Admiralty became convinced that 'there had been serious extravagance in expenditure'. On 22 June, the firm was informed that 'the Admiralty [had] decided not to pay the extra 26000l . . . and not to release the Company from the agreed period of secrecy'.[194]

Moore (now a Rear Admiral) was about to join the Board as Controller. Despite Argo's difficulties, there was no change in the policy on trials.

> It is proposed to purchase five Argo clocks combined with automatic time and range plotters for the 'King George' class, to enable a very thorough comparative trial against the Dreyer gear to be carried out.

But, after Pollen had himself asked twice to be released from secrecy:

> the question of whether it is worth renewing it is under consideration. It is desired to treat the Argo Company similarly to all other contractors, and to dispense with secrecy agreements in future as far as possible.[195]

When the question was raised:

> The Argo Company offered to continue secrecy for 5000l. *per month* [original italics].
> ... They suggested the Admiralty should make them an offer for permanent secrecy or refer it to arbitration. From conversations, however, it was clear that the Company would want much more than the 140,000l. conditionally agreed ... in 1908.

Thus, Argo's 'exorbitant terms' left no reasonable alternative but to dispense with secrecy,[196] a policy which also promised to bring down Argo's prices.

After he became Controller, Moore retained responsibility for the negotiations with Argo, probably because he was thoroughly familiar with the case and with Pollen's habitual lobbying at the highest level. However, Sumida proposes that Moore 'was determined to block the advance of the Argo Company' and resorted to 'underhanded action' to damage Pollen's standing with members of the Board.[197] But, as shown by his minute of 13 August, Moore was now openly determined that the secrecy agreement with Argo must end:

> everything that the Argo Company professes to achieve, can be equally well performed with the Dreyer instruments: except that the Argo Company still advocates 'True Course and Speed plotting' as an essential, whereas the Service and Dreyer prefer the 'Time and Range' and 'Time and Bearing' curve system. (The True Course and Speed system has been tried over and over again and always fails). His [Pollen's] clock may or may not prove better than Dreyer's, under monopoly terms it will certainly be more expensive.

> I do not see any reason for continuing the privileged position of this inventor, he has been handsomely and generously paid for his work in the past, and in my opinion it is full time that he was placed in the same position as all other inventors.[198]

Although there is no record of discussion at a formal Board meeting, Moore's advice was accepted and, on 20 August, Argo was informed that monopoly and secrecy would cease on 31 December and that arrangements would be made for the prompt reassignment of patents; a new quotation for five clocks was requested 'at a price greatly below the £2,400 originally quoted'.[199]

Pollen immediately mobilised support in a bid to reverse the Board's decision. Rear Admiral Peirse wrote to the Second Sea Lord, Prince Louis of Battenberg, who in turn asked Moore for his comments. Moore's handwritten letter of 19 September repeats and expands on the points in his minute. His view was that, as Pollen gained more confidential knowledge, he could press for yet higher monopoly prices and that it was time to shake off 'a chain being forged . . . more and more relentlessly'. Moore considered that the rival fire control systems were functionally about equal, except that, while he was prepared to try Argo's new true-course plotter, he remained sceptical that Pollen would be any more successful than he had been previously. But Moore also emphasised that:

> I am so far from being opposed to Pollen's Clock that I have begged him for his own sake to push on with it & perfect it, as I knew Dreyer was going ahead & I believed Argo Company's work would be more accurately carried out. I have been for nearly a year trying to get contracts placed for 5 Argo Clocks . . . but Pollen has held out always on a prohibitive price based on Monopoly terms.[200]

The Admiralty quickly discovered the difficulties of shaking off Pollen while maintaining secrecy on the dual-rate principles embodied in the Dreyer Table. Beginning in September, Pollen and Isherwood began the process of patenting their course and rate-plotters and, despite the Admiralty's request to withdraw the application for the latter, it was registered as a provisional specification on 12 October. At a conference with Commander C. V. Usborne on the 15th, Pollen further declared, on the basis of the mention of rate-plotting in *Reflections on an Error of the Day* and the adaptation of the *Natal* table to dual-rate plotting, that he had invented rate-plotting independently and that the Admiralty had no claims which could invalidate his application. He did undertake to keep rate-plotting secret until it was made public by some other source,[201] but this was of only temporary value, since, while the provisional specification would not be published, it was the initial step towards open publication as a Complete Specification.[202]

Following his usual practice, in June Pollen had already opened a correspondence with the First Lord, now Winston Churchill, to protest that secrecy was not to be renewed. On 21 October, he sent Churchill an all too characteristic letter. Pollen began by damning the Service system which he had seen while demonstrating the Argo gear in *Orion*, thereby confirming that it was impossible to keep Service secrets while he and his staff were allowed aboard. Then, confusing present capabilities with possible future improvements, he claimed that his clock could keep the range 'with perfect accuracy . . . <u>when we are under helm with the target obscured</u>', which was not true either of the patented or the Mark IV clock. And, he threatened that:

> The day my system becomes public property you have no secret of any kind left in your naval gunnery. In as far as you have adopted a restricted and mutilated form of my system you have obviously no secret of any value.[203]

Yet, despite Pollen's claims and threats, the Admiralty persisted with the intention of purchasing five more clocks for comparative trials; on 26 October, even before the successful trials in *Orion* on 19–20 November, a not greatly reduced price of £2,133 for each clock was agreed. Meanwhile, Churchill, like his predecessors, appears to have had second thoughts about ending Argo's monopoly agreement. On 6 December, during an interview with Pollen's brother, Colonel Stephen Pollen, Churchill requested a quotation 'for a large number of Clocks, the price to be calculated on the basis that the Admiralty should be our [Argo's] only customer'. Moore, who was also present, acknowledged that the Argo clock was mechanically superior, but insisted that its price and the price for monopoly were excessive. On 11 December Argo quoted £1,600 each for 150 clocks to be supplied over the next three years, £50,000 to be paid in advance; Battenburg informed Pollen that, with such prices, there was 'no possibility of coming to an agreement'.[204] The Director of Navy Contracts noted that Elliott Brothers won the order for five range-rate plotters (for use with the five Argo clocks) with a price of £138 10s 0d, while their price for five complete Dreyer Tables (which combined two rate-plotters and a clock) was only £635 each. He therefore urged that the earlier decision to end monopoly should be adhered to.[205] On 19 December, Argo's offer was declined and the decision to end secrecy confirmed; any future orders were not ruled out but they would only be placed on 'ordinary commercial terms'.

## 1913–18

Although the patent for the rate-plotter remained contentious (Argo was warned that it might fall within the scope of the Official Secrets Act),[206] there was for a moment a chance that Argo might establish a new relationship as a normal Admiralty supplier. On 10 January 1913, Pollen informed the DofC:

> we have now completed the jigs and special tools necessary for manufacturing Argo clocks in quantities and are therefore able to make you a more favourable quotation than that submitted some six months ago . . .
> £1150 in lots of 25.[207]

Unfortunately, Pollen was also gathering letters criticising the abandonment of secrecy. While Reginald Plunkett noted on Pollen's letter:

> The request contd. in this letter, wh. I consider wrong, I replied to saying that I found it impossible to comply with.[208]

other officers were more forthcoming and extracts were sent to Churchill by Stephen Pollen on 20 January. The letters contained direct attacks on Dreyer, Jellicoe and Moore and strong criticisms of the Admiralty, which was accused by one correspondent of 'crass stupidity'. The day after they were sent, Arthur Pollen seems to have suddenly recognised the danger and attempted to withdraw them, but the damage had already been done. On 22 January, Churchill's secretary informed Pollen that his action in soliciting criticisms from officers afloat was 'irregular', that the worst extract was 'grossly improper and offensive in its character', and that 'the First Lord was unable to reopen the question of monopoly or the clock'. Then, on 4 February, Pollen approached the Conservative E. G. Pretyman, a former Financial Secretary to the Admiralty, with a view either to raising his case privately with the Prime Minister or 'making a front bench question of it'. Pretymen consulted Jellicoe (who had returned to the Admiralty as Second Sea Lord) and then declined to take any further action.[209] After these incidents, there were no further discussions about additional orders.

In January, the DNO, Tudor, took a more active (though at first uncertain) part in dealing with Argo, by raising with Pollen the concern that the clock features for setting the bearing-rate gave a clear indication of the Admiralty's dual-rate system.[210] On 18 February, Tudor opposed a suggestion by the DofC, F. W. Black, that Pollen might be persuaded by a payment for services rendered to forgo sales to foreign governments. Sumida suggests that:

> Tudor's views carried the day and his scheme for obstructing the foreign sale of the Argo Clock officially adopted.[211]

In fact, after Pollen's recent attempts to sow discontent, it is unlikely that he had any support remaining in the Admiralty, while the question of the bearing-rate dial was not just a ploy. The Navy's opinion was that the clock controls for setting range and bearing rates 'are in no way germane to the Aim Corrector system but were evidently fitted to admit of the clock being used on the Service system'. Pollen maintained that they were 'merely the expression of mathematical truths' and, for good measure, that 'you cannot publish my system without publishing yours, because the whole of your system is involved [sic] from mine'.[212] He would yield nothing to the Admiralty's concerns and, once his lawyers became involved, the correspondence degenerated into lengthy, point-by-point claim and counter-claim.[213] Relations, already bad, grew worse, especially after the dispute became public. *The Naval Annual* for 1913, published in late May or early June, described the main features of the Argo table and clock and pronounced that:

> Mr. Pollen . . . has apparently succeeded in perfecting instruments of incalculable value for finding and keeping the rate at long range.[214]

In mid-June, Pollen informed editors of the end of secrecy and, from 19 June, articles of varying degrees of accuracy appeared in a number of papers, including *The Times*, whose owner, John Walter, had until recently been a major Argo shareholder. Then, on 30 June, a Liberal MP, Robert Harcourt, raised the matter of the Pollen system in a parliamentary question to the First Lord. Sumida proposes that 'the absence of evidence makes it impossible to establish the exact extent of his [Pollen's] involvement with the press and with Harcourt's queries', but himself describes Pollen's connection with Walter.[215] Pollen's previous record also strongly suggests that he was behind the question in the House and, in the unlikely event that he was not, no one in the Admiralty would have believed it.

On this, as on previous occasions, Pollen's actions had undermined Argo's efforts to reach an accommodation with the Admiralty. On 10 June, the company's Board had decided after all to omit the rate dials from their foreign patent applications, at least for the moment, but this was only communicated to the Admiralty at a meeting on 30 June, the day of Harcourt's question to Churchill. The DofC then asked for more excisions and, after further exchanges, Argo concluded that 'the views of the Company and of the Admiralty are irreconcilable'.[216] By 4 August, the Argo gear had been shown 'without reservation to foreign naval Attaches'.

> The Admiralty . . . considered . . . that the action of the Argo Company was most reprehensible . . . all business and other relations were to be broken off with the Company and the Company's name was to be removed from the Admiralty list, and the Fleet and the Australian Navy were informed that no further intercourse was to be held with it.[217]

On 5 September, Pollen and Isherwood included the clock in their applications for French and American patents and, as the Admiralty had feared all along, described both rate dials and, albeit obliquely, their use:

> means are provided for setting up either the target course and target speed or the rate of change of range and rate of change of bearing. In order to determine the target course and target speed, recourse must be had to one of the methods of plotting.[218]

Furthermore, despite Pollen's assurances in November 1912, the complete specification for the dual-rate plotter had been left at the Patent Office on 13 May 1913, even before the final break. The only concessions to Admiralty concerns were that the specification did not describe a separate pencil for clock-range, and that the company applied for foreign patents only on its true-course plotter.[219]

By the end of 1913, Argo had been fully paid for the rangefinder mountings and clocks. In the years 1908 to 1913, the company made a loss of only £3,778 on receipts of some £103,000. Following a 6 per cent debenture issue in 1913, Argo had raised a total of £23,350 in shares and debentures, while the bank balance was £5,710 in the red. However, the firm still held shares in Cooke's to the value of £16,650 while its stock of instruments was valued at £4,554; most importantly, it had completed the development of the Argo system while its only significant income came from the Admiralty. As for Pollen himself, his salary as governing director increased from £1,500 to £2,500 sometime between 1909 and 1911 and he continued to draw it until 1918 or 1919; thus his total income was somewhere between £24,500 and £29,000. In addition, when Argo was registered at the end of 1907, Pollen had already made a profit of £2,930 on his dealings with the Admiralty, while he also received Argo shares and debentures to a value of £4,399. All the debentures were redeemed in 1909, necessitating a payment to Pollen of their value of £3,500.[220] Thus Pollen was well rewarded over many years at the expense of his Admiralty contracts or, latterly, of the Argo shareholders.

The Argo Company began its overseas sales campaign in September 1913. Discussions with Turkey, the United States and France eventually foundered on questions of cost, while the French in any case preferred rate to course plotting. An agreement had also been made with Austro-Hungary, while negotiations were nearly concluded with Brazil and Chile, but all were terminated on the outbreak of war. The Russians also accepted Pollen's analysis. They placed the order mentioned earlier and remained convinced of the superiority of the Cooke-Pollen rangefinder, for which they placed at least one more order, for eight instruments, in 1916. The Admiralty went to some lengths to obstruct this delivery,[221] which suggests that the bitterness from the acrimonious break with Argo in 1913 was long-lasting.

After Jutland, Pollen produced two long memoranda arguing for his system to be reconsidered. Jellicoe submitted them officially to the Admiralty, urging in particular that the latest Cooke-Pollen rangefinder should be examined.[222] Thirty were ordered in March 1918 when Dreyer was DNO, even though, in the same month, the report of the Phillpotts committee noted that, in tests, a 15-foot model had not shown 'any marked advantage over the Barr & Stroud rangefinder at present in use'. This committee had been convened after, for the last time, Pollen had written to an incumbent First Lord, now Sir Eric Geddes; Pollen proposed that instruments about to be despatched for trial to the United States should be inspected by the Royal Navy.[223] The committee was impressed by their 'near mechanical perfection', although they concluded that the instruments were not 'as suited to the service requirements as the present methods in use'. However, Pollen was evidently continuing to hinder his own chances of acceptance:

> Some of the knowledge and most of the experience required for the design ... have been gained in H.M. Service, and it is ... unfortunate that these should be made use of to the public depreciation of Service methods, for which there is no justification.

Nonetheless, the committee concluded:

> It is a matter for regret that the ingenuity and mechanical designing ability displayed is producing these instruments have been lost to the Service . . . The question is for consideration whether the services of the Inventor and his Staff could be utilized in connection with the design of future fire control instruments.[224]

In responding as DNO to the report, Dreyer began:

> I had hoped not to have to minute an Admiralty Docket on the subject of Mr. Pollen's Fire Control Apparatus as I am the inventor of the Dreyer Fire Control Apparatus.

He went on to concur with most of the committee's report, though he insisted that Harold Isherwood could not be spared from the position he now held as Chief Designer in the Mining School. He concluded:

> Mr. Pollen is an enthusiast who always overstates his case ... after ... Jutland he informed everyone of the <u>vast superiority</u> of the Crooke [sic] Range Finder, views which were not found to be justified when it came to be tried ...
>     Mr. Pollen, no doubt with the very best of intentions produced a great feeling of unrest in Naval Gunnery Circles when his

instruments were on trial by his whirlwind eloquence and his journalistic efforts.

I am most strongly of opinion that it would be a grave error to once more put him in touch with the Service.

There were sufficient truths in these statements to convince the whole Admiralty hierarchy, from Geddes and Wemyss downwards. The Deputy First Sea Lord, Rear Admiral George Hope, added a minute that:

Mr. Pollen has always claimed that his methods would produce great results, but he has always underrated the practical difficulties to be met.

Thus Pollen had no significant support remaining in the Admiralty and he was sent a noncommittal letter expressing only polite interest in the outcome of the American trials.[225] In June, he wrote to the First Lord asking for an inquiry leading to the recognition which he believed was his due for the use by the Admiralty of his inventions: but, on 18 December, his request was rejected.[226] After this final exchange, Pollen would have to wait for the sittings of the RCAI before receiving his award for the Argo clock.

The collapse of Argo's commercial relationship with the Admiralty, which Pollen's own actions had done so much to provoke, prevented him from demonstrating his complete A.C. system to the Royal Navy. The outbreak of the war then robbed him of the opportunity to show, by successfully supplying foreign navies, that he had been right all along about the superiority of his system. But was his unwavering conviction correct? Before attempting to answer this question, we must first explore the history and development of the rival Dreyer Tables.

## Notes

1 *IDNS*, p. 77. *PP*, 'The Gun in Battle', February 1913, p. 308.
2 The earliest use found of this term, where it describes the ideal system towards Pollen had been working, is in Argo Co. 'Memorandum', 6 May 1913 in T.173/91 Part II.
3 *PP*, 'Gun in Battle' (1913) [1]. Jon Sumida, 'Pollen, Arthur Joseph Hungerford, 1866–1937', in *DNB* (Oxford: Oxford University Press, 1995).
4 *IDNS*, pp. 78–9 and 102.
5 Pollen to Selborne, 4 February 1901 in T.173/91 Part VII, excerpts in *PP*, pp. 210–11. Precision theodolites were graduated only to 10 seconds of arc: J. A. Bennett, *The Divided Circle* (Oxford: Phaidon, 1987) Plates 107 and 229.
6 *PP*, 'The Pollen System of Telemetry', February 1901, pp. 8–13.
7 Pollen to Selborne, 1901 [5].
8 Patent 6,838/1902, complete specification 22 December.
9 *PP*, 'Fire Control and Long-range Firing: an Essay to Define Certain Principia of Gunnery . . . ', December 1904, pp. 35–7 and 52. Patent 11,535/1904.
10 *PP*, 'Memorandum on a Proposed System for Finding Ranges at Sea and

Ascertaining the Speed and Course of any Vessel in Sight', July 1904, p. 17. Patent 23,872/1904.

11 *PP*, 'Fire Control' (1904) [9] pp. 54 and 39.

12 *PP*, 'Proposed System' (1904) [10] pp. 18–19. *IDNS*, p. 80.

13 *PP*, 'Fire Control' (1904) p. 29. Captain, *Victorious* to Second-in-Command Channel Fleet, 7 December 1904 in 'Vyvyan-Newitt, Siemens and Vickers Electrically Controlled Gunsights', in ADM 1/7832.

14 *PP*, 'Fire Control' (1904) pp. 40–1 and 'A.C.: A Postscript', mid-1905, pp. 55–64.

15 *IDNS* , pp. 85–7. *PP*, 'Jupiter Letters': III, January 1906, p. 83 and IV, 2 February 1906, p. 88.

16 For detailed technical notes on the A.C. and Argo instruments, see 'FCBD', Appendix XII.

17 *PP*, 'Gun in Battle' (1913) pp. 309–11 and 'Notes, Etc. on *Ariadne* Trials', April 1909, pp. 212–13; see also *PP*, 'The Quest of a Rate Finder', November 1910, p. 265. *IDNS*, pp. 86–7.

18 *PP*, 'Jupiter Letter IV' (1906) [15] p. 89.

19 Isherwood told the RCAI that he had worked for Pollen from 1902: T.173/547 Part 3, p. 25.

20 Pollen to Admiralty Secretary, 18 June 1906 with 'One Observer System of Charting' 15 June 1906 in T.173/91 Part VII. 'No clock was ever made until the Natal clock'; Pollen's counsel before RCAI, T.173/547 Part 7, p. 37.

21 Patent 23,846/1906. *IDNS*, p. 123.

22 Pollen to Bacon, 3 August 1907 in T.173/91 Part VII.

23 *PP*, 'An Apology for the A.C. Battle System; being notes for a lecture to the War Course College, Portsmouth', printed December 1907; see especially pp. 140 and 145–50.

24 'The Pollen Aim Corrector', in *Notes, Correspondence, Etc. on the Pollen A.C. System installed and tried in HMS Ariadne*, December 1907–January 1908 in DRAX 3/1, but not in *PP*, pp. 159–71, which prints only Pollen's correspondence with Admiral Wilson.

25 A. H. Pollen, 'Notes on Charts, made before Christmas, sent to Admiral Wilson' pp. 2–3, in *Notes, Correspondence on A.C.* [24].

26 Professor C. V. Boys to Pollen, n.d. but November 1912 in T.173/91 Part II. *IDNS*, p. 230. Patent 14,415/1908 for the transmission system and clutches.

27 'Pollen Aim Correcting System. Points discussed at an interview with Mr Pollen . . . ' with Ewan Macgregor to Pollen, 29 October 1906 in T.173/91 Part VII. *IDNS*, pp. 128–9

28 *PP*, Pollen to Wilson, 24 January 1908, p. 166.

29 H. Isherwood, 'On the Relationship of "Change of Range" to "Time"', in *Reflections on an Error of the Day* in HTN/116A, NMM (not in *PP*). A. H. Pollen, 'Notes of the Torbay Trials of the A.C. System', in *Notes, Correspondence on A.C.*

30 Pollen to Wilson, 1908 [28] pp. 162 and 165. The almost identical courses and speeds were determined by lot: *IDNS*, pp. 129–30.

31 *PP*, Pollen to Admiralty Secretary, 25 March 1908, p. 235. 'Notes on Charts' [25] p. 4.

32 Pollen to Admiralty Secretary, 5 January 1909 in T.173/91 Part II.

33 *IDNS*, p. 138.

34 'The Pollen A.C. Battle System' with Pollen to Secretary, 1909 [32]. For the gyro, see patent 11,795/1909 and draft letter concerning 'Natal' pattern mountings with proposal 'R-F Bearing transmitter', 1911 in DRAX 3/4.

35 Patent 5,031/1909. *PP*, Pollen to Admiral Colville, 1 July 1910, pp. 245–6.

36 *PP*, 'Quest' (1910) [17] p. 265.

37 'A.C. System', 1909 [34].
38 'Fire Control. An Essay by Captain C. Hughes-Onslow RN', Royal Naval War College, n.d. but 1909, Appendix A, p. 5 (and also 'General Remarks . . . ' p. 8) PLLN 1/5.
39 C. I. Thomas to Treasury Secretary, 13 January 1910, in 'Treasury 1091' in T.1/11385, PRO.
40 *PP*, 'Quest' (1910) p. 245.
41 *IDNS*, p. 172. Pollen to Colville, 1910 [35] p. 246.
42 Pollen to Colville, 1910, pp. 247–8. Patent 1,111/1910, applied for 15 January, complete specification 12 August. The table's gyro was probably the same as that used in the rangefinder mounting: Isherwood before RCAI, T.173/547 Part 3, p. 25.
43 *IDNS*, p. 198 and Thomas to Treasury Secretary, 1910 [39].
44 Patent 595/1906 was subsequently abandoned but the description in *IDNS*, p. 82 indicates that it was similar to 2,497/1908.
45 Pollen before RCAI, T.173/547 Part 14, p. 82.
46 *PP*, Pollen to Bacon, 27 February 1908, p. 174.
47 Dreyer before RCAI, T.173/547 Parts 16, pp. 39–40 and 17, pp. 58–9.
48 *IDNS*, Plate 4. Patent 360/1911.
49 Patent 1,111/1910, complete specification.
50 *IDNS*, pp. 201–2.
51 Admiral W. H. May, 'Aim Corrector Trials', 31 May 1910, DRAX 3/3.
52 *PP*, Pollen to Admiralty Secretary, 17 June 1910, p. 253. *Natal* had recommissioned before the beginning of the new trials (*IDNS*, p. 202) but, while she had a new Lieutenant (T), Reginald Plunkett, she retained the same Lieutenant (G), Ralph Eliot (appointed 8 January 1910): *Navy List*, June 1910.
53 Report by Lieutenant R. Plunkett of *Natal*, 4 July 1910, pp. 2–5 in DRAX 3/3. Pollen to Colville, 1910, pp. 245 and 248–9. Pollen to DofC, 25 November 1912 in T.173/91 Part VII. *PP*, 'Quest' (1910) p. 265–6.
54 Pollen to Colville, 1910, p. 249 and *PP*, 'Quest' (1910) p. 268.
55 Argo, 'Memorandum', 1913 [2].
56 *PP*, 'Quest' (1910) p. 268. See also *IDNS*, p. 208.
57 Colville Committee, Enclosure with letter to C.-in-C. Home Fleet, 1 July 1910 in DRAX 3/3. Admiralty Secretary to Argo, 19 August 1910 and Pollen to Admiralty Secretary, 25 August 1910 in T.173/91 Part VII.
58 Plunkett later became the magnificently named Admiral Sir Reginald Aylmer Ranfurly Plunkett-Ernle-Erle-Drax: *DNB 1961–70*, p. 847.
59 Isherwood to Plunkett, 11 August 1910 and Reginald Plunkett, 'Notes on Plotting', n.d. but after *Natal*'s 1910 Battle Practice, both in DRAX 3/3. Excerpts from *Natal*'s log, ADM 53/23982 courtesy Professor Sumida.
60 Pollen before RCAI, T.173/547 Part 2, p. 21.
61 *PP*, 'Quest' (1910) p. 269.
62 Pollen to Plunkett, 22 February and 30 March 1911 in DRAX 3/4. Draft letter by Plunkett in DRAX 3/3 n.d. but after 28 October 1910.
63 *IDNS*, p. 222. Patent 23,351/1912.
64 Patent 7,383/1911.
65 F. C. Dreyer and C. V. Usborne, *Pollen Aim Corrector System, Part I: Technical History and Technical Comparison with Commander F C Dreyer's Fire Control System*, February 1913, p. 34, P. 1024, AL.
66 Phillpotts committee, 'Report of inspection at York of Pollen Fire Control System', n.d. but 1918, p. 2 in DRYR 2/1. *IDNS*, pp. 310–11.
67 Pollen to Henley, 9 December 1910 in T.173/91 Part VII. Patent 362/1911.
68 Henley to Dreyer, 24 July 1911 in DRYR 2/1. *Technical Comparison*, 1913 [65] p. 12.

69 Patent 14,302/1911. For electrical details of the transmitters (which are similar to those in the patent 14,415/1908) see *ART, 1912* pp. 75–7 and Plate 40.
70 Henley to Dreyer, 1911 [68].
71 O. Murray to Treasury Secretary, 5 February 1912 in 'Treasury 2541, 6 Feb.1912' in T.1/11385. Fifteen mountings had probably been delivered before the end of February: *IDNS*, pp. 213–14.
72 Admiralty, *Handbook of the Argo A.C. Range-Finder Mounting 1912*, 18 October 1912, PLLN 1/3.
73 *Technical Comparison* (1913) p. 34.
74 Untitled summary of the Admiralty's case in DRYR 2/1. See also similar statements in 'Answer to the Statement of the Claimant's Case', 25 July 1925, 'Outline of the Admiralty Case', n.d. and 'Claimant's Submission and Observations', all in T.173/91 Part XI. However, the Admiralty's evidence to the RCAI was intended to establish that the Service system owed nothing to Pollen.
75 Admiralty, Gunnery Branch, *Handbook of Naval Range-Finders and Mountings 1921*, ADM 186/253 (reference courtesy John Roberts). The *Iron Duke* class were the exception.
76 *IDNS*, Plate 5. Patent 17,441/1912 applied for with complete specification 4 April. The friction with the rollers prevented the ball from rotating with the disc. Thus, though only when the ball was at or very close to the centre of the disc, there was rotational sliding within their small area of contact, which tended to cause wear at the disc's centre – Gunnery Branch, *The Argo Range and Bearing Clock Mark IV*, January 1914, p. 23, AL.
77 In mathematical terms, these mechanisms performed the vector addition of enemy-speed and own-speed-reversed and resolved the resulting virtual-speed vector into speeds along and across the line of sight.
78 It also mentioned a multiplying linkage for calculating the change-of-range in time-of-flight, but this was never implemented by Argo.
79 Harold Isherwood, 'The A.C. Range and Bearing Clock Mark II', 8 May 1911 (T.173/91 Part VII) accompanying a letter from I. E. Brown, Secretary, Argo Company to Admiralty Secretary, 15 May 1911 (T.173/91 Part III).
80 Pollen to Isherwood, 22 May 1911 in T.173/91 Part III. Pollen and others to RCAI, T.173/547 Part 18, pp. 5, 8 and 9–11.
81 Henley to Dreyer, 1911. 'Statement of the Claimant's Case' in T.173/91 Part XI.
82 Argo to Admiralty Secretary, 26 January 1912 in T.173/91 Part II.
83 Patent 19,627/1911, provisional and complete specification in T.173/91 Part III. Because this patent was not reassigned to Pollen, it was never printed by the British Patent Office. Argo's American patent (1,162,510, filed 5 September 1913) contained essentially identical drawings and text (except for the final claims).
84 *IDNS*, pp. 222 and 229.
85 *Technical Comparison*, 1913, p. 11.
86 *IDNS*, pp. 225, 228–32.
87 *Technical Comparison*, 1913, p. 34.
88 The reasonable assumption that the prototype was the only Mark III is contradicted by Argo, 'Memorandum', 1913, which called it Mark IV.
89 Compare *Technical Comparison*, 1913, p. 38 (d and e) with *Argo Clock Mark IV* [76], the latter being the source for the following technical details.
90 When setting by rates, the 'Target Speed' and 'Angle of Courses' clamps were released.
91 In any moment, Drive II generated change-of-travel-across, which, when divided by range by Drive III, gave change-of-compass-bearing. This is always equal but opposite to the change-of-inclination, and, when own course is steady, it is equal to change-of-course-bearing.

92 Boys to Pollen, 1912 [26].
93 The handle may also have been needed to correct for slippage if the transmitters were too great a load on Drive IV.
94 *IDNS*, pp. 215, 225 and 230. The provisional specification for patent 23,349 applied for 12 October 1912 was, unusually, accompanied by detailed drawings. The complete specification left on 11 April 1913 had an additional Figure 4 showing two extra differentials.
95 Phillpotts 'Report', 1918 [66] pp. 2 and 6.
96 *Technical Comparison*, 1913, p. 36.
97 The averaging receiver was patented by Pollen and Lieutenant Gerard Riley (*IDNS*, pp. 215–16) as 25,768/1912. The cardboard model was seen in 1918 by the Phillpotts committee, who thought it 'very doubtful if this method could cope' with wartime conditions: 'Report', pp. 1 and 3. Before the RCAI, Isherwood disagreed with the Service view that the device was 'of no practical value': T.173/547, Part 15, pp. 112–13.
98 *Technical Comparison*, 1913, pp. 35 and 41. Phillpotts 'Report', 1918, p. 1. Boys to Pollen (1912).
99 *IDNS*, pp. 247–8, 282 and 295–6. For the Russian order, see A. H. Pollen, 'Memorandum on Fire Control', 1916 in T.173/91 Part II.
100 Pollen's gear seems to have been used mainly by the Baltic Fleet. 'Pollen and Russia. A Note by Stephen McLaughlin', 19 March 2004 gratefully acknowledged.
101 E. Wilfred Taylor, 'The New Cooke-Pollen Range-Finder', *Journal of the American Society of Naval Engineers*, XXVI, 3 (August 1914) pp. 813–30. The article does not mention gyro stabilisation of the mounting, or connection to anything other than numerical indicators. *IDNS*, Plate 2 shows this mounting.
102 *IDNS*, p. 247.
103 Patent 11,009/1913, applied for 9 May, complete specification 8 December; also US Patent 1,162,511, filed 14 April 1914.
104 Phillpotts 'Report', 1918, p. 2.
105 British Patent 16,373/1913, applied for 16 July 1913, Complete Specification 16 January 1914, accepted 16 July 1914. US Patent 1,232,968, filed 11 July 1914. DNO's minute of 18 August 1914 quoted in Admiralty to C.-in-C. Home Fleet, March 1916, in 'Fire Control Apparatus: Various Patents', ADM 1/8464/181.
106 Phillpotts 'Report', 1918, p. 6.
107 Information on Kerr courtesy Professor Andrew Lambert. Pollen to Selborne, 4 February 1901 in T.173/91 Part VII.
108 Padfield, *Guns at Sea* [B] p. 221.
109 *IDNS*, pp. 79–80.
110 Lawrence to Selborne with 'Memorandum', both 9 May 1904: Lawrence to Selborne, 27 May and minute by H. D. Barry, 31 May 1904 in 'The Pollen Rangefinder' in ADM 1/7733.
111 Pollen to V. W. Baddeley, 5 July 1904 in ' Pollen Rangefinder' [110]. Minute by W. H. May 13 July 1904 in 'Report of Committees on Control of Fire', in ADM 1/7758.
112 Pollen to First Lord, 14 November and Pollen to Skinner received 24 November 1904 in 'Pollen Rangefinder'.
113 Harding before RCAI, T.173/547 Part 3, p. 31. *IDNS*, p. 84.
114 Admiralty Secretary to Pollen, 3 May 1905 in T.173/91 Part VII.
115 Ewan MacGregor to Treasury Secretary, 25 November 1905 in 'Treasury 21901, 27 Nov.1905' in T.1/11385. *PP*, Pollen to Tweedmouth, 27 August 1906, p. 217.
116 Pollen to Admiralty Secretary, 18 June 1906 in T.173/91 Part II. The machine

was delivered on 14 May 1906: *IDNS*, pp. 88–9. Sumida seems to imply that the machine was a form of clock, since 'computed ranges and bearings', corrected for ballistic factors and time-of-flight, are mentioned; however, he clearly describes the first tactical machine, called the 'crab machine', on pp. 81–2.

117 Pollen's counsel before RCAI, T.193/547 Part 7, p. 27. The two tactical machines were patented as 13,082 and 14,305 of 1906.

118 *Pollen Aim Correction System. General Grounds of Admiralty Policy and Historical Record of Business Negotiations*, Admiralty, February 1913, p. 6, P. 1024, AL.

119 Pollen to Jellicoe, 13 February 1906 in T.173/91, Part I. *IDNS*, pp. 90–1. *PP*, 'Note on the possibility of demonstrating the principle of Aim Correction without . . . instruments . . .', pp. 101–4; the copy in T.173/91 Part VII is dated 21 July 1906.

120 *Admiralty Board Minutes, 7 August 1906* in ADM 167/40. *IDNS*, p. 92. 'Pollen Aim Correcting Apparatus. Notes of a meeting held at the Admiralty in the Board Room on 9th August 1906', T.173/91 Part II. For details of Pollen's commercial and contractual relations with the Admiralty, see 'FCBD', Appendix XIV.

121 Pollen to Admiralty Secretary, 10 August 1906 in T.173/91 Part VII. *Record of Business* [118] p. 7. 'Treasury 14063, 30 Jul. 1906' in T.1/11385; a claim of £210 6s 10d for two-thirds of railway and hotel bills was rejected.

122 Admiralty Secretary to Pollen, 21 August 1906 in T.173/91 Part II. *Record of Business*, p. 7. *PP*, Pollen to Tweedmouth, 27 August 1906, pp. 218–21: also in T.173/91 Part VII.

123 *IDNS*, p. 95. Pollen himself was handed the manuscript of Harding's report and also acquired the typewritten copy with Jellicoe's marginal notes: Pollen's counsel before RCAI, T.173/547 Part 13, pp. 69 and 89.

124 Harding, 'Memorandum upon the Professional and Financial Value of the A.C. System' with Harding to Jellicoe, 4 September 1906 in T.173/91 Part VII.

125 Frederic Dreyer, 'Summary' n.d. but after 1923 and probably 1925, p. 15 in DRYR 2/1. Dreyer to Hughes-Onslow, 19 October 1908 in T.173/91 Part VII.

126 'Memorandum', 1904 [110]. *PP*, 'Pollen System' (1901) p. 12, 'Proposed System' (1904) p. 16 and 'Fire Control' (1904) p. 32. Anita McConnell, *Instrument Makers to the World* (York: William Sessions, 1992) p. 65 for the depression rangefinder.

127 *PP*, 'Notes, Etc., on the *Ariadne* Trials', April 1909, pp. 214–15.

128 Harding before RCAI, T.173/547 Part 14, p. 7. In his evidence, Harding at first claimed that, in 1906, dual-rate plotting was already being discussed as an alternative to course plotting; this is accepted in *IDNS*, pp. 91 and 96. However, under cross-examination, Harding admitted that, in his 'Memorandum', 'The double rate is not represented at all' (T.173/547 Part 14, pp. 9, 11–12 and 34.) The document describes course plotting as 'the analytical method' and contrasts it favourably with 'the synthetic method' of 'determining the rate of change [by] dividing the difference between successive readings at definite periods of time by a convenient multiple of the time taken, or by [noting] the time taken to alter a definite amount'.

129 Harding, 'Memorandum upon A.C.' [124].

130 T.173/547 Part 3, p. 31: see also Part 14, p. 26.

131 *IDNS*, pp. 98–9.

132 Admiralty Secretary to Pollen, 21 September 1906 in T.173/91 Parts II and VII. *IDNS*, pp. 115–16.

133 'Treasury 19317, 3 Nov. 1906' in T.1/11385. Navy Estimates Committee, *Report upon Navy Estimates for 1907–8*, 27 November 1906, FISR 8/10.

134 *IDNS*, pp. 116–19. *PP*, Pollen to Bacon, 27 February 1908, p. 174.

135 Pollen to Bacon, 3 August 1907 in T.173/91 Part VII. *IDNS*, p. 124.

136 Navy Estimates Committee, *Report upon Navy Estimates for 1908–9*, p. 4, FISR 8/11. See also *Navy Estimates 1908–09*, 18 December 1907, CAB 37/90/112, Cabinet Papers, PRO.

137 *IDNS*, pp. 124–6. See also *PP*, Pollen to Wilson, 17 December 1907, pp. 167–71.

138 Pollen to Wilson, 1908, pp. 160 and 165. *IDNS*, p. 131.

139 'Indenture of Agreement . . . 18 February 1908' in T.173/91 Parts II and VII.

140 C. I. Thomas to Treasury Secretary, 15 May 1908 in 'Treasury 9089, 16 May 1908' in T.1/11385.

141 *FDSF I*, p. 137–8. Mackay, *Fisher of Kilverstone* [B] pp. 386–92. Thomas to Treasury, 1908 [140].

142 The agreement provided for new trials only if complete success had not been achieved initially but new designs were submitted subsequently.

143 Correspondence from 2 to 10 March in *PP*, '*Ariadne* Notes' (1909) [127] pp. 225–30. Note that, at some point, the deadline for a decision had been extended from one to two months after the end of the trials.

144 *FDSF I*, pp. 140–2.

145 *PP*, Pollen to Board members, 25 March 1908, p. 231.

146 Pollen to Admiralty Secretary, 1 April 1908 in T.173/91 Part II.

147 *Admiralty Board Minutes, 31 March 1908*, ADM 167/42.

148 *IDNS*, p. 137. The correspondence leading to the new agreement is in T.173/91 Part VII.

149 *PP*, *Reflections on an Error of the Day*, September 1908, pp. 180–1, 183 and 386–7.

150 Alan Rae Smith of Deloitte, Plender, Griffiths & Co., 'The Argo Company Limited', 9 October 1923 with Balance Sheets and Profit and Loss Accounts in T.173/91 Part I, reproduced in 'FCBD', Appendix XV.

151 Pollen to Admiralty Secretary, 5 January 1909 in T.173/91 Part II.

152 *FDSF I*, pp. 159–71.

153 Pollen to Admiralty Secretary, 15 February 1909 in T.173/91 Part VII. *Admiralty Board Minutes, 12* and *18 February* and *4 March 1909*, ADM 167/43. *IDNS*, p. 164.

154 Pollen to McKenna, 22 and 25 March 1909 in MCKN 3/14, McKenna Papers, CC and Pollen to McKenna, 20 April 1909 in T.173/91 Part VII. *IDNS*, p. 164.

155 *IDNS*, pp. 168–9. *FDSF I*, p. 190. Mackay [141] p. 412.

156 Fisher to Arnold White, 4 April 1909 in Arthur Marder (ed.) *Fear God and Dread Nought, Volume II* (London: Jonathan Cape, 1952–9) pp. 241; see also Fisher to George Lambert, 5 April, pp. 240–1.

157 *IDNS*, pp. 164–5. Admiralty Secretary to Argo, 21 April 1909 in T.173/91 Part VII. *Record of Business*, 1913. 'Argo Accounts' [150]. There are no indications that the observer's correcting mechanisms were ever completed.

158 Pollen to McKenna, 20 April 1909 [154]. *PP*, editor's introduction, p. 195. *IDNS*, pp. 169–71.

159 Dreyer before RCAI, T.173/547 Part 16, p. 40 and Part 17, pp. 59–61. Unfortunately, Dreyer's report was introduced only at the hearings and a copy was not included with the other written evidence.

160 *IDNS*, pp. 171 and 166.

161 *Record of Business*, p. 9.

162 *IDNS*, pp. 171–3.

163 Pollen to Admiralty Secretary, 13 April 1910, T.173/91 Part VII. *IDNS*, pp.

172–5 and 183. At the RCAI hearings, Pollen's counsel accepted that Pollen had been present on *Natal* until November: T.173/547 Part 8, p. 63.

164 *IDNS*, p. 165. *Record of Business*, p. 10. *DNOfS*, November 1909, p. 4.

165 'Pollen Aim Correction System. Notes of . . . Conference . . . 10th December 1909' in T.173/91 Part VII. The Linotype Company, which made Pollen's early instruments, had come under American control: Pollen's counsel to RCAI, T.173/547 Part 8, p. 74.

166 Service record, ADM 196/42, p. 64.

167 *IDNS*, pp. 161, 174 and 197–8.

168 DofC to Controller, 18 April 1910, f.1 in MCKN 3/15.

169 *IDNS*, pp. 197–8. Admiralty Secretary to Argo, 11 April 1910, Pollen to Admiralty Secretary, 13 April 1910 and Pollen to McKenna, 13 April 1910, all in T.173/91 Part VII.

170 Pollen to Spender, 12 April 1910 and Pollen to McKenna, 19 April 1910 with Enclosure, 20 April 1910 in MCKN 3/15.

171 DofC, April 1910 [168] f.6; on the same day, the DNO provided his own estimates (also in MCKN 3/15) for manufacturing costs of £800, close to Black's figure of £770. *Board Minutes, 27 April 1910*, ADM 167/44.

172 Admiralty Secretary to Argo with enclosures, 29 April 1910 in T.173/91 Part VII.

173 *IDNS*, p. 201.

174 DofC, April 1910, f.6

175 *PP*, 'Quest' (1910) p. 263.

176 Pollen to McKenna, 20 April 1909 in T.173/91 Part VII. *PP*, Pollen to Admiralty Secretary, 17 June 1910, p. 253.

177 Henley to Dreyer, 13 August 1910 in DRYR 2/1.

178 *PP*, 'Quest' (1910) p. 269. This linkage was patented (7,382/1911); it was not itself suitable for use in a clock and was not subsequently regarded by Pollen as important, even though the patent was not reassigned: Admiralty Secretary to Coward & Hawksley etc., 30 April 1913 in T.173/91 Part II and Argo, 'Memorandum', 1913. The linkage was 'substantially the same invention as the Dumaresq': Pollen's counsel before RCAI, T.173/91 Part 12, p. 103.

179 DofC to Argo, 20 December: Pollen to DofC, 22 December 1910 and Admiralty Secretary to Argo, 19 January 1911 in T.173/91 Part VII.

180 DofC to Argo, 2 May 1911 in T.173/91 Part VII. *IDNS*, p. 215. *Record of Business*, p. 15.

181 *IDNS*, p. 203.

182 Argo to Admiralty Secretary, 17 November 1911 in T.173/91 Part II.

183 DNO's minute, 7 December 1911 in T.173/91 Part III.

184 Typed transcript of draft letter, DNO's marginal note and Controller's minute in T.173/91 Part IV.

185 *IDNS*, p. 221

186 'Argo Accounts'. McConnell [126] p. 74.

187 *IDNS*, pp. 208 and 272, which implies that the 250 £100 shares were all sold and that they were 100 per cent instead of 50 per cent paid. Peirse before RCAI, T.173/547 Part 9, pp. 37–8.

188 *Record of Business*, p. 15. O Murray to Treasury Secretary, 5 February 1912 in 'Treasury 2541, 6 Feb.1912' in T.1/11385.

189 *IDNS*, pp. 221–2. DNO and ITP, 'Local Control in Turrets' 24 May and Admiralty Secretary to Officers Commanding Home Fleet, 7 August 1912 in 'IQ/DNO, Vol. I – 1912', AL.

190 DofC to Argo 7 June and Argo to DofC 10 June 1912 in T.173/91 Part VII. The

plotters were described by Argo as 'Range Plotters only – that is, Range and not Bearing Plotters'. See also *IDNS*, pp. 222–3 and 276.

191 *Record of Business*, p. 17. Contrary to the impression given in *IDNS*, pp. 201 and 222, the contract for the mountings did not give Pollen any right to renegotiate the price.

192 *Record of Business*, pp. 14 and 17. Pollen's salary was £2,500, Isherwood's £1,000.

193 *IDNS*, pp. 222 and 276. 'Argo Accounts'. The profit in 1912 was £15,081 while the accumulated profit since 1908 was £1,991.

194 *Record of Business*, pp. 17–18.

195 *DNOfS*, 30 May 1912, pp. 12–13. Moore presumably meant the four *KGVs* and *Queen Mary* of the 1910–11 programme.

196 *Record of Business*, pp. 17–18.

197 *IDNS*, pp. 223–4 and 276–7. However, the principal source for Moore's behaviour is an unsent letter to J. A. Spender drafted by a disappointed and angry Pollen nearly three months after the event.

198 'Extract from 3rd Sea Lord's Minute', in MB1/T22/174, Papers of Prince Louis of Battenberg in Mountbatten Papers, University of Southampton Library.

199 Admiralty Secretary and C. A. Oliver for DofC to Argo, both 20 August 1912 in T.173/91 Part VII.

200 *IDNS*, pp. 226–7. Peirse to Battenberg, 7 September 1912, MB1/T20/142. Moore to Battenburg, 19 September 1912, MB1/T20/147. *IDNS*, p. 227.

201 Patent 23,351/1912. Pollen to DofC, 25 November 1912 in T.173/91 Part VII. Usborne was now the DNO's assistant responsible for fire control.

202 T. H. O'Dell, *Inventions and Official Secrecy* (Oxford: Oxford University Press, 1994) Chapter 6 (reference courtesy of Dr Anita McConnell).

203 Pollen to Churchill 24 June and 21 October 1912 in T.173/91 Part II. Under helm with the target obscured, the change in own course (from a gyrocompass receiver) could be set manually as the change in target bearing relative to own course. Even if this was done continuously without mistakes, it was approximate because it took no account of the change in target bearing due to speed-across.

204 *IDNS*, pp. 229 and 233–5. (The *Orion* clock was purchased later at the same price: *Record of Business*, p. 16.)

205 Minutes 'Pollen Aim Correction System' (initialled by Churchill) and 'Argo Company, Present Situation' with 'Details of Clocks and rate-plotters on order' by F. W. Black (DofC), n.d. but December 1912 in MB1/T22/174.

206 Admiralty Secretary to Argo, 19 December 1912 in T.173/91 Part VII and in MB1/T22/174.

207 Pollen to DofC, 10 January 1913 in T.173/91 Part II.

208 Pollen to Plunkett, 17 January 1913 in DRAX 3/4.

209 *IDNS*, pp. 235–7.

210 Pollen to DofC, 18 January 1913 in T.173/91 Part II.

211 *Record of Business*, Annex p. 1. *IDNS*, p. 237.

212 Admiralty to Argo, 21 February 1913 in T.173/91, Part II. Pollen to Usborne, 29 April 1913 in T.173/91 Part VII.

213 Correspondence between Coward & Hawksley Sons & Chance and Admiralty Secretary, April to June 1913 in T.173/91 Part VII.

214 *Naval Annual 1913* [B] pp. 319–20.

215 *IDNS*, pp. 241–4.

216 *Ibid.* pp. 241 and 244–5.

217 *Record of Business*, Annex p. 7.

218 US Patent 1,162,510, filed 5 September 1913, p. 1. Also French patent 464.049, demandé 5 Septembre 1913.

219 US Patent 1,123,795 and French patent 464.044; dates as in note 218.

220 'Argo Accounts'. *IDNS*, p. 247. 'Conference 10 December 1909' [165] and Pollen before RCAI, T.173/547 Part 15, p. 62. (For comparison, the salaries of the Directors of Naval Construction and of Naval Ordnance were £2,500 and £1,500, respectively: *Whittaker's Almanac, 1914*, p. 245 – reference courtesy John Covington.)

221 *IDNS*, pp. 247–8 and 295–6. Pollen, 'Memorandum on Fire Control', 1916 [99]. The First Lord made the excuse that Cooke's was seriously behind with Admiralty work; correspondence between Pollen and Balfour in T.173/91 Part VII. At least some of the rangefinders for Russia were 15-foot instruments: McLaughlin [100].

222 'Memorandum on Fire Control' and 'Memorandum II', Enclosures 1 and 2 to Submission . . . of 21.8.16 from C.-in-C. Home Fleet in T.173/91 Part II. Since Jellicoe submitted the memoranda, he did not 'turn a blind eye to Pollen's analysis' in order to deflect criticism of his and Dreyer's part in the rejection of the Argo system: *IDNS*, pp. 307–8.

223 *IDNS*, pp. 309–11.

224 Phillpotts 'Report', 1918, p. 6. For Pollen's public criticism of the Admiralty and particularly Jellicoe, see Beatty to his wife, 24 May 1917, in Bryan Ranft (ed.) *The Beatty Papers, Volume I* (London: NRS, 1989) p. 433 and Browning to Jellicoe, 31 July 1917 in A. Temple Patterson (ed.) *The Jellicoe Papers, Volume II* (London: NRS, 1968) p. 192.

225 'Pollen Fire Control Apparatus', in 'Monthly Record of Principal/Important Questions dealt with by DNO ['MR/DNO'] January to June 1918', pp. 308–10 and 'July to December 1918', pp. 819–29 (copies courtesy Professor Sumida).

226 J. W. S. Anderson to Pollen, 18 December 1918 in T.173/91 Part VII.

# 5

# THE DREYER TABLES

While Pollen always remained an outsider, Lieutenant Frederic Dreyer soon gained a reputation as a promising member of the Royal Navy's gunnery elite. The second son of the Danish-born astronomer John Louis Emil Dreyer, he entered *Britannia* in 1891 and his early career culminated in 1901 when, on the demanding advanced course for gunnery and torpedo lieutenants at Greenwich, he came first in his class of three. Following his 1903 appointment as *Exmouth*'s Gunnery Lieutenant, his ship recommissioned as the flagship of the Channel Fleet and Dreyer quickly became a valued adviser on gunnery matters to Vice Admiral Sir Arthur Wilson. Dreyer also distinguished himself by placing the flagship first in Battle Practice and the Gunlayers' Tests for three years (1904–6) in succession.[1] He represented the C.-in-C. on the Calibration Committee chaired by Percy Scott (Captain Edward Harding was also a member) and, in May 1905, first met Arthur Pollen, who had been invited to witness the Bantry Bay calibration trials, and who gave Dreyer a copy of *Fire Control and Long Range Firing*. The two met again in the spring of 1906, when Pollen presented plans of his system to a group of naval officers, after which he was given a tour of *Exmouth*.[2] On 31 October 1906, he sent Dreyer a copy of the *Jupiter Letters* with a request for 'any reflections you may have'. The latter replied, apologising for the delay, on 15 December,

> but as regards giving you an opinion, as I have never seen your gear and do not know how you have actually overcome the many great mechanical difficulties . . . I must put that off until I have the pleasure of again seeing you.[3]

In his memoirs, Dreyer claimed that the eponymous tables originated in a proposal that he put forward on 10 December, which as Sumida points out, was just before the belated reply to Pollen.[4]

> In December 1906 I submitted a memorandum . . . to Sir Arthur Wilson in which I proposed a chronograph of range-finder ranges

138

... He forwarded this to the Admiralty. I expanded this later into a complete fire-control table.[5]

In fact, the device was originally called a 'Rate of Change Calculator' and it was designed to obtain range-rates directly from a series of ranges.[6] The device was in no sense a chronograph i.e. a means of plotting ranges against time;[7] nor, as Dreyer would claim in 1913, could it provide 'the mean range and rate of change of range'.[8] It was merely a range-rate calculator which, within the existing system, provided a none-too-convenient means for obtaining momentary rates from successive pairs of ranges.[9] It was 'never used in the Service at all';[10] Sumida, justifiably, suggests that 'the Ordnance Department dismissed Dreyer's design as unworthy of serious consideration'.[11]

## ASSISTANT TO THE DNO

By the close of 1906, it was already agreed that Dreyer's next posting would be as an assistant to the DNO, Jellicoe. However, on leaving the *Exmouth* on 7 January 1907, he was first temporarily appointed as gunnery adviser on *Dreadnought*'s Experiment Cruise.[12] In his report, Captain Bacon called 'their Lordships' attention to the great assistance rendered me by Lieutenant Dreyer, whose theoretical and practical gunnery knowledge has been of very great value in carrying out the gunnery practices'.[13] On Dreyer's return in April to join the Ordnance Department, Jellicoe made him responsible for:

1. Non-transferable [turret] mountings except electrical
2. Sighting gear, rangefinders (except experimental)
3. Communications, including fire control.

When Bacon replaced Jellicoe as DNO in August, Captain Edward Harding was still in charge of 'rangefinder experiments', including Pollen's Aim Correction system.[14] Both Harding and Dreyer were in the party that visited Linotype's works at Broadheath, Manchester on 11 June 1907, but, shortly after taking up his new post, Bacon ended Harding's direct involvement with the A.C. system,[15] which gave Dreyer full responsibility for the forthcoming trials in *Ariadne*. These changes may have reflected nothing more than Bacon's high opinion of Dreyer, but Harding's long and close association with Pollen probably also counted against him.

Dreyer's new post gave him the opportunity to submit new inventions directly to the DNO. In June 1907, he put forward two proposals written jointly with his elder brother Captain J. T. Dreyer RA. John Dreyer was well known as an inventor of gunnery devices; in his reports to his successor,

Jellicoe mentioned a range clock (though 'backlash in the gearing has so far delayed the trial'), the cam sight with comprehensive range corrections that would soon be widely adopted, and the Range Corrector.[16] The first proposal was for a 'Position Finder for determining Rate of Change of Range', this rather confusing name having been adopted from the Watkin course plotters used in 'the L.S. [Land Service i.e. coastal artillery] system of Position Finding'. For naval service, the Dreyers proposed a form of time-and-range plot, made on a broad band of paper driven at a constant speed. Two 'bridges' spanned the paper, one fixed, the other able to move in the same direction as the paper. A pencil sliding in the fixed bridge, positioned electrically according to the range transmitted from the rangefinder, plotted successive ranges. After a range had been plotted, an operator followed the mark on the paper with a microscope on the moving bridge. A long rod, pivoted about the plotting pencil, ran through the traveller that carried the microscope; at the moment of plotting the next range, the instantaneous range-rate could be read off a semicircular range-rate scale centred on the pencil, a short extension of the rod acting as a pointer to this scale. In his covering letter, Frederic warned:

> It must be borne in mind that the rate of change of range is a vari-able which alters from instant to instant, which fact makes the drawing of a smoothed curve through a number of points an extremely difficult method and one of more than doubtful reliability.

Instead, he suggested that 'the best method of smoothing the curve is to allow the Range Clock to do so'.[17] The Dreyers seem to have supposed, wrongly, that, if the rates from successive pairs of ranges were set on the clock, the clock-ranges would more closely follow the smooth underlying range curve.[18] This led them to reject what was to be an essential feature of the later rate-plotting tables. Consequently, this invention was left, like its predecessor, with no other purpose than to calculate rates from pairs of ranges.

In his letter to the DNO, Dreyer also stated that: 'Our proposal to use three operators for a 9 ft range Finder is now under trial in the "Excellent"'; the trial was to determine only:

> whether two separate layers for elevation and training, and a third man observing and reading off, will not give better results than are at present obtained with one man laying the instrument, observing and marking off.[19]

However, there was no mention of further adapting the mounting to take bearings. Dreyer requested authorisation for Portsmouth Yard to prepare a conversion kit, and also for Thomas Cooke and Sons (because they manufactured the Land Service Position Finder) to tender for the supply of a 'Rate of Change of range instrument'.[20] In the autumn, probably in November or December, both the rate instrument and the rangefinder mounting were tried out in the *Revenge* by Lieutenant A. T. Johnstone of *Excellent*.[21] Perhaps, when the rate was only changing slowly, Johnstone found that the rate could be measured directly with the bar, but, in any event, this first rate instrument was not mentioned again.

Dreyer appears to have had little time to participate in these trials. In July, on Wilson's recommendation, he was chosen by Fisher to visit the nucleus crews of the Home Fleet to check their equipment and advise on training for the forthcoming gunnery tests.

> I was on the move all the time, coming back to London for a few days every now and again to inform the D.N.O. what gunnery gear [was] needed.
>
> . . .
>
> . . . In the end the nucleus crew ships' average for the Battle Practice was better than that of the fully manned Channel Fleet. Fisher was delighted.

During his absence, his work was looked after by Lieutenant J. C. W. Henley, seconded from *Excellent*.[22]

> In September 1907, Dreyer met Pollen while the inventor was on his way to Portsmouth . . . and Pollen later recalled that Dreyer 'told me he hoped it would be his duty to crab me when the time came.'
>
> The selection of Admiral of the Fleet Sir Arthur Knyvet Wilson to umpire the official trials insured that Dreyer's desire to play a major role in the blocking of Pollen would be fulfilled.

The words in quotation marks are taken from Pollen's testimony to the 1925 RCAI hearing.[23] However, Pollen did not have to rely on memory for the 1907 encounter; he had referred to it in a friendly letter, written to Dreyer on 4 January 1908 to congratulate him on his promotion to Commander, which was included in the written evidence before the RCAI. There is a small but important difference between Pollen's oral evidence and this letter, which read:

> On the occasion of our last meeting going down to Portsmouth you warned me that you hoped it would be your job to crab it if you could . . .
>
> Personally, I am strongly convinced that, unless the system is crab proof . . . the Service ought not to go to any exceptional expense to acquire it.[24]

Dreyer's declared intent to 'crab it' (the A.C. apparatus) rather than to 'crab me' (Pollen), and Pollen's acceptance that this was his proper role, establishes that Dreyer was using the verb in its colloquial sense of 'To criticize adversely . . . pull to pieces'.[25] He undoubtedly intended to test Pollen's gear to the limits necessary to establish its fitness for service, but that is not evidence of a preconceived intent to block Pollen by any means.

Once Wilson had been invited to supervise the *Ariadne* trials, Dreyer, who remained the responsible DNO's assistant, acted as his adviser. However, Dreyer's only contribution to the equipment actually used against the A.C. system in the final trial on 15 January 1908 was the improved method of taking ranges – though this had already been simplified by making the range-taker also responsible for elevating.[26] After the war, Dreyer insisted that:

> Sir Arthur Wilson . . . was the deviser of this virtual course and speed scheme . . . I then pressed him . . . that, in addition . . . he would authorise a time and range diagram.[27]

Also that:

> I was not allowed to try my 'Time and Range' apparatus until the 'ARIADNE' trial was complete.[28]

This is confirmed by Wilson's report:

> In the first experiment [on] the 15th January . . . the 'Vengeance' had found it impossible to plot any virtual course owing to the small change in either range or bearing. This had led to a proposal to deal with similar cases in future by plotting the ranges on a time diagram . . . This I was anxious to try and also the Chetwynd compass.[29]

For bearings:

> we simply used a torpedo director, which had a telescope attached to it. They were bearings not corrected by compass at all.[30]

With only uncorrected relative-bearings available, Wilson was probably fortunate that, despite the flat calm, the almost parallel courses provided an excuse for not completing a virtual-course plot. Since range-rate plotting was not used either, *Vengeance* must have fallen back on the established method of getting a rate by calculation from timed ranges. Thus the trial with *Ariadne* was even more of a sham than has previously been recognised.[31]

Dreyer's main contribution was made in the experiments conducted by Wilson in *Vengeance* between 17 and 21 January 1908. The aloft rangefinder was fitted with a Chetwynd compass and what Wilson called Dreyer's 'push–

pull training gear'. The time-and-range plot was made on simple squared paper, but Wilson, like Dreyer, was concerned about changing range-rate and insisted:

> The object of this diagram was to give the rate of change when bearing is altering very slowly . . . when the bearing is altering rapidly, the time diagram would give a very erroneous forecast.

The preferred method for getting rates from the time-and-range plot was, by a graphical construction, to obtain the means of two successive groups of three ranges, after which the rate could be measured as the slope of the line joining the two mean points.[32] In his own report 'Hints on Battle Firing', Dreyer did not mention virtual-course methods explicitly, but he took the range-rate ideas further. He recommended that, as in the previous year's rate instrument, the plotting paper should be driven by clockwork. And he proposed a second plot on which each mean range-rate (obtained from six ranges) should also be plotted against time; he supposed that a changing rate would appear as a smooth curve.[33]

In later years, Dreyer made much of his third proposal, to set the Dumaresq by a cross-cut (not a term then in use) of range-rate and deflection.[34] However, he did not suggest a time-and-bearing plot, but instead that a single bearing rate could be obtained by calculation.

> Take a series of bearings at intervals of a few seconds apart, noting the times, and after a pause of about one minute, take another set of bearings and times.
> Mean each of these sets . . . and take their difference.

Furthermore, the cross-cut idea is introduced almost as an aside.

> The following method is one of many that can now be employed to keep the Dumaresq properly adjusted.
> Set own speed on the bar as usual.
> Point the sighting vanes at the enemy . . .
> Then pull out enemy's dummy ship until its stem is at the intersection of the line of . . . deflection, and the line of the rate of change of the moment.[35]

Thus Dreyer placed much more emphasis on rates than Wilson, which was certainly in accord with Bacon's recommendation to equip the Fleet with time-and-range boards as the first step in the introduction of plotting.

While still aboard *Vengeance*, Frederic had written to his brother requesting help with the mechanical details of a range-keeper working on virtual-course principles:

the reason why that arose in my mind was that I had Sir Arthur Wilson's instructions to make virtual plots.[36]

John's sketches show a mechanical analogue of virtual course, with a traveller propelled at virtual speed by a long screw. This screw was rotated by a variable-speed drive, for which John Dreyer proposed an arrangement of two cones, one driving the other through a movable belt.[37] Thus even this first Dreyer range-keeper incorporated a variable-speed drive, though of an unusual type. (Whether, as implied by the note scrawled on John Dreyer's diagram during the RCAI hearings, his design had been influenced by Pollen's patents will be considered in Chapter 6.) In February 1908, Dreyer was also corresponding with Elliott Brothers about his proposal to modify the Dumaresq so that the rate could be kept (approximately) during a turn.[38] At this early date, he was alone in showing a concern for rate-keeping (though not for other fire control functions) while the firing ship man-oeuvred. Like Pollen, Dreyer was still a long way from realising his final system, but he had at least initial conceptions for rate plotting and range-keeping on steady courses, and for rate-keeping under helm. It must also have been clear to him that Wilson intended, by almost any means, to secure the rejection of the A.C. gear. Thus early 1908, rather than in 1906 during his previous service with Wilson,[39] seems much more likely as the moment when Dreyer first saw clearly that he could rival Pollen with a fire control system of his own.

In August 1908, he and his brother applied jointly for patents (which were sealed as secret) for the three-operator range-finder mounting and for an improved time-and-range apparatus. This plotter was provided with a rotatable, transparent disc with engraved parallel lines; thus the Dreyers had now accepted that a mean range-rate could be obtained by plotting a series of ranges against time and then measuring the rate as the slope of the tangent to the plot. This disc was the principal novelty in what was later considered 'a very important patent'.[40] Although the patent itself has not been found, the device evidently resembled a 'Time and Range Table (as used in Excellent)', which incorporated all of Dreyer's ideas to date, including a motorised paper drive, the circular disc to measure rate and plots of both range and range-rate.[41] Three of the patented plotters were made at Chatham in 1908,[42] so the resources of the dockyards and the experimental section at *Excellent* were again used to try out ideas originating in the DNO's department in the Admiralty.

In March 1908, Dreyer returned to normal duties with his reputation further enhanced. In a letter to Julian Corbett, Fisher described him as having 'the brain of a Newton!' although 'only 1 in a 100 could understand him'.[43] Yet Dreyer recalled that his situation was an awkward one, though he appears to have forgotten Bacon's insistence that all ships should be equipped first with time-and-range boards.

The Admiralty in 1908 only accepted my 'Time and Range' plotting for use as an adjunct to 'Virtual Course and Speed' plotting . . . Indeed, in 1908 and 1909, as an 'ad hoc' officer . . . in the Naval Ordnance Department . . . I felt constrained to do everything in my power to develop and promote the official 'Virtual Course and Speed' plotting.[44]

In the spring of 1908, he lectured to officers in training at *Excellent*:

in language suited to our indifferent mental capacities, to explain to us benighted 'back-enders' the epoch making 'Vengeance' method of fire control . . . in the heckling which followed [Dreyer] refused to discuss Pollen's A.C.[45]

This hostile reception was reported to Pollen,[46] who, in September 1908, circulated his pamphlet *Reflections on an Error of the Day* to a long list of naval officers. Its attack on range-rate plotting, which also referred to a second curve of rate, was clearly aimed directly at Dreyer's 'Hints'.[47]

That autumn, Captain Constantine Hughes-Onslow wrote to Dreyer requesting information on the latest fire control developments for his War College essay. Dreyer replied directing him to 'the big Fire Control Pamphlet' but also expressing outrage at Pollen's broadcast criticisms.

The latter has stirred up some agitators to believe his auto-system is best but a searching analysis I think reveals that the simple kitchen table methods are better than the complicated machinery game and produce the same results as the latter only does when in adjustment.

Mr. P. has just issued a scurrilous pamphlet in which he has evidently been assisted by some 'failure'.

. . .

It is a great pity that trusting N.O's [naval officers] will go and discuss 'Confidential' matters with any private man and tell him our Secrets.[48]

It is hardly surprising that Dreyer was furious that Pollen was receiving confidential information (including the *Fire Control* pamphlet) and using it to attack Service policy on fire control, for which Dreyer was himself responsible within the NOD. However, his arrogant language so offended Hughes-Onslow that the latter sought Pollen's acquaintance, gave him Dreyer's letter and, in the essay, described the A.C. system very favourably. Hughes-Onslow also joined those prepared to pass confidential information to Pollen; one of the surviving copy of his comprehensive essay on Service fire control developments can be found in the Pollen Papers.[49]

In his pamphlet, Pollen had also insisted that sights should be set automatically; Dreyer's response was that:

> We have tried [auto-sight setting] and now we are trying 'follow-the-pointer' sights.
>
> ...
>
> A lot of rubbish re auto-transmission to the sights is loosely talked of.

The continuing failure of the Vyvyan-Newitt and Siemens automatic sights may well have influenced Dreyer's preference for simple gear, particularly since the problems of setting sights automatically are not very different from those of remotely controlling a plotter arm from a rangefinder. However, his enthusiasm for rate-plotting was also waning.

> Whether the plotting is 'Virtual Course' or is 'True Course of Enemy' is quite a small issue and a matter of fancy waistcoats. The great thing is to use Range and Bearings. I spent a lot of time trying to develop Range Plotting without bearings but happily dropped it before the B.P. and told them all so.[50]

When he was writing, the Fleet had no satisfactory source of bearings. But, in theory, a plot of range-rate against time can yield the speed-across required for a cross-cut; its slope is a measure of the 'second difference [differential]' of range that Dreyer twice mentioned in his evidence to the RCAI.[51] And a simple formula converts the slope into speed-across.[52] To the RCAI, Dreyer described the time-and-range-rate plot as 'only an expedient for the moment': while, in practice, *Excellent* found that it required 'a large number of ranges, which you were not likely to get when the guns were firing'.[53] Thus Dreyer had to fall back on both ranges and bearings, though he too now evidently preferred using them for course plotting.

This conclusion is confirmed by a further Admiralty pamphlet on fire control published in 1909. Its introduction emphasised that plotting remained experimental, and warned that:

> the successful use of Plotting before fire is opened to set the Dumaresq correctly can be greatly discounted by the enemy's Admiral altering course ... 'together' at the moment that either side opens fire.

Nonetheless, much of the text was concerned with manual course plotting, including ingenious though impracticable manual methods for using the new Admiralty-pattern plotter to plot true courses while turning. This plotter was based on a conventional cone-and-roller variable-speed drive, in which the roller's speed of rotation was proportional to its distance from the apex of the cone.[54] The pamphlet also described the new Dumaresq scales intended for keeping the instrument set while altering course.[55] Dreyer certainly wrote the introduction and probably most of the rest of the pamphlet;[56] thus his inventive energies were focused mainly on course plotting and on methods for dealing with course changes. Also, perhaps following Bacon's sudden change of attitude, Dreyer was much less hostile towards Pollen and, after the visit to the Linotype works on 12 July 1909, he reported favourably on Pollen's automatic instruments.

> The Apparatus consists of:- (a) An automatic plotting apparatus combined with a gyro controlled 9 foot Barr & Stroud R.F. similar to that tried in 'Ariadne' but considerably improved. (b) . . . a combined Range Clock and Transmitter, which . . . will, when started, continue to transmit the correct true ranges so long as no alteration of Course and Speed of enemy occurs . . . If this can be made to work satisfactorily it should prove a very valuable piece of apparatus. (c) Range and Deflection Spotting Correction transmitters . . . well worth a further trial now in view of the excellence of Mr. Isherwood's electrical transmission gear . . . (d) . . . apparatus for electrically controlling gun sights for Range and Deflection. This idea has been tried – the Vyvyan-Newitt – and also Siemens Vickers – but . . . is worth another trial.[57]

While Dreyer had been concentrating on course plotting, Norman of *Arrogant* had persevered with dual-rate plotting. On 11 June 1909, Norman's report and the instruments he used were forwarded to the Admiralty, while at some point he also went there to see Dreyer.[58] Yet, even in September, Dreyer was taking out secret patents on two new instruments that still worked not by rates but by simulated courses. (Single examples were constructed by Elliott Brothers.) The first appears to have been some form of tactical plotter 'with an Index or Pointer in the shape of a small bead which could be clipped to a string and caused to travel along a chart at any desired speed . . . in any desired direction'; like the Admiralty-pattern course plotter described in the 1909 pamphlet, it used a 'cone variable speed gear'. The second patent concerned a 'form of range keeper'. During the visit to the Linotype works, Dreyer discussed with Pollen what were described as 'hyperbolic clocks' i.e. clocks that modelled virtual course and so the hyperbolic relationship between range and time; on his return, he was encouraged by the DNO to patent his own ideas.[59] Later reports based on the patent suggest that the mechanism was similar to that proposed by John Dreyer in 1908, although it now incorporated two bars to obtain virtual course and speed from own and enemy ships' courses and speeds. Once again, the virtual movement of the enemy relative to own ship was generated by propelling a traveller at a speed proportional to virtual speed along a single screw aligned with the virtual course.

A direct pinion drive variable speed drive was fitted.[60]

This mechanism may be related to the 'studded disc and . . . small-toothed wheel' used in a portable range clock supplied to the Admiralty by Elliott Brothers.[61]

In September or early October, Lieutenant Joseph Henley, who had already deputised for Dreyer in 1907, returned to the NOD to take over responsibility for fire control, rangefinders, plotting and sights (though all types of gun mounting were now dealt with by another of the DNO's assistants).[62] In November, Dreyer returned to sea. But, by then, he had evidently recognised the importance of Norman's innovations.

## VANGUARD AND THE ORIGINAL TABLE

[In] November 1909 Commander Dreyer went to 'Vanguard' as Executive Officer and rigged up an 'Embryo' Dreyer Table
Time and Range Plot
Time and Bearing Plot
[Vickers] Range Clock
Dumaresq fitted with 2 Cross Sliders, to enable 'Cross Cut' of 2 rates to be used.[63]

This assembly of instruments (it was not yet an integrated table) was completed and tried in the first half of 1910. The failure of the Argo true-course plotter in the *Natal* trials then provided Dreyer with an opportune moment to propose an alternative based on rate plotting. His 'Remarks' of 22 July described the *Vanguard* system. Ranges were plotted on one of the three patented plotters made in 1908, while a standard Admiralty-pattern course plotter was modified to plot bearings from the Chetwynd compass against time.[64] The two 'cross-sliders' fitted to the Dumaresq were celluloid strips at right angles, each with a centrally inscribed black line. In good visibility:

> The Range clock is kept set for 'mean Rangefinder Range of the moment' as shown by the Time and Range Instrument, and the rate as shown by a 'Dumaresq' set by guesswork is first put on, and later this is superseded by the Rate shown by the Range and Time instrument.

Dreyer emphasised that:

> The object of getting the 'Dumaresq' set is to enable the Range Clock to be fed with Rates during periods when Rangefinding is interrupted by smoke etc. but where bearings . . . can be obtained.
>
> . . . ALL systems of Plotting suffer from the defect that they rely on the enemy not altering his course and speed during . . . periods of interrupted Rangefinding.

He declared that:

> This system . . . is meeting with success in this ship, having been used to Ranges over 13,000 yards.
>
> The Range clock is usually started with Rate and mean Range and the Deflection passed to the Guns about 1½ minutes after the first Range is obtained.

With practical experience of rate-plotting at sea, Dreyer was now able to argue against its theoretical disadvantages:

> the general trend of thought afloat in connection with 'Plotting' in the last two years has been too much in the direction of magnifying the importance of small geometrical deficiencies . . . instead of developing the most simple, practical and rapid system most likely to stand the stress of action. Thus, until recently, the general opinion with regard to the Time and Range system has been unduly biased against it by the fact that it often describes a curve instead of a straight line; the fact that it most rapidly and simply produces the mean Rangefinder Range of the moment . . . having been overlooked in favour of this purely Academic point.
>
> . . . the fact that the dots on the two time instruments [may] describe curves . . . does not affect the accuracy . . . as the portions of the curves employed are small.
>
> During the recent P.Z. [tactical exercise] when this ship was continually altering course, a Time and Range instrument would have coped far more successfully with the Range-keeping than any other Instrument now in existence.

However, Dreyer was evidently concerned at this time about clock errors resulting from the transfer of rate from the Dumaresq to the clock only at intervals. His solution was to obtain the clock-rate from an extra Dumaresq set each minute (by reference to the rate from the bearing plot) to 'what the forecasted Bearing will be half-way through that minute'.

Dreyer, once again the principal advocate of rate-plotting, nonetheless acknowledged that the Argo rangefinder mounting and transmission gear were the best means available to make rate plots automatically; he proposed:

that Mr. Pollen may be asked to fit a 9-ft. Barr and Stroud's Rangefinder with his automatic Range Transmission, working a pencil to and fro on a Range bar . . . suitable for being mounted by ship's artificers . . . in this ship. This action could be taken without divulging to Mr. Pollen the nature of this instrument for which a secret patent is held.

Dreyer also recommended that:

As this system shows promise of being a very good one [and as] I was the first to suggest this system which is clearly described at the foot of page 53 of the Pamphlet on 'FIRE CONTROL' . . . G.4023/08,[65]

he should take out further secret patents covering the Time and Bearing Instrument and the method of setting the Dumaresq. Perhaps this was a disinterested suggestion intended to protect Service inventions, but, since the 1908 pamphlet did not mention a bearing plot, it looks more like a deliberate and successful appropriation of Norman's contribution to what, ever afterwards, were known as the Dreyer Tables.

On 13 August, Dreyer received an informal letter from Henley. This and other similar correspondence demonstrate the close and friendly relationship between them; the contrast with Henley's suspicious attitude to Pollen is marked.

Since I last wrote Mr. Pollen appeared one day and informed me that he was preparing a scheme for <u>Automatic Time and ranges</u> Plotting . . .

Mr. P. may have been on this T.&R. scheme for some time but so far we have no information of any patent having been lodged. (Personally I expect he has heard of your scheme through somebody and this has given him the idea).

. . .

In view of Mr. P's sudden attack on T.&R. I concur with you re secret patents and I hope you agree with me that the patent should cover the whole principle of T.&R. & T.&B. so as to keep him out of it.[66]

Sumida has cited this letter as evidence that Moore and others opposed automatic plotting, 'apparently preferring manual methods'.[67] The actual text shows that Henley (like Dreyer) was prepared to make use of 'Mr. P's Auto Receiver' but that the redesigned Argo gear would not be available for over a year. And, even if Moore questioned the practicability of automatic rate plotting in the short term, he was in no doubt that the idea needed protecting. On the same day that Henley wrote to Dreyer, the DNO submitted:

to direct Com[r] Dreyer to take out a Secret patent for the whole system of Time and Range and Time and Bearing worked either automatically or manually . . . This action is considered desirable to protect the Admiralty from any developments of Mr. Pollen or others.[68]

In fact, Dreyer's next technical proposal was not the patent specification but resulted from local control trials, for which *Vanguard* had been selected. The experiments were conducted in August and culminated in a successful Special Battle Practice on the 31st, during which, at ranges sometimes exceeding 7,500 yards, ten hits were made from thirty-nine rounds fired. On 5 September, Dreyer submitted his 'Remarks on Local Turret Control' which recommended an installation comprising a 9-foot turret rangefinder in an armoured hood, a turret Dumaresq, and what he called the 'Time & Range Chronograph, Range Clock & Transmitter Combined' (Figure 5.1). Some features of this combined instrument – the clockwork-driven paper, the rate-measuring disc – had appeared in his earlier patents. It now plotted both observed (rangefinder) and predicted (gun) ranges automatically, the plotting pencils being positioned by long screws. The gun-ranges were generated by 'rate of change clockwork' driving the plotting screw through 'differential correcting gear'; all these, and also the gun-range pencil and transmitter, were mounted on the gun-range scale. This scale, with all its attachments, could slide relative to the fixed scale of rangefinder ranges; the displacement of the gun-range scale was shown on the 'spotting scale'. By sliding the gun-range scale, the gun-range pencil could be 'tuned' to the rangefinder ranges without changing the transmitted gun-ranges; this was useful if hitting had already been established. But normal spotting corrections had to applied in two stages. First, the correction was set on the spotting scale, but, to transmit it, the gun-range pencil had to be brought back into coincidence with the rangefinder ranges by means of the differential. Dreyer did not explain why he adopted this scheme; perhaps its appeal was that it met the functional requirements with only one differential. Nonetheless, he could claim that:

> It is the only instrument yet designed which enables the Range-keeper to be kept instantly tuned up to the 'mean Rangefinder Range and Rate of the moment' by inspection and entirely without calculation.

In this first description, Dreyer even acknowledged that:

> The advisability of fitting a red pencil to U [the gun-range pointer] to obtain a graphic record of the Gun Ranges which might help in correcting the Rate was pointed out to me by Rear-Admiral Peirse

Inspector of Target Practice and Flag Commander W. W. Fisher when describing such a Time and Range fitting to them.[69]

However, when he resubmitted his proposal in October 1910, this frank admission had already been suppressed.[70] Ever after, the origin of this vital feature, which allowed predicted and observed ranges to be compared visually so that the clock-range and rate could be adjusted appropriately, remained unacknowledged.

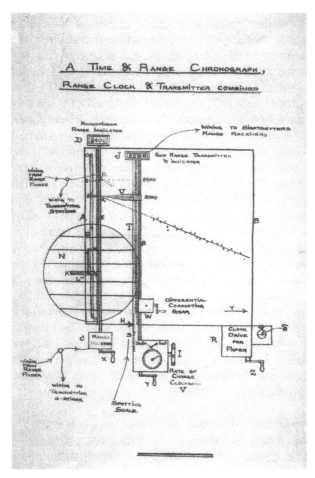

*Figure 5.1* Dreyer's local control instrument, 1910.

The rangefinder (E) and gun (U) ranges were plotted automatically. Gun-range was tuned with the differential W. The gun-range scale and all its attachments were moved bodily, by an amount indicated on the scale S, with the handle I. Range-rate was measured with the engraved glass disc.

Source: Dreyer, 'Remarks on Local Turret Control . . .', in ADM 1/8131 and 8147, PRO.

> The Rate of Change Clockwork can be direct and positive pinion drive as in the combined clock and transmitter being made by Messrs. Elliott Bros. to the designs of Captain Dreyer R.A. and myself, instead of by friction discs, cones and balls, as in other clocks.[71]

First, this must be referring to the virtual-course clock patented in autumn 1909, though thereafter it disappeared from the record. Second, at this time, only Argo was using variable-speed drives incorporating balls; evidently, Dreyer had not forgotten what he had seen during his visit to Linotype the previous summer. Finally, it is apparent that Dreyer was still collaborating with his brother, though this is the last document which acknowledges John's contribution to Frederic's fire control inventions.[72]

While praising the trials conducted by *Vanguard*, Admiral May did not support Dreyer's proposal for plotting instruments in turrets.[73] Even so, Dreyer was now able to use the local control instrument as the basis for a complete dual-rate table on a single base-plate (Figure 5.2); his provisional patent application was submitted on 23 September 1910.[74] This described two automatic plots, for ranges and bearings, placed side-by-side and sharing a common paper drive with manual alternative. The bearing pointer (indicating on a sliding scale) and pencil were mounted on a split nut engaging with the screw driven by the bearing receiver motor; thus bearing plots could always commence with the pencil near the middle of the paper. Bearings were to be received either from a rangefinder or from 'an independent bearing apparatus'. The instrument also incorporated a Dumaresq with celluloid 'cross-sliders'. The range part was very similar to the local control instrument: including the clockwork drive to the 'gun-range indicator'.

When Jellicoe took command of the Atlantic Fleet with his flag in *Prince of Wales*, Dreyer, on 20 December 1910, became his Flag Commander. Since 20 November, Dreyer had been appointed temporarily to the Admiralty,[75] which gave him an opportunity to work on the complete patent specification. On 14 December, he wrote to Keith Elphinstone of Elliott Brothers about the 'rate of change clockwork':

> have you any objection to my using the sketch of this fitment which you are going to send me shortly ... the clockwork of the clock is after all the only part of this apparatus which is yours and if you like I will have that out and put in a cone and roller ... or a disc and roller – any other sort of changeable speed gear in fact.[76]

Thus it appears that Elphinstone had devised the 'direct pinion drive'. However, the Complete Specification of 12 April 1911 described the gun-range screw as being driven by a constant-speed electric motor (the same which powered the plots) and 'a variable speed device [of unspecified type] situated under the Dumaresq', although the remainder of the drive mechanism looks very like that of the local control instrument (see Figure 5.1). It appears, therefore, that this part of the design was far from settled. Dreyer's letter shows that he was largely unconcerned about what type of variable-speed drive was adopted; since he was at sea, the final choice of a conventional disc-and-roller was probably made by Elphinstone alone, as part of the process of realising the patented design as a working fire control table.

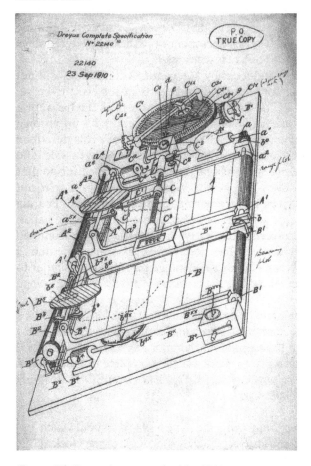

*Figure 5.2* Dreyer's patented table, 1911.

Bearings and ranges were recorded on the nearer and further plots, respectively. Rates were measured with the engraved glass discs. The rate of the range clock was set with the handle C1x, which also positioned the pointer d to indicate the same rate as the Dumaresq enemy bar. The handle $C^0$ tuned the clock range. The knob $C^2$ displaced the whole range screw by an amount indicated on the spotting scale $C^3$.

Source: Patent 22,140/1910, complete specification 12 April 1911, in T.173/91 Part III, PRO.

With the design described in the Complete Specification, applying a simple spotting correction remained a two-stage operation, though the single differential was now provided with a frictionally coupled pointer 'which can be re-zeroed at any time'. The Dumaresq (apparently a modified Mark III) had a fixed dial-plate, while the fore-and-aft bar (with the outer ring on which it was mounted) rotated. The rate set on the range clock was indicated by the small pointer moving in the transverse slot cut in the dial-plate. Hence:

> the Rate need not be actually read off but can be set on the Gun Range Indicator [the clock] by turning the [hand-wheel] so as to keep the pointer opposite to the bows of the dummy enemy's ship.[77]

The essential features of this scheme had been put forward in October 1910 by Gunner J. W. Newland of *Excellent* as part of a proposal for a mechanical connection between a Dumaresq Mark II and a Vickers clock. The DNO decided not to patent the idea,[78] but Dreyer probably heard about it, and read the papers, when attached to the Admiralty in December.

This posting also enabled him to learn about the Anschütz gyrocompass, which was about to undergo trials in his new ship (as well as in *Neptune*).[79] On 2 December, Dreyer submitted a proposal for:

> obtaining, transmitting and plotting . . . the bearings of an Enemy from an Anshutz [*sic*] Gyro Compass Receiver Card mounted inside a Rangefinder mounting or on any other suitable stand . . .
>
> I described this fitting to Mr. Elphinstone of Messrs. Elliott Bros. when visiting their works at Lewisham this afternoon with Lieutenant J.C.W. Henley to inspect the Gyro Compass for the 'Prince of Wales'. Mr. Elphinstone informed me that he could easily incorporate this in the set of Gyro Compass Gear now under manufacture.[80]

Dreyer's proposal, though simple, relied on an operator to transmit the enemy compass-bearings by following the movements of the card of a modified gyrocompass receiver; this was, as he suggested, installed on a standard Barr & Stroud rangefinder mounting.[81] On 21 February 1911, Henley wrote to Dreyer:

> As the T&R & T&B will go to Prince of Wales I think it would be better to get a B&S Transmission as we have already got the Bearing Trans. from the Gyro Rec[r].[82]

At this time, Argo was still some months away from completing the prototype production mounting and were still developing the step-by-step transmission scheme that would eventually be used for the Argo plotters: and, in any case, it was not intended to supply the Argo mounting to pre-dreadnoughts like *Prince of Wales*.[83] Thus, despite earlier expectations, the ranges and bearings for this first Dreyer Table were neither taken nor transmitted with equipment from Pollen's company.

By 1 July 1911, Dreyer was able to advise Elphinstone that 'The Time and Bearing Chrono' had arrived safely in *Prince of Wales*, although their correspondence shows that the design of the range components of the table was still being finalised. Dreyer also requested a 'Connection from Gyro compass to ship's head ring of Dumaresq'; as he later insisted, this was the first mention of the feature that would make the later Dreyer Tables helm-free. Henley had taken up the proposal by 4 July, but on the 10th, he informed Dreyer that, although 'Elphinstone . . . sees no difficulty . . . D.N.O. is rather opposed to making any further alteration to your instrument.'[84] Then, in a letter to Elphinstone dated 19 July, Dreyer proposed another major enhancement, the addition of a bearing clock – though the mechanism he suggested, a hand-worked cone-and-roller drive 'similar to the one you fitted to the Ady. [Admiralty] Screw Bar plotting instrument',[85] was wholly unsuitable for a rate which might be positive or negative. On 24 July, Henley reported that:

> Re: Gyro Connection for Dumaresq or Chrono
> . . .
> Elphinstone said that nearly all the parts of the present chrono are made and that if the Gyro connection were fitted there would entail considerable delay. So D.N.O. decided not to fit it . . . but concurs in the add[n] [addition] if any more instruments are ordered.[86]

Elliotts were then able to complete the installation of the remaining components of the table in *Prince of Wales* by 30 September. After extended trials, and despite an undistinguished placing in Battle Practice,[87] Captain Hopwood submitted a very favourable report, which was fully endorsed by Jellicoe. The heavy underlining in the Captain's letter suggests that the Flag Commander had a hand in its drafting, but it also quoted remarks 'included by the Inspector of Target Practice in his comments on the "PRINCE OF WALES" Battle Practice carried out on 11 November'.

> Commander F.C. Dreyer's Fire Control Instrument appears to be of considerable assistance in obtaining a correct Rate, and in maintaining the mean rangefinder range until fire is opened. The Correct <u>rate</u> was obtained on <u>both</u> runs.

Hopwood's letter mentioned that, during Battle Practice, the lateral movement of the gun-range screw had proved its usefulness when smoke interference forced a change from the fore to the after rangefinder; 'the difference in adjustment between the two rangefinders can be immediately absorbed without calculation'. Attention was also drawn to 'the success with which the Range was kept . . . during a 13 point alteration of own ship's course'.[88]

In 1918, when Dreyer himself was DNO, a lavish *Handbook* on the Dreyer Tables was produced; doubtless at his insistence, it included a photograph of what by then was called the Original Table.[89] The general layout and construction were clearly the same as that illustrated in the complete patent specification. The screws of both plotters were driven by large receiver motors, permitting automatic plotting of ranges and compass bearings transmitted from the rangefinder mounting. The Dumaresq was now the latest model, the Mark VI, which explains why the rate could be kept successfully even through large turns.[90] The Dumaresq had also been raised sufficiently to accommodate the disc-and-roller variable-speed drive. Unexpectedly, the photograph shows clearly that the gun-range screw was driven by a third receiver motor, apparently identical to those for range and bearing. This feature is confirmed by a note (almost certainly by Dreyer) to Hopwood's letter.

Although the instrument . . . worked excellently . . . it would be better . . . to have all future instruments with direct mechanical drive for the range clock portion (instead of electric) as originally designed by the Inventor. This appears likely to be more acceptable in the Service, as Electrical gear is often looked on with suspicion.[91]

This might be seized on as an instance of naval prejudice against new technology, yet Keith Elphinstone had already expressed exactly the same view.[92]

I agree with you absolutely – a mechanical drive is the thing to aim at . . . Now that one has seen the thing at work, I don't see the least difficulty in making the drive mechanical instead of electrical because having had over a quarter of a Century's experience of Electrical Apparatus, I am very keen on cutting out wires and contacts . . . if at all possible.[93]

## THE MARK I BOARD

On 12 October, Dreyer submitted formally through Jellicoe a proposal for a 'Fire Control Board' for use in less important ships, with the suggestion that it should be designated Mark I to differentiate it from the 'Mark II' on trial in *Prince of Wales* (Elphinstone later confirmed that the Original Table had been known for a time as Mark II).[94] Functionally, this 'board' was very like the local control instrument from a year earlier,[95] but with the addition of a Mark VI Dumaresq, modified as in the Original Table. The range-rate pointer was coupled mechanically to a Vickers clock, on which the range scale was replaced by a plain ring with an engraved arrow. By turning a handle to follow the clock hand with the arrow, an operator also drove the screw of the range plot through a tuning differential. The paper was moved by hand, while automatic plotting of rangefinder ranges was proposed only as an option.[96] The surviving sources provide no indication of any immediate actions on this proposal, probably because priority was given to the new table for important ships; however, Dreyer's 'Mark I Board' anticipated the principal features of the later Mark I table.

## THE SEVEN PART RECORDER

On 11 October, shortly after the delivery of the Original Table, Elphinstone wrote to Dreyer:

> I have already got instructions from the D.N.O.'s Office to prepare a specification and Drawing . . . should another instrument be ordered as soon as a report comes in as regards the first one.
>
> . . .
>
> I should be glad if you could criticise the Schedule sent as quickly as possible.

On the 30th, Elphinstone sent 'an amended specification . . . two copies of . . . a perspective sketch I made and a couple of Schedules of the Parts'. In this letter, he also described his only known visit to Argo's premises, on the 26th.

> I was at York on Thursday – we sent up a Gyro Compass Receiver fitted with an attachment to control the Azimuth position of an R.F. and from trials there it looks like a successful application of the Gyro Compass Gear – I hope it will prove to be so in practice at sea.[97]

This occasion was clearly related to the cooperation between Argo and Elliotts, the British agents for Anschütz, that was necessary to fit gyro-compass receivers in the last twenty Argo rangefinder mountings. In his unofficial letter to Dreyer, Elphinstone did not even mention Argo's other work on fire control.

Elphinstone's sketch and schedule (both dated 28 October) were forwarded with Captain Hopwood's letter to the Admiralty on 25 November.

On 7 December, the DNO, Captain Moore, added the following recommendation.

> At a rough estimate the cost of the Argo Co's installation, i.e. rate-plotter and clock will not be less than £1,200 whereas the Dreyer instrument doing the same duties will cost about £300.
>
> It is considered most desirable that the 'Orion' and 'Lion' classes should be provided with these instruments at once. The 'Orion' herself will be fitted with the Argo Co's gear for trial so that it leaves five ships to be provided.
>
> It is therefore submitted that Messrs. Elliott Bros. may be requested to tender for five of the improved instruments.[98]

In his specifications and schedules, Elphinstone called the new design the 'Seven Part Recorder', to emphasise its modular construction. Different equipment schedules were given for ships with and without either Argo rangefinder mountings or gyrocompasses. The general layout was very similar to the Original Table; as previously, the gun-range screw could be shifted laterally by a rack, though now the 'spotting correction' was set on a small circular scale. A gyrocompass receiver controlled an electric motor which applied any change in course to the Dumaresq. The range clock was now coupled mechanically to the gun-range screw through a tuning differential gearbox, while the new bearing clock was connected (by means unspecified) to the Dumaresq. The bearing-rate scales were arranged so that the rate from the bearing-plot could be easily set on the bearing clock. Elphinstone did not mention the Dumaresq as an alternative source of bearing rate, and the design had no means for converting speed-across in knots to bearing-rate in degrees-per-minute.

## Dreyer Table Mark III

The order for five improved tables was placed with Elliott Brothers on 27 February 1912.[99] In December 1911, Jellicoe, on taking command of the Second Division of the Home Fleet, had shifted his flag to *Hercules*. Dreyer continued to serve as his Flag Commander and took the Original Table with him;[100] it was probably still in that ship in February 1916, although, by 1918, it had been replaced.[101] Since he was at sea, Dreyer can have contributed little while Elphinstone developed his ideas from the 'Seven Part Recorder' into a finished design. Working drawings had been completed by May 1912, the first production model being installed, probably in *Monarch*, before the end of the year; in February 1913, she was said to have 'the most up-to-date set of this apparatus . . . afloat'. The remaining four units were fitted in *Lion*, *Princess Royal*, *Thunderer* and (rather than in *Conqueror* as originally intended) in *King George V*.[102] By March 1914, the new design was known as the Mark III table (Figure 5.3).[103]

In December 1912, Dreyer was appointed to command the new cruiser *Amphion*, but, while waiting for his ship to commission (in April 1913), he once again returned to the Admiralty.[104] The assistant to the DNO responsible for fire control was now Commander C. V. Usborne; he had joined the NOD in February 1911 but did not take over from Henley until the following December,[105] so he had had ample time to gain experience. Now, a year later, a number of reports were being produced to justify Admiralty policy on the Pollen Aim Correction system. Dreyer collaborated with Usborne on the *Technical History and Technical Comparison* between the Dreyer and Argo systems: Dreyer contributing a detailed description of the new instrument, which in turn quoted extensively from its instruction pamphlet.

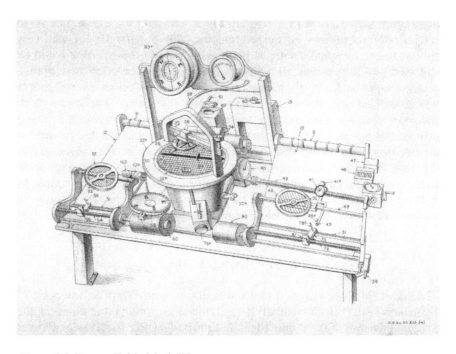

*Figure 5.3* Dreyer Table Mark III.

The modified Dumaresq Mark VI was between the bearing (left) and range (right) plots, with the range and bearing clocks beneath it; 80 and 60 are the receiver motors for ranges and bearings. The rate of the bearing clock was set with the knob and scale 76[A] from the value indicated on the scale 53 of the bearing-rate disc; drum 103 converted between bearing-rate and speed-across. The range clock rate was set with handle 30[A] with reference to the pointer 29. Handle 39 tuned the clock-range, while the unlabelled handle and differential next to the gun-range indicator 46 were used to set spotting corrections.

Source: Dreyer and Usborne, *Technical History and . . . Comparison*, February 1913, Figure 3, AL.

As the accompanying plates showed, Elphinstone had rearranged the main components of the table; the modified Dumaresq Mark VI, with the variable-speed drives of the range and bearing clocks beneath it, was now placed between the two plots. As in the Original Table, the dial-plate of the Dumaresq was fixed, with a slot cut along the length of the arrow representing the direction of the target; the pointer in this slot showed the rate set on the range clock. A compass-ring, graduated in compass-bearings, rotated around the dial-plate. An outer ring, which supported the fore-and-aft bar, was carried by the compass-ring but could also rotate upon it. On the compass-ring, the target arrow indicated enemy compass-bearing, while a pointer at the bow end of the fore-and-aft bar indicated own compass course. An Anschütz gyrocompass receiver was mounted on the panel above the Dumaresq; the panel also carried the Forbes log indicating own ship's speed. A 'relay device' on the back of the panel controlled an electric motor which, through a flexible drive shaft, rotated the fore-and-aft bar relative to the compass-ring by an amount equal to the change in own ship's course. The bearing clock was set to run, at the rate of change of enemy compass-bearing, using the knob and linear scale on the front of the casing; the rate scale was calibrated between ±15°/min. The clock's output shaft was coupled to the compass-ring of the Dumaresq, though a clutch could disconnect the bearing clock so that the enemy compass bearing could be altered by hand.[106] Thus the joint actions of the gyrocompass relay and the bearing clock maintained correctly, without approximation, the enemy-bearing and own-course indicated on the compass-ring.

Once the Argo rangefinder mounting had been fitted for a separate trainer, Dreyer 'expected that the Training Number will get a far larger number of observations than the Range Taker will'. Thus the pencils of the range and bearing plots were controlled separately by the two operators of the Argo mounting, all ranges and enemy compass-bearings being plotted automatically as they were received by the two large receiver motors.[107] As an alternative, ranges from a turret rangefinder could be plotted manually. Dreyer also suggested that:

> It may be found possible to plot the ranges from more than one Range finder at one and the same time

though clearly this was not yet an established method.[108]

In their report on the Pollen Aim Correction system, the Admiralty's Contracts Department insisted:

> It is     only fair to the Service to state that not until the end of 1912 was automatic range plotting made reliable (this was accomplished by Messrs. Elliott Bros.) and that even now in 1913 Mr. Pollen has not yet succeeded in himself producing a reliable instrument for automatic range plotting.[109]

Automatic plotting, of the bearings as well as the ranges transmitted from the Argo mounting, depended on the large receivers developing sufficient torque to drive the plotting screws and attachments. These step-by-step motors were made by Elliotts, but were developed from the designs that the firm had licensed from Anschütz.[110] Perhaps the motors gave some problems in the Original Table, but in the Mark III they evidently proved more reliable than the clutch-based receivers used by Argo.

As before, the rate on the range clock was set by following the Dumaresq indications with the pointer in the slot. The clock drove the plotting screw through a tuning differential (the tuning handle, coupled by shafting, was at the far side of the plot). On the Mark III, the range scale – which extended to 16,400 yards – and screw were fixed. But a second differential gearbox was connected to the far end of the screw, with its output shaft driving the gun-range indicator and transmitter. With the aid of the dial and pointers on this 'spotting' differential, an operator could apply range corrections without moving the range pointer and pencil. Thus the tuning handle and differential were used only to tune the range pointer to the mean of the plotted rangefinder ranges; the pointer and pencil now indicated clock-range, the closest available estimate of the mean rangefinder range of the moment. The spotting differential then converted clock-range into gun-range. Before opening fire, the spotting dial was set with the ballistic range correction obtained from the Dreyer Range Corrector. Then, once firing began, further corrections came from spotting the fall of shot. However, the clock-range pointer and pencil were mounted on a small carriage, movable on the screw by means of a knurled head and dial; hence the clock-range could also be adjusting without altering the gun-range – as might be necessary when changing rangefinders. The output shaft of the spotting differential was coupled mechanically to one of the two range hands on the transmitter to the follow-the-pointer gunsights. This transmitter contained multiple cams, one being selected to match the nature of the charge being fired (full, reduced, sub-calibre or aiming-rifle). By following the first hand with a second coupled to the cam mechanism, an operator generated and transmitted the unequal steps required by the non-uniform graduations of the range-dials of the gunsights.

The range-rate disc with parallel wires measured the slopes of the rangefinder and clock-range plots. Any divergence indicated that the range-rate on the clock was incorrect, and suggested how the Dumaresq range-rate could be adjusted to improve the accuracy of the cross-cut.[111]

Observed enemy compass-bearings were transmitted, in ¼° steps, from the Argo mounting to the bearing plot. This could be narrower than the range plot,[112] since the bearing scale was engraved on an endless loop, while the pointer and pencil (which were attached to a split nut) could be given any starting position. Enemy compass bearing-rate, in degrees-per-minute, was measured with a second rate-measuring disc with parallel wires. This disc was linked to a sliding pointer moving across a set of curves, of constant speed-across, engraved on a drum; the drum was rotated by a shaft connected to the range clock. The curves were constructed so that, at all ranges, the pointer indicated the speed-across that corresponded to the bearing-rate indicated by the scale on the bearing-rate disc. Thus the bearing-rate from the plot could be converted into a speed-across for use in setting the Dumaresq by means of a 'cross-cut'. Or the speed-across indicated by the Dumaresq (usually called the Dumaresq deflection in contemporary documents) could be converted into the bearing-rate set on the bearing clock. Or the bearing-rate from the plot could be compared with the bearing-rate obtained from the Dumaresq speed-across.[113]

The methods of using the Mark III table were set out in its instructional pamphlet. At the start of an engagement:

Set the Dumaresq for guessed course and speed of Enemy and bearing of Enemy . . . as ordered from aloft [and for own speed from the Forbes log].

Set {the fore-and-aft bar} to True Course of own Ship and clutch in the {gyrocompass connection}.

Turn the {rate handle} . . . to keep {the range-rate pointer} opposite to {the enemy bow pointer} (the Range Rates shown by the Dumaresq are thus put on the Range Clock).[114]

Using the tuning handle, set the clock-range pencil to indicate the initial estimated or plotted enemy range. Put on the Spotting Differential 'the anticipated difference between True and Gun Range'. On the bearing clock:

set the Bearing Rate for the range in use as deduced from the Dumaresq Deflection . . .

With both clocks now started and until fire is opened:

turn the {tuning handle} . . . as necessary to keep {the clock-range pencil} by inspection in agreement with the *Mean Range Finder Range of the Moment as shown by the Range Dots* [original italics].

Likewise, if the enemy bearing indicated by the Dumaresq diverges from the mean plotted bearing:

The movement due to {the bearing clock} can . . . be overcome and corrected . . . at any time by manually turning the milled head [which also disengaged the bearing clock from the compass ring].

If clock-ranges or bearings diverge from the plotted values, the table operators propose a new value for range-rate or speed-across, also indicating whether the recommendation is based on a good, fair or indifferent plot. However:

> *It should be clearly understood that the Range Keeper in the Control Position in use is the Master Rate Operator* and therefore no alterations to the Course and Speed of Enemy or any Rate . . . can be made without his permission [original italics].

The control may order either the recommended change or some other value more in accord with observations. If (say) the rate of the range clock is altered, the new value is used unchanged until the control orders a new cross-cut, that is, new settings of enemy course and speed. Then, once again, the clocks are set with the rates (perhaps the changing rates) indicated by the Dumaresq.[115] When firing begins, range tuning at the table may conflict with the range changes ordered by the spotter. Thus every tuning alteration is called up from the table to the Spotting Officer, who can, if he wishes, cancel it by ordering a spotting correction in the opposite sense. Similarly, the control does not order a rate-spotting correction without reference to the officer in charge of the table.[116]

Dreyer emphasised that:

> The Fore and Aft Bar of the Dumaresq being kept Oriented in Space by the connection to the Gyro Compass, THE RANGE CAN BE KEPT WHILE OWN SHIP IS TURNING.

He also pointed out that the bearing clock enabled the Mark III table to keep the rates, and hence ranges and bearing, even if observations of the target were interrupted.

> Whenever the enemy completely disappears *i.e. the moment the bearing operator . . . ceases to receive bearings*, he reads off the Dumaresq deflection [the speed-across] and sets the corresponding true Bearing Rate . . . on the bearing [clock's rate] scale . . . He must then watch the Dumaresq for changes in deflection, so that the correspondingly altered bearing rate may be set on the bearing [rate] scale. The instrument will thus be kept correctly set for bearing of enemy, although the latter is not visible.
>
> NOTE.—Any alteration in course or speed of enemy while out of sight, or any errors in estimating enemy's course and speed, previous to his disappearing on a steady course, will, of course, produce errors in the forecasted range or bearing, or both [original italics].

Dreyer also made a virtue of the 'non-positive' connections between the Dumaresq and the clocks, since they allowed the two parts of the table to be set to different rates.[117] He did not discuss the possibility of errors arising from the manual transfer of range-rate, probably because it was not of practical concern. With the rate lines on the Dumaresq spaced at intervals of 100 yds/min., any changes in rate could normally be followed by the rate pointer in steps of 25 yds/min. i.e. with an equivalent rate error of only 12½ yds/min. Even when two 25-knot ships passed beam-to-beam at 8,000 yards, the interval between these steps was never less than 4.2 seconds. However, if the ship was also altering course unfavourably, this interval could be reduced to 2.3 seconds;[118] this *might* demand steps of 50 yds/min. but, even so, the total error accumulating during a turn of two minutes would have been only some 50–60 yards.[119]

Unlike range-rate, speed-across had to be read from the Dumaresq by eye; since the lines of speed-across were separated by 4 knots, any changes in speed-across could probably be followed in steps no smaller than 2 knots. Each new value was then converted, by means of the graduated drum, pointer and bearing-rate disc, into a new rate to set on the bearing clock. When two 25-knot ships passed on opposite courses separated by 8,000 yards, at no point did the speed-across changed by 2 knots in less than 29 seconds, time enough to make the conversion and set the bearing-rate.[120] In February 1913, a Mark III table was set up in Elliott Brothers' Westminster office to simulate this worst case condition, of two ships on opposite courses inducing rapid changes in range-rate and speed-across. Yet the results showed that operators, at least in ideal surroundings, could transfer rates manually without significant errors. The first test represented two 15-knot ships passing beam-to-beam at 7,000 yards; the target was assumed to become invisible when the range was still 12,000 yards, after which, for almost 10 minutes, the table kept the range and bearing without operator correction until the time of passing beam-to-beam. Yet the range error was then only 70 yards,[121] less than the predicted error from range-rate steps of 25 yds/min., let alone any further errors resulting from steps in bearing-rate.

At sea, and especially in battle, bearings may not have been kept so precisely. The combined effects of the stepwise transfer of bearing-rate and the wander of the gyrocompass induced by large course changes could result in bearing errors of several degrees. However, in typical tactical circumstances, when the speed-across was not high, these errors did not 'feed through' into significant errors in range-rate.[122] In any case, while the enemy remained visible, any bearing errors could be corrected by observation:

> it will be necessary from time to time to unclutch the automatic drive and correct the position of the compass ring. The need for this will be indicated by noticing whether the bearing of the enemy as

shown on the Dumaresq corresponds to the observed bearing recorded by . . . the bearing plot.[123]

If the enemy became obscured, firing ceased – blind firing was not possible before the introduction of the later Gyro Director Training (GDT) gear. Even so, provided 'the enemy is obliging enough <u>not</u> to alter course or speed while out of sight',[124] the bearing clock could keep the bearing, at least approximately, even if own ship changed course. Thus, when the target reappeared, the deflection, range and range-rate would be near enough to correct by spotting the first few salvoes.

Because their rates were set manually, the clocks of the Mark III table cannot be termed automatic. However, because the gyrocompass relay adjusted the Dumaresq automatically (albeit more accurately for small yaws than for large course changes), these tables could be operated irrespective of helm. Thus they can be described as 'helm-free'.

## DREYER TABLE MARK II

As the deliveries of the Mark III tables were commencing,

> it became necessary to decide without awaiting the trials in 'Orion' what form of control instrument should be fitted in 'King George' class. It was decided to order for these ships sets consisting of a Pollen clock and a Dreyer Time and Range table. It was also considered that a Time and Bearing table would not be necessary with the clock . . . As a result of [the *Orion*] trials, the clock was favourably reported on but it was shown necessary to use a Time and Bearing as well as a Time and Range table with it and it was decided that these should be of the Commander Dreyer type and manufactured by Elliott Bros.
>
> The Pollen Time and Range and Time and Bearing tables [*sic*] were not satisfactory . . .

In February 1913, it had already been 'decided to make in Portsmouth Dockyard the necessary apparatus for connecting [Dreyer's plotting] gear to the Argo range-finder mountings and clock', and that the Argo clocks would be supplied to *Ajax*, *Centurion* and *Audacious* (*King George V* class), *Conqueror* (*Orion* class) and *Queen Mary*.[125] By 1918, the combination of Argo clock with Dreyer rate-plotters had been designated Dreyer Table Mark II, but the brief description tells us only that: 'the clock-range screw is run by an electric motor controlled by a commutator from clock-range in argo [*sic*] clock'.[126] The only other information found states that, in early 1914, *Queen Mary* was already fitted with the standard Elliott-type cam-operated follow-the-pointer transmitters as used in the Mark III tables.[127] It appears that the transmission arrangements described in the handbook for the Argo Clock Mark IV were simplified so that clock-ranges were transmitted, in equal steps, to one of Elliott's large receiver motors; the latter then drove the clock-range screw of a dual-rate plotter that was otherwise the same as that in the Dreyer Tables Mark III.

## RANGEFINDER CONTROL

The ships of the *Orion* and *King George V* classes were formed into the Second Battle Squadron (2BS).[128] All these latest battleships were equipped with rate-plotters coupled to either Dreyer or Argo clocks, and, as described in Chapter 3, with multiple rangefinders. As might be expected, the new system of 'rangefinder control . . . has been very largely introduced and developed in the 2nd Battle Squadron' which had 'many more rangefinders than any other'.[129] The system was promulgated to the Home Fleet in a General Order from Admiral Callaghan dated 5 November 1913 as 'a method considered to promise very well', especially, though not exclusively, for the latest ships.

> The readings from as many R.F.s as possible are plotted on moving paper on the Dreyer table, the Argo R.F. being plotted automatically, and the others by hand. If the R.F.s are well together, it has been found that there should be a zone of dots proceeding across the paper, their direction depending on the rate of increase or decrease of the range, and it is then easy to determine by inspection the mean of these ranges.
>
> . . .
>
> . . . alteration of course and speed of the enemy is quickly made apparent in the different aspect of the R.F. plots, from which the clock-range can be corrected, the *correction of the rate being of secondary importance so long as the range is maintained and hitting continued* [original italics].

It was also claimed that the method reduced the dependence on spotting and that after 'straddling, and not being entirely dependent on rate, the maximum rate of fire may be developed'. However, these benefits depended on a constant stream of accurate ranges, which were unlikely to be obtained except:

> under favourable conditions of weather and visibility at ranges below 10,000 yards [when] the rangefinders are well together. These conditions however can *rarely* be those of action as, when the

visibility is good, fire will probably be opened at much greater ranges [original italics].

Ships adopting R.F. control were warned that they 'must be prepared . . . to revert to the alternative system *i.e. maintaining the Range by means of the Rate*' [original italics].[130]

Rangefinder control was more suited to peacetime practice ranges than the much greater ranges experienced during the war.

> The method . . . appears most suitable when concentration renders spotting unreliable, or frequent alterations of course and speed of the enemy makes rate-keeping very hard. But it should be avoided at very long range, and cannot be used unless the conditions admit of good range-taking.[131]

Nonetheless, it firmly established the advantages of being able to plot as many ranges as possible from all the rangefinders that could range on the target.[132] Thus, during 1913, there had been an important change of emphasis, from the automatic plotting of the ranges from one rangefinder to the need (by whatever means) to plot ranges from a number of rangefinders at once. In fact, this had already been anticipated by Dreyer in February 1913; for any future supply of Dreyer Tables, he expected that:

> The Time and Range plot will have arrangements provided to enable the results of several Range Finders to be plotted.[133]

However, he can have had little opportunity to influence subsequent developments once *Amphion* commissioned on 2 April. By June (in the month when he was promoted to Captain) his ship came, and remained, top in the Gunlayer's Test and, subsequently, she was first in her category at Battle Practice. Further advancement soon followed, when, on 27 October, Dreyer was appointed Flag Captain to Rear Admiral Sir Robert Arbuthnot, second-in-command of the 2BS;[134] this was too late for him to have had any influence on the Home Fleet Order of 5 November. Dreyer's new ship was the *Orion*; the Navy, while watching his rapid rise, must have derived no little amusement from his appointment to the only ship with a TS entirely equipped by the Argo Company.[135]

## DREYER TABLES MARK IV AND IV*

Just before he assumed command of *Amphion*, Dreyer submitted to the DNO 'some diagrammatic sketches and a description of some <u>additions</u> which if made to my fire control apparatus would make it more automatic than at present'. He proposed that changes in the Dumaresq range-rate and speed-across should be detected and transmitted by commutator switches to step-by-step receiver motors. The range-rate receiver motor would set the rate of the range clock directly. This was correct in principle, but it is most unlikely that any step-by-step motor could have developed enough torque to drive the roller across the disc. The speed-across receiver motor drove the cone of a cone-and-roller variable-speed drive. The roller was somehow positioned by the range clock, while its shaft set the rate of the existing bearing clock through a third commutator and receiver motor.[136] As described, this part of the scheme was a mathematical nonsense. One glaring flaw may have been due to a simple drawing error but, even after correction, the design is still wrong.[137]

Dreyer does not seem to have recognised any of the problems, theoretical or practical, with his suggestion; indeed, in the *Technical History and Technical Comparison* of February 1913, he represented it and other projected improvements as 'additional parts [that] have already been designed and will probably be included'.[138] The majority of these new features would eventually appear in the next version of the Dreyer Table, the Mark IV, though not always as described. Of the remainder, a single example of a 'corrector which will automatically allow for the "slip" of own ship when turning' was ordered for the first of the new tables but, in July 1914, it was decided that it should 'not be introduced without further experiments';[139] thereafter, it disappears from the record. Range transmission to the guns was never made fully automatic and continued to rely on an operator following a pointer.[140] And, rather than a time-of-flight corrector in the tables, John Dreyer's Range Corrector continued to supply this and other ballistic corrections in the form of a single spotting correction.[141]

In reality, it is unlikely that, in February 1913, the design of any of these additions had yet been taken in hand by Elliott Brothers. With the supply for the *King George V* class and *Queen Mary* already settled, no more tables were now required for new ships until the completion of the *Iron Duke* class and *Tiger* in 1914. Thus priority could be given to the provision of local control tables for use in turrets. The question had been raised in May 1912 and, in August, Dreyer was instructed to work with Elliott Brothers on a suitable design. A prototype was being made at the end of 1913 and, by March 1914, was installed in a turret of *Queen Mary*.[142] By that time, the design of the Mark IV must have begun, since the first of the new tables, for *Iron Duke*, was already under construction, although a letter from Keith Elphinstone dated 14 March gives the impression that many details remained undecided.[143] Nonetheless, by 6 July, the new table had been tested by the DNO's representative and it was decided to order four more sets; it was expected that the prototype would be placed on board *Iron Duke* in mid-August,[144] though this could have been delayed by the flagship's departure for Scapa Flow. The next three Mark IV tables were fitted in *Tiger*, *Benbow* and *Emperor of India*, all completed in October and November; the final unit was supplied to *Queen Elizabeth* (commissioned in December, 1914).[145]

The first Mark IV* was already aboard *Warspite* when she ran her gun trials in April 1915;[146] thereafter until after the completion of *Courageous* and *Glorious* in January 1917, this was the standard model. The only major difference between the two marks was in their range plots. As delivered, the Mark IV plotted ranges from 2,000 to 17,000 yards, whereas the maximum range for the Mark IV* was 20,000 yards.[147] The well-illustrated 1918 *Handbook* has been used by several authors as the principal source for design details.[148] However, it was not promulgated until June 1918, and incorporates many later improvements. Fortunately, the cyclostyled handbook delivered in May 1916 with *Royal Oak*'s Mark IV* table survives in the *Excellent* Museum; its text and illustrations were in turn based on material first prepared for the Mark IV Tables.[149] These and the few other available sources reveal the main features of these automatic Dreyer tables at the time of Jutland, and the more important changes that were made after the battle.

## Bearing plots

As originally fitted, the automatic bearing plots of the Mark IV and IV* tables were similar to those already described for the Mark III (the design shown in the 1918 *Handbook* was introduced much later). However, there were now two larger deflection drums, spanning the full width of the plot. As before, one was graduated with curves of Dumaresq deflection (speed-across). The second drum was inscribed with curves of Gun Deflection, or, more exactly, the component of sight deflection that corrected for travel-across in the time-of-flight.[150] The drums and their pointers were coupled together so that, at all times, the Gun Deflection pointer indicated the correct component of sight deflection for the speed-across and range in use; three interchangeable Gun Deflection drums were provided for full and reduced charges and for sub-calibre firings.

An important change was in the source of bearings. Beginning with the *Iron Duke* class and *Tiger*, all heavy ships were provided with a squat, armoured gun control tower (GCT) protruding above the conning tower. Each ship's principal rangefinder – and, in 15-inch ships, a Director sight as well – were placed under an armoured hood revolving above the GCT.[151] In all these later ships, the Dreyer Tables received target bearings not from the rangefinder but from a special Dumaresq, the Mark VII*, of which two were installed, one on each side of the GCT (except, it seems, in *Tiger*). By 1915, each Dumaresq had been coupled to an Evershed binocular holder; thus the same sighting device was used both as a target indicator and source of bearings. These were transmitted from the Dumaresq, as relative-bearings, to a large step-by-step receiver motor in the Dreyer Table. This motor was coupled to a differential, the other side of which was connected to the motor relay controlled by the gyrocompass; thus the differential output gave the enemy compass bearing and rotated the screw positioning the pencil of the bearing plot.

Like the Argo mounting, the Mark VII* Dumaresq transmitted bearings in relatively coarse steps of ¼°.[152] Furthermore, the gyrocompass relay seems to have had its own imperfections; Midshipman Patrick Blackett of *Barham* found that:

> The chief disadvantage . . . lies in the fact that the gear actually operating the bearing plot is large and heavy – necessitating a powerful 'relay-system' from the Gyro[-receiver] to eliminate yaw . . . 'hunting' takes place, which tends to render a plot of little value.[153]

This 'relay' (we would now call it a servo-follower) was of a new design that could correct even for large initial misalignments between the motor shaft and the gyro-receiver. Elphinstone claimed that it 'has the advantage of working with extreme accuracy'.[154] However, like most contemporary relays, it depended on the action of a delicate switch to control the motor; even with careful adjustment and maintenance, the motor could, as in *Barham*, overshoot and then 'hunt' back and forth about the correct position. These fluctuations appear to have been large enough to obscure small changes in enemy compass bearings. Before Jutland, some ships may have taken up a suggestion by *Queen Elizabeth* to increase the movement of the bearing pencil for each degree change in bearing; this had been prompted by 'the small bearing rates involved by the increase of range at which actions are likely to be fought'.[155]

## Range plots

In March 1914, it was intended that the Mark IV table should plot the ranges from several rangefinders using a pneumatic device invented by Lieutenant Macnamara; Elphinstone was then working on a scheme to prevent the 'recording points' from jamming should two records be made simultaneously at the same position.[156] The whole device must have been very complex, and, in May 1914, the prototype was ordered of a simpler, keyboard-operated device designed by Commander J. Brownrigg. On 6 July, it had been decided to inform Elliotts that no order would be placed for the Macnamara plotter,[157] and, on 7 August (after favourable reports had been obtained verbally), to order nine more Brownrigg keyboards immediately.

> At present the plotting tables in H.M. Ships are provided with no means of plotting a number of rangefinders and the need for some such instrument is urgently required.[158]

Subsequently, the Brownrigg device became the standard fitting until after Jutland. It had four rows of ten keys, each key being coupled to a needle which perforated the paper from beneath; each key and needle corresponded to a step in range of 50 yards. The range-bar was notched so that the carriage for the keys could be located quickly and accurately in 1,000-yard increments; once positioned, the keys could be used to perforate the paper for ranges from 1,000 yards below the nominal position to 950 yards above it. The Brownrigg keyboard was the only means of plotting ranges on the Dreyer Tables Mark IV and IV*. It was best suited to multiple Barr & Stroud range receivers. These had a buzzer or other indicator to draw attention to each new range, which then remained on the receiver until the next 'cut';[159] nonetheless, the keyboard operator still needed to record each range as soon as possible after it had been received. Thus manual range plotting from multiple receivers had superseded the automatic plotting of ranges from a single Argo mounting on the earlier Dreyer Tables.[160]

By early 1915, the battles of the Falkland Islands and the Dogger Bank had shown that, in good visibility, firing could commence at the limits of the gun range. In August, it was decided to fit the range scales of the Mark IV table with sliding numeral strips so that, through small windows cut in the scales, they could be read either from 2,000 to 17,000 yards or from 10,000 to 25,000 yards. This required the fitting of a 'pedalling clutch' by which the clock-range pencil could be shifted by 8,000 yards without changing the gun-range. Similar modifications extended the maximum ranges of the Marks III and IV* to 24,400 yards and 28,000 yards respectively.[161]

## The Electrical Dumaresq and clocks

Other than the idea of electrical transfer of rates, Elphinstone's design for the Electrical Dumaresq and clocks for the Mark IV table owed nothing to Dreyer's erroneous proposal of December 1912. On the Dumaresq, the enemy bow pointer was replaced by a downward-extending 'contact stem'; the stem carried four metal plungers that pressed on the pattern of contacts let into the top face of a circular 'contact plate' The centre of this plate stood at or near the intersection of a line of range-rate and a line of speed-across on the dial-plate. Two 20V electric motors, one for range-rate, the other for speed-across, controlled the position of the plate. The range-rate motor also set the rate of the range clock directly. The speed-across motor was coupled to one end of a lever, while the other end was linked to the bearing clock roller. The pivot between them was positioned by a spiral cam which, through a connection to the clock-range screw, was rotated according to change of range.[162] The spiral cam was cut so that this C.B. (change-of-bearing) gear divided speed-across by range and maintained the rate of the bearing clock.

The two motors were controlled by electromagnetic switches that were energised when electric circuits were completed between the contacts on the stem and on the plate. If the stem and plate were exactly aligned, all four stem contacts lay in a circle of insulation on the plate, so the motors were switched off. But if the Dumaresq then generated a new range-rate or speed-across (or both), the stem moved. Power was then switched to at least one motor so that the plate was driven back into alignment with the stem. The plate became known as the 'poached egg . . . which insists on impaling itself on the fork'.[163] Elphinstone had devised a novel, dual-axis 'follower' which enabled the rates of both clocks to follow the indications of the Dumaresq automatically. The Electrical Dumaresq was also adjusted automatically by the gyrocompass relay for changes of own course (as in the Mark III table). Thus the Mark IV can be described as both automatic and helm-free.

The clocks of the Mark IV table remained of the conventional disc-and-roller pattern. There were substantial mechanical loads connected to both clock roller shafts: but, since the 20V motors could supply ample torque to move the rollers against friction with the disc, the assembly force could be made large enough to minimise slippage. In 1918, the standard check 'to test the automatic features of the electrical dumaresq and clock' of the Mark IV and IV* tables was to simulate two 28-knot ships on opposite courses passing each other at a minimum range of 7,000 yards; it was expected that, after a 12-minute run without any operator intervention, the range would return to its initial starting value of 13,200 yards. Although the *Handbook* does not give specific limits for acceptable errors,[164] they were evidently expected to be small whereas, since this test produced a large change of range-rate, it would have resulted in a substantial range lag if the assembly force had been insufficient.

## Jutland to the Armistice

In July 1916 an experimental typewriter was tried for identifying the ranges from each particular rangefinder . . . Supply of these to existing tables was made in 1917.

Thus the Brownrigg keyboard was replaced by the typewriter, which was the only means of plotting described in the 1918 *Handbook* for all tables. The new typewriter provided nine characters (T, C, R, •, Y, X, Q, B and A), thereby enabling 'the plotting officer to obtain an idea of the relative reliance to be placed on each . . . rangefinder'.[165] So, by 1918, even the Mark III tables had been converted from automatic plotting to manual plotting of the ranges from many rangefinders.[166]

On 24 October 1915, Frederic Dreyer transferred to *Iron Duke* as Jellicoe's Flag Captain, while both officers returned to the Admiralty at the end of 1916, Dreyer becoming DNO on 1 March 1917. While he himself was mainly preoccupied by the successful development and supply of new armour-piercing shell, he also 'set up a Fire Control Staff, which included scientists, and did valuable work'.[167] Despite his duties in the Grand Fleet, Dreyer had continued to invent and, in 1916, proposed a 'Wind Dumaresq for the Dreyer Fire Control Table':[168]

> in the first half of 1917 complete wind Dumaresqs were supplied for use with the Dreyer table, together with deflection totalisers [for] Dumaresq deflection corrected for range, deflection due to wind, uncorrected drift and spotting corrections. [169]

These additions were probably designed under Admiralty auspices; in use, the deflection totaliser was criticised as 'much too slow'.[170] The gunnery officers of the Grand Fleet were also developing their own ideas.

> In August 1917, after various experiments by individual ships, it was determined that a gun-range pencil must be provided on the range-plot. This pencil shows continuously the actual gun-range in use, and a comparison between gun-range and clock-range is valuable in keeping the range.[171]

The screws required to work these pencils are shown in the schematic diagrams for the 1918 *Handbook* but cannot be seen in the photographs, so any necessary new fittings were probably still being supplied when the handbook was promulgated on 25 June 1918.[172] This was five days after Dreyer had been succeeded as DNO by Captain Henry R. Crooke; Dreyer himself became Director of Naval Artillery and Torpedoes with responsibility for the Gunnery and Torpedo Division of the Naval Staff.[173]

In contrast to the evident agreement reached over the gun-range pencil, the Admiralty's attempts to develop an improved bearing plot were overtaken by much more radical ideas originated in the Grand Fleet:

> until the Mark V. table for 'Ramillies' . . . bearings were transmitted in ¼° steps. In the Mark V . . . these were reduced to 4-minute steps . . . This necessitated a special form of bearing transmitter which was manufactured by Messrs. Elliott. This table was erected in 'Ramillies' in July 1917. Orders were placed for bearing trans-mitters and for improved bearing plotting gear . . . for all capital ships, but owing to the introduction of the Gyro Director training gear, which embodied this improvement, but used the gun director as the bearing transmitter, this order was cancelled.

This 'GDT' gear had been devised initially by a Committee of the Grand Fleet, which, after the inconclusive action of 17 November 1917, had been established to evolve:

> an instrument, which, by a combination of the gun-director, Gyro compass, and the bearing clock of the Dreyer table, enabled the Director to be kept on for direction when the enemy was hidden, provided that he had been effectively engaged before his disappearance.
>
> . . .
>
> . . . in July 1918 a complete instrument was supplied by H.M.S. Excellent to H.M.S. Emperor of India for trial . . . Approval to place the order for 24 capital ships with Messrs. Elliott, who had prepared the designs, was given in January 1919.[174]

However, when the 1918 *Handbook* was being prepared, even the GDT prototype had not yet been completed. This explains why it described the improved bearing plot as a standard-pattern fitting on all tables. In fact, the cancellation of the new bearing plotting gear meant that, apart from the prototype supplied to *Ramillies* and, perhaps, a few early production models,[175] most Dreyer bearing plots ended the war still receiving bearings in ¼° steps.[176]

## DREYER TABLE MARK I

In February 1916, the Ordnance Council awarded Dreyer £5,000 for his contributions to fire control. The list of the 'Ships in which Dreyer's Fire Control is fitted or is being fitted', drawn up for his application, included the following:

MARK I (Simple Mechanical Table . . . )
Marlborough
Dreadnought
Bellerophon
Vanguard

Superb
St. Vincent
Collingwood
Temeraire
Neptune
Colossus
New Zealand

Australia
Erin
Inflexible.[177]

This was the first mention of such a table since the Mark I Board of 1911. Notice the gap after the first four ships. Three battlecruisers – *Invincible, Indomitable* and *Indefatigable* – did not appear here, nor under any other mark. Furthermore, the equivalent list from the 1918 *Handbook* contained only the same three 12-inch battlecruisers. *Indomitable* was still missing.[178]

A handbook for the Mark I was published in 1916,[179] but, since a copy has not been found, it is necessary to rely mainly on the 1918 *Handbook*. The table was built around the Dumaresq Mark VI*, for which the first production order was placed on 11 October 1914. Like ordinary Dumaresqs, the Mark VI* had a fixed fore-and-aft bar and a rotating dial. But it retained a slotted dial-plate and pointer, so range-rate could still be transferred (through a flexible shaft) to the clock by following the bow of the Dumaresq's enemy bar.[180] The range-plot was similar to the other Dreyer tables, except that the paper was hand-driven. However, it extended across the full width of the Mark I and, from the start, was capable of plotting up to 20,000 yards (later extended to 28,000 yards) – just like the Mark IV* table, first supplied in the spring of 1915. These dates suggest that deliveries of the Mark I tables began some time in 1915. Their manufacture would also have maintained the production tempo at Elliott Brothers in the last nine months of 1915, when only two Mark IV* tables were required for commissioning heavy ships (*Barham* and *Canada*). Thus the list from February 1916 may represent the planned installation schedule for Mark I tables, with only the first four ships then having been fitted.[181] There is no definite information on the extent of progress by the time of Jutland. Only *Bellerophon* explicitly mentioned a Dreyer Table in one of her reports, while, in the TSs of *New Zealand* and *Indomitable*, ranges were plotted with coloured pencils, which suggests they were using manual plotting boards.[182] Thus, it is almost certain that, at the Falkland Islands and the Dogger Bank, none of the 12-inch battlecruisers present had Dreyer Tables. It is also quite possible that, at Jutland, all the ships of both the Second and Third Battle Cruiser Squadrons had to rely on the pre-war system based on the Dumaresq Mark VI, Vickers clock and manual plotting. And, if the 1918 *Handbook* is correct, *Indomitable* served throughout the war without a Dreyer Table of any description.

At first, the Mark I range-plot probably had a Brownrigg keyboard. Range was kept by a Vickers clock on the same lines as proposed by Dreyer for the Mark I Board. The 1918 *Handbook* shows a standard-pattern bearing plot (of the type which was cancelled) and a deflection totaliser squeezed in next to the Dumaresq.[183] There could never have been space for the old style of bearing plot and it is unlikely that the Mark I tables were given any priority in the distribution of the few completed new-style plotters. Without a bearing plot, the deflection totaliser would have been much less useful. Probably, until the war's end, the majority of Mark I tables dealt only with range.

The Mark I table was followed by the short-lived Mark I*, which was very similar apart from the addition of a coupling between the Dumaresq Mark VI* and a gyrocompass relay. This in turn led to the Mark III*, which became the standard table for use in cruisers. It replaced the Vickers clock with an electric clock similar to that in the Turret Tables. As described in the 1918 *Handbook*, it was originally designed to use the cancelled bearing plot, but the design was subsequently altered to incorporate the GDT gear. This in turn required a bearing clock, which was set for rate by hand using values read off a graduated drum. Thus, with its gyrocompass connection to the Dumaresq, range and bearing plots and hand-set rates on the bearing clock, the Mark III* in its final form was, functionally, a direct descendent of the Mark III.[184]

## CONSTRUCTION

In comparison with the enclosed and largely maintenance-free designs of the Argo Company, the mechanical construction of the Dreyer Tables was much less sophisticated. Gear wheels were held on their shafts by tapered pins which were hand-made, non-interchangeable and could be shaken out by prolonged firing.[185] Chain drives and flexible shafts were liable to wear, which caused backlash. Although not usually serious,[186] the effects were magnified in the change-of-bearing gear at low ranges, to the extent that accurate results could not be obtained below 5,000 yards. Regular lubrication, especially of the parts driven by the variable-speed drives, was essential although, because of the open construction, the oil attracted dust, so frequent cleaning was also a necessity. In the clock mechanisms, the cast-iron clock discs had to be kept completely free of oil.[187] Also, it was vital to move the hardened steel rollers only when the discs were rotating, otherwise the rollers developed flats and had to be replaced. The rough surface of the cast iron appears to have been well chosen to maximise friction: but it may have been more liable than a hardened steel disc to develop a recess at its centre.

> In this event, the recess should be removed by turning up the disc in a lathe.[188]

Electric relays might stick, but the Mark IV and IV* tables had switches to permit hand-setting of rates.[189] In 1917, an American assessment of British fire control methods reported:

In considering the system used in the British Service for plotting . . .
we can say that it impresses us as very complete though somewhat
cumbersome . . . It is believed that as a simple matter of design, the
whole system is not well worked out. The parts are clumsy, and large
in parts where there is absolutely no necessity for them to be. The
marking pencils do not mark until the ships' officers take the
holders out themselves and build others on board ship.[190]

On the other hand, as Dreyer and Usborne emphasised in 1913:

the whole apparatus is so simple that it can easily be repaired . . .
with the resources of the ship.[191]

Further, during the war, it was also possible for ships' gunnery officers to
modify their tables, either to correct design flaws, or in the course of
developing new techniques, for example in concentration firing and gyro
director training.[192] It is very difficult to imagine how any changes could have
been made in the Fleet to the Argo instruments.

The Dreyer Tables certainly needed frequent maintenance and well-
trained operators, both of which the Royal Navy could normally be expected
to provide. Their mechanisms may also appear somewhat crude, especially
to modern eyes, though that is neither here nor there. Provided that they
were kept in working order and operated correctly, they functioned as their
designers intended. And, most importantly, any errors in their predictions
were insignificant in comparison with the inaccuracies of the data with which
they had to work.

## Notes

1 John Brooks, 'Dreyer, Sir Frederic Charles (1878–1956)', in *Oxford DNB*.
Examination certificates in DRYR 1/2. Dreyer, *Sea Heritage* [B] pp. 32, 45, 47–8,
52–3 and 57.

2 'Calibration of Guns. Report of Committee, &c', in ADM 1/7835. *IDNS*, p. 122.

3 Pollen to Dreyer 31 October and Dreyer to Pollen 15 December 1906 in T.173/
91 Part VII.

4 *IDNS*, p. 122.

5 *Sea Heritage* [1] p. 55.

6 Dreyer, 'Change of Range', 10 December 1906 in DRYR 2/1 and T.173/91 Part
III.

7 The term was first used in 'Remarks on Local Turret Control by Commander
F.C. Dreyer R.N. . . .', 5 September 1910, in 'Local Control of Turret Guns.
Special Firing carried out by HMS "Vanguard" . . .', in ADM 1/8147.

8 Commanders F. C. Dreyer and C. V. Usborne, *Pollen Aim Corrector System Part
I. Technical History and Technical Comparison with Commander F.C. Dreyer's
Fire Control System*, Gunnery Branch 1913, p. 5 in P. 1024, AL.

9 'It was a crude instrument, I confess . . . it was not actually a graph'. Dreyer
before RCAI, T.173/547 Part 16, p. 13.

10 Captain Tower before RCAI, T.173/547 Part 11, p. 7.
11 *IDNS*, p. 122.
12 Jellicoe to Dreyer, 11 December 1906 in DRYR 3/2.
13 Captain R. H. Bacon, *Report on Experimental Cruise*, 16 March 1907, p. 5, ADM 116/1059.
14 *DNOfS*, July 1907, pp. 27 and 49, AL. The 'Aim Corrector System' is mentioned in the section headed 'Rangefinders'. *Sea Heritage*, pp. 56–7.
15 *IDNS*, pp. 121 and 123. Pollen and Harding before RCAI, T.173/547 Part 14, p. 82 and Part 3, p. 34. Harding remained in the DNO's department until 11 December 1908: service record, ADM 196/62, p. 355.
16 *DNOfS*, July 1907, pp. 20, 22 and 23. For the 'Dreyer sights', see Admiralty, *The Gunnery Pocket Book 1932* (reprinted 1938), pp. 60–1.
17 F. C. and J. T. Dreyer, 'Position Finder for Determining Rate of Change of Range' with Dreyer to DNO, 2 July 1907 in T.173/91 Part III.
18 For technical analysis of the Dreyer Tables, see 'FCBD', Appendix XVIII.
19 *DNOfS*, July 1907, p. 26
20 McConnell, *Instrument Makers to the World* [B] pp. 64 and 78.
21 *Technical Comparison*, 1913 [8] p. 5 and Tower before RCAI, T.173/547 Part 11, pp. 7–8.
22 *Sea Heritage*, pp. 58–9 and Henley before RCAI, T.173/547 Part 3, p. 66.
23 *IDNS*, pp. 121–4. Pollen before RCAI, T.173/547 Part 14, p. 84.
24 Pollen to Dreyer, 4 January 1908, in DRYR 2/1 and T.173/91 Part III.
25 *Shorter Oxford Dictionary*.
26 Admiral of the Fleet Sir A. K. Wilson, 'Rate of Change of Range Experiments' in Admiralty, Gunnery Branch, *Fire Control*, 1908, p. 28, in ADM 1/8010 and T.173/91 Part I.
27 Dreyer before RCAI, T.173/547 Part 16, p. 22.
28 Dreyer to Vice Admiral Sir Frederick Field, 12 November 1923 in DRYR 2/1. See also 'Some Comparisons between the Argo Clock and the Fire Control Table in "Monarch"' n.d. but late 1912, T.173/91 Part VII and *Technical Comparison*, 1913, p. 6.
29 Wilson, 'Rate Experiments' [26] pp. 26–7.
30 Dreyer before RCAI, T.173/547 Part 16, p. 22.
31 *Cf. IDNS*, p. 130 for time-and-range plotting on 15 January.
32 Wilson, 'Rate Experiments', pp. 26 and 46 and Dreyer, 'Hints on Battle Firing', p. 52, in *Fire Control*, 1908 [26]. The actual time-and-range plots made in *Vengeance* on 17 January are in ADM 1/8010.
33 Dreyer, 'Hints' [32] pp. 52–3
34 For example, see *Technical Comparison*, 1913, p. 10.
35 Dreyer, 'Hints', pp. 50 and 53–4. Another means of keeping the Dumaresq adjusted was a cross-cut of range-rate and virtual-course (speed not required). Dreyer later claimed that he had tried this in *Vengeance*: 'Some Comparisons . . .', 1912 [28] and *Technical Comparison*, 1913, p. 6.
36 Dreyer before RCAI, T.173/547 Part 17, p. 3.
37 John to Fred. Dreyer, 17 January 1908 with attached figures in T.173/91 Part III.
38 Elliott Sales Manager to Dreyer, 7 February 1908 with drawing E.S. 1165, 6 February 1908 in T.173/91 Part III.
39 *IDNS*, p. 121.
40 *The Time and Range System, Report of J. Swinburne, F.R.S.*, 5 March 1913, pp. 3 and 8, AL (copies of this report and related correspondence provided by Professor Sumida and gratefully acknowledged). The patents were 16,463 of 4 August and 16,912 of 11 August 1908, respectively.

41 'Fire Control, An Essay by Captain C. Hughes Onslow, RN', Royal Naval War College, n.d. but 1909, Section III, PLLN 1/5 and in HTN/116B, NMM. See also 'Notes re Admiralty Letter . . .' 9 February 1916, p. 1 accompanying G. K. B. Elphinstone to Director of Navy Contracts, 14 February 1916 in 'Fire Control Apparatus, Various Patents', ADM 1/8464/181 and Dreyer to RCAI, T.173/547 Part 16, pp. 43–5.

42 'Remarks by Commander F.C. Dreyer R.N. on the question of how best to obtain and maintain the gun range in action', 22 July 1910 in T.173/91 Part III and ADM 1/8147.

43 Fisher to Corbett, 10 March 1908 in *IDNS*, p. 135.

44 Dreyer to Field, 1923 [28].

45 *IDNS*, p. 149.

46 Pollen before RCAI, T.173/547 Part 14, p. 65.

47 *PP, Reflections on an Error of the Day*, September 1908, pp. 180 and 386–7.

48 Dreyer to Hughes-Onslow, 19 October 1908, typed transcript of what was probably a handwritten letter, in T.173/91 Part VII.

49 *IDNS*, pp. 151 and 178. Hughes-Onslow [41] Appendix A. The Pollen Papers also contain the confidential *Handbook for Fire Control Instruments 1906*.

50 *PP, Reflections* (1908) [47] p. 190. Dreyer to Hughes-Onslow, 1908 [48].

51 T.173/547 Part 16, p. 43 and Part 17, p. 71.

52 See the Appendix (p. 304, this volume).

53 Dreyer before RCAI, T.173/547 Part 17, pp. 18–19.

54 Unlike the disc-and-roller, the cone-and-roller was unsuited to rates that could be positive or negative.

55 Admiralty, Gunnery Branch, *Information regarding Fire Control, Range Finding and Plotting*, 1909 in Ja 010, AL.

56 Dreyer to Field, 1923.

57 Extract from Dreyer's report read to RCAI: T.173/547 Part 17, p. 60.

58 *Technical Comparison*, 1913, p. 10. Dreyer before RCAI, T.173/547 Part 17, p. 45.

59 Dreyer and Pollen before RCAI, T.173/547 Part 17, pp. 61–4 and 108–10. Harold Isherwood, 'On the Relationship of "Change of Range" to "Time"', in *Reflections on an Error of the Day* in HTN/116A (not in *PP*).

60 Swinburne, 1913 [40] pp. 3–4 and 8. Elphinstone to Director of Navy Contracts, 18 March 1914, in 'Fire Control Patents' [41] and 'Notes', 1916 [41].

61 Admiralty, Gunnery Branch, *Manual of Gunnery for His Majesty's Fleet 1920*, November 1920, p. 27, AL.

62 *DNOfS*, November 1909, p. 41.

63 Frederic Dreyer, 'Summary', n.d. but 1925, p. 11 in DRYR 2/1.

64 The range bar, fixed at right angles to the driving screw, was recalibrated in degrees.

65 Dreyer, 'Remarks', 1910 [42]. The frequent underlining is typical of Dreyer's writings.

66 Henley to Dreyer, 13 August 1910 in DRYR 2/1.

67 *IDNS*, p. 218.

68 DNO's Minute 13 August 1910; also Dreyer to Captain Eustace, *Vanguard*, 12 October 1910 in 'Invention of Rangefinding System', in ADM 1/8131.

69 Dreyer, 'Local Control', 1910 [7].

70 'Description' accompanying Dreyer to Eustace, 1910 [68].

71 Dreyer, 'Local Control', 1910.

72 Admiral Sir Desmond Dreyer confirmed that the 'Dreyer Table . . . was developed by my father with considerable help from his brother . . . later Major-

General J. T. Dreyer': 'Early Development in Naval Fire Control', *The Naval Review*, July 1986, p. 238.

73 Admiral W. H. May to the Secretary of the Admiralty, 1 October 1910, in 'Local Control of Turret Guns' [7].

74 Patent 22,140/1910, Provisional Specification 23 September 1910, Complete Specification 12 April 1911, in DRYR 2/1 and RCAI, T.173/91 Part III.

75 *Sea Heritage*, pp. 62–3. Jellicoe to Dreyer, 10 November 1910 in DRYR 3/1 and 3/2.

76 Quoted by Dreyer before RCAI, T.173/547 Part 17, p. 105.

77 Patent 22,140/1910, Complete Specification [74] pp. 6–7, 10 and diagram. The quoted passage does not appear in the Provisional Specification.

78 'Invention for a device for applying the Dumaresq to the Range Clock', in ADM 1/8131.

79 Fanning, *Steady As She Goes* [B] p. 177.

80 Dreyer to DNO, 2 December 1910 in T.173/91 Part III.

81 Dreyer before RCAI, T.173/547 Part 17, pp. 82 and 86.

82 Henley to Dreyer, 21 February 1911 in DRYR 2/1.

83 *DNOfS*, May 1912, p. 15. *ART 1912*, p. 75.

84 Dreyer to Elphinstone, 1 July 1911, Elphinstone to Dreyer, 3 and 4 July and Henley to Dreyer, 10 July 1911 in T.173/91 Part III. Dreyer, 'Summary', 1925 [63].

85 'Extract from Letter dated 19/7/11 from Com. Dreyer' in T.173/91 Part III. Dreyer before RCAI, T.173/547 Part 16, p. 54.

86 Henley to Dreyer, 24 July 1911 in T.173/91 Part III.

87 *Prince of Wales* was seventh out of nine ships in the Battle Practice of the Atlantic Fleet and Fifth Cruiser Squadron: Admiralty, Gunnery Branch, *Results of Battle Practice in His Majesty's Fleet 1911*, AL.

88 Hopwood to VAC Atlantic Fleet, 20 November 1911 and VAC Atlantic Fleet to the Secretary, Admiralty, 25 November 1911 in T. 173/91 Part III.

89 *Handbook of Captain F.C. Dreyer's Fire Control Tables 1918*, Plate 45, AL. Reproduced in William Schleihauf, 'The Dumaresq and the Dreyer', *Warship International*, 38, 1–3 (2001), p. 16.

90 'The parts to complete the Dumaresq to Mark VI' were sent from Elliotts before the end of October: Elphinstone to Dreyer, 30 October 1911, T.173/91 Part III.

91 Hopwood to VAC Atlantic, 1911 [88].

92 Elphinstone had been a director of Theiler and Co., telegraph instrument makers, before the firm combined with Elliott Brothers: H. R. Bristow, 'Elliott, Instrument Makers of London . . .', *Bulletin of the Scientific Instrument Society*, 36 (1993) p. 11. John Bradley, 'Elphinstone, Sir (George) Keith (Buller) (1865–1941)', in *Oxford DNB* (draft gratefully acknowledged).

93 Elphinstone to Dreyer, 11 October 1911 in T.173/91 Part III.

94 Elphinstone to Dof C, 1916 [41].

95 A drawing of the latter was attached to Dreyer's letter.

96 Dreyer to Jellicoe, 12 October 1911 with 'Description of the Apparatus' in T.173/91 Part III.

97 Elphinstone to Dreyer, 11 and 30 October 1911 in T.173/91 Part III.

98 Elliott Bros. 'Seven Part Recorder' revised 28 October 1911 (with sketch): Jellicoe to Admiralty Secretary, 25 November 1911 and DNO's Minute, 7 December 1911, all in T.173/91 Part III.

99 Dreyer, 'Summary', 1925, p. 13. 'Details of Clocks and rate-plotters on order' attached to F. W. Black, 'ARGO COMPANY, Present Situation' n.d. but probably December 1912 in Mountbatten Papers, MB1/T22/174, University of Southampton.

100 *IDNS*, pp. 220–1: *Technical Comparison*, 1913, pp. 12 and 39.

101 'Ships in which Dreyer's Fire control is fitted or is being fitted' attached to 'Recommendations of the Admiralty Members of the Ordnance Committee at a Meeting 10.2.16 concerning Dreyer's award', DRYR 2/1. Here, the five ships which received the new table are listed under the heading 'Mark II', but they are headed by *Hercules*, marked by an asterisk. By 1918, *Hercules* had a Mark I table: *Handbook 1918* [89] p. 3.

102 Dreyer, 'Summary', 1925, p. 13. *Technical Comparison*, 1913, pp. 11, 12 and 55.

103 Elphinstone to DofC, 1914 [60].

104 Dreyer to DNO, 19 December 1912 in T.173/91 Part III. *Sea Heritage*, p. 72. Dreyer to Jellicoe, 14 June 1913 in DRYR 4/3.

105 *Navy Lists*. Usborne's service record, ADM 196/45 p. 118

106 *Technical Comparison*, 1913, pp. 39, 41–2, 46, 50 and Figures V/1, 3, 6 and 7. *Handbook 1918*, pp. 17, 49 and Plate 23.

107 All five ships with Dreyer Tables Mark III were early recipients of Anschütz gyrocompasses: Fanning [79] p. 178.

108 *Technical Comparison*, 1913, pp. 42–4, 46–7 and Figure V/9.

109 *Pollen Aim Corrector System: General Grounds of Admiralty Policy and Historical Record of Business Negotiation*, February 1913, p. 3, P. 1024, AL.

110 *Technical Comparison*, 1913, Figure V/9. Hugh Clausen, 'Notes on Step by Step Transmission System' (Evershed and Vignolles Ltd 1962) p. 11, CLSN 1/7.

111 *Manual of Gunnery 1915*, p. 8. *Technical Comparison*, 1913, pp. 41–2, 45–6, 49 and Figure V/1, 3, 5, 6 and 7.

112 15 compared with 36 inches: *ibid.* p. 48.

113 *Ibid.* pp. 42, 44–5, 49–50 and Figures V/1, 3, 7 and 8. *Handbook 1918*, p. 18, Plates 6 and 23. Admiralty, Technical History Section, *The Technical History and Index*, 'Fire Control in H.M. Ships', December 1919, p. 27, AL. For additional technical details of the Mark III and later Dreyer Tables, see Schleihauf [89].

114 The {} brackets show where descriptions have been substituted for reference letters. The [ ] brackets, as usual, indicate other interpolations.

115 *Technical Comparison*, 1913, pp. 42–5.

116 *Home Fleet General Orders*. '14. Fire Control Organisation', 5 November 1913 (p. 3) with Enclosure No. II, 'Instructions defining the latitude allowed to the transmitting station officer . . .' in DRAX 1/9. Any correction to deflection or range-rate ordered as a result of spotting was, presumably, applied to the Dumaresq of the Dreyer Table as a change in the cross-cut.

117 *Technical Comparison*, 1913, pp. 41 and 46–7. He even suggested that, by allowing the rate to lag somewhat, the operator could correct for 'slip': 'Some Comparisons . . .' 1912.

118 'FCBD', pp. 189–90 and Appendix III.

119 'FCBD', Appendix XXII shows that the same simple approximate relationship between error-rate and rate step size still applies when own ship alters course, though in extreme conditions the approximation is less exact.

120 If, at the same time, own ship was altering course in the more unfavourable direction, steps of 4 knots may have been used for a time: 'FCBD', Appendix XVIII-11. At 8,000 yards, a speed-across of 2 knots was equivalent to 0.5°/min.; in a two-minute turn, a bearing-error of about 1° could accumulate.

121 *Technical Comparison*, 1913, p. 61 and Figures 11 and 12. The test was repeated for two 30-knot ships. Until just before the passing point, the table kept the range as accurately as before, but the range error then increased to 140 yards in only one minute. However, the bearing rate was then 16.6°/min. which exceeded the maximum rate of the bearing clock.

122 The range-rate error (in yds/min.) is 0.6 times the product of bearing error (degrees) and speed-across (knots): 'FCBD', Appendix XVIII-9.

123 *Handbook 1918*, p. 49.

124 'Some Comparisons . . .' 1912.

125 *Technical Comparison*, 1913, pp. 11–12: *Record of Business*, 1913 [109] p. 15.

126 *Handbook 1918*, p. 15. In 'Ships . . . fitted', 1916 [101], the tables with Argo clocks are called Mark III*. By 1918, this number had been adopted for a more modern table.

127 Elphinstone, 'Notes' 1916.

128 Parkes, *British Battleships* [B] pp. 521, 528 and 538. 'Practices of Ships fitted with Director firing', 15 May 1914 in 'IQ/DNO III, 1914'. *Sea Heritage*, pp. 74–5.

129 C.-in-C. Home Fleet G.0360/14, 'Practices of Ships fitted with Director Firing', 15 May 1914 and '"Colossus" Report on Rangefinders', 20 May 1914, in 'IQ/DNO III, 1914'.

130 *Home Fleet*, 'Control Organisation', 1913 [116] p. 3 and Enclosure No. I, 'Remarks on Rangefinder Control'.

131 Admiralty, Gunnery Branch, *Manual of Gunnery (Vol. III) for His Majesty's Fleet, 1915*, pp. 17–18, AL.

132 However, quadrupling the number of rangefinders only halved the uncertainty in the range: P. G. Pugh, 'Dreadnought fire control', November 1993 (unpublished paper, copy courtesy of the author) p. 2.

133 Addendum (February 1913) in *Technical Comparison*, 1913, pp. 47–8.

134 *Sea Heritage*, pp. 72–5. Dreyer to Jellicoe, 14 June 1913 in DRYR 4/3.

135 *Orion* does not appear in 'Ships . . . fitted', 1916, which suggests that it still relied on the Argo rate-plotter. The wording of the March 1918 report by the Phillpotts committee seems to imply that the Argo plotter was still in the ship, but the *Handbook* of June 1918 lists *Orion* as having a Dreyer Table Mark II.

136 Dreyer to DNO, 19 December 1912 in T.173/91 Part III.

137 The proposed partial correction would drive the roller from the speed-across receiver and the bearing-rate commutator from the cone: 'FCBD', Appendix XVIII-14.

138 *Technical Comparison*, 1913, pp. 47–8.

139 DNO's Minute 'Dreyer Fire Control Apparatus', 6 July 1914 in 'IQ/DNO III, 1914', p. 617.

140 *Handbook 1918*, p. 72 and Plate 31.

141 *Technical Comparison*, 1913, p. 47. The 'Dreyer Corrector' was still used in 1930: see 'Pamphlet on the Dreyer Tables Mark III*, 1930' (p. 3 and Plate 1) and 'Pamphlet on the Dreyer Tables Mark IV*, 1930' (p. 7 and Plate 2) in 'Guard Book for Pamphlets on Dreyer Tables', AL.

142 DNO and ITP, 'Local Control in Turrets', 24 May 1912 and Secretary of the Admiralty to C.-in-C. Home Fleets etc. 7 August 1912 in 'IQ/DNO I, 1912', pp. 248–55. See also DNO's minutes of 30 July and 3 August 1914 in 'IQ/DNO III, 1914'. 'Captain F.C. Dreyer's Fire Control System for Local Control', 1913 in P. 1024, AL. For details of the production turret tables, see Schleihauf, pp. 176–83.

143 *Technical Comparison*, 1913, p. 47 (1912 Addendum). DofC to Elphinstone, 10 March and Elphinstone to DofC, 14 March 1914, sheet 3 in 'Fire Control Patents'.

144 'Dreyer's Fire Control Apparatus', 6 July and '"Iron Duke" Gunnery and Torpedo Exercise Programme' 11 July 1914 in 'IQ/DNO III, 1914', pp. 617 and 587.

145 Parkes [128] pp. 545, 551 and 577 for completion dates. 'Ships . . . fitted', 1916. *Handbook 1918*, p. 3.

146 'Report on *Warspite*'s Gun Trials', 15 April 1915 in Ships' Cover 294A/58a, *Queen Elizabeth* class, NMM.
147 *Handbook 1918*, pp. 3 and 22 (the range scale was 400 yards per inch and the speed of paper 2 inches per minute). *Technical History*, 1919 [113] p. 27. 'Ships . . . fitted', 1916.
148 *IDNS*, pp. 218–20 and Plates 7 and 8. Padfield, *Guns at Sea* [B] pp. 224–7 and 231. Hartcup, *War of Invention* [B] pp. 12–13. Schleihauf, *passim*.
149 Elliott Brothers, London, 'Captain F. C. Dreyer's Fire Control Apparatus Mark IV*. As fitted in HMS Royal Oak', May 1916, *Excellent* Historical Library. Many of the figures are captioned 'Captain Dreyer's System Mark IV. HM Ships Iron Duke & Class and Tiger' and are dated from August to December 1914.
150 *Ibid.* pp. 14–15, 44–9 and Figures XII and XIII.
151 Brooks, 'Mast and Funnel Question' [B] pp. 50–6.
152 '*Warspite*'s Gun Trials' [146]. Elphinstone, 'Dumaresq Instruments Designs & Patents. Notes as to History', 31 January 1916 in 'Fire Control Patents'. Dreyer (who was Captain of *Iron Duke*) described the binoculars to the RCAI: T.173/547 Part 17, p. 31. 'Dreyer's Apparatus Mark IV*' 1916 [149] pp. 44–6, 50A–51A and Figures XIII and XIX dated December 1914. *Tiger* at Jutland, 'not having the Mark VII [*sic*] Dumaresq', could not make bearing plots of any value: Gunnery Report, 30 October 1916 in 'Jutland Despatches', ADM 116/1487. For the Dumaresq in *Valiant*'s GCT, see Peter Liddle, *The Sailor's War 1914–1918* (Poole: Blandford Press, 1985) p. 108.
153 'Rate of Change of Bearing Instrument' with P. M. S. Blackett (transcribed by Dr N. Blackett) 'Naval Diary 1914–1918'. *Barham* had a Mark IV* table. John Brooks, 'The Midshipman and the Secret Gadget', in Peter Hore (ed.) *Patrick Blackett; Sailor, Scientist and Socialist* (London: Frank Cass, 2003) pp. 86–90.
154 Elphinstone, 'Notes', 1916, p. 7. 'Dreyer's Apparatus Mark IV*', 1916, pp. 39–40 and Figure IX. *Handbook 1918*, p. 64 and Plate 28.
155 *Technical History*, 1919, p. 27.
156 Elphinstone to DofC, 1914, sheet 6.
157 'Dreyer Fire Control Apparatus', 6 July 1914 in 'IQ/DNO III, 1914', p. 617.
158 'Tender for Brownrigg Plotters', 7 August 1914 in 'IQ/DNO III, 1914', p. 433. Four of the nine must have been for the remaining Mark IV tables. The other five were perhaps for the first five Mark IV*s rather than for only some of the existing Mark II and Mark III tables (five of each).
159 The receivers were Mark II* in 13.5-inch, Mark III in 15-inch ships: Admiralty, Gunnery Branch, *Handbook for Fire Control Instruments, 1914*, pp. 24–5 and Plates 68 and 69, ADM 186/191. *ART 1914*, p. 74 and *1915*, p. 228. Admiralty, Gunnery Branch, *Handbook of Range-Finders and Mountings 1921*, pp. 105–7 and Plates 57 and 57A, ADM 186/253; in later Mark III installations, the shutter was replaced with a lamp illuminating the word 'cut' at the receivers.
160 Since the Brownrigg keyboard perforated the range plot from beneath, it could, in theory, have been fitted to the older plotters, but there is no evidence for this.
161 *Handbook 1918*, pp. 17 and 22. No source mentions a similar modification to the Mark II tables.
162 'Dreyer's Apparatus Mark IV*', 1916, pp. 25–8 and 36 and Figures IV and VII. *Handbook 1918*, pp. 51–5, 61 and 87 and Plates 22 and 24–7. Schleihauf, pp. 26 and 198. John Brooks, 'The Admiralty Fire Control Tables', in Antony Preston (ed.) *Warship 2002–2003* (London: Conway Maritime Press, 2003) p. 70.
163 Dreyer before RCAI, T.173/547 Part 16, p. 84. See also Tower before RCAI, T.173/547 Part 12, p. 103.

164 *Handbook 1918*, p. 87. Schleihauf, pp. 231–3 has drawn attention to some discrepancies in this test; for example, for a passing range of exactly 7,000 yards, the starting and finishing ranges should have been 13,335 yards. These were the result of using 2,000 rather than 2,026.7 yards per mile in converting knots into yds/min. and may give some indication of the expected errors i.e. of the order of 100 yards in range, 10 seconds in time or (as also given by Schleihauf) 20 minutes in bearing.

165 *Technical History*, 1919, p. 27. *Handbook 1918*, p. 29 and Plate 12. Schleihauf, p. 22.

166 *Pace IDNS*, pp. 218–19, the typewriter was a late development; the Original Table had plotted automatically.

167 *Sea Heritage*, pp. 96 and 234–5. Chatfield, *Navy and Defence* [B] p. 157.

168 Undated list (but after 12 December 1923) of 'Rear Admiral Dreyer's Inventions' in DRYR 2/1; see also the *Handbook of the Dreyer Tactical Appliances 1915* in DRYR 1/3.

169 *Technical History*, 1919, p. 27. The Wind Dumaresq, when set with own speed and course and true wind and direction, indicated the components of 'wind-you-feel' along and across the line-of-sight.

170 'Third Interim Report' in Admiralty, Gunnery Branch, *Reports of the Grand Fleet Dreyer Table Committee 1918–1919*, 1919, p. 10, ADM 186/241.

171 *Technical History*, 1919, p. 27.

172 *Handbook 1918*, p. 2; compare Plates 2 and 3 (Mark I) and 8 and 9 (Mark IV/IV*).

173 *Navy Lists. Sea Heritage*, p. 236. O. Murray, memorandum 27 June 1918 in 'Re-organisation of Naval Staff Division 1917–1921', ADM 116/1803.

174 *Technical History*, 1919, pp. 28–9.

175 Sufficient units were available for the photographs in the 1918 *Handbook*.

176 After the war, GDT gear was fitted to all Mark IV and Mark IV* tables and to the table in *Ramillies*; all were then designated Mark IV*. Mark V was reserved for the table in *Hood*, which was more elaborate. Schleihauf, pp. 188–9, 200 and 221.

177 With 'Extract from Recommendations of the Admiralty Members of the Ordnance Council at a Meeting 10.2.16 concerning Dreyer's award' in DRYR 2/1. See also Dreyer to Field, 1923.

178 *Handbook 1918*, p. 3.

179 *Technical History*, 1919, p. 28.

180 Elphinstone, 'Dumaresq History', 1916 [152] p. 11; this does not mention the Mark I table. *Handbook 1918*, pp. 13 and 46 and Plates 3, 21 and 22.

181 As would be expected, *Marlborough*, the only 13.5-inch ship without a fire control table, is at the head of the list. However, there is no apparent reason for the remaining order.

182 Captain, *Bellerophon*, 10 October 1916 in *OD*, p. 385. Nigel Steel and Peter Hart, *Jutland 1916. Death in the Grey Wastes* (London: Cassell, 2003) pp. 75 and 213.

183 *Handbook 1918*, pp. 13 and 29 and Plates 3, 21–2 and 39.

184 For the Mark III* in its original and final forms, see Schleihauf, pp. 174–5 and 193–7. Bearings, as the *difference* between observed and predicted (clock) values, were plotted by the GDT gear.

185 *Handbook 1918*, p. 10. 311: 'Remarks on the Action of 17th November 1917', in *Grand Fleet Gunnery and Torpedo Orders*, p. 196, ADM 137/293.

186 Each measurable backlash was expected not to exceed 25 yards: Schleihauf, p. 228 for the Mark V table.

187 'Pamphlet on Mark IV* 1930' [141] pp. 47, 50–2 and 55.

188 *Ibid.* p. 14. The clock discs rotated at fifteen revolutions per minute.
189 'Dreyer's Apparatus Mark IV*', May 1916, Additions to Book.
190 USN Office of Naval Intelligence, *British Fire Control System – Plotting Methods*, 10 August 1917, pp. 8–9 (NARA: RG38-U-2-e, Register 9124) quoted in Schleihauf, pp. 221 and 223.
191 *Technical Comparison*, 1913, p. 56.
192 'Third Interim Report', *Dreyer Table Committee* [170] pp. 5–11.

# 6

# INFLUENCES AND CHOICES

Having followed separately the developments of Pollen's A.C. system and the Dreyer Tables, we can now address two crucial questions. First, what were the influences that shaped the rival systems? In particular, what debts in principles and technique did each owe to the other and, indeed, to the older manually worked system that had preceded them into service? Second, what were the critical choices in fire control made by the Admiralty: and what considerations determined, and perhaps justified, those choices?

Even Pollen's first proposals from 1901 contained features already anticipated by service developments. Two-observer rangefinders had been tried unsuccessfully afloat in *Arethusa*. Enemy courses were plotted by the Watkin Position Finders in service with the coastal artillery.[1] The suggestion of plotting own as well as target course was novel, as was the vague mention of gyroscopic correction for yaw (though the latter was not seriously considered again until the *Jupiter* trials). At first, Pollen believed that the primary purpose of his two-observer rangefinder and plotter would be as a tactical aid; however, his two papers from the latter half of 1904 (especially 'Fire Control and Long Range Firing') show that, by then, he was aiming for a complete fire control system. A new element was a clock; in July 1904, it was apparently only for ranges, an idea partly anticipated by Percy Scott's proposal of late 1903 for an integrating range clock. However, by December, it had become a 'change of range and bearing machine'.

After the *Jupiter* trials of early 1906, Pollen was fortunately able to change tack and, thanks to the recent appearance of the Barr & Stroud 9-foot rangefinder, to propose a gyroscopically stabilised mounting transmitting ranges and yaw free bearings to an automatic straight course plotting table. These ideas were original, as the Admiralty acknowledged during the contract negotiations in 1906. Pollen also proposed transmitting elevation and deflection directly from the (non-existent) clock to the gun sights, but this was a year later than the trials of the Vyvyan-Newitt sight in the Channel Fleet, which Pollen probably heard about when he was being advised by Beresford's gunnery officers. There is no evidence that Argo ever constructed its own automatic sights and, ultimately, the Argo Clock Mark IV transmitted ranges to Vickers Follow-the-Pointer sights (either directly or through the range plotter of the Dreyer Table Mark II).

As delivered to *Natal* in 1909, the newly redesigned plotter was still automatic only when making a straight-course plot. Captain Ogilvy urged that it be converted into a helm-free, true-course plotter. But the attempt failed, to the extent that, subsequently, Pollen abandoned further attempts at a true-course plotter for about eighteen months. Instead, though well after Dreyer's patent application, Pollen produced his own version of a dual-rate plotter, which he acknowledged was a satisfactory alternative to a straight-course plotter.

The final versions of the Argo rangefinder mounting and the clock (Mark V), and the true-course plotter (Mark IV), all depended on Anschütz gyrocompass receivers: while the clock and plotter also relied on the Forbes speed log. Thus, eventually, the whole Argo system was helm-free, but only because it could depend on technology from other suppliers to the Royal Navy.

After discarding the Argo Clock Mark I, which worked by modelling virtual-course, Isherwood began again on known principles. The Mark II of 1911 used a dumaresq-type linkage to obtain a range-rate; and it set the range-rate on a variable-speed drive, which then generated the change-of-range. These were the same principles embodied in the well-established combination of Scott/Vickers clock and Dumaresq. However, unlike the clockwork-driven Vickers clock, the new Argo clock, like its predecessor, was powered by an electric motor. And, since the rate of Isherwood's new slipless drive could be altered with minimal force, the Argo version of the dumaresq linkage could set the rate of the range clock directly and continuously. The idea of automatic range generation then led Argo to propose that bearings could also be generated and applied automatically to the dumaresq. Thus the Argo Clock Mark IV could keep both ranges and bearings without operator intervention, though only while own ship held her course. Isherwood's design was a great advance, both functionally and mechanically. Even so, the variable-speed range clock and the Dumaresq linkage had long been parts of the Service system, with which Pollen had been familiar since 1904. Furthermore, the Argo Clocks Mark IV and V had dials for setting both range and bearing rates. These had been requested by Henley in May 1911, as soon as he had been informed of Argo's proposal for automatic bearing generation; these dials allowed the dumaresq to be set by the cross-cut that was already known to the Service in 1908.

In a turn, the patented clock design held the inclination constant, the same approximation first proposed by Dreyer in 1908 and used from late

1910 in the Mark VI Dumaresq. True helm-free operation – that is, range and bearing being kept automatically without operator intervention, whether own ship was on a steady, yawing or changing course – was only achieved with the Argo Clock Mark V of 1913. Like the Dumaresq on the earlier Dreyer Table Mark III, this depended on a gyrocompass relay to maintain the correct indications of own compass-course and enemy compass-bearing on a compass-ring. There is no direct evidence that Pollen learned of the details of either the Dumaresq Mark VI or the Dreyer Table, though, given his acquaintance with Rear Admiral Peirse and many other sympathetic officers,[2] it is more likely than not. However, even if Argo arrived at similar principles independently, they had no claim to priority of invention.

We turn next to the sources of ideas that influenced Dreyer. In the early days, the most important was his brother John. For their 'Position Finder' of 1907, the Dreyers proposed that ranges should be plotted automatically against time on a broad paper band moving as a constant speed. Automatic plotting was not new; it had long been used in Watkin position finders and Pollen was developing his own version for the *Ariadne* gear. Nonetheless, this was the first proposal for a time-and-range plot and for a device (the pivoted bar and scale) for measuring range-rate, though the Dreyers did not then accept that a mean range-rate could be obtained from the plot itself. However, during the *Vengeance* experiments of January 1908, Frederic made the time-and-range plot on simple squared paper; he obtained the range-rate graphically and the bearing-rate by calculation, and used them to set a Dumaresq by a cross-cut, though his 'Hints' suggest that the method may already have been common knowledge. Dreyer also proposed a plot of range-rate against time and he seems to have hoped that, in the absence of accurate bearings, the speed-across could be derived from its slope. This plot was included in the patent applied for jointly by John and Frederic in 1908, which also introduced the rate-measuring 'grids' that were characteristic of the later Dreyer Tables. The time-and-range-rate plot, though theoretically correct, did not work in practice and Frederic abandoned the idea at about the same time that Norman of *Arrogant* first plotted bearings as well as ranges against time. For the remainder of his service in the NOD, Frederic's plotting efforts were directed mainly towards manual methods of course plotting, though these differed little from those proposed by Pollen.

Between 1908 and 1910, John Dreyer also helped his younger brother in the mechanical design of two virtual-course or 'hyperbolic' clocks. Since 1906, Pollen and Isherwood had been proposing clocks which simulated virtual-course, and, thanks to his membership of the DNO's department, Frederic Dreyer was probably familiar with their 1906 patent. However, in January 1908 (a month before Pollen applied for his second clock patent) only John Dreyer was contemplating using a variable-speed drive to generate a movement proportional to virtual speed. By the following year,

Argo too had adopted variable-speed (though not yet 'slipless') drives for its Mark I clock; however, the virtual movement was generated from two components at right angles, a quite different arrangement from the single 'traveller' still used by the Dreyers. In the event, none of these hyperbolic clocks had any significant influence on subsequent clock designs.

Frederic did not take up dual-rate plotting wholeheartedly until after he had learned of Norman's experiments in the *Arrogant*. After Dreyer had joined *Vanguard*, his first improvised system led in turn to the proposal for a local control instrument, to his patent, and to the Original Dreyer Table. Dreyer acknowledged, though only briefly, his debt to Peirse and W. W. Fisher for the suggestion of the vital clock-range pencil. In his initial proposals, he had no choice but to accept that only Pollen had the technology to transmit ranges from a rangefinder and plot them automatically. At first, this was also true of target bearings, though Dreyer was quick to seize on the new Anschütz gyrocompass as an alternative source of bearings. He was also well placed to appropriate Gunner Newland's idea of follow-the-pointer transfer of range-rate from the Dumaresq. Dreyer's patent was realised by Elliott Brothers as the Original Dreyer Table. This also included a modified Dumaresq Mark VI, the latter embodying the principles which Dreyer himself had originated early in 1908. However, the initial clockwork 'direct pinion drive' was dropped. Instead, a constant-speed electric motor supplying plenty of torque (a feature that had already been seen in the Argo Clock Mark I) drove the whole table. Probably, Keith Elphinstone alone chose a conventional disc-and-roller variable-speed mechanism for the range clock; this same type was then used for both the range and bearing clocks of all the subsequent Dreyer Tables. And, although remote plotting of ranges and bearings had previously been feasible only with Argo's special receivers, Elliotts were now able to adapt the Anschütz receiver motors for the same purpose.

In deciding the question of plagiarism that may have occurred in 1911, the period from May to October is critical. On 15 May, Argo sent to the Admiralty the proposal for the Argo Clock Mark II. This described the new slipless disc-and-ball variable-speed drive, set automatically for rate from the dumaresq linkage. The proposal also mentioned, though only briefly, 'the addition of a simple linkage and another variable speed drive' by which bearings, like ranges, could be generated automatically.[3] By 22 May, Henley had asked Pollen for an outline sketch of the bearing arrangements, which was probably received on the 27th. But it seems that no further progress had been made on the bearing clock by 26 June, since it was not mentioned in the provisional patent specification then forwarded to the Admiralty.

By the beginning of July, the first parts of the Original Dreyer Table were being delivered to Dreyer's ship, *Prince of Wales*, then at Cromarty. On the first of the month, Dreyer wrote to Elphinstone and suggested for the first time that a connection from a gyrocompass could keep the Dumaresq adjusted automatically during an alteration of own course; this idea must count as one of Dreyer's most important innovations in fire control. Elphinstone replied on 3 and 4 July; his letters show that he was meeting regularly with Henley to discuss the table, but none of the actual correspondence (which includes a letter from Henley to Dreyer on the 10th) contains any evidence that Henley described Argo's proposals to Elphinstone or Dreyer. Then, on 19 July, Dreyer wrote from Cromarty requesting that a bearing clock, in the unsuitable form of a cone-and-roller drive, should be added to the Original Table – though he did not indicate the source of its bearing-rate. Only an excerpt from this letter was placed in evidence before the Royal Commission on Awards to Inventors. This could suggest that the remainder contained some compromising or embarrassing remarks about Pollen or Argo's designs: except that Dreyer himself produced the whole letter during the RCAI hearings in 1925 without any damaging revelations.[4] Meanwhile, on 18 July, Lieutenant George Gipps (who, with the Admiralty's permission, was employed by Argo as a technical adviser) sent a circular letter to seventy-two serving officers – including Dreyer – seeking opinions on Argo's proposals for turret control.[5] The letter was accompanied by a description of a 'Change of Range' clock incorporating a 'reversible linkage' that clearly had the same properties as a dumaresq linkage. There was no mention of a dividing linkage or a change of bearing clock, though there was perhaps a hint of the latter's function in Gipps claim that 'we have all the geometric data needed to discover ranges, bearings or change of either'.[6] In his evidence to the RCAI, Dreyer denied that this letter influenced his proposal of the 19th, not least because it would have taken about three days to reach Cromarty. We know that he wrote to Henley about it on 22 July, and that Henley replied on the 24th, deploring Argo's attempt 'to obtain opinions and suggestions from sea which they will patent and then attack the Admiralty with'. Nonetheless, of the Argo clock itself, he wrote:

> I think their design is going to be a great improvement on the old, and I hope to get one for trial.

However, he gave no details of the design itself.[7]

After this until October, there is a gap in the surviving correspondence as Elliott Brothers completed the construction of the Original Dreyer Table and Argo proceeded with the design and began the construction of the prototype Argo Clock Mark IV. Since the decision had a profound effect on the general mechanical layout, it was probably at this time that Isherwood dropped the dividing linkage and adopted a pair of variable-speed drives for the generation of change-of-bearing. On 11 October, Elphinstone wrote to Dreyer about modifications to the Original Table that he had been discussing with Henley. Elphinstone also stated that he and Elliott's drawing office had started work on the new design that eventually became the Dreyer Table Mark III; he enclosed the first schedule for what he soon dubbed the 'Seven Part Recorder'. On 28 October, once he had received Dreyer's comments, Elphinstone completed his sketch of the new design, which, together with revised and extended schedules, was sent to Dreyer with a letter dated 30 October, a Monday. In this informal letter, Elphinstone also referred to his visit to Argo at York on the previous Thursday, the 26th, to discuss the fitting of an Anschütz gyrocompass receiver in the Argo rangefinder mounting, but he wrote nothing about Argo's other developments.[8] Meanwhile, Henley had visited Argo on 11 October and had inspected the working drawings and some parts of the clock under construction.

Only these two separate visits by Henley and Elphinstone are corroborated by the RCAI evidence. Yet, on the last but one day of the 1925 hearings, when counsel were already summing up, Pollen's own counsel suddenly announced:

> The letter of Sir Keith Elphinstone was one of the secret documents which I was not allowed to show to Mr. Pollen. Mr. Pollen now tells me that when Captain Henley went to York to see the Argo clock, Sir Keith Elphinstone was with him.

And, a little later:

> Mr. Pollen tells me that Sir Keith Elphinstone was constantly up there [York] all through that year and was shown everything in connection with the Argo clock. He was looked upon as an Admiralty contractor.[9]

However, earlier in the RCAI hearing, Pollen had been cross-examined about Henley's visit on the 11th but had said nothing about Elphinstone being present. Pollen's recollections of other visits had also already proved unreliable under cross-examination; he had at first insisted that Dreyer had accompanied Captain Craig on a visit to Broadheath on 15 February 1910, whereas in fact Dreyer had already joined the *Vanguard* and the second visitor had been the recently appointed Henley. Pollen exaggerated the progress on the clock by stating that, at the time of Henley's visit on 11 October 1911 the 'main part of it [the clock] was constructed',[10] whereas on 17 November 1911, Argo advised the Admiralty only that the 'designs of [the] clock are now approaching completion and we hope to demonstrate it at work by the end of January'.

The prototype was eventually exhibited at Argo's London offices from February to April 1912. On 8 July, the Admiralty was sent a copy of Argo's complete patent specification dated 4 April.[11] After further modification, the Argo clock was installed in *Orion* for trials. Meanwhile, at Elliott

Brothers, working drawings of the Dreyer Table Mark III were completed in May 1912 and the first table had probably been fitted in *Monarch* by the end of the year. Neither Henley nor Elphinstone were called before the RCAI in 1925 (Henley was then serving in the Mediterranean),[12] but Dreyer himself stated that:

> there was no information which reached me until long after the Mark III Table was designed – in fact, until it was under manufacture – as to what the Argo clock was. [13]

The uncertain origins of the Dreyer Table Mark IV can be traced to December 1912, when Dreyer submitted his proposal for an additional cone-and-roller drive and step-by-step transmitters and motors, by which he hoped to make the Mark III 'more automatic than at present'. He retained the disc-and-roller bearing clock, but thought he could set it for rate from the cone-and-roller. However, his ideas were both impracticable and wrong in principle. By this time, the mechanism of the Argo Clock Mark IV was well known in the Admiralty and, we must suppose, to Dreyer. Since this also used a pair of variable-speed drives in the generation of change-of-bearing, it probably had some influence on Dreyer's proposal, though clearly he did not understand properly how it worked. But he gave no hint whether he was only trying to realise the same principles by other means, or whether, albeit erroneously, he was trying to circumvent the Argo patent.

When in 1914 Elphinstone took up the design of the Mark IV Tables, he also employed electrical means to enable the Dumaresq to set the rates automatically on the disc-and-roller clocks, though otherwise the two-axis electric follower owed nothing to Dreyer's 1912 proposal, nor to anything designed by Argo. However, like the Argo Clock Mark V of 1913, the Dreyer Table Mark IV obtained the bearing-rate by dividing speed-across by range with a mechanism based on a lever and a spiral cam. The Argo patent claimed only for a lever pivoted at one end and a cam cut according to a simple reciprocal function. In contrast, the pivot of the Elliott lever moved between the ends of the lever, so its cam was cut to a different function of range and the Argo patent was not infringed.[14] Even so, the similarities do pose the question of whether Elphinstone obtained the broad principle from Argo. In seeking an answer, we shall also see how Dreyer reacted as 'his' tables became more and more the work of Elphinstone and Elliott Brothers.

The Argo patent was applied for, with a provisional specification, on 16 July 1913, while the similar complete specification was left on 16 January 1914. In February 1914, the Admiralty had asked the Patent Office for notice of Argo patents as soon as they were submitted. This request had been refused, the Patent Office insisting that patents remained confidential until accepted and published.[15] However, it did undertake to supply copies of Argo patents immediately on publication,[16] and 16,373/1913 was accepted on 16 July 1914. Thus even if it had been published immediately,[17] it could not have reached the Admiralty until after the first Mark IV table had been completed.

In March 1914, at the request of the Director of Navy Contracts, Elphinstone made some suggestions concerning patent cover for the Dreyer Tables, including the new Mark IV then being designed. Dreyer had already submitted a complete patent specification that included his spurious proposal from the end of 1912,[18] but Elphinstone realised that it was not correct and what was needed in its stead:

> assuming that a certain . . . deflection is adjusted on the Dumaresq dial . . . any subsequent alteration of the Range would only cause [the] Roller to travel longitudinally on the shaft . . . and no alteration to the Rate of Change of Bearing . . . would result, which I do not think is correct.
>
> The Device appears to me to call for a system of proportional levers whereby alteration to either the deflection or the Range alters the Rate of Change of Bearing.

He described the scheme he then adopted as 'a special application of a Device which has been used for a long time for a particular purpose'.[19] Although Elphinstone mentioned another Pollen patent in his letter,[20] he did not refer to 16,373/1913. However, a copy had evidently reached the Admiralty by August, when a minute by the DNO (Captain Singer) suggested, optimistically, that it had been anticipated by Dreyer's erroneous 21,480 of 1912.[21]

When the subject of patent cover was raised again in 1916, Elphinstone specifically drew 'attention to Mr. A.H. Pollen's Patent 16373/13, Claim I, where Apparatus is mentioned on lines somewhat similar to that [used in the] Tables, Mark IV and IV*'. He went on to propose that, although the device actually adopted was 'a special application of a known mechanical method [it] might possibly be worth protecting'.[22] Dreyer, on the other hand, took the view that it was 'too late to take out a New Patent . . . as it would be invalidated by Mr. Pollen's Patent . . . 16373'.[23] However, in early 1916 Dreyer was applying for an award from the Ordnance Council for his contributions to fire control. On 1 February 1916, he declared:

> In the case of each of the inventions described in [my] patents, I took out a provisional specification . . . before communicating with the Firm, so that the prior claims of the Admiralty should be clearly established.
>
> The actual details of such machines when made are of little importance, and could be designed by any good Firm of Instrument Makers to whom the invention was communicated.[24]

He was awarded £5,000 on 10 February,[25] but this did not persuade him to give any more credit to Elphinstone:

> The fact, as mentioned by Mr. Elphinstone, that in my Secret Patent No. 21,480 of . . . 1912, the example quoted . . . is not quite automatic, is unimportant.[26]

At the RCAI hearing in 1925, Dreyer was seeking a further award and was prepared to acknowledge only Elphinstone's 'assistance' in elaborating the plans for the first table, although he was obliged to admit that he had had no part in devising the 'poached egg'.

> The designers chose to suggest another method; but I think that is only a detail.[27]

## Questions of plagiarism

This chronology can now be used in judging what was and was not plagiarised by Dreyer and Elphinstone from Pollen and Isherwood. Once Dreyer took over responsibility for Pollen's A.C. system from Harding in mid-1907, he must have learned all about Pollen's proposals and patents, including those for 'hyperbolic' clocks. The clocks of this type designed by John and Frederic Dreyer in 1908 and 1909 also worked on virtual-course principles, but they were mechanically very different from their A.C. contemporaries. In 1907, the Dreyers may have had Pollen's automatic course plotter in mind when they first proposed an automatic time-and-range plotter, but, since they called it a 'Position Finder', they may just as well have been influenced by the well-established Watkin land-service gear. After the *Ariadne* trials, Frederic took automatic plotting no further and, once time-and-range-rate plotting proved impracticable, concentrated on attempts, eventually unsuccessful, to devise manual alternatives to the automatic course plotting advocated by Pollen. While Frederic Dreyer was still in the NOD, he expressed a high opinion of Argo's transmission gear and, in July 1910, he recommended its use in making rate plotting automatic. However, in the end Pollen's gear was not used in any of the Dreyer Tables, since Elliott Brothers developed more reliable step-by-step motors derived from Anschütz technology. The Original Dreyer Table of 1911 was powered by a speed-regulated electric motor, a form of drive that had been used in 1910 for the *Natal* clock and plotter; however, an electric motor was the obvious alternative to the clockwork proposed by Dreyer in his provisional patent.

Thus, up to the Original Dreyer Table as built by Elliott Brothers, Pollen's influence on Dreyer's ideas had been slight, problematic or led nowhere. Thus if, as Sumida suggests, Dreyer and Elphinstone resorted to plagiarism in 1911, it must relate to features of the new Argo Clock (eventually the Mark IV) that were copied for their next design, the Dreyer Table Mark III and its precursor, Elphinstone's 'Seven Part Recorder'. There is no doubt that, in proposals sent to Henley at the Admiralty in May 1911, Argo was first to describe a 'bearing clock' that ran at a rate derived from the dumaresq speed-across, and that closed the loop by adjusting the enemy course-bearing of the dumaresq. In May, Argo intended to use some form of dividing linkage and a single variable-speed drive; however, this scheme was soon replaced by a pair of drives that was functionally equivalent but mechanically quite different. In this form, the design had been largely completed by November 1911. During this period, Henley and Elphinstone met often, while both men corresponded regularly with Dreyer at Cromarty. Yet the RCAI evidence bundles contain nothing to show that Henley had betrayed Argo's confidence, either in corresponding with Dreyer or in his discussions with Elphinstone. Dreyer also firmly denied that he knew anything of the Argo clock until the following year. And the bearing clock described in Dreyer's letter of 19 July was nothing like either of Argo's designs; it was based on an unsuitable cone-and-roller drive, and Dreyer did not say how the bearing-rate was to be obtained. On the other hand, it is curious that Dreyer did not call either Henley or Elphinstone in support of his 1925 claim for a further award. So did Dreyer receive some information about the Argo bearing-clock in correspondence that was subsequently lost or destroyed, and did this then inspire his own request to add a bearing-clock to the Original Table? It is impossible to be certain that he did not hear something about Argo's proposal for a bearing clock. But the sheer inadequacy of his own proposal strongly suggests that, at most, he learned of the general idea of a bearing clock, but nothing about the actual Argo implementation.

In early July, Dreyer had made the important and original suggestion of a connection from the gyrocompass to the Dumaresq, the essential for helm-free prediction. Once the Original Table had been completed, Elphinstone set about incorporating the gyrocompass connection and a bearing clock in the next table. The first stage in its evolution was the Seven Part Recorder, as documented in the schedules of 11 October, and the revisions and sketch made on the 28th. By then, the two design teams were proceeding on very different lines, both functionally and mechanically. Argo's clock was built around three (perhaps already four) of its disc-and-ball slipless drives. While courses were steady, it generated ranges and bearings automatically. However, if own ship turned, enemy bearings had to be set by hand. The Seven Part Recorder also had range and bearing clocks, each a single disc-and-roller; for the bearing-clock, this type of variable-speed drive, already used in the Original Dreyer Table, was an obvious and necessary improvement on Dreyer's cone-and-roller. Both clock rates were set by hand; there was provision for obtaining the bearing-rate from the plot, but not from the Dumaresq. And Elphinstone included a gyrocompass receiver and relay motor for adjusting the Dumaresq automatically in a turn. Thus, apart, perhaps, from the presence of a bearing-clock, there were no other features of the Seven Part Recorder that can be attributed to Argo.

What then of Pollen's implication that the Elphinstone took advantage of many opportunities to copy from Argo? Pollen had been told officially at the start of 1911 that the Admiralty wished the two systems to be 'developed independently and then tried in comparison with each other'. And the inventor was in regular contact with serving officers, who could confirm that Dreyer and Elliott Brothers were working on a rival system. It is, therefore, hard to credit that he would have revealed any details of his clock to his principal competitor, whether or not Elliotts was an Admiralty contractor. There are also several reasons for doubting Pollen's version of events in 1911. First, his last-minute claims to the RCAI seem to have been prompted by seeing a letter of Elphinstone's referring to a visit to York by Henley – yet in fact the only relevant letter by Elphinstone is that dated 30 October, which referred to his own visit on the 26th and does not mention Henley or, indeed, any Argo equipment other than the rangefinder mounting. Second, although Elphinstone's sketch and schedule revisions for the Seven Part Recorder were dated two days after his visit to York, his letters to Dreyer establish that he had been working on the design since before the 11th, and that the new versions had been prompted only by the receipt of Dreyer's comments. Third, in earlier evidence Pollen had been wrong about a previous visit by Henley in 1910: he had exaggerated the state of completeness of the clock in October, and he had not mentioned Elphinstone when describing Henley's visit on the 11th.

But was it only that Pollen's memory of fourteen years earlier had played him false? Pollen had trained as a barrister,[28] and must have known that, if his counsel could interject fresh assertions during the summings-up to the RCAI, they would not require supporting evidence nor be tested by cross-examination. Not only are there many reasons for judging that his claims were untrue, but also there must be a strong suspicion that they were deliberately and knowingly introduced at the last moment to mislead the Commission. Even if that was not the case, nothing in the Seven Part Recorder came from Argo except (and even this is not certain) the general idea of a bearing clock. There are no grounds for accusing Elphinstone of plagiarising Argo's designs in 1911, not least because he almost certainly did not have the opportunity.

Once the prototype Argo Clock Mark IV had been put on display from February 1912, its functionality and even some details of its internal mechanisms must have become known to many, including Dreyer and Elphinstone. The latter completed the design of the Dreyer Table Mark III in May. Functionally, it was similar to the Seven Part Recorder, though the

197

mechanical layout was different. The only major addition was the graduated drum that allowed conversion between speed-across and bearing-rate. Thus the rate of the bearing clock could now be set either from the bearing plot or, for the first time in a Dreyer Table, from the Dumaresq. It may seem unlikely that the idea of generating change-of-bearing from Dumaresq speed-across did not occur to Dreyer or Elphinstone until they learned how the Argo clock worked, but it cannot be entirely discounted. Yet, apart from this general resemblance in principle, the rival designs remained as far apart as ever, both mechanically and functionally. In the Argo Clock Mark IV, thanks to the slipless variable-speed drives, conversion of speed-across and rate-setting were automatic – though bearings were generated automatically only on a steady course. On the Dreyer Table Mark III, the drum converted speed-across into bearing-rate, though all rate transfers were manual. However, the Dumaresq was adjusted automatically when own ship yawed or turned. Thus, every detail contradicts the conclusion that Elphinstone's clock bore 'an unmistakable resemblance to the disc-ball-roller arrangement of the Argo clock'. Once again, only a general idea, in this case of deriving the rate of the bearing clock from Dumaresq speed-across, was perhaps obtained from Argo.

In December 1912, Dreyer submitted his proposal for additions to make the existing Mark III table more automatic. The design of the Argo Clock Mark IV, now known in detail at the Admiralty through Argo's complete patent specification, may have suggested the use of an extra variable-speed drive in the generation of bearings. If so, the Argo influence went no further. In Dreyer's scheme, the two drives were connected differently, though also incorrectly, and the rates were transferred electrically, not mechanically. If it was a deliberate attempt to be as different as possible, it certainly succeeded.

In the spring of 1914, Elphinstone was designing the Dreyer Table Mark IV, including the C.B. gear that used a spiral cam to position the central pivot of a proportional lever. By that time, he probably knew all about Argo's earlier proposals and patents. In 1911, the firm had suggested in general terms the use of 'a simple linkage and another variable speed drive' in the generation of bearings. Argo's complete specification for the Mark IV clock also described a cam and centrally pivoted lever, though it was employed in generating the non-uniform steps required for transmitting ranges to follow-the-pointer sights. However, Elphinstone had not yet seen any details of the Argo Clock Mark V; in the generation of bearings, this used a different form of cam-and-lever in which the lever had a fixed pivot at one end. Perhaps, in devising his own change-of-bearing gear, Elphinstone put together Argo's vague proposal from 1911 for a simple linkage (or lever) with its mechanism from the Mark IV clock, though he himself said that his inspiration derived from a mechanism known 'for a long time' in another application.

Thus Argo's influence on the Dreyer Tables was often uncertain and mostly restricted to general ideas. It is possible, but not proven, that Dreyer's own request for a bearing clock was inspired by hearing something of Argo's idea, and that, when Elphinstone was designing the Dreyer Table Mark III, the idea of using Dumaresq speed-across came to him from Argo rather than independently. In designing the C.B. gear, Elphinstone perhaps remembered Argo's unspecific idea from 1911 for a linkage, or adapted a mechanism that was used for a different purpose in the Argo Clock Mark IV; however, he claimed that he made use of long-familiar mechanical principles. A more probable case of Argo influence appears in Dreyer's defective scheme of late 1912 for making the Mark III table more automatic. However, it was a technical dead-end and none of its Argo features had any influence on Elphinstone's bearing-clock for the Mark IV Table.

Is the reuse of general ideas still plagiarism? If it is, then such a charge could also be levelled at Pollen and Isherwood. There were many points at which the A.C. system was influenced by Service developments, or depended upon them. The two-observer rangefinder and automatic plotting of enemy course had land-service antecedents, while the idea of automatic sights (which Argo probably never realised itself) was not original. Had it not been for the new Barr & Stroud 9-foot rangefinder, Pollen would have had nothing to propose after the *Jupiter* trials except further development of the discredited two-observer system. The Argo rangefinder mounting, the true-course plotter and the Argo Clock Mark V all depended on the Anschütz gyrocompass for helm-free operation; the gyrocompass connection to the Mark V clock may also have been suggested by the Dreyer Table Mark III. Following in-service experience with its predecessor, the new Argo rangefinder mounting of 1914 had a second seat for a trainer. Most importantly, after the abandonment of the Argo Clock Mark I, the starting point for the design of the later clocks was the long-familiar integrating range clock, set with range-rate from a dumaresq-type linkage.

But, in this case of two rival teams working on the same problem at the same time for the same customer, highly charged accusations of plagiarism obscure rather than illuminate the actual process of engineering design and development. Isherwood and Elphinstone both had to depend on other inventions for the data supplied to their clocks and plotters. Both were constrained by the same fundamentals, expressible most concisely in the equations for the range and bearing rates. They were working within a shared context of contemporary mechanical and electrical technology, sometimes at the limits of what was possible. Both were aware of earlier and current developments in fire control, notably the Dumaresq and the integrating clock (based on a variable-speed drive) for generating range from range-rate. After the false start of the Argo Clock Mark I, Isherwood began again with these familiar elements; then, in only a few months, he made important advances, the perfected slipless drive leading to the conception of the range-and-bearing clock. Dreyer then asked for a gyro-compass connection to the Dumaresq and, with or without some knowledge of the Argo proposals, that a bearing clock be added to the next table design. Elphinstone succeeded in realising both ideas in the helm-free clock of the Dreyer Table Mark III, though its rates were still transferred manually. Isherwood's Argo Clock Mark V was automatic as well as helm-free. Finally, Elphinstone produced his own automatic clock based on the Electrical Dumaresq, a device having no resemblance to anything devised by Argo. Both engineers employed rather similar lever-and-cam dividers, but Elphinstone's had probably been designed independently on well-known lines.

When he was asked to compare the Pollen and Dreyer systems as they existed at the beginning of 1913, James Swinburne FRS wrote of the Argo clock:

> It looks as unlike the Dreyer apparatus as it well could; but it is really on almost the same lines.[29]

This was even more the case after another phase of development of both systems. To plagiarise is 'to take and use another person's ... inventions ... as one's own'.[30] This is not an appropriate description of the normal process of incremental development followed by both Isherwood and Elphinstone. Both made important innovations. Both made use of earlier ideas, but were always obliged to adapt them to their own purposes. Both ended with automatic, helm-free clocks that solved the fire control equations. Yet, despite the common principles, their implementations were radically different. Neither were plagiarists; both were original and talented designers.

## THE ADMIRALTY'S CHOICES

Even Pollen's very first approach, in 1901, was characteristic of his long relationship with the Admiralty. First:

> He brought originally merely ideas worked out partially on paper but without demonstration in the shape of apparatus.[31]

Second, his technical claims (in this case for angular accuracy) were extravagant. Third, even though his ideas were not especially original, he represented them as a secret which the Admiralty should buy. Fourth, he bypassed the responsible department, that of the DNO, by going straight to the First Sea Lord and First Lord, and by circulating a pamphlet promoting his scheme to serving officers (in this case in the Mediterranean Fleet).[32] No doubt mindful of the earlier rejection of two-position rangefinders, the Admiralty chose then not to pay for secrecy. In 1904, Pollen and his father-in-law again applied to the most senior members of the Admiralty hierarchy, which did nothing to lessen the personal dislike of the DNO, Barry. However, faced with the limited accuracy of existing one-observer rangefinders, the Controller, Admiral May, was willing to try two-position instruments once more. Pollen was also fortunate that, in early 1905, Barry was replaced by Jellicoe who, on Harding's over-enthusiastic advice, was prepared to finance the equipment for the *Jupiter* trials (to the tune of £5,300). Pollen then proved unable to complete all the instruments that he had promised: while the rangefinder and plotter that were delivered were almost entirely unsuccessful. As Pollen later admitted, 'no crazier scheme was ever put forward'.[33]

Yet, despite this fiasco, Jellicoe and the Controller, now Rear Admiral Jackson, were still prepared to consider Pollen's new proposals for a gyro-controlled rangefinder mounting and automatic plotter. These were certainly novel but, even though they were entirely unproven, Pollen not only demanded further development funds but also pressed for an extraordinary contract. This covered only the mounting and plotter and, while it allowed the Admiralty the option of choosing whether or not to place a production order, if the Admiralty decided to do so it was committed to paying £100,000 to preserve secrecy and monopoly supply. This was an enormous sum, the amount awarded by a grateful nation only to its most senior commanders,[34] or the price demanded by the agent of the Wright Brothers for a whole air force of fifty flyers.[35] With Harding's continuing support, in November 1906 Pollen received £6,500 for new trial instruments, though he was already regarded as someone who could not be trusted with Service secrets. The negotiation of the full contract was protracted and became acrimonious even before Jellicoe was superseded by Bacon in July 1907. Bacon was certainly sceptical of the value of complex fire control instruments, questioning 'how far mechanisms should supersede the human brain'. Even so, both the early Navy Estimates for 1908–9 and Wilson's initially cordial relations with Pollen show that, at first, the Admiralty expected to adopt Pollen's gear; even Dreyer's intention to 'crab' the gear meant only that it would be rigorously tested. However, Wilson's attitude changed once he had understood the contractual terms demanded by Pollen and that the system was far from complete; he conducted the *Ariadne* trial with the sole purpose of demonstrating that his manual, virtual-course plot was just as satisfactory. Dreyer no doubt provided all the assistance required of him, but his time-and-range plotting was not actually tested until after the trial itself. Given the increasing pressures to reduce the Estimates, Bacon would not have opposed the decision (permissible under the contract) to reject Pollen's system. However, the DNO preferred Dreyer's simple time-and-range plotting to Wilson's over-elaborate scheme, though subsequent efforts (including Dreyer's) were directed towards unsuccessful attempts at manual course plotting.

The sham of the *Ariadne* trials and the Admiralty's dealings with Pollen afterwards must be deplored. Yet the Admiralty still chose to pay Pollen £11,500 to fund further development and maintain secrecy. At the beginning of 1909, Pollen announced the availability of the complete A.C. system, though Bacon wanted to try only the redesigned rangefinder mounting. The Board, however, on which Jellicoe now sat as Controller, chose to purchase a complete set of instruments. Fisher and Bacon may have attempted to delay the invitation to tender, but Pollen's political pressure on the First Lord overcame any opposition. Yet, as soon as the Admiralty began discussion of the new trial, it became apparent that some parts were still being developed and others were non-existent. Nonetheless, Argo received an order, eventually worth about £9,800, for the principal instruments. Shortly afterwards, despite Pollen's efforts to provoke a quarrel, his relationship with the DNO's department improved dramatically after Bacon, Craig and Dreyer had been favourably impressed on first seeing the actual A.C. instruments. Fisher's personal hostility to Pollen does not seem to have influenced subsequent events and discussions on a production contract began while he and Bacon were still at the Admiralty. However, when he handed over as DNO to Captain Moore at the end of 1909, Bacon remained convinced that the most useful component of the Argo system was the rangefinder mounting.

During his time as DNO, did Bacon really display 'obstinacy and technical ignorance' and a determination 'from the start to prevent the adoption of Pollen's ... system'? In March 1908, Bacon certainly questioned the value of elaborate instruments. In responding to Pollen's arguments for a fully automatic system of fire control, he declared:

> The flexibility of the powers of a man either cerebral or mechanical has to be balanced against the rapidity of operation of a machine. The liability to error of both from different causes is a variation of the problem and the available spare men must be balanced against the available spare machines.[36]

Even in 1909, after the Argo instruments for the *Natal* trial had been ordered, the DNO admitted to 'a hatred of complication'. But he was not as opposed to the mechanisation of fire control as Sumida has suggested. Bacon had not found that *Dreadnought*'s 9-foot rangefinders were wholly unsatisfactory, only that they required '"finders" [auxiliary telescopes for finding the target] of much greater aperture';[37] this rather minor criticism is not enough to infer in Bacon a general 'distrust of fire control instruments and faith in spotting'.[38] In September 1908, Bacon's decision to reject the Petravic gyro-firing gear is supposed:

> to have been prompted by the same distrust of gyroscopes that had

operated in the case of the *Ariadne* trials. The Naval Ordnance Department even declined to support the work of Percy Scott.[39]

In fact, such distrust was amply justified by the unsuccessful Petravic trials. Furthermore, at most Bacon did not support further development of the early elevation-only form of director, and was himself responsible for placing the order with Vickers that produced the first practicable Director, as fitted in *Neptune* in December 1910.[40]

In 1908, Bacon's dislike of complicated instruments could well have been influenced by the recent failure of direct sight-setting gear and by problems with the early Vickers clocks. But, while he was still DNO, the latter were overcome, continuous aim with turret guns was mastered and trials began of follow-the-pointer sight-setting gear; this Vickers gear was needed to keep the range on the sights when the rate was high and was an important technological precursor of the Director itself. Bacon also placed the order for the prototype Evershed target indicator. These were not the achievements of a technically ignorant officer obstinately opposed to any form of fire control instrumentation. In early 1908, Bacon doubtless concurred with the decision – taken under considerable financial duress, though, curiously, this is not even mentioned by Sumida as a contributory cause – to deny Pollen a production order. Other causes were more immediate technical priorities, Pollen's unyielding attitude, his all-or-nothing contract and the incomplete and experimental state of his system. But nothing suggests that Bacon opposed the funding of further development, a policy in which Pollen at first cheerfully acquiesced. Subsequent experience showed that Bacon had also judged correctly in his initial preference for manual time-and-range plotting rather than manual course plotting,[41] in placing most value on the Argo rangefinder mounting, and in doubting whether a monopoly agreement was in the Admiralty's interests. Compared with Jellicoe, Bacon was from the start more wary of Pollen's claims, though even Jellicoe became increasingly exasperated by the inventor's promotional efforts. In view of the disappointing outcome of the *Natal* trials, there can be little doubt that any large order placed in early 1908 would have been premature; it is even arguable that, in recommending an order for the rangefinder mounting as he left office in late 1909, Bacon's proper scepticism had at last been overcome too soon by Pollen's persuasive powers.

Shortly after Bacon handed over to Moore at the end of 1909, Wilson also replaced Fisher as First Sea Lord, but Admiralty policy on fire control did not change. Moore followed Bacon's advice. Tough negotiations followed, but, in April 1910, a production order for forty-five rangefinder mountings was placed; worth £60,750, it was more than sufficient for 'all ships of "Lord Nelson" and "Indomitable" classes and later'.[42] The contract allowed for an advanced payment of £15,000 and, while the price per mounting was less than Pollen had proposed, it was sufficient to cover manufacturing costs, an adequate profit and continuing development of the rest of the system – at the rate of expenditure declared by Pollen himself. If Wilson had been opposed to any monopoly agreement (Pollen is the only source for this), he did not remain adamant for long; nor are there any signs that, subsequently, he 'played an important role in the disruption of the development of the Pollen system'.[43]

The Admiralty placed the order before the *Natal* trial of the complete A.C. system in June 1910. The mounting proved to be far from reliable under service conditions.[44] The Mark I clock probably worked well enough as a mechanism, but had to be stopped before its range and bearing could be corrected from observations or altered after a change of own course. Pollen himself chose to design an entirely new rate-based clock. The attempt to convert the straight-course plotter into a true-course plotter had failed, while even Pollen now acknowledged that rate plotting was 'a good alternative . . . to straight line plotting'. He also declared that, with both methods, 'you must have a steady course'.[45] This was certainly true of straight-course plotting; since the Argo mounting was then only yaw-free, no useful course plot could be made while own ship was turning. For the same reason, no time-and-bearing plot was possible while altering course, but the time-and-range plot gave at least an indication of the change in range-rate, and it still allowed comparison between clock-range and mean rangefinder range. Thus Dreyer had cause for claiming that a time-and-range instrument was the best available means of coping with continually altering course.

In Moore's later words to Battenberg: 'after the Natal trials all that was successful of the Pollen gear was accepted i.e. The gyro-controlled Range Finder'.[46] At that time, no further choices were required relating to Argo. The Navy could only wait until the firm produced proposals for its new clock and demonstrated, if it could, that true course plotting was, after all, feasible. However, for the first time, Dreyer's proposals provided an alternative to Pollen's. Thus Admiralty policy was to encourage Argo and Elliott Brothers to develop their clocks and rate-plotters independently, so that they could be tried in comparison with each other.

By the end of 1911, the Original Dreyer Table had been tried successfully in *Prince of Wales*. Elphinstone was designing the Dreyer Table Mark III, while Argo was well advanced with both the prototype Argo Clock Mark IV and its own rate-plotter. Moore and the Controller (Rear Admiral Briggs) were agreed on holding comparative trials with five sets of equipment from each supplier. In February, the order was placed with Elliott Brothers for Dreyer Tables for the three battleships (other than *Orion*) and two battlecruisers that were due for completion during 1912. By April, Moore had decided that, even though the new Argo clock had not yet been tried, the five sets from Argo would be fitted in the very latest battleships and battlecruiser, the *King George V* class and *Queen Mary*. But, despite Moore's commitment to Argo and his persistent efforts, no agreement on terms could be reached with Pollen. Probably by June, certainly by August, Moore's patience was at an end. The true extent of Argo's financial problems remains obscure, but Pollen's demands for further large payments only drew attention to what the Admiralty considered had been extravagance and mismanagement of his company's affairs.[47] Faced with Pollen's own request for the early abandonment of secrecy, his 'prohibitive price' and demands for 'hush money', Moore recommended that secrecy and monopoly should not be renewed and that, if Argo were to remain an Admiralty supplier, they must operate under normal commercial terms.

At this crisis in their commercial relationships, Pollen's negotiating position was also much weaker because, as Moore reminded Battenberg in September:

> If there was no other system achieving equal results with Pollens then there would be no choice (or very little) for us; but there is another system; it is almost identical, it is Dreyers.

Plotting was not then the issue; Moore doubted that a new true-course Argo plotter would be a success, particularly at sea in a fleet, but:

> If he can produce one there would be no objection to trying it in conjunction with the Clock & Rangefinder, and Mr. Pollen is quite mistaken in thinking I oppose this.

Since the rival rate-plotters were functionally similar (price was another matter), the only important technical choice was between the clocks. Moore accepted that both depended on the data supplied by the Argo rangefinder mounting.

> Both place data thus obtained upon a clock which . . . transmits the corrected range . . . & both clocks keep the rate of clock adjusted as the bearing of enemy alters.
>
> . . .
>
> I believe that both Dreyer's & Pollens' [*sic*] systems will produce about equal results – Dreyer's is the more developed at present, but Pollen's workmanship is probably better.[48]

Moore went no further in differentiating between the functions embodied in the rival designs, but the differences are made clear by Dreyer in the comparison, written towards the end of 1912, between the Argo and *Monarch* (Dreyer Mark III) clocks.

In the 'Monarch' Clock, alterations in own ship's course are made automatically by the Fore and Aft bar of the Dumaresq being activated by the Gyro Compass.

In the Argo Clock, alterations in own ship's course have to be supplied manually, the operator having first to remember to raise some clips and then remember to lower these clips when ship is steady. If own ship is yawing badly or making small alterations in course for station keeping the manipulation of the Argo Clock will become even more difficult.

. . .

If the case occurs . . . of the enemy disappearing in smoke, rain or fog, and own ship alters course, but the enemy is obliging enough not to alter course or speed while out of sight, there is a far better chance of having the correct range with the 'Monarch' table than with the Argo Clock when the enemy reappears.

Dreyer did not draw attention to any other deficiencies of the prototype Argo clock, though these must have been well understood, since its trials were delayed in part by alterations suggested by naval officers: but, in any case, most had probably been rectified before the *Orion* trial.

As always, Dreyer emphasised that:

The 'Monarch' Clock can be 'Tuned up' throughout to the 'Mean Rangefinder Range of the moment' BY INSPECTION.[49]

He also made the most of manual transfer of range-rate by claiming, optimistically, that it permitted an allowance for 'slip' during a turn. He did not even mention the errors which might arise from the manual, stepwise transfer of range- and bearing-rates. However, the tests carried out at Elliott's offices in February 1913 were soon to demonstrate that, at least in ideal operating conditions, manual rate transfer did not result in significant errors, even when rates were changing rapidly. When, in December 1912, Dreyer first proposed making his table more automatic, he was probably chiefly concerned with eliminating the chance of operators' mistakes.

Dreyer's comparisons give only one side of the technical argument, though his criticisms of the Argo clock were legitimate. Moore, in contrast, took the view that the pros and cons were finely balanced, and he persisted with the policy of purchasing five more Argo clocks, despite the high price of £2,133. Thus, in the autumn of 1912, no technical choice had been made. But Moore had initiated a profound change in the commercial relationship with Argo. Many years' experience had shown, and the recent negotiation had only confirmed, that the existing contract allowed Pollen to threaten to take abroad not only his own system but also all that he had learned of Admiralty methods. The longer secrecy was maintained, the more knowledge he acquired. It was time, Moore argued, to break the chain.

It was not long before Moore's fears were confirmed when Churchill received Pollen's declaration that, if the Argo system became public, 'you have no secret of any kind left in your naval gunnery', and, for good measure, by claiming to have invented rate-plotting himself.[50] The Director of Navy Contracts urged that 'the decision already reached be adhered to . . . Otherwise all experience goes to show that exorbitant terms for monopoly will have to be paid to Argo Company'.[51] The Argo rate-plotter proved to be both expensive and unreliable, but the Admiralty continued to discuss the possibility of further orders for the Argo clock on commercial terms. In January 1913, the firm at last quoted a price that might well have been acceptable.[52] At that critical moment, Pollen made his final attempt to go over the heads of the responsible departments to the First Lord. This not only exposed his crass efforts to foment discontent in the Service, but also showed conclusively that, even after twelve years, he lacked any conception of how to conduct business with the Admiralty. After this and with the dispute over patents festering, there was little prospect of establishing a new relationship similar to that enjoyed by other suppliers. Involving the Press and inciting questions in Parliament could only make matters worse.

Furthermore, the technical comparisons were unchanged or swinging further in favour of the Dreyer system. In February, the Admiralty knew nothing of the helm-free Argo Clock Mark V. The need to make the Dreyer clock automatic had been recognised, although Elphinstone had not yet begun the new design which would correct Dreyer's initial, faulty conception. Argo were on the point of completing the prototype Mark IV true-course plotter, but it was never tried by the Royal Navy. This omission could have been due entirely to the worsening relationship. However, the requirements for a plotter were also changing; the preference for plotting ranges from several rangefinders, and the related development of rangefinder control by the Second Battle Squadron, made the true-course principle less and less relevant.

The new plotting requirements had already been recognised by Dreyer and Usborne in their *Technical History and Technical Comparison*.[53] Their report claimed that Usborne alone was responsible for the critical comparisons of the rival systems and for the concluding 'Summary'; however, the criticisms were against requirements defined by both officers in an earlier chapter. The Admiralty should not have appointed Dreyer as a judge of his own cause; the report was not an impartial assessment, but a justification of the Admiralty decision of January not to reopen the question of the clock, and, in effect, a recommendation to take no action once the true-course plotter was complete. But, even if the criticisms may have been biased, were the final conclusions also unfounded?

In his 'Summary', Usborne emphasised that a fire control system for all action conditions had to work with inaccurate or intermittent target data.

What we require is a method which gives the hitting range in the shortest time, and which can be relied on to cope with all the difficulties which may arise in action.

As far as can be seen, Commander Dreyer's Fire Control instrument and system fulfils this requirement completely.

If no ranges and no bearings are obtainable, then the instrument is suitable for employing estimation only.

If ranges are obtained, no matter from what range finder, then the instrument makes the best possible use of them, combining the information gained from them with estimation.

If both ranges and bearings are obtained, then the instrument deduces therefrom the enemy's course and speed with even better accuracy than does the A.C. system.

If spotting proves impracticable, the instrument is ready for working by mean range finder ranges.

In criticising the Argo system, Usborne correctly pointed out that had only 'a continual verbal communication from the plotting table to the clock' and that it was impossible 'to see at a glance if the ranges transmitted to the guns are in accord with those coming down from the range finders'. Furthermore, it had:

no means of applying 'meaned' ranges to the clock . . . only actual ranges . . . The enemy's speed can only be obtained by measuring on the plot the distance between any two dots or minute circles . . . one cannot make use of the mean or average position of such dots.[54]

But was Usborne also correct in claiming that rate plotting was more accurate at determining enemy course and speed? By 1913, enemy compass bearings could be obtained from the Argo mounting, which now had a separate trainer to keep it on the target. Thus, bearings could be taken frequently or even continuously in good conditions: and as often as possible in poor visibility or rough weather. However, the accuracy of the individual bearings received at the plotter was limited not only by the skill of the trainer, but also by any tendency of the mounting servo to 'hunt', by wander of the gyrocompass induced by turns and roll, and by the rather coarse ¼° transmission steps. Even so, every bearing observation could be recorded on the Dreyer time-and-bearing plot. At the same time, the ranges from the Argo mounting could be plotted automatically by the time-and-range plot, while ranges from turret and other rangefinders could be recorded manually. In contrast, the Argo true-course plotter could plot only the ranges from the Argo mounting and only the bearings taken simultaneously with those ranges. Consequently, at any moment after plotting commenced, the Dreyer Table's separate range and bearing plots would have more, usually many more, plotted points than an Argo true-course plot. And, as Usborne noted, speed measurement from the Argo plot had its own additional inaccuracies.

Usborne also addressed the claim that 'Rate plotting is bad, because ranges plotted against time are always on a curve, and its direction cannot be truly read off'.

> This criticism is, in its theoretical sense, true, a time and range plot is always a curve, but the curvature is so slight that in nearly all practical cases it is both negligible and imperceptible . . .
> The worst case is that . . . where ship and enemy are on opposite courses. This, by the way, is a highly improbable situation, but one much quoted by the exponents of the argument.

He could also have pointed out that, even in this worst case, the high curvature is encountered only close to point where the range reaches its minimum. He did state, however, that 'the observer always has the knowledge of which way the curve must be bending theoretically to help him', and that:

> the operator will be in no wise put out by the curvature of the rate plot, but will recognise in it the fact that the ships are nearly abreast, and that the rate is about to change sign.[55]

Usborne could perhaps have conceded that, in the rare and fleeting circumstances when an enemy on a roughly opposite (and not too distant) course was first sighted near the point of minimum range, true-course plotting *might* have been more accurate. But, in all other cases, his claims for the superior accuracy of rate-plotting were justified. Before any enemy course, let alone speed, could be perceived on the true-course plot, the rate plots could give initial values first of mean range and then of mean range and bearing rates. If necessary, these could be used at once to open fire, even before a cross-cut gave a first estimate of enemy course and speed. And, as plotting proceeded, at any moment the enemy speed and course obtained from a cross-cut of rates would be more accurate than the values obtainable from a true-course plot. Furthermore, only the Dreyer time-and-range plot permitted continuous visual comparison between the ranges predicted by the clock and the mean rangefinder range.

Usborne did not address explicitly the other causes of curvature in rate plots, alterations of course by own or enemy ship. However, similar arguments in favour of rate-plotting still apply. If the enemy altered course, the consequent changes in range and bearing rates would be perceptible more quickly on the rate plots. Furthermore, even while the enemy was turning, it was possible to tune the Dreyer range and bearing clocks in small steps to keep the predicted and observed values close together; the range and range-rate steps would have been similar to those used for spotting corrections. During a turn by own ship, the accuracy and frequency of ranges and bearings would be reduced, while disturbances to the gyrocompass would add to the bearing errors. It would still have been possible, if a large range deviation developed (the enemy might also alter course at the same time) to tune the range clock of the Dreyer table to the mean rangefinder range.[56] In contrast, while own ship was turning, the Argo true-course plot was affected by the increased errors in ranges and especially in bearings, and by the fluctuations in own speed; hence it produced the 'confused plot' described by the Phillpotts committee.

It has been suggested that:

> Captain Dreyer's gear was not 'helm-free', and could not, in practice, carry over information about a given target from one own-ship course to another: rather, it would have to start again and build a fresh database to establish the new rate of change of range.[57]

As own ship altered course, the Dumaresq of the Dreyer Table Mark III was adjusted continuously and automatically; the change-of-bearing from the gyrocompass was sometimes accurate only to a few degrees but, even then, this did not result in significant errors in normal tactical circumstances. Thus changes in range, enemy bearing and inclination were kept through the turn, based on the enemy course and speed set on the Dumaresq when the turn began. Thus, in fact, the Dreyer Table did 'carry over information . . . from one own-ship course to another'. As always, any significant deviations between predicted and observed ranges and bearings could be corrected by tuning. In comparison, during turns the Argo Clock Mark IV had to be set by hand for change of enemy bearing. These changes could be obtained by direct observation or, indirectly, from the change in own course registered by the gyrocompass. However, the second method, though it could be used even when the enemy was obscured, was only approximate; quite apart from the limited accuracy of the gyrocompass, it did not allow for the change in enemy-bearing due to speed-across.

Although the functional analysis was restricted to the steady-course case, the technical assessments available to the Admiralty in 1913 provided sound arguments that, in action, the Dreyer Tables, which integrated the rate-plotting and predicting functions in a single, closed-loop system, would be superior to Argo's separate true-course plotter and clock. Furthermore, Dreyer time-and-range plotting was already proving well suited to the technique of rangefinder control. Yet, as his technical lead slipped away,

Pollen seemed, in the first half of 1913, to go out of his way to poison what remained of his relationship with the Admiralty. Finally, in the summer of 1913, Argo was removed from the list of suppliers to the Royal Navy.

Should this embittered ending be attributed to Moore's inveterate opposition from the moment that he became DNO? Moore (with the DNO, Tudor) must have been mainly instrumental in securing the final break with Argo – though the policy was not opposed by senior Admiralty officers, even those, like Jellicoe and Battenberg, who had in the past been sympathetic to Pollen. But Moore's words and actions throughout 1910 to 1912 indicate that he wished to support, not oppose, Pollen. He placed both major orders with Argo. The large order for rangefinder mountings also preserved monopoly supply and paid for the firm's running expenses at the level declared by Pollen. In 1912, Moore was not 'a determined opponent of true-course plotting';[58] while sceptical, he was prepared to try it if Pollen could produce such a plotter. But, by that time, Moore's own assessment, and the advice he received (though Dreyer's was hardly disinterested), convinced him that the Dreyer Table was now an effective alternative. Thus the new Controller was not prepared to forgo the advantages of competition or to continue with Argo's exceptional treatment. But his opposition was then to the existing commercial and contractual arrangements. It became absolute only when Pollen's continuing intransigence confirmed his unwillingness to establish a new relationship as a normal Admiralty contractor.

Both 'The Quest for Reach' and 'A Matter of Timing' have proposed that the Admiralty's decisions in favour of the Dreyer Tables was also motivated by the expectation of close-range battle against the High Seas Fleet. However, these conclusions rely on flawed comparisons between the functional characteristics of the Pollen and Dreyer systems as they existed around the end of 1912. First, two of the main advantages claimed for the Argo system are that rates, even if they were changing rapidly, were transferred accurately and automatically within the clocks, and that true-course plotting represented a steady enemy course as a straight line, even in conditions when changing rates would produce curved rate plots. Since the shorter the range, the more rapid the change of rates, the Admiralty should have looked more, not less, favourably on Pollen's system if they had really expected to fight only close-range engagements. Second, 'A Matter of Timing' states that 'Pollen had perfected the leading elements of his "helm-free" mechanized system of fire control in the fall of 1912', and implies that the contemporary Dreyer Table was suited only to conditions 'when courses were straight' and was inappropriate 'to an action involving frequent changes of course and shooting at long range'.[59] Yet, in 1912, it was the Dreyer Table, not the Argo Clock, that was adjusted automatically from the gyrocompass for change of course; nor does the article explain why the Argo system (with its reliance for plotting on simultaneous ranges and bearings from a single rangefinder) was better at coping with the increased observational errors to be expected at long ranges. Furthermore, Sumida acknowledges the 'absence of direct evidence' for his conclusions,[60] which are contradicted by the many sources showing that the Royal Navy actually hoped to play at long bowls – though, of course, only in good visibility. The rangefinders would then be rather inaccurate. But nonetheless the Dreyer Table would still be able to obtain first a mean range, then a mean range-rate and deflection, and finally enemy course and speed more quickly than an Argo plotter. In poor visibility, fire had to be opened almost immediately the enemy was sighted, using a gun range based on an estimated range or, at best, the mean of a few rangefinder ranges; only the Dreyer Table could cope with such conditions. The Admiralty's decision in its favour did not mark an end to the quest for reach, but a recognition that, unlike the Argo system, the Dreyer was 'a practical instrument designed to meet the real requirements of Naval action',[61] at long range if possible but also at short range if necessary.

Thus, in mid-1913, the Admiralty had compelling reasons for its final choice of the Dreyer Tables as designed and manufactured by Elliott Brothers. The reasons were not only technical. Under Keith Elphinstone, the firm had built up an easy and close relationship with the Admiralty, beginning with simple instruments like the Dumaresq and progressing to much more complex devices like the Anschütz gyrocompass and the fire control tables themselves. Elliotts were prepared to develop ideas originated by naval officers and to charge prices with a level of profit acceptable to the Department of Naval Contracts. In return, it was assured of the production contracts and the recovery of its development costs.

But while Elliott Brothers was in many ways a typical Admiralty supplier, Pollen and his Argo Company were always unusual. When the Contracts Department produced its historical record of the Admiralty's business relations with Pollen, they began:

> This case has been an exceptional one.
>     . . . Usually inventions of importance for naval purposes . . . are brought to the Admiralty in a more or less complete state . . . ready for trial.
>     . . .
>     . . . where an inventor brings his invention direct to the Admiralty in an immature state, and wishes the Admiralty to assist in its development, he obviously cannot expect to receive so great a reward if he had borne the expense and risk himself.
>     . . . Mr. Pollen's case is of the latter class.[62]

The exceptional nature of the relationship is also strongly indicated in the minutes of the Board of Admiralty. These hardly ever mention suppliers, even those as vital to the Navy as Vickers and EOC. Yet, between 1906 and

1910, Pollen and the Argo Company appear in the minutes of no fewer than eight meetings of the Board.[63] Pollen's prominence was no doubt partly due to his habit of bypassing the responsible departments and taking his case direct to the First Lord and, indeed, to other politicians, including those in opposition. This behaviour did nothing to promote harmonious relationships with successive Directors of Naval Ordnance. Nor did Pollen's threats, repeated regularly from 1904, to take abroad not only his own inventions but also the knowledge and experience acquired from the Royal Navy. Apart, perhaps, from Jellicoe's earlier months as DNO, Pollen was always treated warily by successive directors and their assistants; hence he and his representatives were at times excluded from any trials at which they might learn of Service secrets. Yet, despite everything, Pollen was awarded a succession of contracts which, in large part, paid for the development of the Argo system. Pollen himself was also generously rewarded as Argo's governing director.

Sumida has proposed that 'the co-operative relationship of Pollen and the Admiralty can be regarded as an early attempt to create the kind of state and private partnership in defence procurement that would later become characteristic of the post-World War II military-industrial complex'.[64] On the contrary, the period before the First World War provides many examples of successful cooperation between the Admiralty and private firms,[65] including that with Elliott Brothers, which continued through two world wars and, indeed, to the end of the era of mechanical fire control computers. The contrast between Elliott Brothers and Argo is marked. In 1913, the Director of Naval Contracts concluded: 'With regard to ... giving encouragement to inventors in the early states of their work [the] Admiralty does adopt that policy in some cases', but in the case of the Argo Company,

> the policy was the reverse of successful. Experience shows that there are very considerable advantages in insisting on inventors ... getting all the experimental work done themselves and bringing before the Admiralty a finished and prepared piece of practical mechanism instead of a theory worked out on paper only ... It may in some cases mean paying a higher price for a good and successful invention.[66]

Likewise, after the war, the experience with Argo was remembered as 'not at all satisfactory and encouraging' and as an indicator of how *not* to conduct cooperative relations.[67] From Jellicoe onwards, Pollen had convinced successive DNOs and Controllers that he should be paid for secrecy and for the development of his system, yet had continued to declare that he possessed unrestricted rights not only to his own initial concepts but to the serviceable instruments developed at Admiralty expense. Towards the end, he even laid claim to Service ideas which he had initially ridiculed. It is a remarkable tribute to Pollen's powers of persuasion that his relationship with the Admiralty, so full of tensions and contradictions, lasted as long as it did. When it eventually ended, the final rupture was largely provoked by Pollen himself.

## Notes

1 Dreyer before RCAI, T.173/547 Part 16, pp. 91–4 and Part 17, p. 98.
2 Pollen remained in close touch with Rear Admiral Peirse throughout the second half of 1912, when the ex-ITP was active on his behalf, while also participating in the trials in *Orion. IDNS*, pp. 225–32 and 245.
3 This dividing linkage is unrelated to the dumaresq linkage.
4 T.173/547 Part 17, p. 90.
5 *IDNS*, pp. 215–17.
6 Gipps to Dreyer, 18 July 1911 with enclosure in T.173/91 Part II.
7 Dreyer before RCAI, T.173/547 Part 16, pp. 57 and 63. Henley to Dreyer, 24 July 1911 (mentions Dreyer to Henley of Saturday the 22nd) in DRYR 2/1.
8 Elphinstone to Dreyer, 11 and 30 October, the latter with attachments dated 28 October in T.173/91, Part III.
9 T.173/547 Part 18, pp. 105–6. In 1925, Henley was a Captain and Elphinstone had been knighted.
10 Pollen and Dreyer before RCAI, T.173/547 Part 14, p. 60, Part 15, p. 89 and Part 16, pp. 40–2.
11 Argo to Admiralty Secretary, 17 November 1911 and Argo 'Memorandum', 6 May 1913 both in T.173/91, Part II. 'Detailed Reply' with Coward & Hawksley etc. to Admiralty Secretary, 7 May 1913 in T.173/91 Part VII.
12 T.173/547 Part 18, pp. 57–8 and 104. The minutes do not reveal why Elphinstone was not called.
13 T.173/547 Part 16, p. 63.
14 'FCBD', Appendix XVIII-16.
15 The Patent Office insisted on preserving the confidentiality of unaccepted patents, even during the First World War. T. H. O'Dell, *Inventions and Official Secrecy* (Oxford: Oxford University Press, 1994) p. 71.
16 DNO's minute, 'C.P. 11614/13. Pollen Patents; Question of Civil Proceedings Against Argo Co.', 2 February 1914 in 'IQ/DNO II, 1913'. Admiralty, Contracts Branch, *Pollen Aim Correction System. General Grounds of Admiralty Policy and Record of Business Negotiations*, 1913, Annex p. 9 in P. 1024, AL.
17 Two of Pollen's other patents, 23,352 and 25,768 of 1912, were accepted in December 1913 and marked as printed in the same month. The print date on 16,373 is just '1914'.
18 Secret patent 21,480, applied for 20 September 1912. The provisional specification was mainly concerned with 'the control of own ship's bar by the gyrostat compass': J Swinburne, *The Time and Range System*, March 1913, pp. 4 and 8 in P. 1024, AL (the number and date on p. 8 are incorrect).
19 Elphinstone to DofC, 18 March 1914, pp. 4 and 6 in 'Fire Control Apparatus, Various Patents', ADM 1/8464/181. Unfortunately, there are no clues to what was 'the particular purpose'.
20 2,497/1908, published with the other withheld Argo patents on 6 November 1913.
21 DNO's Minute, 18 August 1914 quoted in Admiralty to C.-in-C. Home Fleet, 1 March 1916 in 'Fire Control Patents' [19].

22 Elphinstone, 'Notes', 9 February 1916, p. 7 with Elphinstone to DofC, 18 March 1916 in 'Fire Control Patents'

23 Enclosure (b) with Dreyer to C.-in-C. Home Fleet, 7 March 1916 in 'Fire Control Patents'.

24 Dreyer to C.-in-C., 1 February 1916 in 'Fire Control Patents'.

25 'Extract from Recommendations of the Admiralty Members of the Ordnance Council at a Meeting 10.2.16 concerning Dreyer's award': Dreyer to Vice Admiral Sir Frederick Field, 12 November 1923; both in DRYR 2/1.

26 Dreyer to C.-in-C. 7 March 1916 [23].

27 Dreyer before RCAI, T.173/547 Part 16, pp. 83 and 85. Argo patent 16,373/1913 was not considered by the Commission.

28 *IDNS*, p. 76.

29 Swinburne [18] p. 6.

30 *Concise Oxford Dictionary*.

31 *Record of Business*, 1913 [16] p. 2.

32 *PP*, editor's introduction, p. 8.

33 *PP*, 'The Gun in Battle', February 1913, p. 309.

34 To Lord Roberts for turning the tide of the Boer War and to Beatty and Haig after the First World War (though Jellicoe received only £50,000). T. Jackson, *The Boer War* (London: Channel 4 Books, 1999) p. 143. Roskill, *Beatty* [B] p. 293.

35 David Edgerton, *England and the Aeroplane* (London: Macmillan, 1991) p. 3.

36 *IDNS*, p. 133.

37 Captain R. H. Bacon, *Report on Experimental Cruise*, 16 March 1907, pp. 28, 84–5 and 96–8, ADM 116/1059.

38 'QfR', p. 64. Since *Dreadnought* did not fire 4-gun salvoes at 15 second intervals, the assumption that 'such rapid fire greatly increased the value of spotting' is also unfounded.

39 *IDNS*, p. 153.

40 Brooks, 'Scott and the Director' [B] pp. 168–9.

41 For a fleet containing but one dreadnought battleship (the *Invincibles* would join during 1908) and equipped to fire accurately only in tactical circumstances which limited range-rate and change-of-rate, this choice was an adequate first step in the introduction of plotting methods.

42 *ART 1912*, p. 75.

43 *IDNS*, pp. 196, 220 and 268.

44 Even so, there was no lack of commitment in utilising the mounting. From the *Lion* and *King George V* classes to the *Iron Duke* class and *Tiger*, it was placed atop the conning tower under an armoured hood (the Argo Tower) that was the focus of the ship's fire control: Brooks, 'Mast and Funnel Question' [B] pp. 44–53.

45 *PP*, 'The Quest of a Rate Finder', November 1910, p. 269.

46 Moore to Battenberg, 19 September 1912, Mountbatten Papers, MB1/T20/147, University of Southampton.

47 There is a marked contrast between Pollen's finances and the prudent policies followed by Barr and Stroud in the early years of their company: Moss and Russell, *Range and Vision* [B] pp. 24 and 32–3.

48 Moore to Battenberg, 1912 [46].

49 'Some comparisons made between the Argo Clock and the Fire Control table in "Monarch"', n.d. but 1912, T.173/91 Part VII.

50 Pollen to Churchill, 21 October 1912 in T.173/91 Part II.

51 F. W. Black, 'Argo Company, Present Position' n.d. but late 1912 in MB1/T22/174.

52 However, if clocks were to be purchased in lots of twenty-five, a decision would have been required to supply them to all major ships, not just the latest dreadnoughts.

53 Commanders F. C. Dreyer and C. V. Usborne, *Pollen Aim Corrector System Part I. Technical History and Technical Comparison with Commander F.C. Dreyer's Fire Control System*, Gunnery Branch 1913, pp. 38, 48 and 55 in P. 1024, AL. For the dates of writing between February and April, see *IDNS*, pp. 240–1.

54 *Technical Comparison*, 1913 [53] pp. 62 and 35–6.

55 *Ibid.* p. 61.

56 In effect, to resort to rangefinder control.

57 Gordon, *Rules of the Game* [B] pp. 366–7 citing Nicholas Lambert.

58 *IDNS*, p. 220.

59 'MoT', pp. 91, 94 and 130–1.

60 *Ibid.* p. 130.

61 *Technical Comparison*, 1913, p. 62.

62 *Record of Business*, 1913, p. 2.

63 From 1905 to 1913, Elswick and Vickers appear once (31 July 1905) among other firms invited to tender for the *Invincibles*. Pollen or the Argo Company are named in minutes for 7 August and 18 September 1906, 31 March and 16 April 1908, 17 and 18 February and 4 March 1909 and 27 April 1910. ADM 167/39, 40, 42, 43 and 44.

64 'QfR', p. 81.

65 For the Admiralty's reliance on the research of private firms, see Nicholas Lambert, *Fisher's Naval Revolution* [B] pp. 152–3.

66 Report by the Director of Navy Contracts, 2 June 1913 in 'IQ/DNO II, 1913', p. 159. This concerned the Submarine Sound Signalling system invented by J. Gardiner: see Willem Hackmann, *Seek and Strike. Sonar, Anti-submarine Warfare and the Royal Navy* (London: HMSO, 1984) p. 10.

67 Minute by DNO, 21 March 1919 in 'Ford Fire Control System', 'MR/DNO III, January–June 1919', p. 6.

# 7

# INTO BATTLE

The early battles of the First World War soon confirmed that fire control had to cope with both extremes of visibility. In the first month of the war, on 28 August 1914, Beatty's battlecruisers fought an action in which three German light cruisers were sunk, two by the flagship, *Lion*. Despite this success, the conditions in the Heligoland Bight confirmed pre-war apprehensions about visibility in the North Sea.[1]

> The enemy first appeared . . . at about 7,500 [yards] ships being on closing courses. . . . when the 'Commence' was sounded, no range had been taken, nor was it possible to take any afterwards.
> . . .
> The range on the sights on opening fire was 6,000 but this was rapidly spotted down to 5,200 and first straddle was obtained at a range of about 5,000.

Since the Argo Tower's training gear had broken down with the first salvo, plotting was out of the question. *Lion*'s Captain Chatfield also considered that 'the gunlayers were probably unduly hurried' and that 'under short visibility conditions . . . slow and deliberate firing with turret guns will be as effective as rapid and great waste of ammunition will be avoided'.[2] His report resulted in the Admiralty issuing orders 'to avoid waste of ammunition';[3] this emphasis was to have unfortunate consequences during *Lion*'s next major engagement.[4]

At the Battle of the Falkland Islands (8 December 1914), Vice Admiral Sturdee used the superior speed and armament of *Invincible* and *Inflexible* to force an engagement at ranges long enough to overwhelm Vice Admiral von Spee's two armoured cruisers with little damage to the British ships.[5] The action began, with good visibility, at close to the maximum range on the battlecruisers' sights (16,400 yards) and continued (with one break of three-quarters of an hour) for more than four and a half hours; they expended 1,173 rounds of 12-inch shell.[6] Throughout, Sturdee chose to remain to windward, so that his ships were severely handicapped by their own smoke and were obliged to make frequent course changes. At one point, they turned about to cross the German wake and, then and later, were on opposite courses to their targets;[7] after the sinking of *Scharnhorst*, *Inflexible* was even forced by the flagship's smoke to turn out of line without orders.[8]

> Owing to the long ranges, smoke from funnels, and frequent changes of course, the practice was not uniformly accurate, and sometimes even wild, especially for direction; but whenever a steady course was maintained for any length of time, the effect of the fire on the enemy was evident.[9]

*Invincible's* gunnery report emphasised that, from the fore-top (her principal fire control position):

> Range taking was impossible during the greater part of the action, due to funnel smoke, gun smoke, etc.
>     Rangefinder was on several occasions covered with spray from shell bursting short.

Ranging from turrets was even more problematic, and often impossible, while, without directors, aiming with the turret gunsights was also badly affected. Furthermore:

> Great difficulty [was found] in keeping the shot on the target due to the rate constantly changing. This appears to have been due to the enemy zigzagging, and at the long range these alterations of course, in and out, could not be detected by eye or by rangefinder.
>     . . .
>     It was often very difficult to see overs, or hits, unless a bright flame accompanied the hits.[10]

For most of the action, *Invincible's* foremast suffered from considerable shaking following an 8.2-inch hit on the starboard strut,[11] yet the effect on rangetaking from the top with the Argo rangefinder was not even mentioned explicitly in her reports – nor was the making of range plots. It appears that rangefinding was so difficult, due to smoke and the long ranges, that few usable ranges were obtained; thus, particularly with the enemy zigzagging, most reliance had to be placed on spotting.

The Battle of the Dogger Bank, on 24 January 1915, was a protracted stern chase to the SE, Hipper (leading in *Seydlitz* and followed by *Moltke*, *Derfflinger* and *Blücher*) being pursued by Beatty's five battlecruisers, in order *Lion*, *Tiger*, *Princess Royal*, *New Zealand* and *Indomitable*.[12]

> The day was so clear that only the shape of the earth prevented one from seeing everything on it.[13]

With a light wind from the NE, Beatty took the orthodox lee position, in which the smoke from his own ships would not interfere with gunnery.[14] At 8.52, *Lion* opened on *Blücher* with a single shot at the unprecedented range of 20,000 yards; *Tiger* and *Princess Royal* also selected the same target shortly thereafter: but *New Zealand* and *Indomitable* were already falling behind. *Princess Royal* also could not keep up; *Lion* pressed ahead, accompanied by *Tiger*. However, *Tiger*'s fire was largely ineffective, which Beatty attributed to her failure to obtain 'that proportion of short shots which is usually considered essential for effective control';[15] it also appears that other British battlecruisers made similar mistakes:

> it is absolutely misleading to think hits will be seen, at any rate at long range. Shorts are the only guide, and the great value of them must be impressed on control officers.[16]

Furthermore, *Tiger* also ignored Beatty's signal at 9.35 to fire at opposite numbers, leaving *Moltke* free to concentrate with *Seydlitz* on the British flagship. The critical moment came at about 9.50, when a hit from *Lion* started a cordite fire which gutted both after turrets in *Seydlitz*. Unfortunately, as Chatfield admitted:

> The mistake made was in not at once going into Rapid Independent and putting forth our whole volume of fire regardless of ammunition expenditure. Enemy would then have been overwhelmed and never recovered.

Thus *Seydlitz* was able to continue firing with her fore and starboard-wing turrets and *Lion*'s shooting was soon severely disrupted.

> The enemy's fire was slow at first but got faster, and at the end was a maximum. *Lion*'s fire was fairly quick at first, but got slower, due to the enemy's shorts interfering with gunlaying, spotting and control, until eventually it was almost impossible to return the fire...
>
> ...
>
> [*Seydlitz*] and *Moltke* at the end fired about 2 salvoes a minute i.e. from their 7 [surviving] turrets, 14 shots a minute at *Lion*, whose rate of fire at that time was about 2 rounds a minute.[17]

After 10 o'clock, *Lion* continued to bear the brunt of the German fire. From 10.35, she was struck repeatedly until, at about 10.50, the port engine had to be stopped and she was forced to quit the line without light or power. Although the flagship was left with nothing except two signal halyards, Beatty still attempted to control his force, but *Lion*'s final confused flag signals turned his other ships NE'wards to concentrate on and sink the already-stricken *Blücher*;[18] thus Hipper's three true battlecruisers were able to escape, though not before inflicting significant damage on *Tiger*. In all, *Seydlitz* and *Moltke* were both hit three times, whereas *Lion* received between thirteen and seventeen hits and *Tiger* four or five.[19]

Despite his initial advantage in numbers and weight of fire, Beatty had been unable to obtain a decisive result; it had taken an hour and a half even to reduce *Blücher*'s speed. When *Lion* pressed forward without effective support from either *Tiger* or *Princess Royal*, Hipper's weaker force was able to achieve a decisive concentration that, eventually, knocked out the British flagship and the chain of command. Also, Beatty's ships did not gain the advantage expected from their lee position; the wind blew spray from the bows and from enemy shorts onto the instrument glasses, while the smoke from the German ships was carried almost directly down-range, causing severe interference to ranging, aiming and spotting, although Hipper's ships were also badly affected.[20] Furthermore, much of the firing was at ranges close to the limits marked on the sights; the *minimum* range recorded in *Lion*'s TS was a momentary 14,825 yards at 10.29½. The Argo gear could transmit ranges only up to 16,000 yards; longer ranges were conveyed by voice-pipe,[21] and could have been plotted only by improvised means. *Tiger* also reported that 'very few ranges were obtained and no attempt was made either to obtain or keep a rate'.[22]

> Little use could be made of the rangefinders as few cuts could be obtained, whilst the range was too great for accurate readings to be taken; time and range plotting was impracticable.[23]

In contrast, a bearing plot was maintained in *Lion* until about 10 o'clock. This probably helped her to open with, and then keep, a correct deflection. However, the officer commanding the Fore TS concluded:

> On the whole I do not consider that the Dreyer table has justified its existence and that until rangefinders have been made more accurate and the difficulties of spray, etc. in turrets, overcome [more] energy should be devoted to the bearing plot, which if the yaw can be eliminated, should give accurate results.[24]

Since the yaw was taken out in the Argo mounting before transmission to the Mark III table, this comment implies that the gyro stabilisation was only partially effective.

By zigzagging, *Lion* threw out her opponents' fire for a short time and both Beatty and Chatfield recommended alterations of two points (one point at high speed) with small helm to this end. The former added:

> This has often been practised and will in no way interfere with our gunnery

which indicates confidence in the helm-free operation of the Dreyer Tables Mark III and IV, and in the compensation for course-change incorporated in the Dumaresq Mark VI. However, against a zigzagging target:

> Rates and Dumaresqs become almost useless . . . Rangefinders may help but spotting must be the primary aid for keeping on the target.[25]

After the Dogger Bank action, Chatfield concluded:

> It is certain that Battle Cruisers, and probably Battleships, may have to open fire at much greater ranges than 15,000 yards, and that rapid fire will be employed by the enemy at 18,000, which must be answered by rapid fire.[26]

Beatty's emphasis, while showing a surprisingly complacent view of his ships' gunnery, was quite different.

> The Falkland Is. fight, and 24th January, have proved that hits can be made without difficulty [sic] at 19 or 20000 yards, but this range is not decisive and the percentage of hits is too small.
> . . . we must try and get in closer without delay. Probably 12,000 to 14,000 yards would suit us well, this being outside the effective range of enemy's torpedoes and 6" guns.[27]

These divergent views would have an important bearing on their next encounter with Hipper's battlecruisers.

## GERMAN FIRE CONTROL

At the Dogger Bank, the fire control system in the German battlecruisers had proved all too effective, even from a disadvantageous position. In these ships, fire was normally directed from the fore control position, an armoured tower in the rear of the conning tower, though there was a reserve armoured position aft, and small spotting tops on the masts. The control positions were linked by telephone and voice-pipe to the transmitting stations beneath the armoured deck; gunnery data and orders were thence transmitted electrically to the turrets by fire control instruments from Siemens & Halske.[28] All the battlecruisers at Jutland were fitted with Zeiss 3-metre stereoscopic rangefinders. One type was installed in turrets with prismatic objectives protruding through the roofs. A second type, on which particular reliance was placed, was mounted with its tube rotating above the roof of each control tower; extension tubes brought the images down to the rangetaker in the tower.[29] The rangetakers were carefully selected for good three-dimensional vision and, paradoxically, the very difficulty of using the instruments demanded that they were rigorously trained:

> to qualify as rangetakers [the] maximum errors allowed [with the 3-metre] at the end of the course are 400 metres at 20,000 yards, and 200 metres at 10,000 metres, *i.e.* 2 per cent.[30]

Thus it appears that, in service, these instruments were, at 20,000 yards, as accurate as the Barr & Stroud 9-foot coincidence rangefinders at 15,000–16,000 yards. In addition, stereoscopic rangefinders were sometimes able to obtain ranges when coincidence instruments could not, notably when a target was almost shrouded in smoke.[31]

In German ships, ranges were transmitted electrically from the rangefinders to the control positions by the *Basis Gerät*,[32] but mean range and rate were never obtained by any form of plotting. From 1908, range-rate only was obtained from the *EU-Anzeiger*, while a similar but separate instrument indicated deflection; both worked on the same principles as the Dumaresq, though neither had any special features to assist in keeping the rates during a turn by own ship.[33] From 1912, range-rate was set on a range clock; the more recent model described in wartime intelligence reports was probably the *Aw-Geber C.12* Elevation Telegraph, which converted clock-range into elevation, the latter then being transmitted directly to follow-the-pointer gun-sights.[34]

All the German battlecruisers at Jutland were fitted with a training director, which transmitted target bearing from a periscopic sight in the control position to follow-the-pointer receivers in the turrets; thus the instrument also served as an accurate target indicator. One model was designated *Rw-Geber C.13*,[35] while *Derfflinger* at Jutland had the then new *C/XVII* (or *C.17*?). The control officer viewed his target through binocular eyepieces, while a separate trainer used a monocular eyepiece at the side – though *Seydlitz* found the latter 'was useless nearly the whole time, so that the Gun Control Officer had to serve the Director Gear himself'.[36] *Derfflinger*'s main director was also supplemented by a periscope in the fore-top; its bearing was transmitted to the main instrument, where the trainer could follow the aloft pointer if he could not see the target himself.[37]

Unlike training, gun laying remained the responsibility of the individual layers, who were accustomed to aim continuously and preferred to fire their own pieces once the fire gong had sounded;[38] thus, at Jutland, several British observers described the German salvoes as rapid ripples.[39] The Germans used a rather different (and potentially more rapid) method of bracketing from that used by the Royal Navy. Attempts to estimate the distance over were forbidden but:

It is desirable that we should train our assistant observers to such an extent that when short shots occur they will be able to tell the fire commander with certainty what size of bracket will suffice.[40]

When straddling, about 25 per cent of shots were kept falling short. Spotting was assisted by electric 'hit-indicators', which sounded buzzers in the top, control and TS when the salvo was due to fall; however, these seem to have been far from reliable.[41] German sources all indicate that, to find the target, they fired single salvoes, spotting each before firing the next. Rangetaking continued between salvoes and was used to check the rate. But, once the target had been straddled consistently, they fired a burst of rapid unspotted salvoes before, inevitably, the rate was lost.[42]

Between the Dogger Bank and Jutland, the Germans introduced an instrument which calculated the mean of the ranges received from up to eight rangefinders. The officer in charge could switch out any rangefinders giving abnormal results; he also reported 'the change of range per minute calculated from the difference of the range-finder readings'. This instrument, called the 'Mittlungs Apparat' in intelligence reports, provided a mean range to set on the range clock,[43] and an alternative value for range-rate to that obtained from the EU-Anzeiger. At Jutland, Derfflinger had also been supplied with a new instrument invented by Commander Paschen of the Lutzow, which kept both range-rate and deflection. This was probably the device called the EU/SV-Anzeiger,[44] which may, like the British Dumaresq Mark VI, have kept the rates approximately through a turn by holding the inclination constant.[45] However, when repeatedly altering course, the German Navy seems to have relied less on its rate instruments and clocks and more on its stereoscopic rangefinders. After Jutland, Seydlitz reported:

> The electric clock was used only in the first part of the engagement [the Run to the South]; afterwards the movements of the ship were so frequent and sudden that regular shooting by electric clock was impossible. Firing was continued in connection with the . . . Basisgerat . . . in [the] forward gun control tower.[46]

Thus in these conditions the Germans used a form of rangefinder control.

Soon after the war began, the Royal Navy obtained and promulgated full details of German practices conducted in 1912–13. Between April and July 1913, nearly all the fully worked-up battleships and battlecruisers carried out practices in which speeds were 12–16 knots, the ranges were long and the targets were three old battleships, moored in line.[47] Ranges were from 12,250 to 16,000 yards and rates reached 325 yards per minute. Some ships made only one hit from thirty-six rounds fired but, under less demanding conditions, others obtained over 10 per cent. In addition, the rates of fire per gun equate to salvoes fired every 27–43 seconds, intervals which are consistent with breaking into rapid fire as soon as the target had been straddled. In 1921, *Derfflinger*'s gunnery officer wrote that:

> Before the war no man in our navy had thought it possible to fight effectively at a range of over 150 hm. [16,250 yards] I can still remember . . . war games . . . in which on principle all shooting at more than 100 hm. [10,950 yards] was ruled out as ineffective.[48]

Nevertheless, when hostilities began, the German Navy had given most of its heavy ships an opportunity for practice at long ranges, and to observe the effects of their fire falling on and around actual ship targets.

Unlike British fire control instruments, which had many origins, the instruments of the German system were mostly developed by the firm of Siemens & Halske, under the direction of the physicist August Raps.[49] As a system, it was rather simpler and better integrated, but the completed British system had greater redundancy and, therefore, resilience to damage. It also provided greater functionality, notably a director that could be mounted aloft and that controlled elevation as well as training. Both systems used similar devices for rate-keeping. However, only the British system had rate plots, for both bearings and ranges; the latter plot appears superior to the '*Mittlungs Apparat*' in dealing with anomalous ranges, and in determining mean range and range-rate, and, uniquely, it permitted a graphical comparison of observed and predicted ranges. On the other hand, length for length, the German stereoscopic rangefinders were probably more accurate at long ranges, while, once shorts had been obtained, their spotting procedures could straddle more quickly.

These comparisons have been against the British system that was being fitted in new ships when the war began. Thus it is now timely to identify any changes to British fire control methods and procedures that followed the introduction of the Director and the Dreyer Tables.

## BRITISH FIRE CONTROL 1914–16

In British 'super-dreadnoughts', the principal fire control position was atop the conning tower, either in the 'Argo Tower' (the revolving armoured hood protecting the rangefinder on the Argo mounting) or, in the later classes, in a fixed, armoured gun control tower. However, spotters were still stationed aloft, where the director sight was also located. In 15-inch ships, a second director sight and the principal rangefinder were placed in a large armoured hood that rotated above the GCT.[50] Beginning with the *King George V* class and *Queen Mary*, there was only one transmitting station for the main armament.[51] But, while there were many detailed differences in the communication arrangements of successive classes, the data conveyed between control positions, TSs and the turrets remained much the same, though gun range and deflection were now also transmitted to the director sights. In each TS, the Dreyer Tables integrated the functions previously performed by separate instruments, namely the Vickers clock, the Dumaresq and one or two manual plotting boards.

Thus the responsibilities of the officers in control positions and transmitting stations did not change as the Dreyer Tables became more widespread. The TS kept the clock-range tuned to the mean rangefinder range of the moment, and informed the control of all tuning corrections (which would be countermanded if necessary by a pseudo-spotting correction). From the slopes of the plots, the TS could also propose changes to the range-rate and speed-across i.e. to the Dumaresq settings of enemy course and speed. However, these changes were not applied to the Dumaresqs until accepted by the control as consistent with observations of the enemy. Likewise, the control ordered corrections to range, range-rate and deflection as determined by their own or other observations of the fall of shot.

The Director introduced a new means of laying, training and firing the guns under the control of a master gunsight, but all the equipment needed to aim and fire independently from each turret remained in place. In ships with an Evershed installation, an Evershed receiver could indicate the designated target to the Director trainer. However, quite a number of ships – notably *New Zealand*, *Iron Duke* and *Tiger* – were not fitted with Eversheds until after Jutland. The last two probably had the older Barr & Stroud bearing receivers in their turrets but not at the Director;[52] if so, their director trainers had to find their targets either from verbally conveyed target bearings, or even from descriptions of the target positions in the enemy line. This deficiency may well have contributed to *Tiger*'s poor shooting at the Dogger Bank.

The *Grand Fleet Battle Orders*, first issued shortly after Jellicoe took command in August 1914, stipulated:

> On a clear day and unless the enemy opens fire earlier, 13.5-inch guns ships will open deliberate fire at 15,000 yards, 12-inch gun ships at 13,000 yards.[53]

Once Scapa Flow had been made a safe anchorage, the ships of the Grand Fleet for the first time began regular practices at such ranges, initially at rocks and, from 1915, at battle-practice targets towed at up to 17,000 yards, sometimes with 'relatively difficult change of range problems'; ships fired both individually and concentrating in pairs.[54]

In contrast to German methods, the training of British rangetakers had been neglected until just before the war, and thereafter may not have been given sufficient priority in all squadrons. The Grand Fleet order issued after the Battle of the Dogger Bank had declared that, since so few ranges had been taken:

> The gun was, in fact, used as its own rangefinder and rate keeper.[55]

Frederic Dreyer, then still Captain of *Orion*, feared that, as a result, rangefinding practice would be neglected and while he continued to encourage the training of rangetakers – 'a tedious business requiring great patience and persistence' – he did not expect his efforts to have much impact outside his own Second Battle Squadron.[56] On the other hand, he also noted:

> An inspection of a few of the Rangefinder Plots of the Fleet leads one to believe that excellent results can be obtained roughly speaking up to 15,000 yards in clear weather, and good results from 15,000 to 17,000 yards and fair above that.[57]

Dreyer was also unimpressed by other aspects of the gunnery of Beatty's ships at the Dogger Bank.

> The <u>unsupported Spotting</u> of the Battle Cruisers does not seem to have been very good.[58]

In fact, it is clear that, in general, 'their reputation for gunnery was very very shaky indeed' and 'that the Battle Cruisers' shooting was rotten'.

> An officer posted to *Invincible* reported back to *Barham*'s first-lieutenant that 'he was shocked by the standard of efficiency he encountered.'[59]

Undoubtedly, the battlecruisers, based in the Forth, found practice hard to get.[60] However, there also seems to have been a feeling in the Grand Fleet that they did not try hard enough.

> Ships from the Forth, visiting Scapa for gunnery drills, found that 'the Battle Cruisers' name up here is mud, owing to the inefficiency of their gunnery and the general casualness and lack of concentration with which they appear to treat the war.'[61]

In November 1915, Jellicoe wrote to Beatty:

> I am afraid you must have been very disappointed at *Lion* and *Tiger*'s battle practice results. I can't understand how a control officer of experience could have made such a blunder as that made by *Lion*'s . . . I fear the rapidity ideas were carried to excess in one

case (*Queen Mary* I think). Also the RF operators were bad. It is most difficult for you to give them proper practice I know.

Even before the war, Beatty's battlecruiser orders had emphasised the importance of maximising the rate of hitting and had recommended breaking into rapid independent after the first or second straddle.[62] Now Beatty responded, with the same complacency that he had shown after the Dogger Bank:

> Yes indeed it was a terrible disappointment the battle practice of *Lion* and *Tiger* ... The other three were not bad but undoubtedly as you say we could do with much more practice at sea ... I do not think you will be let down by the gunnery of the battle-cruisers when our day comes.
>     ... on the subject of rapidity of fire [I] feel very strongly ... and think we should endeavour to quicken up our firing ... the Germans certainly *do* fire 5 to our 2.

Jellicoe's response was that:

> I ... am very glad you think all will be well ...
>     I am all for rapidity of fire, but my only fear is that ships may break into rapid fire *too soon*, as *Queen Mary* I think did. It's all right even if not hitting *if short* but no use *if over* [original italics].[63]

Thus Beatty's ships were still neglecting shorts and were now compounding the mistake by breaking into rapid fire before they had reliably straddled their targets. Perhaps some of the battlecruisers improved before Jutland, but, on 7 May 1916, Beatty wrote to Jellicoe:

> I am sending you the results of the recent firings. The *Tiger*'s was as usual unsatisfactory.

Although Beatty was at last considering a replacement,[64] Captain Pelly was still in command when, as Beatty and so many others had anticipated so eagerly, their day came.

## Notes

1 *FDSF II*, pp. 50–4. Roskill, *Beatty* [B] pp. 82–5. Beatty's despatch, 30 August 1914 in *Beatty Papers, Volume I* [B] pp. 122–6.
2 'Remarks on Cruiser Action of 28th August' with Captain Chatfield to VAC First Battle-Cruiser Squadron, 31 August 1914 in ADM 1/8391/286. See also *Beatty Papers I* [1] pp. 127–9.
3 DNO's minute, 8 September 1914, in ADM 1/8391/286.

4 For Admiralty concerns about shortages, particularly of cordite, see Iain McCallum, 'Achilles Heel? Propellants and High Explosives, 1880–1916', *War Studies Journal*, 4, 1 (1999), pp. 76–8 (copy gratefully acknowledged).

5 *FDSF II*, pp. 121–3: Halpern, *Naval History of World War I* [B] pp. 98–9.

6 'Gunnery Remarks', Enclosure A with *Invincible* to C.-in-C., 18 December 1914 and *Inflexible*, 'Report on Action . . . off Falkland Islands', 11 December 1914, in ADM 137/304. *Inflexible* fired 660 rounds.

7 Vice Admiral Sturdee, 'Report of the Action off the Falkland Islands', 8 December 1914 and 'Scale Plan of Action' in ADM 137/304. *Invincible* to C.-in-C. [6] and *Inflexible*, 'Report' [6]. 50. 'Report of action off the Falkland Islands', *Grand Fleet Gunnery and Torpedo Orders*, p. 15, ADM 137/293.

8 Sturdee [7] stated that: 'Under the circumstances, the independent action taken by the "INFLEXIBLE" was quite justified'.

9 *Inflexible*, 'Report'.

10 *Invincible*, 'Gunnery Remarks' [6]. C.-in-C.'s telegram, 2.1.14 [*sic*] in 'Action off the Falkland Islands. Methods of firing . . .', ADM 1/8408/6.

11 'Damage caused to H.M.S. "Invincible" by Gunfire . . .', with *Invincible* to C.-in-C. Sumida does not mention the hit on the mast, stating only that 'the Argo mounting had been placed at the top of the fore-mast, where vibration from the high speed . . . and funnel smoke rendered it useless': *IDNS*, pp. 297–8.

12 *FDSF II*, pp. 156–74: Roskill [1] pp. 108–120: James Goldrick, *The King's Ships were at Sea* (Annapolis, MD: Naval Institute Press, 1984) pp. 248–302.

13 William Goodenough, *A Rough Record* (London: Hutchinson, 1943) p. 92.

14 Captain of *Neptune*, 'Empress of India firings', 17 November 1913, in ADM 1/8346. Admiral Callaghan, 'Conduct of a Fleet in Action. Commander-in-Chief's Instructions' (supplementary to Admiralty instructions of October 1913) in THU/107, NMM.

15 Beatty to Pelly, 11 February 1915 in *Beatty Papers I*, pp. 246–7. *Tiger* also failed to use her 'time-of-flight arrangements'.

16 Chatfield to Beatty, 'Remarks on the Action, 24th January 1915', 2 February 1915 in *Beatty Papers I*, p. 232.

17 *Ibid.* pp. 231–2; despite his own report, Chatfield also regretted 'the general impression there has been since 28th August that ammunition expenditure must not be excessive'. See also Chatfield, *Navy and Defence* [B] pp. 126–7.

18 Gordon, *Rules of the Game* [B] pp. 94–5. Goldrick [12] pp. 272–5. Moore to Beatty, 7 February 1915 in *Beatty Papers I*, pp. 219–20.

19 John Campbell, *Warship Special 1. Battlecruisers* (London: Conway Maritime Press, 1978) pp. 24, 44 and 50 for hits on German ships. Tables of hits on *Lion* and *Tiger*, 25 May 1917 in 'BCF War Records', Volume VII, ADM 137/2135.

20 Chatfield to VAC, 1BCS, 27 January 1915 and Pelly, 'Gunnery Notes' in *Beatty Papers I*, pp. 211 and 241. Hipper's despatch in Hugo von Waldeyer-Hortz, *Admiral von Hipper* (London: Rich & Cowan, 1933) p. 152.

21 *Lion*'s gunnery reports with the copy of Chatfield, 'Remarks', in ADM 137/305.

22 Pelly, 'Gunnery Notes' [20] p. 241.

23 '51. Remarks on Action on 24 January 1915' in *GFG&TO* [7] p. 17.

24 *Lion*'s gunnery reports [21].

25 Beatty, 'Notes re Lessons Learned . . .' in *Beatty Papers I*, p. 224. See also Chatfield, 'Remarks' [16] p. 232 and Chatfield to Beatty, 27 January 1915 in *Beatty Papers* I, p. 212.

26 Chatfield, 'Remarks', p. 234.

27 Beatty 'Lessons' [25] p. 225.

28 Von Hase, *Kiel and Jutland* [B] pp. 77–9. Naval Staff, Intelligence Department,

*Report on Interned German Vessels. Gunnery Information*, February 1919, pp. 8 and 18, ADM 186/240. Hartcup, *War of Invention* [B] pp. 12 and 14.

29 *Interned German Vessels*, 1919 [28] pp. 8, 17 and 34–5. Naval Staff, Intelligence Division, *Reports on Interned German Vessels, Part V Gunnery Material*, October 1920 (C.B. 1516E), pp. 7–9, ADM 186/243. *Seydlitz*, 'General Experience', in 'Jutland, Later Reports', f.272, ADM 137/1644. Naval Staff, Intelligence Department, *German Gunnery Information Derived from the Interrogation of Prisoners of War*, October 1918 (C.B. 01481), pp. 18 and 22, Ca 0108, AL. Von Hase [28] pp. 79 and 148.

30 Admiralty, Gunnery Branch, *Handbook of Stereoscopic Rangefinders. 1919*, March 1919, p. 8.

31 Admiralty, Gunnery Branch, *Progress in Gunnery Material 1922 and 1923*, November 1923, p. 56, ADM 186/259. Unfortunately, no rangefinder trials compared 9-foot coincidence with 3-metre stereo rangefinders at 15,000–20,000 yards.

32 Literally 'base- or pedestal-gear' but frequently used to include the transmitter as well. von Hase, p. 79. Admiralty, *German Navy, Part IV Section 4, Target Practice, Rangefinders and Control of Fire*, July 1917 (C.B. 1182A) p. 16, Ca 0106, AL. *Seydlitz*, 'Experience' [29].

33 Padfield, *Guns at Sea* [B] p. 228. *Information from PoWs*, 1918 [29] pp. 16–17 and Plate 3. *EU (Entfernungs Unterschieds) Anzeiger* means range difference indicator and is the term used by Padfield and von Hase; the intelligence report calls the instrument an *EU Pielscheiber* (range difference bearing disc).

34 *Information from PoWs*, 1918, p. 16. Karl Lautenschläger, 'The Dreadnought Revolution Reconsidered', in Daniel Masterson (ed.) *Naval History, The Sixth Symposium of the U.S. Naval Academy* (Wilmington, DE: Scholarly Resources, 1987) p. 135. Von Hase, pp. 82–3.

35 Von Hase, pp. 79–81. For installation dates see Lautenschläger [37] p. 135 and Campbell [19] pp. 19, 22, 43 and 49. German terms for the training director were *Zielgerät* (target-gear) – Lautenschläger – and *Richtungsweiser Sehrohre* (direction-indicator periscope) – *German Gunnery Material*, 1920 [29], p. 5.

36 *Seydlitz*, 'Experience', f.271. See also Padfield [33] pp. 252 and 271.

37 Von Hase, pp. 155–6.

38 *Information from PoWs*, p. 19. Von Hase, pp. 82–3.

39 'C.-in-C.'s Despatch', 18 June 1916 in *OD*, p. 2. Brooks, 'The Midshipman and the Secret Gadget' [B] p. 84.

40 *German Target Practice*, 1917 [32] pp. 5 and 11.

41 Von Hase, p. 134. *Seydlitz*, 'Experience', p. 272 for breakdown soon after engaging at Jutland. Paul Schmalenbach, *Die Geschichte der deutschen Schiffsartillerie* (Herford, 2nd edition 1975) p. 91 illustrates a combined range and fall-of-shot clock (*Entfernungs- und Aufschlag-Meldeuhr* or *E.A.-Uhr*) but the latter feature is not as described by von Hase, so this instrument was probably introduced after Jutland. Grateful thanks to Andrew Smith for copies, notes and translations from this book.

42 *German Target Practice*, 1917, p. 11. Von Hase, pp. 84, 145, 148–9 and 160.

43 *Information from PoWs*, 1918, p. 16 and Plate 3. Von Hase, pp. 79 and 132.

44 Von Hase, pp. 131–3. Padfield, p. 228; the illustration on p. 250 is from Schmalenbach [41] p. 91.

45 'TCBD', pp. 488–90.

46 *Seydlitz*, 'Experience', f.272.

47 Admiralty War Staff, Intelligence Division, *Germany. Results of Firing Practices, 1912–13* December 1914, pp. 14–15, 24–7, 34–5 and 44–53, ADM 137/

4799. Four *Nassaus*, four *Helgolands*, *Kaiser* and *Friedrich der Grosse*, *Moltke* and *Von der Tann* took part in the practice.

48 Von Hase, p. 153.

49 Hartcup [28] pp. 12 and 14.

50 For details of each class, see Brooks, 'Mast and Funnel' [B].

51 Admiralty, Gunnery Branch, *Handbook of Fire Control Instruments 1914*, pp. 6–7, ADM 186/191.

52 *Ibid.* Plates 69 and 96 (*Iron Duke*).

53 'Extracts from Grand Fleet Battle Orders', 18 August 1914 in *Jellicoe Papers, Volume I* [B] p. 59.

54 Dreyer, *Sea Heritage* [B] pp. 90–1 and 95. 'The Log of Captain F.C. Dreyer R.N. H.M.S. "Orion". 1914', DRYR 5/1. Midshipman P. M. S. Blackett, 'Naval Diary 1914–1918' (transcribed by Dr Nicholas Blackett) for 16 November 1915 and 31 January 1916. Quote from 'MoT', p. 124.

55 *GFG&TO*, 51 [23] p. 18. See also the similar H. F. Memorandum, '66. Remarks on Action of 24th January 1915', 5 February 1915, p. 18, in ADM 137/1943.

56 Draft letter from Dreyer to unnamed recipient, 26 March 1915 in DRYR 1/3.

57 'A few notes on the determination of the most advantageous range at which the Grand Fleet should engage the High Sea Fleet', n.d. (but probably after October 1915) in DRYR 1/3.

58 That is, unsupported by rangefinding: draft of 26 March 1915 [56].

59 Interview with Admiral Royer Dick (at Jutland, a midshipman in *Barham*) and papers of Rear Admiral S. Tillard cited in Gordon [18] pp. 30 and 51. The second quotation is from 'The Diaries of Stephen King-Hall', in L. King-Hall (ed.) *Sea Saga* (London: Gollancz, 1935) p. 436.

60 Chatfield, *Navy and Defence* [17] p. 138.

61 S. King-Hall quoted by Gordon, p. 30.

62 Beatty, '1st B.C.S. – General Gunnery Memorandum', 5 March 1914 in DRAX 1/9.

63 Jellicoe to Beatty, 18 and 23 November 1915 and Beatty to Jellicoe, 21 November 1915, in *Jellicoe Papers I* [53] pp. 188–9. At the Dogger Bank, the three leading German ships fired 976 rounds, their British opposite numbers, 869: Campbell, pp. 24, 44 and 50 and *GFG&TO*, 51. Perhaps Beatty's 5:2 ratio was based on *Lion*'s experience of the concentrated fire of *Seydlitz* and *Moltke*.

64 Beatty to Jellicoe, 7 May 1916 in *Beatty Papers I*, p. 308.

# 8

# JUTLAND AND AFTER

On 22 May 1916, the five *Queen Elizabeth* class battleships of the Fifth Battle Squadron (5BS) arrived in the Firth of Forth. On the same day, the Third Battle Cruiser Squadron (3BCS) left for Scapa Flow; there, they would calibrate their guns and adjust the new Directors in *Inflexible* and *Indomitable* before, with the squadron flagship *Invincible*, putting in some much-needed firing practice. *Queen Elizabeth* herself went straight into dock, the commander of the 5BS, Rear Admiral Hugh Evan-Thomas, transferring his flag to the *Barham*. Thus Beatty now had under his command four of the most powerful battleships then in service. He had been campaigning for this augmentation to the Battle Cruiser Fleet (BCF) since the previous February. Yet, he did not bother to meet with Evan-Thomas, or even to favour him with a copy of the Battle Cruiser Fleet Orders; thus Evan-Thomas was given no insights into the battlecruisers' action-doctrine, which was so much freer than that to which he was accustomed in the Grand Fleet.[1]

Only eight days later, the opening British moves of the Battle of Jutland were ordered by the Admiralty on 30 May, after a marked increase in wireless traffic indicated that an operation by the German battlefleet was imminent. At 10.30 p.m., the squadrons of the Grand Fleet (among them the 3BCS, commanded by Rear Admiral the Hon. Horace Hood) left their anchorages in Scapa Flow and the Moray Firth. Half an hour later, Beatty's six battlecruisers put to sea, followed by the four fast battleships. The German plan was to advance northwards to the entrance to the Skaggerack, with the five battlecruisers of Hipper's First Scouting Group (1SG) acting as bait ahead of the main High Seas Fleet (HSF) commanded by Vice Admiral Reinhard Scheer; it was hoped that submarines already in position off the British bases would sink some ships as they came out and that, subsequently, the whole German force might intercept and destroy British squadrons detached from the main Grand Fleet. Hipper left the Jade at 1.00 a.m. on 31 May, the squadrons of the HSF weighing anchor at 2.30 a.m. Only one of the German submarines succeeded in firing torpedoes (to no effect) while none provided any useful information on British movements. In fact, Beatty's force was heading eastwards to reach a position due west of the Jutland

231

Bank at about 2.30 p.m.; his ships would then turn towards a rendezvous with the Grand Fleet some seventy miles further to the NNW. Initially, Beatty and Jellicoe had little cause to believe that they would not meet as planned. Due to the now notorious misunderstanding between Captain Thomas Jackson (Director of Operations) and the intelligence staff of Room 40, the Admiralty signalled at 12.30 p.m. that, an hour before, the German flagship was still in the Jade.[2] The wording of the signal did not, however, rule out the possibility that the 1SG was already out.

At 12.30 p.m., Beatty's ships were still heading east in cruising formation. His flagship, *Lion*, led the First Battle Cruiser Squadron (the 1BCS: *Princess Royal* followed by *Queen Mary* and *Tiger*). The Second Battle Cruiser Squadron (*New Zealand* and *Indefatigable*) were two miles broad on *Lion*'s port bow, while the 5BS (*Barham* leading *Valiant*, *Warspite* and *Malaya*) had been stationed five miles fine on the port quarter. At 1.30,[3] to prepare for the coming port turn towards the rendezvous, Beatty repositioned the 5BS NNW of *Lion*, still five miles distant, and the Second Battle Cruiser Squadron (2BCS) three miles ENE.[4] Andrew Gordon argues convincingly that these dispositions show that Beatty had no thought for any encounter other than the anticipated meeting with the Grand Fleet. However, they left his most powerful, though slowest, squadron, the 5BS, well separated from the battlecruisers and in the opposite direction from that in which the enemy would most likely be sighted and pursued.[5]

At 2.15, Beatty made the general signal that turned all his squadrons to NbyE. But at 2.20 or thereabouts, the light cruiser *Galatea* reported by wireless that she had sighted two enemy cruisers bearing ESE.[6] At 2.25, a flag signal from *Lion* ordered the accompanying destroyers to 'Take position as Submarine screen when course is altered to S.S.E.'. Flags were again used at 2.32 to signal a turn by all squadrons to SSE, but without a searchlight repeat to the distant 5BS. According to the British 'Messages', Evan-Thomas did not order the 5BS to turn about to SSE until 2.40, though the report of *Barham*'s Captain Craig gave the time as 2.38.[7] Thus the distance between the battlecruisers and the 5BS had now increased from five miles to some nine or ten miles.[8]

The question of responsibility for this separation became a matter of bitter controversy. From *Galatea*'s first wireless message, Evan-Thomas was aware of the presence of a pair of enemy ships, but his orders were to look out for the approaching Grand Fleet, while Beatty's other forces hardly needed the support of the 5BS to deal with two cruisers. There are good reasons for believing the carefully worded statement of Evan-Thomas' nephew that:

> my uncle to the end of his life was quite certain that NO executive signal [course SSE at 2.32] was received by *Barham* at this time, and that no 'informative signal' giving any clue to the battle-cruiser

movements [the signal to the destroyers at 2.25] was ever reported to him on the bridge.[9]

It only became apparent after 2.35 that the battlecruisers, already shrouded in dense funnel smoke, were turning about. Evan-Thomas then had to decide what to do without any prior guidance or clear orders. Despite the urging of Captain Craig (and, perhaps, the Flag Commander),[10] he probably did hesitate for a few minutes, but that hardly justifies the savage criticism that he subsequently received.[11] As Gordon says:

> the onus would not have devolved upon Evan-Thomas's initiative if *Lion*'s signalling had been conducted professionally and in accordance with Grand Fleet Battle Orders.[12]

*Lion*'s signallers were still commanded, as at the Dogger Bank, by Beatty's Flag Lieutenant, Ralph Seymour. Their failure to make sure that *Barham* had received and acknowledged the order for course SSE was the primary cause of the *increase* in the separation of the 5BS from the battlecruisers. But, by focusing attention on Evan-Thomas' delay in turning, Beatty (whether deliberately or not) obscured the fact that, even before the turns, his own dispositions had already created an *initial* separation of five miles.[13]

At 2.39, *Galatea*'s wireless announced:

> Urgent. Have sighted large amount of smoke as though from a fleet bearing N.N.E.

and, at 2.51:

> Urgent ... Smoke seems to be seven vessels besides Destroyers and Cruisers. They have turned North.[14]

The British commanders now had confirmation that, at very least, the 1SG was at sea; by 3 o'clock, Jellicoe had ordered steam for full speed and complete readiness for action. Yet, while Beatty now knew the German position and course, at least approximately, he did nothing to dispose his forces in readiness for action. With his two weakest ships three miles to the NNE and closest to the enemy, he continued on course SSE until he turned his squadrons together at 2.52 to SE, at 3.01 to E and at 3.13 to NE. All three turns were ordered only by flags as general signals, but they probably could not be read from *Barham*; Evan-Thomas held on to the SSE until 3.05, and then cut the corners by altering to ESE and, at 3.14, to E. At 3.21, Beatty broadcast his course and speed by wireless and, at the same nominal time, Evan-Thomas ordered his ships to conform i.e. NE at 23 knots. As early as June 1916, Beatty had the gall to blame Evan-Thomas for not closing on the battlecruisers,[15] yet the succession of general signals clearly establishes that Beatty intended that the 5BS should follow parallel courses. Nonetheless, it is regrettable that Evan-Thomas abandoned his independent effort to close the battlecruisers.

At 3.15, Hipper (in the flagship *Lützow* leading *Derfflinger*, *Seydlitz*, *Moltke* and *Von der Tann* in line) turned from NNW (not N as reported by *Galatea*) to NW.[16] The two sides were now converging rapidly; at 3.20, two columns of British battlecruisers were first sighted from the 1SG, while the German ships were visible from *Lion* by 3.25, and may have been spotted earlier from the 2BCS.[17] Yet, in the forty-five minutes since *Galatea* had reported 'smoke as though from a fleet', Beatty had taken no steps to form his line or even to concentrate his forces in anticipation of this critical moment. The 5BS were some six miles on *Lion*'s port beam;[18] as Andrew Gordon concludes:

> Having hustled for the 5th BS, and won, VABCF was about to engage the 1st Scouting Group no better off than if the battleships had stayed in Scapa, and it was substantially his own fault.[19]

Just as seriously, the two thinly armoured battlecruisers of the 2BCS were on the flagship's starboard bow, about three miles closer to the 1SG. Yet, even with the 5BS out of range, Beatty still appeared to have an advantage in numbers and weight of fire. But, with the range already falling towards 23,000 yards at about 3.30,[20] he now had little time in which to manoeuvre his battlecruisers into an effective battle formation.

## THE RUN TO THE SOUTH: FIRST PHASE

At first sighting, the visibility from the two sides was, at its best, not much different, though it was more patchy for the British:

> the weather was misty in patches, the visibility varying from 12 to 6 miles; wind west, force 3; sea calm.[21]

Beatty took the initiative at 3.30 with a general signal by flags turning his squadrons E at 25 knots. This signal and its repeat by flags was evidently not read by the 5BS, which continued NE until the order to turn E was repeated by searchlight at 3.35. This further signalling failure by *Lion* left the 5BS trailing about eight miles on *Lion*'s port quarter.[22] But the double repeat is also the final evidence that Beatty had intended from the start to keep the battleships at a distance on parallel courses. Indeed, Captain Roskill concluded uneasily that Beatty was motivated by a fear that they might otherwise steal the battlecruisers' thunder.[23]

To form his six battlecruisers into line of battle, Beatty's first thought had been an order to the 2BCS to prolong the line ahead, but the flag hoist at 3.29 was not made executive. Instead, at 3.34, they were commanded to form in line astern, which obliged them to make two sweeping turns to starboard and port before hauling into line at 3.45;[24] at 3.35, Beatty also slowed slightly to 24 knots. Meanwhile, with his line of retreat threatened, at 3.35 Hipper had ordered a turn away in succession of fifteen points to SE. By 3.40, *Lützow* had probably steadied on the new course when he called for a speed of 18 knots, having already ordered a distribution of fire from the left.[25] Between the leading ships, the range was, therefore, now closing at almost 550 yds/min.[26] Subsequently, the German battlecruisers made only one more course alteration, of two points together to SSE at 3.45, 'to close the enemy more rapidly'. The approximate courses of both sides after 3.30 are shown on Figure 8.1. When the Germans opened fire at 3.48, their targets and ranges were:

| | | |
|---|---|---|
| *Lützow* | 16,800 yards | *Lion* |
| *Derfflinger* | 16,400 yards | *Princess Royal* |
| *Seydlitz* | 16,400 yards | *Queen Mary* |
| *Moltke* | 15,500 yards | *Tiger* |
| *Von der Tann* | 17,700 yards | *Indefatigable*[27] |

Thus *New Zealand* had been missed out; perhaps *Von der Tann* had found it difficult to keep on one target while the 2BCS twice reversed course.

At 3.43, *Lion* hoisted the flag signal ordering the battlecruisers to form a line of bearing NW. I hope a brief aside to explain this formation will help in understanding the next few hectic minutes on the British side. In simple line-ahead, each ship followed in the wake of the leader. In battle, provided the wind and the enemy were both somewhere on the same side, one's own funnel and gun smoke was carried onto the non-engaged side and did not interfere with gunnery. But smoke interference was potentially a problem if the wind blew from any point in the arc from dead ahead, through all points on the non-engaged side, to dead astern. If ships were then in line, either they could be enveloped in the smoke from those ahead, or the smoke from ahead was carried between each ship and its target. Either problem could be solved by forming a line of bearing, inclined towards the enemy, at an angle to their common course. The direction of the line was specified as a compass bearing from the guide, normally the leading ship. If formed correctly, each ship had the smoke from all those ahead on her non-engaged side (though her own smoke could still cause problems in her after turrets).

At 3.43 and 3.46, *Lion* made two small turns to starboard, while at 3.45, the line of bearing signal was hauled down (made executive). According to the British records, the Germans opened fire at 3.47 and *Lion*'s signal to reply was made immediately; thus German times were about one minute fast

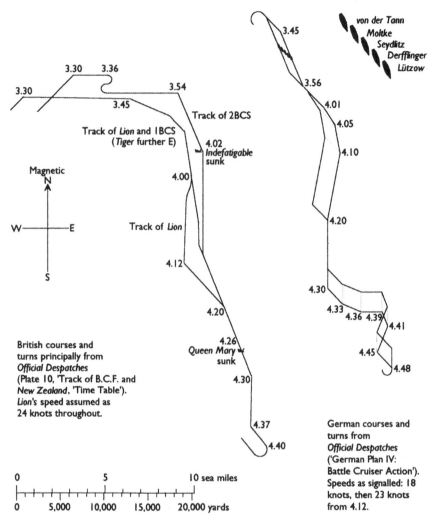

*Figure 8.1* The Run to the South: approximate courses of the battlecruisers.

on the British. Literally at the last minute (3.46), Beatty made his only fire distribution signal, for *Lion* and *Princess Royal* to concentrate on the leading German ship.[28] This implied that the remaining battlecruisers should engage ship-to-ship, but, according to their signal logs, it was not received by *Tiger* or *New Zealand*.[29] *Lion* also made a general flag signal to all ships to alter course together to ESE. In the British 'Messages', it was timed at 3.45, but, according to the Vice Admiral's 'Narrative', it was made at 3.47 in the same hoist as the five-flag for 'open fire'.[30] In the absence of any other orders, a line-of-bearing NW was formed from an easterly course by all the ships astern of *Lion* (the guide) fanning out to port, though the manoeuvre required almost seven minutes to complete.[31] If the flagship's course had still been E, the rear ships would have turned almost directly towards the enemy;[32] not only would this have sharply increased the range-rate but also it would have ensured that only their forward turrets could bear. However, since *Lion* was at the same time turning to starboard, and may have ordered a simultaneous turn together to ESE, the remaining battlecruisers were probably able to infer that they should form the line-of-bearing either by turning to starboard by different degrees (*Lion* and the 1BCS) or by holding to course E (2BCS, as shown on their course chart).[33] If, on the other hand, the course signal was delayed for as much as two minutes, it may have been made because some battlecruisers had not responded as desired, though, after such a delay, its intent may have been far from clear. In any case, the method chosen to form the line-of-bearing was too slow; at best, only *Princess Royal* can have reached the line-of-bearing NW from *Lion* when firing began. Furthermore, it did practically nothing to counter the rapidly falling range.[34] Although *Lion* herself had turned away two points to ESE, the move had been countered by Hipper's almost simultaneous turn inwards to SSE. Thus, at 3.47, the calculated range-rate between the two flagships was –570 yds/min. While the time of the signal altering course together to ESE must remain uncertain, the conflicting records themselves suggest that, once again, *Lion*'s inept signalling organisation had sown confusion in Beatty's line, this time in the last critical minutes before they went into action.

Lion and *Princess Royal* returned the German fire immediately (both ships timed their first salvoes at 3.47½) but *Tiger* did not open until a minute or so later, with *Queen Mary* about two minutes later still. *New Zealand* followed at 3.51. The targets and initial ranges were as follows.

| | | |
|---|---|---|
| *Lion* | 18,500 yards | *Lützow* |
| *Princess Royal* | 16,000 yards | *Lützow* |
| *Queen Mary* | ~17,000 yards | *Seydlitz* |
| *Tiger* | 18,500 yards | *Moltke* |
| *New Zealand* | 18,100 yards | *Moltke* |
| *Indefatigable* | ? | *Von der Tann*[35] |

Since it is now generally agreed that the actual range was about 16,000 yards,[36] at least four of the British battlecruisers opened with ranges that were far too high. Also, *Queen Mary* and *Tiger* were shooting at their opposite numbers so, despite Beatty's numerical advantage, *Derfflinger* was not under fire. Both *Lion* and *Princess Royal* recorded initial target bearings of Red 42 (42° on the port bow); thus all their turrets could bear on the enemy and they had probably already turned to ESE. However, a survivor from *Queen Mary* recalled that she opened fire with only her fore turrets, while, assuming that the 2BCS were still on course E, their after turrets could not engage. It is therefore likely that *Tiger* was similarly handicapped.[37]

Beatty's own despatch confirms that smoke interference was a problem during the approach – and that the general visibility was not.[38] However, its times are very different from those in the 'Narrative' still to be found in his personal records. Thus he appears to have deliberately misrepresented his conduct of the approach, probably to forestall anticipated criticism of his tactics.

> At 3.30 p.m. I increased speed to 25 knots and formed the Line of Battle, the 2nd Battle Cruiser Squadron forming astern of the 1st Battle Cruiser Squadron ... I turned to E.S.E., slightly converging on the enemy, who were now at a range of 23,000 yards, and formed the ships on a line of bearing to clear the smoke ... The visibility at this time was good, the sun behind us and the wind S.E.[39]

Furthermore, all other sources describe the wind as a light westerly breeze, though they differ somewhat in the extent and timing of a shift from NW to SW.[40] This wind would have piled up the smoke astern while on course E, and carried it onto the engaged side, especially after the turns towards ESE – hence the line of bearing NW. Yet, even before it was formed, *Lion*, at the head of the line, should not have been troubled by smoke, while her smoke evidently did not affect *Princess Royal*; the second British ship sighted '5 Enemy Battle Cruisers in sight' at 3.34.45 and, at 3.42, she chose the 'Right hand ship ("Lutzow" class)' as her target. Her initial range was by far the most accurate of Beatty's ships, while her rate of –400 yds/min. was the most accurate known from either side.[41]

> I think that at this time all the battle cruisers except 'P.R.' had underestimated the rate; we had [in *Tiger*].[42]

In marked contrast, *Tiger*'s 'Gunnery Record' does not even begin until 3.44 (Table 8.1).

*Table 8.1* The start of *Tiger*'s Gunnery Record

| GMT | Gun range | Object | Remarks |
| --- | --- | --- | --- |
| 3.44 | | | Enemy reported in sight from 'Lion'. |
| 3.45 | | | Sighted enemy B.C.S. apparently 3, 'Derflinger' [*sic*], 'Seydlitz' and 'Moltke'. |
| 3.48 | | | Enemy opened fire. |
| 3.50 | | | 'Lion' opened fire. |
| 3.51 | 18.500 | 4th ship from right, 'Seydlitz' class | Considerable interference from own T.B.Ds' smoke. |

Even after *Tiger* opened fire:

> The top reported that the funnel smoke of our battle cruisers ahead
> made their view very bad.[43]

Information about *Queen Mary* is necessarily scarce. Though next ahead
from *Tiger*, she opened fire later, and, although she was regarded as the
crack gunnery ship of the BCF,[44] her initial range was about a thousand yards
too high. Furthermore, like *Tiger*, she fired at her opposite number in the
German line. Yet (subject to ensuring that no ship was left unfired at) Grand
Fleet orders emphasised the importance, if numbers permitted, of
concentrating on an enemy's leading ship or ships;[45] this was the distribution
scheme assumed, without orders, by *Princess Royal* at 3.42 and by the 2BCS,
and ordered from *Lion* at 3.46. It seems unlikely that *Queen Mary* and *Tiger*
would have chosen differently; probably, they did not in fact do so. If *Queen
Mary*, like *Tiger*, could not at first see *Lützow*, *Seydlitz* and *Moltke* would
have appeared to have been their correct targets. Evidently, by the time of
her first salvo, the mistake was apparent in *Tiger*, but, with smoke interference from both battlecruisers and destroyers, there was neither time nor
opportunity for either ship to change target. Thus Beatty's delay in
reforming his line 'to clear the smoke' had particularly bad effects on these
two ships. Not only did they select the wrong targets, but also they were able
to begin ranging and plotting only a few minutes (three in the case of *Tiger*)
before their opponents opened fire, while, even then, they were still not free
from smoke interference. It is not surprising that their opening ranges and
rates were inaccurate. In accordance with BCF Battle Orders, *Queen Mary*
and *Tiger* could perhaps have done more on their own initiative to avoid the
smoke from ahead. However, the Orders stipulated that:

> It is desirable that ships should not haul out more than one point
> [which may not have been enough] and that no movement should
> inconvenience others [difficult to avoid when the 2BCS were trying
> to haul into line on the port quarter].[46]

Without a lead from the flagship, both ships seem to have just followed in
her wake.

Since *New Zealand*'s Captain was 'rather impressed by the little smoke
interference there was', the 2BCS must have come into line on *Tiger*'s port
quarter. However, their violent manoeuvres created conditions of heel,
vibration and rapidly changing bearings which made ranging impossible; it
was not until 3.45 that *New Zealand* 'Commenced ranging on the 4th ship
from the right'.[47] With the 1BCS making 24 knots, the 2BCS also had to
recover the speed lost in the turns. When *New Zealand* opened fire, her
engines were making over 300 revolutions per minute, more than she had

managed at the Dogger Bank, so the ranging of the 2BCS continued to be disrupted by vibration.[48]

*Lion*'s rangetakers had none of the difficulties experienced by those in the four rear ships, yet they failed conspicuously to match the standard set by *Princess Royal*. *Lion*'s TS record contains only two rangefinder ranges from the period of the approach: 20,000 yards at 3.42 and 18,500 yards at 3.46. From the calculated rates, it can be estimated that these ranges were too high by, respectively, 900 and 1,600 yards. Yet her TS did not even accept the implied rate of –375 yds/min. When fire was opened at 3.47½, the rate in use was only –150 yds/min., while the opening range was still 18,500 yards, as though, since 3.46, there had been no rate at all. And the other recorded rates suggest that, throughout the approach, the estimate of enemy course was insufficiently converging by as much as four points.[49] It appears that, despite Beatty's reassurances to Jellicoe, the whole fire control organisation of his flagship was no more efficient than it had been during the practices of late 1915.

Somehow, Beatty himself seems to have been aware of the German course, since he reported it by wireless to Jellicoe at 3.45 as S 55° E; this was barely 3° different from their SE'ly course held until a minute before.[50] However, he may not have been aware of the serious gunnery implications. Admiral Goodenough, though an admirer, admitted that the pre-eminence of 'that ardent spirit Lord Beatty' did not derive from 'great professional knowledge, certainly not of gun or torpedo'.[51] Unfortunately, at this critical moment, Beatty was unable to turn to his Flag Captain, on whose gunnery expertise he customarily relied.[52] Chatfield recalled:

> I was on the compass platform . . . Beatty remained for a time on his own bridge . . . with [his staff]. I wanted him to come on the compass platform and sent a message to Seymour, telling him to advise Beatty that the range was closing rapidly and that we ought almost at once to be opening fire . . . But I could get no reply, the Vice-Admiral was engaged in an important message to the Commander-in-Chief. 18,000 [*sic*] yards. I told Longhurst [the gunnery commander] to be ready to open fire immediately.[53]

Thus Chatfield implies that Beatty was preoccupied with signalling and had not yet realised that they were already within the range at which (in Chatfield's opinion formed after the Dogger Bank) they must expect a rapid and accurate fire from the German ships. Another possibility is that Beatty deliberately chose to ignore Chatfield's conclusions and to follow his own intention to press in to 12,000–14,000 yards, in which case their separation denied Chatfield a final opportunity to warn against such a dangerous tactic.

Beatty, it seems, never explained what had been in his mind, but Hipper was in no doubt about the consequences of his headlong approach.

The fact that the English Battlecruisers, [possibly] on account of bad light conditions or perhaps forming line of Battle too late, delayed opening fire, allowed us too to withhold our fire until the enemy was in effective gun range (15,000–16,000 yards). The possibility of obtaining a rapid gunnery superiority . . . is principally to be attributed to this delay in opening fire which compelled the enemy to remain a longer time within effective gun range.[54]

The light also favoured the Germans, especially for spotting, since they were 'against a dark grey background, whilst we were silhouetted against the Western sky'.[55] The effects of the fire from the 1SG were quickly felt; by 3.52, both *Lion* and *Tiger* had been hit twice.[56] Hipper held his course SSE, which brought the range down to less than 13,000 yards; then, at about 3.54–6, he turned *Lützow* away to SE and ordered his ships to follow in her wake.[57] Even before she was hit, at 3.49 *Lion* began a series of unsignalled turns away,[58] so there was no possibility of even the 1BCS completing the formation of a regular line of bearing. *Lion*'s director layer had problems because with these 'alterations of course the ship was now yawing considerably'.[59] By 3.55, *Lion* had steadied on a course SbyE, which she held until 4.00; thus, after reaching a minimum below 13,000 yards at 3.54, the range between the leading ships opened at a rate of more than 430 yds/min.[60]

Without signals from the flagship, Beatty's other battlecruisers were left, as required in BCF Orders, to use their 'initiative and judgement' in following his movements. *Princess Royal* also 'gradually altered to southward', but she seems to have got into *Lion*'s smoke, as well as being subjected to *Derfflinger*'s undisturbed fire; thus she was unable to make anything of her accurate opening range and rate, even though her ranges were comparable with *Derfflinger*'s until 3.55; her fire was then badly disrupted by two hits at 3.56, one of which put her Argo Tower out of action.[61] She was hit again at about 4 o'clock. *Queen Mary* made the first British hits, on *Seydlitz*, at 3.55 and 3.57, the second of which burned out the after superfiring turret; *Queen Mary* evidently had few problems with smoke from ahead, which suggests that, compared with *Princess Royal*, she made a wider turn. Her survivors did not recall any hits on their ship until much later,[62] but *Tiger* took another six hits from *Moltke*, after which Q and X turrets were incapable of accurate fire for the rest of the battle.[63] Also, *Tiger*'s gun ranges continued downwards after 3.55 to reach a minimum of 10,500 yards just after 4 o'clock, while, at 4.04, *Moltke*'s range was 11,500 yards and still falling;[64] furthermore, each ship was probably hit once by the other at this time. Probably while avoiding smoke interference, *Tiger*'s course appears to have taken her considerably closer to the enemy line than the rest of the 1BCS.

At the rear of the British line, the 2BCS were still headed E at 25 knots when firing began and remained on this course until [3.54], when they turned six points to SSE.[65] These courses kept them well clear of smoke from the

1BCS to starboard, while the turn altered the rate from almost -800 yds/min. closing to under +300 yds/min. opening, and allowed the after turrets to bear. But their large turn probably disrupted ranging and aiming, thereby increasing the difficulty of recovering from the large initial range errors; neither *New Zealand* nor *Indefatigable* made any hits before or after their turn.[66]

At 4 o'clock, the 1SG was ordered to turn together to SEbyS; if they were already headed SE, this would have been a turn towards.[67] At the same nominal time, both flagships found each other's range. *Lützow* was hit twice while a single hit wrecked *Lion*'s Q turret. Her TS record of target bearings shows that, at this moment, *Lion* turned away rapidly by almost three points so that, at least momentarily, A and B turrets were not bearing: though, by 4.04, despite three more hits, she had been brought back onto a new course S.[68] *Lion*'s sudden swing to starboard was confirmed by her Captain.

> It was at this moment [after Q turret had been knocked out], seeing that the range was decreasing and not wishing to let it do so, I told Commander Strutt to steer 5 degrees to starboard. Strutt gave the order. The Chief Quartermaster, however, misheard it as ordering him to give the ship 5 degrees of port helm. I suddenly saw the ship swinging off to starboard rapidly and had to bring her back and increase speed to resume our station. The ships astern, having seen the large flame shooting up, thought we were steering off because of the damage!
>
> At 4.25, soon after we resumed our position ahead of the 'Princess Royal' ... the 'Queen Mary' ... blew up .[69]

Meanwhile, the range from *Von der Tann* was falling to a minimum of 13,450 yards; thus she was firing her 5.9-inch as well as her 11-inch guns. At about 4.02, she succeeded in straddling *Indefatigable* with two 11-inch salvoes in quick succession; at least two shells from each were observed to hit and, shortly after the second salvo, *Indefatigable*'s magazines exploded.

As the two lines drew apart at the end of this first phase of the Run to the South:

> From the *Lützow* it appeared about this time [c.4.05] as if the British flagship hauled out of line, with a list of 10 degrees to starboard; she seemed to disappear at times behind the other vessels wrapped in a thick pall of smoke ... At times the enemy's fire ceased altogether and the tactical cohesion of the British line appeared to be seriously shaken.[70]

Beatty's line was in disarray; he had lost a battlecruiser to a numerically inferior opponent, and he had been decisively beaten in the gunnery duel, his ships making only six hits, while receiving at least twenty-two.[71] The 1SG had been able to seize and retain gunnery superiority mainly thanks to Beatty's tactics. At the start, he had failed to concentrate his squadrons; consequently, when the enemy was sighted, the battleships were too distant to give support and the weak 2BCS was dangerously exposed. After a brief uncertainty, Beatty turned all his squadrons across the wake of the 1SG before ordering the 2BCS to prolong the line astern. Although this move obliged Hipper to turn about, he was then able to make an easy approach at 18 knots with his opponents clearly in sight abeam; he made only one more course alteration to close more rapidly. Yet, with the range falling rapidly, Beatty held his course, and his speed of 24 knots, so that he had insufficient time and sea-room:

- to get the 2BCS into line;
- to form the line of bearing that avoided mutual smoke interference;
- to order his distribution of fire;
- to allow all his ships to range and to plot unimpeded, despite any patches of poorer visibility;
- lastly, to keep the enemy at the long ranges that exploited the advantages conferred by his heavier guns.

Beatty probably did not realise fully just how quickly time was running out. *Lion*'s few ranges were misleadingly high, while Chatfield implies that the Vice Admiral had not been paying them sufficient attention. When the Germans opened fire, the light conditions were already in their favour. But as the British ships were forced to reply, their other disadvantages were the direct result of Beatty's conduct of the approach:

- they were already within their opponents' effective range;
- they were still trying to reform their line in accordance with *Lion*'s confusing signals;
- the 2BCS were struggling to keep station;
- some ships were still hampered by smoke from ahead (which interfered with their own rangetaking much more than their opponents');
- not all their turrets were bearing;
- only *Princess Royal* had obtained an accurate opening range and rate;
- frequent course changes disrupted aiming and ranging;
- despite their numerical superiority, one of their opponents was not even under fire.

Having lost gunnery superiority, it was not possible to recover. And, without tactical direction from the flagship, the vulnerable ships of the 2BCS, probably to avoid smoke from ahead, strayed dangerously close to the 1SG. Once *Von der Tann* found the range, the deadly combination of her effective armour piercing shell, *Indefatigable*'s weak armour and the dangerous handling of ammunition in the BCF quickly led to her cataclysmic destruction.

## THE RUN TO THE SOUTH: SECOND PHASE

After the sinking of *Indefatigable*, Hipper turned his ships together at 4.04 to SbyE but his leading ships were soon obliged to cease firing as the range continued to increase; at 4.08, it reached 20,775 yards from *Derfflinger*. At 4.07 or a little later, the 1SG again altered together to the slightly converging course of SbyW. They increased speed to 23 knots at 4.12, while *Lützow* probably altered one point away to S before, at 4.18, Hipper ordered his other ships to follow in his wake. They then held a steady course until 4.27.[72]

By 4.10, Beatty's ships were probably all headed S with *Lion* (as Chatfield confirms) still out of line to starboard of *Princess Royal* and *Queen Mary*. *Tiger* and *New Zealand* were further astern, with, for a time, *Tiger* nearer to the enemy. Despite smoke interference from destroyers, *Lion* and (as far as can be known) *Queen Mary* continued firing at their opposite numbers, while *New Zealand* was now engaged with *Von der Tann*.[73] *Tiger* was attempting to keep her guns on the *Moltke*, but, due to her damaged turrets and a suspect director, she could fire her shots only in ones and twos, while some of these were probably aimed at *Seydlitz*.[74] *Tiger* had neither an Evershed installation, nor a Mark VII* Dumaresq in her GCT; thus, once her Director became unreliable, she was especially ill equipped to keep all her guns on the same target. Between 3.55.15 and 4.15.28, *Princess Royal*'s record contains only one range (19,100 yards at 4.06.50) and no indication that she changed target; however, von Hase of *Derfflinger* implies that she had done so even before *Indefatigable* was destroyed, while, even if this was not the case, it is most unlikely that *Princess Royal* left her opposite number undisturbed after the British line was reduced to five ships.[75]

At about ten past four, the 5BS was at last able to open fire, initially at *Von der Tann*, which was hit almost immediately at a range of 19,000 yards. The battleships were soon concentrating in pairs, delivering 'a regular hail of 15-inch projectiles'; *Moltke* received two hits at about 4.16.[76] Meanwhile, Beatty turned *Lion* to a course SE so that, from 4.12, the range to *Lützow* began to close rapidly at about –700 yds/min. Although apparently without the aid of signals from the flagship, Rear Admiral Brock in *Princess Royal* responded appropriately by altering to SSE; thus, by 4.19–20, *Lion* had regained her position at the head of the line, when she too turned SSE. At this time, Hipper also altered away, so the subsequent rate works out at just over –250 yds/min.[77] During this new approach by the British ships, *Lützow* was hit twice at 4.15, probably by *Lion*, and *Seydlitz* once by *Queen Mary* at 4.17.[78] However, as the range fell, at 4.15–17 the 1SG were able to reopen fire.

Once more the 'Lion' was covered by the German fire, receiving several hits and, due partly to a still fiercely burning fire from an earlier hit, she became so enveloped in smoke and fumes as to be at times invisible from ships astern of the 'Lützow'.

Although von Hase confirms that *Lion* could not be seen from *Derfflinger*, *Lützow*'s next astern, the reason he gives is somewhat different:

At [4].17 I again engaged the second battlecruiser from the left. I was under the impression that it was the same ship as I had engaged before, the *Princess Royal*. Actually, however, it was the *Queen Mary* . . . this was due to the fact that, just as I was finding my target, Admiral Beatty's flagship, the *Lion*, was obliged to fall out of the enemy line for a time, and, owing to the heavy smoke covering the enemy line, could not be seen by us.

Von Hase cannot be correct about the time at which *Lion* fell out of line, but he verifies that she had still not regained the head of the line. Unfortunately, *Seydlitz* did not make the same mistake in identifying her target, so both she and *Derfflinger* concentrated on *Queen Mary*.[79]

Beatty's ships remained in the windward position, from which smoke interference would again be a problem if they did not form a line of bearing inclined towards the enemy. They now had the worst of the visibility; in the first version of his despatch, Beatty wrote:

The visibility to the North Eastward had become considerably reduced and the outline of the ships very indistinct. This, no doubt, was largely due to the constant use of smoke balls or charges by the enemy, under cover of which they were continually altering course or zig-zagging.

The reference to imaginary smoke balls was omitted from the published version of his despatch, while the only German ships that needed to zigzag were those under the hot fire from the 5BS.[80] Nevertheless, there is no reason to doubt the deterioration in visibility, though it was as bad for the battleships as for the battlecruisers.[81] *Lion*'s high ranges (she recorded rangefinder ranges of 23,000 yards at 4.12 and 21,000 yards at 4.16) are explicable, at least to some extent, by her position out of line and the increased difficulty in rangetaking. Nonetheless, their fall represented an average rate of −525 yds/min., not that much less than the calculated value. Unfortunately, this trend was largely disregarded; the rates in use just before and after *Lion*'s turn to SSE were still only −200 and −150 yds/min., though the small rate reduction indicates that *Lion*'s fire controllers were beginning to recognise their mistake.[82] Likewise, the surviving records from Beatty's other battlecruisers suggest that none had yet realised how fast the ranges had been falling.

The first hit by the 5BS on *Von der Tann* temporarily damaged her steering gear; this, or her zigzagging to throw out the battleships' fire, seems to have taken her out of line to port, since, by [4.16½], *New Zealand* had lost sight of her and shifted her fire to *Moltke*. A minute later, *Von der Tann* engaged and even made one hit on *Barham*, but, at 4.20 and 4.23, *Von der Tann* also received two more hits. Campbell, though without explanation, attributes these to *Tiger*. But *Tiger*'s erratic fire was straying towards the head, not the rear, of the enemy line, while, if *Von der Tann* was obscured from *New Zealand*, she would have been even more difficult to see from *Tiger*. It is much more likely that these hits were due to the rapid and accurate fire of the 5BS, which also scored another two hits on *Moltke* at about this time.[83] In that case, following the three hits made early in their renewed approach, Beatty's battlecruisers made no further hits on the 1SG in this second phase of the Run to the South and soon lost gunnery superiority; at 4.24, *Lion* received two hits from *Lützow*.[84] But, more seriously, and despite *Princess Royal* not even being under fire, the shooting of the British battlecruisers did nothing more to take the pressure off *Queen Mary*. She had probably already been hit twice by *Seydlitz* before, at 4.21, the right gun of Q turret was put out of action; von Hase spotted *Derfflinger*'s first straddle at 4.22.40, when his rate was −330 yds/min. and range 15,200 yards. After spotting the fall of the next three salvoes, he ordered rapid fire, which produced six salvoes with an average interval of only twenty-two seconds; at 4.26, after two further hits, *Queen Mary* was sunk by explosions in her fore and midships magazines.[85]

Shortly after 4.25, *Princess Royal* might have hit back, since her ranges were beginning to converge on *Derfflinger*'s. But then there was an unexplained gap of almost six minutes in her salvo record. Since Beatty originated a wireless signal at 4.25 ordering her to 'Keep clear of smoke', it appears that, once again, she strayed into the flagship's smoke. *Princess Royal* may have responded to the signal by turning to SE for a time.[86] She now became the target for *Derfflinger*; Campbell mentions three more ill-documented and largely ineffective hits on the British ship, but only one has been added here to the German total.[87]

Meanwhile, the second and third hits on *Von der Tann* had disabled both her fore and after turrets; she was forced to turn her midships turrets back to *New Zealand* and, at 4.26, made a hit on X barbette, though fortunately it did not penetrate. Nonetheless, Hipper's two rear ships were still in danger from the fire of the 5BS, while his line was now also threatened with an attack from British destroyers that, since about 4.20, had been forming up ahead of *Lion*.[88] Only a minute after the destruction of *Queen Mary*, Hipper began a withdrawal – by turning away together four points to SE – that continued until 4.38. Beatty in *Lion* also turned away, but only by two points, and soon returned to much the same course as before,[89] towards the advancing but as yet unsighted High Seas Fleet.

After the destruction of *Queen Mary*, *Tiger* narrowly avoided her remains by hauling out to port. *Tiger* changed target to *Seydlitz* but herself became the target for *Seydlitz* as well as *Moltke* and received three further hits. Her ranges fell to improbably low values (a minimum of 11,800 yards at 4.33.30) but it does appear that, once again, she got closest to the enemy. Against *Moltke*, *New Zealand*'s ranges did not begin to decrease decisively until after she had passed the wreck of *Queen Mary* on its starboard side. *New Zealand*'s ranges did not fall as far as those of her consorts, while there are several gaps in her salvo record;[90] thus it appears that she remained somewhere on their starboard quarter and that, as would be expected, their smoke interfered at times with her fire. As in the first phase, she made no hits on either of her targets.

In the second phase of the Run to the South, the 5BS scored at least five, probably seven, hits on *Von der Tann* and *Moltke* at long range. The 1SG must be allowed at least another twelve hits on the British battlecruisers, as well as the hit on *Barham*. Whereas, if the two hits on *Von der Tann* are discounted, the British battlecruiser tally was only three. These three were all made at the start, when ranges were long, and hint at what might have been accomplished if the approach had been less precipitate. Unfortunately, these early successes were not sustained, though for different reasons. *Lion*'s ranges were again too few, while her transmitting station ignored their clear downward trend; the rate in use was insufficiently closing until after her turn from SE to SSE. Shortly after 4.25, *Princess Royal* might have found the hitting range, had she not, at the critical moment, got into *Lion*'s smoke.[91] *Tiger*'s previous damage rendered her target selection uncertain and her fire ragged and ineffective. *New Zealand*'s own gunnery record shows that she was slow in reducing the range and suggests that she suffered from smoke interference once she did so. On the other hand, her ranges show that she was the only British ship that detected how rapidly Hipper was withdrawing.

When *Lion* initiated the new approach by turning SE at 4.12, her rangefinder range of 23,000 yards was almost certainly too high. Once again, her inaccurate rangetaking, by exaggerating the distance between the opposing lines, was about to have serious tactical consequences. The flagship's steep approach without signals pushed *Princess Royal* and the ships astern onto a converging course that closed the range too quickly. When Beatty's ships once more found themselves unexpectedly within the German's effective range, *Lion* was only just regaining her position at the head of his line, while there are no signs of any concerted attempt to form the line-of-bearing N (or even E of N) that would have prevented mutual smoke interference. Yet again, Beatty's impetuous tactics had failed to exploit the advantage of his heavier guns; they had left his ships still forming line under fire, while at least two of them would soon be hampered by smoke. Now the Germans also had the better visibility. Worst of all, because Beatty initiated the approach with *Lion* still out of line, the flagship was partly obscured and *Derfflinger* mistakenly selected the third ship as her target. And, because the fire of the other British battlecruisers was too ineffective to punish the German mistake, *Derfflinger* and *Seydlitz* were allowed to continue almost undisturbed with their fortuitous concentration on *Queen Mary*.

Beatty's tactics in both phases of the Run to the South had failed to prevent mutual smoke interference and to maintain 'that steady course that is so important for gunnery' – especially for ranging and aiming. But were the British coincidence rangefinders also inherently inferior to the stereoscopic instruments used by their opponents? Certainly, when the British were unable to take ranges through their own smoke, the Germans could still range on the smoke itself. Furthermore, at the ranges encountered during the approaches – in excess of the 16,000 yards – the inherent accuracy of the Barr & Stroud instruments probably fell off more rapidly than those from Zeiss; also, on average, the German rangetakers were better trained than their British counterparts. But, at the beginning of the Run to the South, *Princess Royal*'s opening range and rate were as accurate as any, while a good rate required a sequence of consistent plotted ranges.[92] Her ranging shows that, when the visibility was reasonably good and the speed not excessive,[93] a competent rangetaker could obtain good results with the Barr & Stroud coincidence rangefinder. It then follows that poor rangefinding by the other British battlecruisers was due, in varying degrees, to smoke, high speed and untimely changes of course, and to poor training and insufficient practice in rangetaking.

Beatty's conduct of both approaches imposed too many avoidable disadvantages on his ships. However, these difficulties were compounded by others which Beatty could do nothing about, and which, conversely, handed advantages to Hipper. In the leeward position, the 1SG were not troubled by their own smoke, so Hipper had more tactical flexibility. As firing began, the light from the German line was better for spotting, and perhaps for rangefinding too; in the second phase, the 1SG had much better visibility. They twice quickly gained the upper hand, but this was not only because they were first to straddle. The German's most rapid rate of fire was so impressive that, after Jutland, the Royal Navy assumed its opponents had fired multiple salvoes in quick succession, even while still finding the target.[94] In fact, before straddling, they and the British mostly fired at similar rates. For example, the first five or six salvoes from *Lion*, *Princess Royal*, *Lützow* and *Derfflinger* were fired with average intervals of 38, 53, 45 and 48 seconds respectively. The distinguishing feature of the German firing was their use of rapid, and if necessary unspotted, fire – but only when the target had already been consistently straddled. *Lützow* and *Von der Tann* both fired in this way,[95] but the system is described most clearly by von Hase. After *Queen Mary* blew up and the 1SG began to withdraw, *Derfflinger* fired eight salvoes at *Princess Royal* with an average interval of fifty-two seconds. The first straddled but subsequent salvoes fell short.

> Each time we had to wait for the splashes. When these were observed new orders had generally to be given for deflection, rate and elevation.

But when, at the start, von Hase's sixth salvo straddled *Princess Royal* at 4.52:

> now I had found the target . . . the transmitting station was to give the order 'Salvoes-fire!' to the heavy guns once every 20 seconds . . . While the firing was going on any observation was out of the question . . . Naturally such furious rapid fire could only be maintained for a limited time . . . It was not long before our salvoes fell over or short, as a result of the enemy altering course . . . Each salvo was then directed afresh and this continued until the target was again straddled. And then the devil's concert began again on the order 'Good, Rapid'.

In fact, *Derfflinger*'s first burst of rapid fire after only one straddle may not have obtained any hits, whereas, against *Queen Mary*, von Hase waited for the third straddle before ordering 'Good, Rapid'.[96] The gunnery records for the Run to the South from the British battlecruisers contain no such sequence of repeated straddles followed by a rapid burst fired at a steady rate. The only ship that got close to the maximum German rate of fire was *New Zealand*. When she opened fire at 3.51, she broke immediately into rapid salvoes fired mostly at thirty second intervals;[97] from this wild fusillade – undoubtedly another case of taking 'the rapidity ideas . . . to excess' – she made not one hit. In contrast, *Barham* waited to straddle before she 'fired four more salvoes rapid and straddled again'.[98] But the key to success was first to straddle consistently; this not only confirmed that you had the range and rate, but also disrupted your enemy's efforts to straddle in return; once gunnery superiority had been lost, it could not be regained.

## THE RUN TO THE NORTH

After 4.27, as Hipper withdrew eastwards, the British battlecruisers began to check fire, First *Lion* (at 4.33) and lastly *Tiger* (4.39). However, the 5BS were able to continue firing intermittently while, with one brief turn away, continuing on a course just W of S. At 4.38, Hipper turned back decisively from E to SSE and, at 4.44, the 1SG opened fire on the battleships; the two squadrons were soon heavily engaged, and both *Barham* and *Seydlitz* were hit.[99]

As Beatty's forces continued southwards, the Second Light Cruiser Squadron (2LCS) had been scouting ahead. At 4.33, Commodore William Goodenough's flagship, *Southampton*, flashed by searchlight the startling report 'Battleships S.E.' and, at 4.38 announced by wireless:

> Urgent. Priority. Have sighted Enemy battlefleet bearing approximately S.E., course of Enemy N.

In the face of overwhelming numbers, Beatty now had to withdraw and, if possible, lead the High Seas Fleet under the guns of the Grand Fleet. Thus at 4.40, he made the general signal by flags to alter course in succession sixteen points to starboard; this took the battlecruisers onto course NWbyN. However, this order cannot have been meant for the 5BS, still some seven or eight miles astern. At 4.45, *Lion* turned three points to a course N that would take the battlecruisers between the 5BS and the enemy, but would also avoid any risk of collision.[100]

At 4.42, the German C.-in-C., Scheer, had turned his battleships two points, from N in line ahead into columns of divisions. They were, in order of steaming:

> Third Squadron, Fifth Division: *König, Grosser Kurfürst, Markgraf, Kronprinz*
> Third Squadron, Sixth Division: three *Kaiser* class
> First Squadron, First Division: *Friedrich der Grosse* (Fleet flagship) and four *Helgoland* class
> First Squadron, Second Division: four *Nassau* class
> Second Squadron: six pre-dreadnoughts.

At 4.45, Scheer ordered 'Distribution of fire from the right ship to ship' and, a minute later, 'Open fire' – though his intentions must have been hard to fathom when, reading from his right, the 5BS were steaming S, the battlecruisers had turned north and, closest of all, the 2LCS were more or less head on to the German columns.[101]

At 4.48, according to the British 'Messages', Beatty ordered the 5BS by flags to 'Alter course in succession 16 points to starboard'. This time was two minutes before his battlecruisers would cross the line of fire between the battleships and the 1SG; perhaps for this reason, Hipper seized his opportunity to turn about – also to starboard – and at 4.51 ordered 'Course N' (Figure 8.2).

One object of the 5BS's turn-about was to form astern of the battlecruisers. Andrew Gordon proposes that Beatty ordered the battleships to

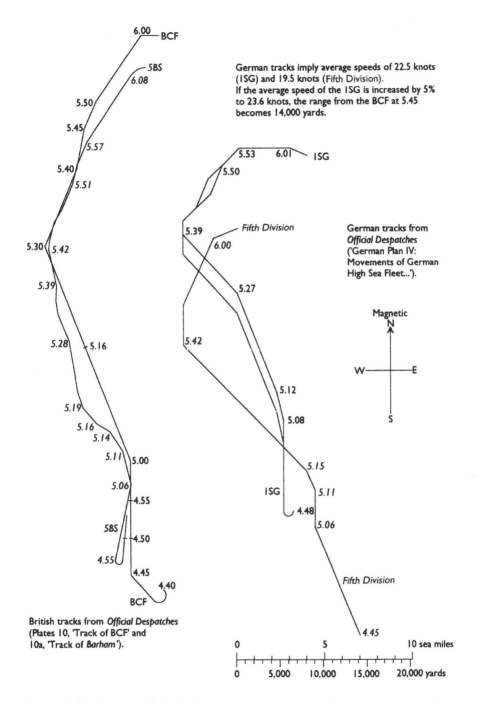

*Figure 8.2* The Run to the North.

turn away to starboard because he intended, as soon as he had passed them, to turn sharply to port; this turn is indeed shown on Marder's Chart 6, while Campbell times the turn by the battlecruisers at 4.54.[102] Yet the BCF's own track chart shows a steady course N from 4.45 until 5.00, and then a turn away to NNW.[103] If this is correct, it is still possible that Beatty was thinking ahead. But a more likely explanation is that, having already decided to pass between the 5BS and the enemy, he intended further to relieve the pressure on the battleships by ordering them to turn away from the enemy. Another, less heroic, possibility is that *Lion's* shaky signalling organisation, now under extreme pressure to keep up with the rapidly changing situation, merely repeated to the 5BS the same signal that had been made generally at 4.40. Whatever the actual reason for the signal, Gordon concludes convincingly, from a wealth of evidence, that it was hoisted only at 4.48, that it was still flying when the flagships passed at 4.50, that due to yet another signalling error in *Lion*, it was not hauled down (made executive) until 4.53, and that only then did Evan-Thomas lead his ships round to starboard; as a result, the 5BS ended up some 4,000 yards (two sea-miles) closer to the High Seas Fleet.[104]

In his report, Evan-Thomas stated that, after the sixteen-point turn, the 5BS 'altered course a little further to starboard to follow and support the battlecruisers', while *Barham's* chart shows her on a course NbyE from 4.55. At 5.01, just after her turn from N to NNW, *Lion* ordered the 5BS, yet again only by flags, to 'Prolong the line by taking station astern', but *Barham* did not respond until 5.06, when she made the first of three two-point turns away.[105] As *Valiant's* report confirms:

> At 5.13 p.m . . . the Fifth Battle Squadron . . . was altering course slowly to port to get astern of our Battle Cruisers.[106]

Evan-Thomas' delay in turning away may have been due to difficulty in reading *Lion's* flag signals: to uncertainty about the flagship's new course and, therefore, how far the 5BS should turn: to a quixotic attempt to draw the German fire: or some combination thereof. It would certainly have been better if *Lion* had made a clearly readable signal to turn immediately onto a parallel course. Whatever the explanation, the outcome was that the distance between the battlecruisers and the 5BS had now increased by another mile;[107] the battleships, especially *Warspite* and *Malaya* in the rear, were now in deadly danger.

From the start of the Run to North, it is difficult to determine who was firing at whom. After Beatty's battlecruisers completed their sixteen-point turn, *Lion* was first to open fire again at 4.48, possibly at *Moltke* or *Von der Tann* just before they put their helms over.[108] The British ships fired at ranges from 17,000 to 21,000 yards, though *New Zealand* managed only two salvoes, the second at [4.54], before her target (perhaps again *Von der Tann*) went out of range. Soon the 1SG could no longer be seen in the smoke and mist and *Lion*, *Princess Royal* and *Tiger* ceased firing at 5.04, 5.02 and 5.09 respectively; no hits had been made. Hipper re-engaged ship-to-ship at about 4.57 with the visibility still in his favour and, between 4.58 and 5.02, *Tiger* was hit once and *Lion* three times. Campbell is probably correct in attributing these to *Lützow* and *Seydlitz*,[109] although the German Third Squadron could also have a claim.

When the battleships of the High Seas Fleet were ordered to open fire at 4.46, those that obeyed immediately were probably firing at the 2LCS. However, at about 4.50–1, some of the Third Squadron targeted *Lion* class battlecruisers, while others engaged the 5BS.[110] Andrew Gordon cites no fewer than eight eyewitnesses from the 5BS who were convinced that, as they turned about, the Germans concentrated their fire on the turning point. *Malaya*'s Captain turned short for this reason, while Midshipman Patrick Blackett in *Barham*'s A turret was of the same opinion.[111] In fact, the Germans probably had little choice, particularly those firing at the leading British battleships, which, as they turned away, would have disappeared behind those still approaching the turn; if the Germans were to keep firing, they had to transfer their fire to the next turning ship. The ship itself provided the point of aim. To obtain the range of the turning point, the Germans could either rely on their rangefinders, or set the enemy-bar of the *EU-Anzeiger* at right angles to the line of fire. However, determining the deflection was difficult, because of the rapidly changing inclination and speed of the target; this probably explains why, despite many near misses, none of the 5BS was actually hit as they turned. But *Barham* did not escape for long, and between 4.58 and 5.10, she received three damaging hits. Also, the British battlecruisers were drawing out of range or sight of the Third Squadron, so that the 5BS were now their sole targets.[112]

From the 5BS, *Malaya* sighted the enemy battlefleet before the turn at 4.53, but they were not visible from *Barham* until a few minutes afterwards. *Barham* and *Valiant* then renewed their engagement with the 1SG, while *Warspite* and *Malaya* opened fire on the *Königs* of the Third Squadron; however, after she had fired only three salvoes, *Warspite*'s target was right aft and she transferred to the battlecruisers; she did not sight the battleships again until 5.20. Nearly all the reports from the 5BS emphasise the difficulty of seeing the enemy through the smoke and mist at ranges of 17,000 to 20,000 yards, and that they themselves were silhouetted against a bright horizon. On the other hand, the Germans found that their gunlayers were blinded when the sun broke through underneath the clouds, while even the 5BS were now beyond the effective range of the 1SG. *Barham* was not hit again after 5.10 and *Valiant* remained unscathed. The 5BS were already striking back; between 5.06 and 5.10, *Seydlitz* (*Valiant*'s principal target) received three 15-inch hits; *Derfflinger* was hit at 5.19, and, between 5.13 and 5.30, *Lützow* was hit three times. *Malaya* should probably be credited with the two hits on

*Grosser Furfürst* at 5.09 and the hit on *Markgraf* at 5.10, while the *Markgraf* also received another two untimed hits during the Run to the North.[113] But, despite their strenuous efforts – at 5.10, Evan-Thomas had optimistically signalled his intention to proceed at 25 knots – the 5BS were neither closing the gap to Beatty's battlecruisers, nor shaking off the pursuing Third Squadron. The German battleships were able to concentrate their fire on Evan-Thomas' two rear ships and particularly on *Malaya*:

> six salvoes were falling round the ship per minute, and at one time, counting some which were probably meant for 'Warspite', *nine* salvoes fell in rapid succession.[114]

*Malaya* was first hit at 5.20, but her worst time was from 5.27 to 5.35, when she took at least five hits; but for prompt action, a serious fire in the starboard 6-inch battery could well have spread to the magazines. Campbell allows only two hits on *Warspite*, at about 5.27, but, as Gordon points out, this tally is strongly belied by the testimony of her executive officer; it should probably be at least four.[115] With his rear ships in grave danger of a crippling hit, at 5.30 Evan-Thomas gave the order that permitted each of his ships to 'Proceed at your utmost speed'.

At this critical moment, Beatty's battlecruisers were not even distantly engaged. At 5.10, when the battleships were already trailing astern, he had reduced speed, but only from 25 to 24 knots, which did nothing more than prevent the gap from increasing further.[116] By that time, all his ships had ceased firing, while, at 5.15, they vanish from the German chart and were not sighted again (briefly) until 5.48.[117] Yet, in his report, Beatty alleged that:

> Between 5 and 6 p.m. the action continued on a Northerly course, the range being about 14,000 yards

adding that he had personally observed a damaged battlecruiser quitting the enemy line. As Captain Harper realised, this could not possibly have been the range throughout the Run to the North, though it was probably about right towards the end. After 'a first-class row', Beatty gave Harper a direct order to make the range 14,000 yards in the Jutland record. Marder's verdict was that:

> It is difficult to understand [Beatty's] position . . . the gallantry of his leadership was surely beyond question. Besides, closing in would obviously have been foolish . . . the German fleet was on his quarter and would soon have finished any of his ships that might have lost speed as a result of further damage.

Roskill makes much the same excuse, adding:

One can only surmise that he [Beatty] was trying to forestall criticisms of himself for not closing the range – which in fact no one had made.[118]

In reality, Beatty had left each ship of the 5BS, and *Malaya* in particular, at imminent risk of being finished off after a crippling hit. Beatty's own orders and his flagship's inept signalling had done much to open up the three-mile gap between his battlecruisers and battleships. But he then neither slowed down sufficiently to allow the 5BS to close the gap, nor, while generally holding his course towards the Grand Fleet, did he keep in touch with the 1SG. Thus Hipper's ships were left free to join in the cannonade at the 5BS. Fortunately, this German fire probably had no direct effect, but the presence of the 1SG divided the fire of the 5BS at a time when it needed to be directed solely at disrupting the shooting of the Third Squadron. Beatty's gallantry remains beyond question. But he should be criticised for once again failing to use all the fire power at his disposal, for leading his battle-cruisers out of action for the best part of half an hour, and for leaving the battleships under his command unsupported while they alone fought off the whole German battlefleet. Furthermore, his despatch again shows that Beatty himself had recognised that he was vulnerable to criticism of his tactics.

After 5.15, Scheer's battleships had been on course NW as they attempted to close the range to the 5BS. However, the German charts suggest that, soon, only their forward turrets could bear; by about 5.44, they had turned N and would soon turn further to starboard; the 5BS suffered no more hits after 5.35. Hipper, following a direct order from Scheer to 'Take up the chase', turned the 1SG together from NNW to NW at 5.26, although, at 5.39, he made the first of a series of turns onto courses N and east of North.[119] At 5.25, Beatty made the general signal 'Prepare to renew the action', but this can have been intended only for the battlecruisers, since he knew that the '5th B.S. were still firing hard'. Since 3.09, the Grand Fleet had been pressing on SEbyS at 20 knots in their cruising formation of six columns of battle-ships, with the cruiser line spread out ahead across their line of advance. As they fell back, Beatty's forces were led by *Falmouth*, flagship of the Third Light Cruiser Squadron (3LCS); between 5.30 and 5.33, she sighted cruisers (*Black Prince* and one or two others) on the starboard wing of the battlefleet's screen.[120] At some time between 5.27 and 5.35, Beatty's battle-cruisers turned NNE; the immediate effect was to close the range and, at 5.40, *Lion* was able to reopen fire at the 1SG. At this time, Beatty estimated the Grand Fleet's position to be just west of north.[121] Thus, his change of course would keep his ships between the Germans and the Grand Fleet; if his gunnery was successful, he might also push Hipper, and Scheer coming up astern, onto more easterly courses. Further turns to starboard would also be needed if the Grand Fleet held its present course, since, once Jellicoe and

Beatty joined forces, the proper position for the fast ships was in the van of the British battle line.

The visibility and light was now increasingly in favour of the British ships. At 5.44, after spotting the second straddling salvo at a gun range of 14,500 yards, *Lion* fired five rapid salvoes at about thirty second intervals; it was probably one of these that scored the hit on *Lützow* at 5.45. At 5.42, the 5BS also turned to NNE (and would stay on this heading until 6.08).[122] They continued to engage both the 1SG and the Third Squadron; at about 5.55, they obtained one or two hits on *Derfflinger* and two on *Seydlitz*, and also a hit on *König* at 6.03. It is also convenient to include here the hit on *Lion* by *Lützow* at 6.05. The 5.45 hit on *Lützow* was the only one made by the British battlecruisers during the Run to the North, whereas they received five, all but one early on. The 5BS took fifteen hits (assuming four on *Warspite*). These caused extensive damage but their ability to fight their heavy guns was almost unaffected. Fortunately for the reputation of British gunnery, the shooting of the 5BS was excellent, despite the odds against them. Campbell identifies twelve or thirteen 15-inch hits on the 1SG, plus five more on the Third Squadron. These heavy shells added considerably to the damage inflicted on Hipper's battlecruisers. All were now badly holed. The after superfiring turret in *Seydlitz* had been burned out earlier, while the guns of the starboard wing turret could be elevated only as a pair. And, by the end of the Run to the North, due to hits and failures with run-out gear, *Von der Tann* had not a single working turret gun.[123]

## AROUND WINDY CORNER

The 3BCS, which only the day before had been at gunnery practice,[124] had been stationed initially about ten miles ahead of the Grand Fleet's cruiser screen. At 4.05, Jellicoe ordered Hood to 'Proceed immediately to support B.C.F.' An hour and a half later, due to the differences in the dead reckoning between the Grand Fleet and the BCF, Hood was out of sight to the east of the High Seas Fleet and in danger of sweeping right past as they and Beatty ran northwards. However, at 5.27, the cruiser *Chester*, positioned some four or five miles on Hood's starboard beam, turned to the westward towards the sound of gunfire, and soon encountered the four light cruisers of the German Second Scouting Group (2SG), which were positioned to the NE of Hipper's battlecruisers. Under a heavy fire, *Chester* was forced to retire, but Hood turned to assist and, at 5.55, the 3BCS opened fire. Their engagement with the 2SG lasted only about five minutes in poor visibility at ranges of about 10,000 yards. Rates were high and changed rapidly, particularly when the German cruisers turned about to fire torpedoes; *Inflexible*'s rate swung from 800 closing to 900 opening. Nonetheless, both *Pillau* and *Wiesbaden* were hit, the latter in the engine room as she turned; she was brought to a complete stop and left to become a helpless target for the approaching Grand Fleet.[125] This action shows that, at medium ranges, the quite simple fire control systems in the 3BCS could obtain hits even when, due to opposite and changing courses, the rate was changing rapidly.

Rear Admiral Friedrich Bödicker, commanding the 2SG, had only dimly glimpsed his assailants and at 6.00 reported that he was under fire from enemy battleships. Five minutes earlier, Hipper could see nothing of Beatty's ships firing from his left, while the heavy guns of the 3BCS were probably audible from somewhere on his starboard bow; in addition, British cruisers and destroyers were appearing to the N just as the German flotillas were heading E towards the 3BCS. At 5.55, Hipper turned the 1SG E and then, at 5.59, ordered them to turn about together to starboard so that he could fall back on his own battleships. (Perhaps, despite the times in the 'German Signals', this drastic reversal was prompted by Bödicker's report.) At 6.10, Hipper executed a second turn-about and hauled into line ahead of the Third Squadron; on Scheer's orders, their flagship the *König* (Rear Admiral Paul Behncke) was acting as guide to the High Seas Fleet. Still under fire from an invisible 5BS, she had edged away to starboard until her course was ENE. But, despite the brief sighting of the light forces attached to the Grand Fleet, neither Hipper nor Scheer realised that the whole British battlefleet was bearing down upon them.[126]

At 5.56, Beatty had sighted the leading battleships of the Grand Fleet bearing N about five miles – just at the time that, due to Hipper's turn E, the 1SG were presumably becoming indistinct in the mist. At 6.00, Beatty also turned E and at 6.07 to ESE, though by then the enemy had again all but disappeared. Nonetheless, he kept up the pressure on the heads of the German lines that had been pushing them away from the advancing Grand Fleet. Even at 6 o'clock, Jellicoe's battleships were still in their cruising formation of six columns of divisions, numbering First to Sixth from port to starboard, with *Iron Duke* leading the Third Division. Beatty's courses took his battlecruisers across the heads of these columns so that, once Jellicoe formed his battle line, they would be in position to take up their proper place in the van.[127] Evan-Thomas, still astern of the battlecruisers on course NNE, did not sight Jellicoe's starboard column, the Sixth Division led by *Marlborough*, until shortly after 6.06. He assumed that her division was already leading the battle line, so, between 6.08 and 6.11, he hauled round to SEbyE, also with the intention of forming up ahead.[128] But Jellicoe was still waiting for information on the position and course of the enemy battlefleet before he deployed from columns into line. From 4.45 until after 6 o'clock (which included the time when the battlecruisers were out of action), Beatty had neglected to provide any further reports of the enemy. After 5.00, even Goodenough had remained silent until, at 5.40, *Southampton's* wireless again transmitted her position and the apparent enemy course (NNW, then N at 5.50). However, differences in dead reckoning put the 2LCS further to the E of *Iron Duke* than was actually the case, while other reports reaching Jellicoe from his cruisers were contradictory.

At this stage it was not clear whether the enemy battlefleet was ahead of our battlefleet or on the starboard beam.

His own columns were still headed SEbyS with their guides disposed abeam i.e. on a line-of-bearing NEbyE from *Marlborough*. Another consideration for Jellicoe was that, characteristically, he had already asked his Flag Captain, Frederic Dreyer, to determine the direction for engaging the enemy that would give the best visibility for gunnery; Dreyer had reported that 'the most favourable direction was to the southward, and would draw westwards as the sun sank'. At 6.02, '[i]n order to take ground to starboard' Jellicoe turned the column guides to S, the ships astern to follow in succession. But 'it was soon realised that the enemy battlefleet must be in close proximity . . . and the fleet was turned back [at 6.06] to S.E. preparatory to deployment to port'; at 6.08, the destroyers were disposed accordingly.[129] Deployment to port involved the port guide immediately leading its column onto the designated course and the other guides turning together onto the line-of-bearing; then each column in turn hauled into line, astern of the preceding columns.[130] Since this unavoidably resulted in a *loss* of ground to starboard, it appears that, even before 6.02, Jellicoe had decided to deploy on his port column, the First Division led by *King George V*. But this was only the half of it; he still had to decide on the best course for his battle line.

Just before the turn S, visual contact was made between the British flagships; at 6.01, *Iron Duke*'s searchlight demanded of Beatty 'Where is Enemy's B.F.?' *Lion* replied, though not until 6.06, 'Enemy's B.Cs. bearing S.E.'. This was not what Jellicoe really needed to know, though Beatty's easterly heading gave some indication of German courses. At 6.10, *Barham* reported 'Enemy's battlefleet S.S.E.', though Jellicoe did not mention her signal in his despatch. Also at 6.10, he repeated his question to Beatty, who responded at 6.14 'Have sighted Enemy's battlefleet bearing S.S.W.' Jellicoe could now deduce that the German battleships were approximately south of him, though he could still only guess their course. But he could wait no longer and at 6.15 ordered the deployment to port, course SEbyE, by the famous signal 'Equal speed, Charlie London'.[131]

As the guides of the British columns put their helms over, the 1SG had completed their second turn-about; they were now headed about NE or ENE, followed by the line of German battleships curving away to the south.[132] Thus, once the majority of the British battleships had turned NEbyE, they were on similar courses to the German van, with a separation of about six miles.[133] After the light forces preceding Beatty's and Jellicoe's dreadnoughts had met, many had been squeezed into the space between the two lines; now, amidst confusion 'like Piccadilly Circus with the policemen on strike',[134] the cruisers and destroyers had to take up their positions relative to Jellicoe's line. But so too did the battleships of the 5BS and the battlecruisers led by Beatty and Hood. And, cutting across the confusion of wakes, Sir Robert Arbuthnot's flagship *Defence*, accompanied by *Warrior*, seemed intent only on the destruction of the crippled *Wiesbaden*. The two armoured cruisers had been at the centre of the Grand Fleet's cruiser line. At about 5.47, they had sighted the 2SG and, after turning to port, had opened fire, though their salvoes fell short. They then swung through about 120° to starboard before, at 6.05, re-engaging their target, which 'appeared to be crippled, and soon nearly stopped'. Arbuthnot continued to close, even though, after about 6.07, his ships – all too conspicuous under clouds of coal smoke – were being straddled by salvoes from the 1SG and the Third Squadron.[135]

Jellicoe's deployment signal indicated to Beatty that he should move to a position ahead of *King George V*. However, at 6.15, Arbuthnot's reckless advance took his ships across *Lion*'s bows, obliging her to veer to port; the BCF's chart shows them turning at this time from ESE to a course ENE, which they then held until 6.25. However, the turn was probably necessary anyway to avoid getting too close to the German line. Arbuthnot's passage did not interfere with *Lion*'s gunnery for long; between 6.16 and 6.21, she fired ten salvoes at *Lützow*, with rapid fire ordered at a range of 8,250 yards after straddling with the sixth. *Lützow* was hit twice and it was probably this burst of firing that forced Hipper to turn sharply together at 6.20 to SE. The 1SG could not reply effectively, but at about 6.22, *Princess Royal* (which fired only four salvoes between 6.11 and 6.31) received two hits from *Markgraf*, one of which put X turret out of action.[136]

By 6.19, Evan-Thomas had realised that *Marlborough* was not leading the Grand Fleet and that the battleships were deploying on the far, port column. He therefore decided that his battleships must haul into line astern of the Sixth Division, commencing with a large turn in succession to port. The timing (at 6.18 according to *Warspite* but at 6.23 on *Barham*'s Track) and extent of this turn, or even whether it was made with or without a signal, remain uncertain.[137] However, well before it began, Arbuthnot had wheeled his ships further to starboard and was now attempting to escape while making for his position in rear of the line. But *Defence* could not evade the salvoes raining down on her; at 6.20, as she was coming between the 5BS and the enemy on an opposite course, she was hit by two heavy salvoes in quick succession, blew up and disappeared.[138]

*Warrior* seemed likely to soon share her fate, but the 5BS, then commencing their turn at what became known as 'Windy Corner', were already drawing the German fire. *Barham*'s Captain Craig was convinced that the Germans were again concentrating on the turning point, although, despite 'a hailstorm of splashes', his ship escaped unscathed. But *Warspite*, after turning to port, had to turn violently to starboard to avoid colliding with *Malaya* and then *Valiant*. Her steering jammed, and she completed almost two complete circles before escaping to the north. German battle-ships deluged these circles with salvoes as they passed; *Warspite* took seven heavy hits on her port side and, probably, another four to starboard, plus an unknown number of 5.9-inch hits as well.[139] Yet she survived, although she was unable to rejoin the line. And, by providing such a tempting distraction, she enabled *Warrior* to stagger out of action, though the cruiser foundered later after all her survivors had been taken off. The remaining three ships of the 5BS had joined the line by about 6.30 but, after Windy Corner, they saw little of the German line, other than occasional glimpses through the mist and smoke.[140]

We must now move to the other end of the arena between the lines. After his brush with the 2SG and the disabling of *Wiesbaden*, Hood led the 3BCS westward to join up with Beatty. As they sighted *Lion* on the port bow at about 6.13, there was some confusion as the three battlecruisers dodged torpedoes fired by German destroyers and, momentarily, *Invincible* appeared to stop with clouds of steam pouring from her escape pipes; her gunnery officer later reported that 'her helm jammed when put "hard-a-port"'. But she quickly got under way again and led *Inflexible* and *Indomitable* (in that order) round to port; they were apparently heading south when sighted from *Lion* at 6.20. In his despatch, Beatty claimed that he then ordered the 3BCS to take station ahead. However, no such signal appears in the British 'Messages', while the course adopted by Hood, probably SEbyE, was more southerly than Beatty's until the latter turned to SE at 6.25 in support.[141] Thus Hood seems to have been acting on his own initiative as he completed his turn and engaged the 1SG, abeam on a similar course. While his ships' targets are not certain, their reports suggest that *Inflexible* fired first at *Derfflinger* (opening range 8,000 yards) before, two minutes prior to *Invincible*'s end, shifting to *Seydlitz*. *Indomitable* seems to have fired at only one target, probably also *Derfflinger* (opening range 9,500 yards).[142] Between them, they made three hits on *Derfflinger* and, later, one hit on *Seydlitz*. In that case, the eight hits on *Lützow* between 6.26 and 6.34, major causes of the extensive flooding forward that eventually would sink her, were the work of *Invincible*.[143] At the start of this engagement, the 3BCS were invisible in the mist, so they were undisturbed by enemy fire. However, a few minutes before *Invincible* was lost, she was hit several times, once aft, while *Indomitable* was also straddled – though neither she nor *Inflexible* were hit. By this time, *Invincible* had broken into the rapid fire that accounts for her many hits.

> A few moments before the 'Invincible' blew up Admiral Hood hailed the Control Officer in the Control Top from the fore bridge: 'Your firing is very good, keep at it as quickly as you can, every shot is telling.'

Unfortunately, *Invincible* was by then a clear target for *Lützow*. With her fire controlled from the after position, Hipper's flagship straddled with the second salvo (fired with a DOWN correction of 400 metres), while a shell from the third penetrated the roof of *Invincible*'s Q turret at about 6.34; the magazines ignited and she was torn in two.[144] Although von Hase of *Derfflinger* also claimed a part in her destruction, he added that the ship that was sunk was firing at him; alternatively, *Derfflinger* may have been responsible for the salvoes that surrounded *Indomitable*. Whichever was the case, von Hase's description epitomises the dangerous efficiency of German gunnery. At 6.29, as soon as 'the veil of mist in front of us [had] split across like the curtain of a theatre', the rangetaker next to von Hase in *Derfflinger*'s fore control obtained a range of 9,000 metres (9,800 yards); this was used for the first salvo, which fell 'Over. Two hits!'. Immediately von Hase ordered rapid fire, and once again his salvoes followed each other at twenty second intervals.[145] Whichever German battlecruiser made the fatal hit, it is evident that their Zeiss rangefinders had enabled them to straddle their targets quickly, and that rapid fire from one or perhaps both soon made hits. Campbell's time for the first hit on *Lützow* suggests that *Invincible* may have required more salvoes to straddle, but then she too used rapid fire to devastating effect. The results were not as immediately spectacular, but they ensured that *Lützow* would follow *Invincible* to the bottom.

Meanwhile, five divisions of British battleships processed steadily NEbyE before swinging to starboard onto SEbyE; *Iron Duke* made the turn at about 6.22, *Marlborough* at 6.34.[146] Jellicoe had ordered the deployment only just in time since, as it began, heavy shells had been falling around the Fifth and Sixth Divisions, though these must have been 'overs'. Thereafter, the whole line was untroubled by German fire, not least as they passed through the potentially vulnerable turning point. Scheer and Hipper were still unaware of their presence, even though *Marlbourough* fired seven salvoes at the German line from 6.17 (range 13,000 yards), *Agincourt* opened on a battlecruiser at 6.24 (at 10,000 yards) and the hapless *Wiesbaden* provided a target for a number of other battleships. While Hipper had swung SE, Behncke turned less sharply to starboard; by 6.30, battleships of the Third Squadron (the *Königs* and *Kaisers*) could be seen from all except the four leading British battleships; fifteen were able to engage ships of either the 1SG or the Third Squadron. Many could fire only a few salvoes at ranges mostly between 10,000 and 13,000 yards:[147] but Dreyer's *Iron Duke* gave what Campbell describes as 'a fine display of speedy and accurate firing' against *König*.[148] The target was sighted at 6.26 but fire was not opened until 6.30.25, time enough for the Dreyer Table Mark IV to establish the enemy course as 'slightly converging'.

Error reported by Rangefinder Plot was 500 yards. Range 11,000 yards. Bracket used 800.

After four salvoes (at intervals of 35, 40 and 50 seconds), the third and fourth were spotted as hits; rapid fire was then ordered, the next three salvo intervals being 30, 25 and 23 seconds. The rate of the last three salvoes then slowed as *König* turned away into the mist,[149] but not before she had received seven direct hits.[150] *Iron Duke* was not under fire. Nonetheless, she provided yet one more demonstration that the essence of effective shooting was careful rangetaking to obtain a reasonably accurate mean range and, if possible, a rate: deliberate fire to obtain consistent straddles: and only then rapid salvoes to blanket the target before it could evade them.

The German line was now crossed, its head under fire from an arc of British battleships and battlecruisers, mostly visible only as gun flashes, extending from N round to E. After their single-minded pursuit of Beatty and Evan-Thomas, Hipper and Scheer had blundered unknowingly into the full might of the Grand Fleet; only at the last moment was their predicament confirmed by intelligence obtained from the captured crew of the destroyer *Nomad*.[151] With much the worse of the visibility, the 1SG and the Third Squadron were now in grave danger of destruction, unless they could be extricated without delay.

### THE REMAINS OF THE DAY

Under heavy fire from their invisible opponents, Hipper and Behncke were already veering further away to starboard; if the other squadrons had followed them in succession, each would have been exposed in turn to the full fire of the British line. Presciently, the German Navy's tactical orders provided for an 'action-turn-together' onto an opposite course (*Gefechtskehrtwendung*).[152] Although the instruction assumed a more orderly formation than Scheer's extended, curved line, at 6.36 he commanded that the manoeuvre be executed as a turn-together to starboard onto an opposite course; after three minutes, he clarified his intention with a general signal 'Course W'. As quickly as they had appeared, what had been the German van vanished in the murk. Neither then nor later did Jellicoe himself see more than three or four German dreadnoughts at one time.[153] Although *König*'s turn-away had been seen from *Iron Duke*, he now had little more idea than previously of Scheer's formation and course. At 6.44, Jellicoe tentatively turned the guides of his columns one point to starboard, but more decisively to S at 6.55.[154]

At 6.25, *Lion* had turned to course SE, and then to ESE at 6.35 and SSE at 6.45.[155] By 6.50, she had drawn clear of the leading battleships, which were bearing three miles NNW (i.e. astern) from *Lion*. *Inflexible* and *Indomitable* had been turning to starboard in an attempt to regain contact with the enemy, but Beatty now ordered them to prolong the battlecruiser line astern; *Indomitable* then took the lead of the 3BCS.[156] At 6.53 Beatty reduced speed to 18 knots. Historians now accept, despite Beatty's denials, that shortly afterwards, at about 7 o'clock, *Lion* led the whole BCF through a complete circle; furthermore, it seems that Beatty's reason for commencing the turn was to maintain visual contact with the battlefleet.[157] The BCF then hauled round to starboard until, by 7.08 or even later, they were headed about SW; although still to the east of the First Division, this course would soon begin to take them across the heads of the battleship columns.[158]

About forty minutes earlier, *Falmouth* (flagship of the 3LCS) had found herself between the lines and had courageously attacked the leading battlecruisers of the 1SG with her 6-inch guns. The report of Rear Admiral Napier stated:

> About 6.30 p.m., 'Invincible' blew up . . . Shortly after, the enemy Battle Cruisers turned to westward, and [we] were left without an enemy to engage.[159]

But he did not see fit to inform Beatty until, probably no later than 6.45, *Lion*'s searchlight questioned:

> What is bearing of Enemy's Battle Cruisers? Reply: Last seen 1820 [*sic*]. Altered course to W., engaged by 3rd B.C.S.

Yet Jellicoe did not receive this vital intelligence from Beatty until 7.00 – and then in the less useful form 'Enemy are to Westward'.[160]

Even if Jellicoe had known more of the German withdrawal, he could hardly have anticipated that, at 6.55, Scheer would order a second 'action-turn-together' that soon must result in his 'T' being crossed once more. Indeed, as the contemporary British charts show, their commanders did not realise that this is what had occurred. Marder speculated that Scheer was trying to slip around the rear of the British fleet, but Scheer's own words suggest only that he deliberately drove into the British line from abeam, a tactic that worked for Nelson but was next to suicidal in the dreadnought era.[161] Once again in contrast to Beatty, Goodenough (who had attached the 2LCS to the 5BS at the rear of the line) warned Jellicoe at 7.00 of the German approach, though he gave their course as ESE. The crippled *Lützow* was now attempting to limp back to port, so the German line was now led by only four battlecruisers. Scheer's advance was met by fire from all along the British line, commencing at about 7.05 in the rear (ranges from the Fourth to Sixth Divisions were between 9,000 to 11,000 yards) and about 7.15 in the van and the BCF. The battlecruisers' ranges (mostly over 16,000 yards) were similar to those in the leading battleship divisions so, despite his more westerly course, Beatty was too distant to keep the 1SG under fire for long (*Lion* fired only four salvoes between 7.13 and 7.16).[162] By the time that the German ships reappeared, the visibility was already difficult even for the British. In Jellicoe's words:

> Ships fired at what they could see, when they could see it.

In these circumstances, *Thunderer*'s Captain reported:

> Objects came into view and disappeared again in about 3 minutes. A quick R.F. reading, used immediately, was the only practicable method.[163]

The Germans could see nothing but the flashes of British guns and it was soon clear to Scheer that he must withdraw immediately. As cover, at 7.13 he urged the remainder of the 1SG:

> Battlecruisers at the enemy! Give it everything!

His third *Gefechtskehrtwendung* commenced at 7.18, as his destroyers began their attacks with torpedoes. Scheer's battleships, with the battlecruisers taking position on the port quarter, were again extracted without loss, though not without severe damage; the battlecruisers received twenty-five hits (fourteen on *Derfflinger* alone), the Third Squadron eleven and even the older *Helgoland* was struck once. In contrast, only the *Collosus* suffered, though not seriously, from a pair of hits made by a single salvo from the 1SG. All the torpedoes missed, but they had forced Jellicoe to turn away two points to port at 7.22 and again at 7.25; by 7.35, all his divisions had ceased firing. For the second time, the German battlefleet had vanished into the gathering gloom. They continued westward until, at 7.27, Scheer ordered a turn to SW; by 8.10, the battleships were headed S in two columns, the pre-dreadnoughts of the Second Squadron forming the more westerly line. The 1SG was still closest to the enemy on a course converging slightly on Scheer's.[164]

Beatty's battlecruisers had not been threatened by the German torpedo attack and were able to continue SW'wards across the heads of the battleship columns. His despatch reported:

> we re-engaged at 7.17 p.m. and increased speed to 22 knots. At 7.32 p.m. my course was S.W., speed 18 knots, the leading enemy Battleship bearing N.W. by W. Again after a very short time the enemy showed signs of punishment...The Destroyers at the head of the enemy's line emitted volumes of grey smoke, covering their capital ships as with a pall, under cover of which they undoubtedly turned away, and at 7.45 p.m. we lost sight of them.

As Jellicoe assumed in his own despatch, this implied that the BCF continued to punish the enemy dreadnoughts until they disappeared, whereas the BCF gunnery reports show that they had ceased firing before 7.25.[165] A wireless signal originated at 7.30 in *Lion* but not despatched until 7.40 gave the enemy bearing – NWbyW – and added that they were 'distant 10 to 11 miles'; however, the British 'Messages' do not give a time-of-receipt by *Iron Duke*. The battlecruisers and battleships were no longer in visual contact, but a second signal originated at 7.45 and relayed by searchlight through *Minotaur* and *King George V* – with the same enemy bearing but also a course of 'about S.W.' – was received in the flagship at 7.59. Thus Beatty knew their course before losing sight of the enemy. Yet he had already reduced his speed to 18 knots and, when he turned towards the enemy at 7.45, it was by only two points, to WSW. In the meantime, at about 7.35 Jellicoe had formed the battleships into a single line ahead on course SbyW, and by 7.43 his course was SW at 17 knots.

Beatty's next wireless signal to the C.-in-C. would later become a major bone of contention.

> Urgent. Submit van of Battleships follow Battle Cruisers. We can then cut off whole of enemy's battlefleet.

If the signal despatched at 7.40 failed to reach Jellicoe, then, when this exhortation arrived at 7.54, he had only a vague notion of Beatty's whereabouts, and no idea about the enemy's position or course. In any case, the vital course information did not arrive until 7.59; it is unlikely to have been a coincidence that, one minute later, Jellicoe ordered the guides of his divisions to turn four points to starboard onto course W, and informed Beatty by wireless that he had done so. Since Beatty was still heading WSW, the battleships were now on a steeper approach to the enemy; also, because most of Scheer's ships had already turned S, Jellicoe's columns were for a time approaching the German lines at right angles. Also at 8 o'clock, Beatty belatedly ordered his light cruisers to 'Sweep to the Westward and locate the head of the Enemy's line before dark' (sunset was at 8.19). Within ten minutes, the 3LCS sighted 'Ships bearing N. by W.': and, between 8.15 and 8.17, Beatty at last turned the battlecruisers W. But he held this course only for four or five minutes before turning away again to WSW and, at 8.25, to SW.[166]

Almost as soon as they turned westward, the battlecruisers sighted the German columns; the opening salvo was fired by *Princess Royal* at 8.18 and the final shots (probably not a full salvo) by *Tiger* at 8.36. Campbell describes one hit on *Derfflinger* and five on *Seydlitz*, plus a single hit on the pre-dreadnought *Schleswig-Holstein*. While the BCF gunnery reports do not in all cases support Campbell's attributions for these hits, *New Zealand* claimed to have engaged *Seydlitz*; we must hope she made at least some of the three hits credited to her,[167] since, otherwise, she made not a single hit during the whole battle.[168] Once more under a heavy fire to which they could not reply, the Germans again turned westward to break off contact, even though they turned S again (the 1SG at 8.42) and, at 9.10, to about ESE. Much to their surprise, the BCF did not follow them.[169] In the mean time, at 8.07, *King George V* (flagship of the Second Battle Squadron) received Jellicoe's order '2nd B.S. follow our Battle Cruisers'. However, the BCF were out of sight and remained so until 8.30, then their gun flashes could be made out ahead. By that time, Jellicoe had ordered his divisions – the two divisions of the 2BS followed his movements – to turn from W to WSW (8.21), back to W (8.25) and finally, at 8.28, to SW, the same course as that of the battlecruisers. The British fleet then continued SW until 9.01, when the battleship divisions followed their guides to S; the battlecruisers turned S between 9.24 and 9.30.[170] It was now dark, and Beatty did not know that he had crossed the heads of the German columns before turning onto the same course as the enemy. Thus the two fleets had narrowly missed making contact again before the light failed. During the night, despite fierce fighting between the light forces, Scheer succeeded in taking his heavy ships across the wakes of Jellicoe's columns. By dawn, the High Seas Fleet was struggling back to its harbours, leaving the Grand Fleet in possession of an empty ocean. But, as far as gunnery between dreadnoughts was concerned, the battle had ended the previous evening.

Jellicoe was much criticised for the turns away after 7.20 that avoided the German torpedoes. Although long since agreed with the Admiralty and incorporated in the *Grand Fleet Battle Orders (GFBOs)*,[171] the tactic undoubtedly broke off contact with the enemy when there was little time to regain it before nightfall. But, by blaming Jellicoe – and also by focusing attention on whether the BCF turned through a complete circle at 7 o'clock – Beatty and his partisans effectively distracted attention from his own less than thrusting performance after he joined up with Jellicoe. Beatty received essential intelligence concerning Scheer's course after the first 'action-turn-together', but he kept it to himself for ten to fifteen minutes, gave no orders to his light cruisers to follow up *Falmouth*'s sighting, ended the attempt by *Indomitable* and *Inflexible* to retain contact with the 1SG, and continued to lead the battlecruisers to the far flank of the British fleet. The thirty-two-point turn may have been a mistake, but it had begun as a deliberate turn to keep Jellicoe's leading battleships in sight. When the High Seas Fleet unexpectedly reappeared, Beatty was too far off to engage his proper targets, the 1SG,[172] for very long – contrary to the impression given by his despatch. Unlike the battleships, the BCF were not troubled by torpedoes and were able to continue SW and, subsequently, WSW. But these courses, and a speed of only 18 knots, were too cautious to close an enemy last seen some ten miles NWbyW on a course SW. It was Jellicoe who turned boldly W at 8 o'clock, even though he risked the Germans crossing the Ts of his columns. Also at 8 o'clock, but at least half an hour too late, Beatty ordered his light cruisers westward to seek out the enemy. He did not turn the battlecruisers W until 8.15, when he almost immediately sighted the German columns. His targets soon retired westward but, as the sun set, Beatty also veered away towards the support of the Grand Fleet.

Even if Beatty had reported *Falmouth*'s enemy course immediately or given a lead by turning S and W, the next clash of the battlefleets would probably have been no less confused and indecisive. But his inaction suggests that he had been concerned only to reach his position in the van, and not at all with maintaining contact with a fleeing enemy. Furthermore, after the Germans had again retreated into the smoke and mist, Jellicoe had closed more aggressively in seeking out the enemy forces. If Beatty had kept up his attack after 8.30, more damage would have been inflicted (perhaps *Seydlitz* would then have foundered during the night), contact might not have been lost before nightfall, and Scheer might not have been able to slip away during the night. In view of the late hour, poor visibility and Scheer's unwillingness to stand and fight, the action of 31 May could never have been another Trafalgar. Scheer's escape was in part due to Jellicoe's reluctance to turn towards oncoming torpedoes. But Beatty must bear his share of responsibility, because of his own failures in reporting, reconnoitring and pursuing the enemy.

## LESSONS FOR FIRE CONTROL

After Jutland, the *Grand Fleet Gunnery & Torpedo Orders* (*GFG&TOs*) acknowledged the usefulness of the Dreyer Tables in difficult conditions:

> Notwithstanding the bad light and mist, some ships obtained good ranges which proved of great value, and it was again proved that every conceivable method should be employed to gain data with which to feed the fire control table. The difficulties introduced by enemy and our own alterations of course, speed, etc. make this imperative. The deflection must also be watched closely.[173]

However, when ships were ordered to forward Dreyer Table charts to the Admiralty, only *Lion* is known to have sent in a bearing plot, while *Ajax*, *Monarch*, *Revenge* and *Warspite* all stated clearly that they had not made bearing plots.[174] Supporters of Pollen, like Herbert Richmond, took the view that Dreyer, as Jellicoe's Flag Captain, could and did stifle any criticisms from the Fleet of 'his' tables.[175] However, Beatty and Chatfield bore no responsibility for the Navy's fire control equipment and were quick enough to criticise the British armour-piercing shells;[176] if they believed that the Dreyer Tables had in any way failed them, they would surely have seized on the excuse. In fact, the Battle Cruiser Fleet's own committee concluded:

> The action . . . appears to show that more value was obtained from rangefinders by some ships than by others, and that at such times as the enemy was on a steady course undoubted assistance was received from the plot.
>
> It is again strongly emphasised that the enemy system of continuously altering course defeats any system of fire control based on rate-finding, for the reason that by the time the plot has established a rate it is no longer applicable.

Chatfield's committee also mistakenly concluded that 'the enemy has a system of ranging by a succession of rapid salvoes' and they recommended that 'a "ladder" system of salvoes' should be adopted.[177] Jellicoe established two committees with representatives from the BCF and the Grand Fleet, one chaired by Dreyer, the other by Joseph Henley (now Captain of *Marlborough*) and their recommendations were combined into the new spotting rules promulgated on 24 September 1916. Essentially, pairs of rapid salvoes were fired in succession, all salvoes separated by 400 yards, until the target was crossed, after which a 200-yard correction in the opposite direction was expected to straddle. The printed version also included specific provisions for the correction of range and rate together (normally in steps of 200 yards and 100 yds/min. respectively) when the enemy altered course after he had been straddled.[178]

> The development of [the] spotting rules and afterwards the solution of the problem of concentration of fire, constituted the main work of the Fleet during the latter half of 1916, and in 1917 and 1918. The progress has been enormous.[179]

Action ranges from 15,000 to 18,000 yards were assumed.[180] Practices were conducted at up to 24,000 yards, while the new technique of 'throw-off' firing allowed gunnery to be tested while employing realistic tactics at full speed, including frequent changes of course by both sides.[181] By mid-1918:

> It is considered to be definitely established that at normal fighting ranges the range and bearing plots alone cannot be expected to provide either an accurate rate or a prompt indication of changes of enemy's course, and that it is therefore necessary to devote increased attention to direct estimation of inclination.[182]

Although 13.5-inch as well as 15-inch ships had been provided with 15-foot range-finders,[183] it was accepted that 'small rangefinder spreads were the exception'.[184] Nonetheless, the *GFG&TOs* warned against:

the neglect of the range plot which on numerous occasions during throw-off firings provided information which could have been utilised to great advantage.

... many [plots] were excellent and afforded throughout a good indication of the rate and true range; on the other hand some present large and varying differences between hitting gun range and mean plotted range.[185]

They also insisted that the range plot 'is of immense value as a check on gun range, and especially so when fire has been opened at short notice'. It also had a new importance as a means of recording the ranges in use by consorts in concentration firing.[186]

In contrast, the original bearing plot was probably of only marginal utility. An American naval officer with the Grand Fleet found that: 'The bearing plot instrument is not generally taken seriously',[187] while the post-war *Technical History and Index* admitted that: 'Bearing plots have not been an unqualified success'. However, in 1918 the Grand Fleet committee was already at work on the Gyro Director Training gear, which plotted bearings transmitted from the Director in steps of four minutes. It also introduced an important new principle, that of the 'straight-line' plot, in which a straight line up the middle of a narrow strip of moving paper always represented the target compass bearing predicted by the bearing clock. Each observed compass bearing was plotted as its *difference* from the current predicted value; thus, as well as showing the deviation of observed and predicted values, the slope of the mean line through the plot of observed bearings also indicated the error in the clock rate.[188] This enhanced version of Dreyer rate plotting would soon be taken up as the basis for plotting in a new generation of fire control tables.

## THE DREYER TABLE COMMITTEE

In September 1918, Beatty set up the Grand Fleet Dreyer Table Committee. Its First and Second Interim Reports concerned the Mark V table then being built for HMS *Hood*; the committee criticised the excessive number of fittings obscuring its plot, but concluded only of this plot that: 'A considerable alteration in design is therefore necessary'.[189] However, it also expressed concern about:

*The drive of the Frictional Clock Disc.* – Many complaints have been received that this disc is not sufficiently strong for the work now imposed on it. It is considered that the power of the motor should be greater, and that the diameter of the shaft carrying the roller should be increased.[190]

In fact, the first clear indication of a problem, the result of inventive gunnery officers modifying their tables, can be found almost a year earlier:

**Overloading the Dreyer Table.** Attention is drawn to the necessity of circumspection in adding fittings to the Dreyer Table; if driven by the rate disc it is essential that they should be fitted with great care and thoroughly tested to ensure against overloading and slipping, as occurred in one ship.[191]

Even so, the standard tables did not suffer from significant slippage, even when the rate changed rapidly while under helm.

In certain firings [during the first quarter of 1918] the range and deflection were maintained very successfully during turns of twelve points and upwards.[192]

In October, the committee was instructed to consider two much broader questions. The first, which was addressed in its Third Interim Report of 29 January 1919,[193] concerned 'standardising the alterations which are being made by various ships to their Dreyer Tables'. The request was repeated for the strengthening of the friction drive in the Mark IV and IV* tables, to allow for new fittings on the range plot. Notwithstanding the inadequacies of the old bearing plot, the report emphasised that:

The measurement of rate of change of bearing is considered of great importance owing to the accuracy with which bearings can be observed, even when the visibility is poor . . .
. . . bearing observations can be obtained *continuously* and *accurately* [original italics].

It accepted that 'The Gyro Director Training Gear . . . will standardise the arrangements for dealing with rate of change of bearing', though it also acknowledged that 'the present system of correction' of the gyrocompass, with which 'oscillations take place when course is altered', must be improved.[194]

Concerning the time-and-range plot, the committee adopted the more pessimistic of the conflicting views in the *GFG&TOs*.

*Experience has shown, and it must be accepted, that it will very seldom, if ever, be possible to obtain the rate of change of range from rangefinders* [original italics] . . . The frequent alteration of course at high speed which are now the accepted conditions of action will preclude the rate . . . being obtained with sufficient rapidity from a time and range plot.

The setting of the enemy bar must, therefore, be obtained from the rate of change of bearing and the inclination found by inclinometer, observation or outside reports (*e.g.* aeroplane) . . .

. . .

. . . It is considered that the primary object of plotting the rangefinder observations is to enable them to be 'meaned' by inspection for the purpose of checking gun range . . . and to allow the value of the rangefinder readings to be assessed.[195]

Thus, to determine enemy course and speed, the committee rejected the cross-cut of range-rate and speed-across (the latter derived from bearing-rate), favouring instead a cross-cut of inclination and speed-across. In the last year of the First World War, the direct measurement of inclination (the angle between enemy course and the line-of-sight) appeared to be particularly promising. In addition to observations from aeroplanes, rangefinders were being adapted for this purpose and several simple inclinometers were being tested, while an automatic instrument with integral calculator was under construction. However, whatever the optical details, all inclinometers in the firing ship depended on measuring the small angle between two widely separated features on the target, for example, its masts or bow and stern; then, if the target range and the distance between these features were known (the latter depended on recognising the class of ship correctly), the inclination could be calculated as an angle less than 90°. However:

The chief defect which is common to all inclinometers is that by the instrument itself it is impossible to say on which side of 90° the inclination lies. It is therefore essential that the inclinometer should be worked in close conjunction with the rangefinder and gun range plots.[196]

And, when the inclination was close to 90°, even a substantial change of course resulted in only a small change in the measured angle.

Despite the known difficulties, the committee repeated its preference for inclinometers over range-rate plotting in its Final Report. Submitted on 1 February 1919, this addressed the second question of 'the Fleet's requirements for the future development of Fire Control Tables generally'. However, although true-course plotting was considered, it was decisively rejected as an alternative to separate plots of ranges, bearings and, now, inclination.

When observations and information of the enemy's movements and fall of shot becomes so good and rapid as to enable a correct track to be plotted, these results can be set direct on the clock, and the necessity of plotting for gun control purposes vanishes.

While the committee had no interest in reviving the Argo plotter, it proposed that the new table should be a 'combination of all the good points of the Dreyer table, Ford clock, and Argo clock';[197] in particular, the committee accepted that, in the Dreyer Tables,

> The drive of the automatic Dumaresq . . . is not the best available type of variable speed gear.

They also recommended that the range and bearing plots should be of the straight-line type, and that two time-and-range plots were needed to deal with the increased amount of range information.[198]

## THE ADMIRALTY FIRE CONTROL TABLES

In most respects, the first of the new generation of fire control tables, the Admiralty Fire Control Tables (AFCTs) Mark I fitted in *Nelson* and *Rodney*, followed the recommendations of the Grand Fleet Committee. The final design had no fewer than three time-and-range plots and two time-and-bearing plots, all on the straight-line principle. Thus there was no 'adoption of . . . true-course plotters . . . after the war'.[199] Nonetheless, the clock was based on the Argo-type variable-speed drive, although the linkages which generated the speeds along and across were more like those in the Ford clock.[200] However, the committee's enthusiasm for the direct measurement of inclination, as a complete replacement for range-rate plotting, proved premature; a fully satisfactory inclinometer did not enter service until 1927. As finally developed, the AFCT clock had a pair of 'suggestion wires' for making the cross-cut of range-rate and speed-across so long advocated by Dreyer, but an inclination projector extended the principle by providing for the alternative cross-cut of inclination and speed-across.[201]

In recommending the Final Report to the Admiralty, Beatty had proposed that the design be undertaken by a committee of experts which should include both Isherwood and Elphinstone.[202] As originally formed, the Fire Control Tables Development Committee had only Service members. But the final design, which was not completed until 1925, was a cooperative effort by this committee, designers on the staff of Elliott Brothers, and the Low Power and Fire Control section of the department of the Director of Torpedoes and Mines. Isherwood (assisted by H. F. Landstad, a senior draughtsman from Argo) worked within the last-named section during 1920 and 1921 on mechanical design. Unfortunately, no clear indications have been found of when Elliotts began to contribute to the design process nor, therefore, of whether Isherwood and Elphinstone (now Sir Keith) had worked for a time in collaboration.[203]

The reports of the Grand Fleet committee were submitted just as Frederic

Dreyer was leaving the Admiralty in February 1919 to serve as Chief of Staff during Jellicoe's Empire Mission. However, he returned in April 1920 to take up his previous duties (under the title of Director of the Gunnery Division) for two more years.[204] Since no details had then been finalised, he had plenty of opportunity to influence the design of the new tables. Yet, a year after his return, Dreyer had only one concern about the way the development was proceeding.

> D. of G.D. was for a long time very anxious as regards the effect of the very complex proposals for the new Fire Control Table, but eventually arrived at the conviction that they were necessary in order to face the problems with which we are confronted.[205]

After the first trials of the prototype AFCT Mark I at the end of 1925, Dreyer, now a Rear Admiral and back at the Admiralty as Assistant Chief of the Naval Staff (ACNS), reaffirmed that:

> I am quite sure that the Policy pursued and the money expended in connection with these experimental Tables are fully justified.[206]

Sumida suggests that, after Dreyer returned as DofGD, 'the design process was well under way, but political circumstances [the presence of Beatty as First Sea Lord] were also such as to limit severely his powers of interference' and that, as ACNS, he 'had good reason to be circumspect in his remarks' because of the recent exposure by the Royal Commission on Awards to Inventors of 'the plagiarization of the Argo Clock'.[207] These interpretations might be justified if the Argo fire control system had been the basis for the AFCT Mark I. In reality, as a complete system, there is some justification for Dreyer's claim that the AFCT 'was in fact only a rearrangement of my "Dreyer Table"',[208] despite the clear Argo influence on the clock. Thus Dreyer had no reason to interfere with the development of the Mark I, or to dissimulate his enthusiasm over the outcome; not a hint has been found that he did not give the new table his full support.

Later marks of AFCT were, in the main, supplied only to newly constructed cruisers and battleships. However, the Mark VII was developed specially for the capital ships that were comprehensively reconstructed, and supplied to *Warspite*, *Queen Elizabeth*, *Valiant* and *Renown*. *Hood* was the only ship with the final development of the Dreyer Table, the Mark V. As for the remaining eight capital ships retained under the Washington Treaty, their Mark IV* tables were updated and elaborated along the lines recommended by the Dreyer Table Committee;[209] like the table in *Hood*, they were still in place in September 1939 and, in the ships that survived, appear to have served until the end of the Second World War. Refitting ageing battleships was not a priority; even so, the retention of these old fire control

273

tables does suggest that they remained at least adequate in the task for which they had been designed some thirty years previously.

## Notes

1 Gordon, *Rules of the Game* [B] pp. 43–51 and 54–8. Correspondence between Beatty and Jellicoe, 21 February to 7 May 1916 in *Beatty Papers, Volume I* [B] pp. 294–308.
2 *FDSF III*, pp. 37–40, 45–7 and Chart 1. Gordon [1] pp. 72–3.
3 All times are Greenwich Mean Time, and henceforth are *post-meridiem* in the twelve-hour clock format employed in the contemporary reports of Jutland.
4 'Record of Messages Bearing on the Operation', *OD*, Appendix II. Except that positions are given in latitudes and longitudes rather than the original codes, this appendix is the same as Admiralty, Naval Staff, Communications Division, *Battle of Jutland. Record of Messages Bearing on the Operation*, 23 September 1919, ADM 186/625. This earlier record, 'compiled by the Signal Division of the Naval Staff . . . from the Signal, W/T and Cypher Logs of Fleet Flagships, Senior Officers of Squadrons and a large number of private ships, and also from the Admiralty Log', was completed before Beatty became First Sea Lord on 1 November 1919.
5 Gordon, pp. 69–70, 74–7 and 97.
6 The 'cruisers' were actually destroyers: V. E. Tarrant, *Jutland. The German Perspective* (London: Arms and Armour Press, 1997) p. 65. Tarrant (p. 7) acknowledges that he relied heavily on the German Official History: see Admiralty, Naval Staff, *The Battle of Jutland (The German Official Account) from Der Krieg zur See, 1914–1918, North Sea, Volume V* by Captain O. Groos, translated by Lt. Com. W. T. Bagot RN, 1926, AL.
7 British 'Messages' [4]. *Barham*, 'Captain's Report', *OD*, p. 198. Commander Michael Craig Waller, 'The Turn to the S.S.E.' (unpublished note, copy gratefully acknowledged) points out that the BCF's own track charts in *OD* time their turn SSE at 2.35.
8 See Gordon, Chapter 6 for a comprehensive analysis of all aspects of this episode.
9 Quoted by Gordon, p. 687.
10 Gordon, p. 82. *FDSF III*, p. 61.
11 Even recently, Nigel Steel and Peter Hart, *Jutland 1916. Death in the Grey Wastes* (London: Cassell, 2003) p. 64 concluded that 'Evan-Thomas was . . . guilty of an egregious blunder'.
12 Gordon, p. 92.
13 Gordon, pp. 97–9. Brooks, 'The Midshipman and the Secret Gadget' [B] pp. 76–9.
14 British 'Messages'; both messages ended with *Galatea*'s position.
15 *Beatty Papers I* [1] p. 368.
16 'Summary of the More Important German Wireless Messages and Visual Signals Relating to the Battle of Jutland', Appendix 10 to Tarrant (pp.272–303). Henceforth, where not stated otherwise, the times of changes in course and speed and other orders or messages are taken from flag signals in the British 'Messages' (times of despatch) and these 'German Signals' (times received). Normally, flag signals could be acted on soon after they were hauled down (made executive). Nonetheless, these times are only approximate and not always consistent – both records contain signals with times of despatch or receipt

that are earlier than their times of origin. But, even when available, times from individual ships' reports are no more accurate, in part because of differences in their clocks. Thus all times have to be read with an implied 'about' preceding them.

17 Tarrant [6] p. 69. The British 'Messages' state that *New Zealand* sighted five enemy ships at 3.15, but her own report (*New Zealand*, 'Time Table', *OD*, pp. 159–61) states that their smoke was not seen until 3.24. Comparison of this time table, and other reports from *New Zealand*, with the times in the British 'Messages' suggests that they correspond quite well before 3.45 but that all subsequent times from *New Zealand* are about six minutes fast: see also Campbell, *Jutland. An Analysis* [B] pp. 39 and 48. Where her times have been corrected in this account, they are given in square brackets.

18 *FDSF III*, Chart 4. *Narrative of the Battle of Jutland* (London: HMSO, 1924) p. 13.

19 Gordon, p. 101. VABCF is Vice Admiral Commanding Battle Cruiser Fleet.

20 'Record of Events during Action of May 31st compiled from Records kept in Control Tower and Transmitting Station. H.M.S. Lion' in 'Gunnery Range and Rate of Fire Reports', BTY 6/6, Beaty Papers, NMM. This contains surprisingly few rangefinder and gun ranges; it was not included in the *Official Despatches*.

'Battle of 31st May: Narrative of Events' in 'Action with the German High Sea Fleet . . . VABCF's Personal Records', BTY 6/3. Another copy of this tabulated 'Narrative' is in DRAX 1/57.

These important sources are seldom cited.

21 'Gunnery Officer of H.M.S. *Tiger*' in H. W. Fawcett and G. W. W. Hooper, *The Fighting at Jutland* (London: Chatham, 2001 – first published London, 1921) p. 397. See also *New Zealand*, 'Captain's Report', *OD*, p. 162 and PO Sheppard, 'Notes on Jutland' in *Beatty Papers I*, p. 356.

22 *FDSF III*, Chart 4.

23 Roskill, *Beatty* [B] p. 155.

24 VABCF's 'Narrative' [20]. *New Zealand*'s 'Time Table' [17].

25 The fire distribution order in 'German Signals' [16] is timed at 3.30 but its position suggests a misprint, probably for 3.39.

26 For ranges, courses and rates throughout the battle, see 'FCBD', Appendix XXVI.

27 *German Account* [6] pp. 57–8. The course (110 or SEbyE) and bearing (57) given by Commander Paschen of *Lützow* – Steel and Hart [11] p. 80 – do not conform with the other German sources.

28 *Lion*'s 'Record' [20]. VABCF's 'Narrative'.

29 Sir Julian S. Corbett, *History of the First World War Based on Official Documents . . . Naval Operations, Volume III* (London: Longmans Green, 1923) p. 334.

30 VABCF's 'Narrative' confirms that the order was by Blue Pendant ('alter course together' – *FDSF III*, pp. 34–6).

31 This interpretation is largely based on the note of 19 June 2001 by Captain Peter Grindal RN on fleetwork and line-of-bearing manoeuvres, which is gratefully acknowledged.

32 Corbett [29] Map 23 shows all the battlecruisers astern of *Lion* fanning out to port between 3.45 and 3.50 before converging again onto a single track curving away to the South.

33 *OD*, Plate 9a, based on 'Tracing of track followed by Second Battle Cruiser Squadron . . .' in ADM 137/303. *FDSF III*, Chart 4 – and the many books published subsequently that clearly base their charts on Marder's – shows only the 2BCS fanning out to port.

34 If Beatty had turned the battlecruisers in succession to SE and then together to ESE, he would have both reduced the rate and formed the line-of-bearing in about four minutes – Grindal [31].

35 *Lion*'s 'Record'. Gunnery records of *Princess Royal, Tiger* and *New Zealand* in 'Jutland Despatches. Gunnery Notes', ADM 116/1487; expurgated versions in *OD*, Appendix I. *Tiger*, 'Captain's Report', *OD*, p. 155. Report by Midshipman J. L. Storey of *Queen Mary*, 3 June 1916 in ADM 137/302 stated that *Queen Mary* began firing at 3.53.

36 Campbell [17] p. 39. Corbett, p. 334. Chatfield, *Navy and Defence* [B] p. 142.

37 *Lion*'s 'Record'. *Princess Royal*'s gunnery record [35]. Recollections of Midshipman J. H. Lloyd-Owen (X turret) in M. W. Williams, 'The Loss of HMS Queen Mary at Jutland', in D. McLean and A. Preston (eds) *Warship 1996* (London: Conway Maritime Press, 1996), p. 113. Campbell (p. 39) concluded that not only *Tiger* but also *Lion* commenced with forward turrets only.

38 'The visibility was good but not abnormal': Midshipman N. G. Garnon-Williams, stationed in *Lion*'s conning tower. Garnon-Williams Papers, 85/26/1, Imperial War Museum [IWM].

39 'VABCF's Report', 12 June 1916 in *Beatty Papers I*, p. 326 and *OD*, p. 132.

40 Von Hase, *Kiel and Jutland* [B] pp. 153–4, 'Report by the Commander-in-Chief of the German High Sea Fleet . . . 4 July 1916', Appendix III, *OD*. 'Narrative from H.M.S. *Indomitable*' (p.239) and *Tiger*'s Gunnery Officer (p. 397) in Fawcett and Hooper [21]. Admiral Pelly, *300,000 Sea Miles. An Autobiography* (London: Chatto & Windus, 1938) p. 165. *New Zealand*, 'Captain's Report' [21].

41 *Princess Royal*'s gunnery record. 'Narrative from Officers of H.M.S. *Princess Royal*' in Fawcett and Hooper, p. 18. *New Zealand*'s gunnery record [35] gives –200 yds/min. *Derfflinger*'s opening rate was –220 yds/min.: von Hase [40] pp. 145–7.

42 *Tiger*'s gunnery officer.

43 *Tiger*'s gunnery record [35] and *Tiger*'s gunnery officer, pp. 397.

44 Midshipman G. M. Eady, 'Account of Jutland', in 'Life in the Battle Cruiser Fleet 1916', Eady Papers, 86/58/1, IWM.

45 Pelly to Beatty, 31 January 1915 (summarised to justify *Tiger*'s firing for a time at the leading enemy ship during the Battle of the Dogger Bank) in *Beatty Papers I*, pp. 213–14.

46 'BCF Orders', 18 February 1915, *Beatty Papers I*, p. 257.

47 *New Zealand*, 'Captain's Report', p. 162. *New Zealand*'s gunnery record.

48 Eady, 'With the Battle-Cruiser-Fleet at Jutland', in 'Life in the BCF' [44]. Eady claimed 327 rpm and 29.7 knots but these figures must be exaggerated. On trial, *New Zealand* managed 26.39 knots at 300 rpm: Roberts, *Battlecruisers* [B] p. 80. For the effects of vibration on gunnery, see Chatfield [36] p. 109.

49 *Lion*'s 'Record'.

50 S 55° E was a True Course: 'Remarks on Lord Jellicoe's Comments', in 'Observations on the Narrative of the Battle of Jutland', ADM 116/3188.

51 William Goodenough, *A Rough Record* (London: Hutchinson, 1943) p. 91.

52 Roskill [23] p. 131.

53 Chatfield, pp. 141–2.

54 Hipper to Scheer, 'Lessons from the Skaggerak Battle' in DRYR 6/10 and ADM 137/1644.

55 'The Diaries of Stephen King-Hall', in L. King-Hall (ed.) *Sea Saga* (London: Gollancz, 1935) p. 451. After opening fire 'They had the advantage of light . . .': Garnon-Williams [38]. Chatfield, p. 141.

56 Campbell, pp. 40–1, 67 and 73–4.

57 'German Plan IV. Battle Cruiser Action', *OD*, Plate IV. The separate case of maps with the *Official Despatches* included seven German Plans that were drawn originally to illustrate the report of the C.-in-C., Admiral Scheer, to the Kaiser (*OD*, Appendix III). Where, as here, the 'German Signals' are ambiguous, the German courses shown on 'Plan IV' have been assumed; there are significant differences from Marder's Charts 4 and 5 in *FDSF III*.

58 The British 'Messages' contain no course signals from Beatty between 3.45 and 4.40.

59 PO Sheppard [21].

60 'Track of BCF II.0 P.M. to IX.24 P.M . . .', *OD*, Plate 10; originals in ADM 137/303 and 137/2147 and in DRAX 1/57. *Lion*'s 'Record'.

61 'BCF Orders' [46]. *Princess Royal*, 'Captain's Report' and RA1BCS, 'Notes on Action', *OD*, pp. 151 and 147. *Princess Royal*'s gunnery record lists five salvoes up to 3.51.15 but then only two more in the next four minutes, the last at 12,800 yards; Beatty signalled 'Increase the rate of fire' at 3.55. Von Hase, pp. 145–52 and Sketch I; *Derfflinger*'s range at 3.54 was 12,575 yards.

62 Campbell, pp. 41, 70 and 80–3. Williams [37] p. 122.

63 Campbell, pp. 71–5. For the effects of hits on Q and X turrets, see Lt.Com. Macnamara to Captain Pelly, 4 June 1916 in BTY 6/6.

64 *Tiger*'s gunnery record. *German Account*, p. 62.

65 *New Zealand* 'Time Table'. In her gunnery record, *New Zealand* recorded a minimum range of 10,800 yards at 3.56. Marder's Chart 4 and its many derivatives show the battlecruisers fanning out at different times to port and starboard to form a complete line of bearing NW, then turning together, preserving the line of bearing, to southerly courses, and continuing thus until after the sinking of *Indefatigable*. Four things are wrong. First, the line of bearing could not have been formed as shown in response to just one signal. Second, there is no record of the signal that would have been necessary for the turn together. Third, on southerly courses, the line of bearing NW did not prevent smoke interference. Fourth, *Indefatigable* would therefore have been hidden behind the smoke of her five consorts at a range of some 18,000 yards, which is far higher than the ranges reported by *New Zealand* or *Von der Tann*; however, the 'Track of BCF' [60] does indicate that, when she sank, *Indefatigable* was about NNW from *Lion*.

66 Since *Moltke* was the target of *Tiger* as well as *New Zealand*, each ship's fall of shot may well have confused the other's spotting.

67 As shown on the 'German Plan IV' [57]; however, the *German Account*, p. 60, states that 'Hipper . . . bore away one point'.

68 Campbell, pp. 41–2, 64–9 and 78–9. *Lion*'s 'Record'. VABCF's 'Narrative'. 'Track of BCF' shows a turn only from SbyE to S at 4.00.

69 Chatfield, p. 143. In fact, the range-rate in *Lion*'s 'Record' was an increasing one of 400 yds/min. opening. In a letter to Keyes dated January 1923 (in KEYES/15, British Library), Chatfield gave a different and more likely explanation of what may have been, at first, a small turn to throw out the enemy fire: 'Lion actually made one considerable swing to Starboard about 2 Pts owing to Comd (N) saying Port 5 & then forgetting he had done so'. This is a common error – Grindal.

70 *German Account*, pp. 61–2; also Campbell, pp. 60–2 and Steel and Hart, p. 92.

71 Campbell, Chapter 5. The ricochets which struck *Lion* and *Tiger* (the latter 'probably hit in the first 10 minutes' ) – pp. 67 and 75 – have not been included in the German total.

72 *German Account*, p. 63. 'German Plan IV'. Both time the turns two to three minutes later than the 'German Signals'.

73 'Track of BCF'. *Lion*'s 'Record'. VABCF's 'Narrative' (4.05) and British 'Messages' (4.11). 'Officers of *Princess Royal*' [41] p. 30. *New Zealand*'s 'Time Table' and gunnery record. *Princess Royal* submitted a track chart after Jutland (Enclosure 13 in ADM 137/303 and *Official Despatches*, Plate 12) but the courses shown (ESE from 3.45 to 4.10 and then SbyE until 4.38) cannot be reconciled with other sources.

74 *Tiger*'s gunnery records. *Tiger*'s gunnery officer, pp. 397–8.

75 *Princess Royal*'s gunnery record. Von Hase, p. 150.

76 *Barham*, Captain's Report' [7] p. 199. VABCF's 'Narrative' and 'VABCF's Report' [39] p. 326. *German Account*, p. 64.

77 'Track of BCF'. VABCF's 'Narrative'. *Lion*'s 'Record'. 'Officers of *Princess Royal*', p. 19. For rates, see Chapter 2.

78 Campbell (pp. 48 and 79–80) attributes the hits on *Lützow* to *Princess Royal*. The ranges at 4.15 were 21,275 yards (*Lion*'s 'Record') and 18,500 yards (*Princess Royal*'s gunnery record).

79 *German Account*, p. 66. Von Hase, pp. 154 and 159.

80 'VABCF's Report', pp. 326 and 328. Compare with the extract from Beatty's report in 'Jellicoe's Despatch . . . as published . . . 4th July 1916', in *Jellicoe Papers, Volume I* [B] p. 293.

81 Jellicoe to Beatty citing Evan-Thomas, 4 June 1916 in *Beatty Papers I*, p. 319.

82 *Lion*'s 'Record'.

83 Campbell, pp. 75 and 85–94. *Tiger*'s gunnery officer, pp. 397–8.

84 VABCF's 'Narrative'. Campbell, pp. 67–9.

85 Williams, pp. 122–5 and 132. Von Hase, p. 160 (who claimed, almost certainly wrongly – p. 157 – that *Queen Mary* was firing full broadsides at *Derfflinger*). *Pace* Campbell, pp. 62–4, *Seydlitz* made three hits but these include that at 4.21; 'FCBD', Appendix XXVI-15.

86 *Princess Royal*'s gunnery record. British 'Messages'. 'Officers of *Princess Royal*', p. 30.

87 Von Hase, pp. 162–4. Campbell, pp. 69–71.

88 Tarrant, pp. 91–2. Campbell, pp. 50 and 76.

89 The bearings in *Lion*'s 'Record' suggest turns to starboard and then to port three to four minutes earlier than shown on 'Track of BCF'.

90 Williams, p. 129. *Tiger*'s and *New Zealand*'s gunnery records. Campbell, pp. 47–8 and 73–5.

91 Once again, *Princess Royal* did not live up to the ferocious reputation of her Captain, Walter Cowan, for which see Gordon, pp. 28–9.

92 She did not repeat this feat during the approach to the second phase. By then, the visibility from the British line was the poorer, while her principal range-finder in the Argo Tower remained out of action, even though the tower's training gear had been repaired: *Princess Royal*, 'Captain's Report' [61] p. 151.

93 *Princess Royal* required less than three-quarter power to make 24 knots: Roberts [48] p. 80.

94 'Advance Report of [BCF] Gunnery Committee', 22 June 1916 in *Beatty Papers I*, p. 347.

95 *Lion*'s 'Record'. *Princess Royal*'s gunnery record. Campbell, pp. 40, 61 and 364. *German Account*, p. 61. *Lion*'s average interval for her first 20 salvoes was 43 seconds, *Lützow*'s for her first 31 was 38 seconds. *Lützow* fired salvoes alternately from her fore and after turrets: PO Sheppard.

96 Von Hase, pp. 162–4 and 148–9. When ranges were less than 13,000 m., two salvoes from the secondary armament were fired between heavy salvoes.

97 *New Zealand*'s gunnery record.

98 Blackett's 'Naval Diary', in Hore, *Patrick Blackett* [B] p. 5.

99 Battlecruisers' gunnery records [35]. 'RA5BS Report', *OD*, p. 193. 'Track of *Barham*', *OD*, Plate 10a. Campbell, p. 55, 76 and 80.

100 'Track of BCF'. 'Track of *Barham*' [99]. Gordon, p. 129 states that otherwise they 'would have passed very close green-to-green'.

101 Campbell, p. 16. 'Track of BCF'. Gordon, p. 127.

102 Gordon, pp. 131–3. *FDSF III*, Chart 6. Campbell, p. 54, also states that the turn 'avoided the immediate vicinity of *Queen Mary*'s wreck, but this is not borne out by his (p.105) or Marder's charts. (*Lion*'s 'Record' does have two alterations to port (at 4.50 and 4.53) and an alteration to starboard at 4.56: but the first cannot be correct.)

103 'Track of BCF'. Commander Michael Craig Waller, 'The Turn to the North' (unpublished note, copy gratefully acknowledged).

104 Gordon, pp. 136–40 and 147. *Barham*, 'Captain's Report', p. 199. The last two times are based on the 'British Messages' and *Barham*'s reports and track; they are one minute earlier than Gordon's.

105 Gordon, pp. 405–6. 'RA5BS Report' [99]. 'Track of *Barham*'.

106 *Valiant*, 'Captain's Report', *OD*, p. 206.

107 Estimated by plotting the *OD* tracks of the BCF and *Barham* at the same scale. These suggest that the distances between flagships were 3.4 sea miles at 4.55, increasing to 4.3 miles at 5.16. Chatfield (p.144) stated that 'we met and passed close to the Fifth Battle Squadron'.

108 *Lion*'s 'Record'. PO Sheppard. Chatfield, p. 145.

109 Battlecruisers' gunnery records. Tarrant, p. 102. 'German Messages' for 4.57. Campbell, pp. 96–7 and 124–5.

110 Tarrant, p. 101 and particularly Gordon, pp. 142–6 and Appendix IV.

111 Brooks, 'The Midshipman and the Secret Gadget' [13] p. 82.

112 Without explanation, Campbell (pp. 126–30) attributes the hits on *Barham* to *Derfflinger*. Gordon, p. 618.

113 5BS reports in *OD*, pp. 192–220. British 'Messages' for 5.20. Tarrant, pp. 105–7. Campbell, pp. 134–45.

114 *Malaya*'s 'Diary of Events', *OD*, p. 218.

115 Campbell (pp. 130–3) again without explanation attributes the hits on *Warspite* to *Seydlitz*. He lists thirteen hits on *Warspite* made after 6.15, but numbers 3 and 13 correspond to the first two described by Commander Walwyn (pp. 173–9). Gordon, pp. 413 and 672. 'Experience in . . . *Warspite*', Fawcett and Hooper, p. 143.

116 Jellicoe had informed Beatty in February 1916 that the best speed of the *Queen Elizabeths* was less than 24 knots: *Beatty Papers I*, p. 295–7.

117 'German Plan V. Movements of German High Sea Fleet and Approximate Position of British Fleet . . .', *OD*, Plate V.

118 'VABCF's Report', pp. 134–5. *FDSF III*, p. 86. Roskill, p. 162.

119 'German Signals', 'German Plan V' [117] and 'German Plan VI. Diagram of Important Phases . . .', *OD*, Plate VI, though all three differ in detail. See also Tarrant, pp. 107–9.

120 VABCF's 'Narrative'. *OD*, 'Track of *Iron Duke*' (Plate 6a), 'C.-in-C.'s Despatch and Narrative' (pp. 6, 12, and 15–16), 'RA2CS Report' (p. 270), 'RA3LCS Report' (p. 185). Gordon, p. 430.

121 VABCF's 'Narrative'. *Lion*'s 'Record'. 'VABCF's Report', p. 135.

122 *Lion*'s 'Record'. Campbell (p. 135) says the 'shell at 1745 was probably from *Princess Royal* – but she fired only three salvoes before, at 5.46, changing target to the right hand ship: *Princess Royal*'s gunnery record. 'Track of *Barham*'.

123 Campbell, Chapter 7.

124 Gordon, p. 431.

125 Campbell, pp. 36, 59 and 111–13. Tarrant, pp. 115–17. Captain Heaton Ellis, *Inflexible*, to VAC BCF, 10 June 1916 (contains gunnery information not in *Inflexible*, 'Captain's Report', *OD*, pp. 169–71) and report of Lt. Com. (G), *Indomitable*, both in BTY 6/6.

126 Tarrant, pp. 109–17. Between 5.51 and 6.10, the 'German Plans V and VI' do not show the 1SG courses that would be expected from the 'German Signals'. Like Marder's Chart 8, the plans show the 1SG on SW'ly courses for a time.

127 'VABCF's Report', p. 330. 'Track of BCF' (which shows the Grand Fleet bearing NbyE, 6 miles at 5.56). Battlecruisers' gunnery records.

128 'RA5BS Report', p. 194. 'Track of *Barham*'.

129 'C.-in-C.'s Narrative' [120] p. 16. Dreyer, *Sea Heritage* [B] p. 145.

130 Though not applicable here, the quickest method of deploying from column into line was for all columns to turn onto the line-of-bearing, which became the new course: see also Campbell, p. 120.

131 'C.-in-C.'s Narrative'. *Sea Heritage* [129] p. 146.

132 'German Plans V and VI' do not agree on the course (the 'German Signals' imply a course E).

133 At 6.15, *Marlborough* estimated the range of a *Kaiser*-class battleship as 10,000 yards ('Gunnery Report', *OD*, p. 70) but opened fire at 6.17 at 13,000 yards ('VA1BS Report', *OD*, p. 65).

134 'Narrative of *Nicator*', Fawcett and Hooper, p. 355.

135 *Warrior*, 'Captain's Report', *OD*, pp. 290–4 and 'Narrative', Fawcett and Hooper, pp. 161–9.

136 'VABCF's Report', p. 331. 'Track of BCF'. *Lion*'s 'Record'. Campbell, pp. 153, 160, 170–2 and 183.

137 'RA5BS Report', p. 194. *Warspite*, 'Captain's Report' and chart, *OD*, pp. 202–3 and Plate 17. 'Track of *Barham*'. Gordon, p. 447. British 'Messages', 6.18.

138 'VA1BS Report', *OD*, p. 65. *Warrior*, 'Captain's Report' [135].

139 *Barham*, 'Captain's Report'. *Warspite*, 'Captain's Report' [137]. Tarrant, p. 129. Campbell's hits 3 and 13 (pp.173–8) were probably received earlier.

140 Narratives from *Engadine* in Fawcett and Hooper, pp. 69–73. The 5BS reports in *OD*, pp. 192–220.

141 British 'Messages', 6.12. Reports of SO3BCS (Captain of *Indomitable*) and Commander H. Dannreuther in *OD*, pp. 163–9. The former gives the course as 153 (about SbyE) but *Indomitable*'s chart (*OD*, Plate 13) shows SEbyS. 'VABCF's Report', p. 331 and VABCF's 'Narrative'.

142 Lt. Com. (G) *Indomitable* and Captain Heaton Ellis [125]. *Inflexible* opened with 'practically no rate' at what she thought was a *König* class battleship (apart from the fifth turret between the funnels, these ships had a profile not unlike *Derfflinger*'s) and, at 6.28, shifted to the next astern, a ship 'apparently firing from 5 turrets' (see also *Inflexible*'s gunnery officer, Fawcett and Hooper, pp. 226–30). *Indomitable*'s report gives an opening rate of -100. It implies that she could see the three leading ships of the 1SG and fired only at the centre one. 'FCBD', Appendix XXIX.

143 Campbell (pp. 183–7) assumes that *Inflexible* made some of the hits on *Lützow* and that *Indomitable* made the hits on both *Derfflinger* and *Seydlitz*.

144 Dannreuther and 'SO3BCS Report' [141]. Commander Gunther Paschen of *Lützow* in Steel and Hart, pp. 229–30. *German Account*, p. 110.

145 Von Hase, p. 183.

146 *Iron Duke*'s track charts time her turn at either 6.21 or 6.23: *OD*, Plates 2 and 6a. *Marlborough*'s track, Plate 7a.

147 'C.-in-C.'s Narrative' and reports of SOs of Squadrons and Captains in *OD*, pp. 17–18, 52–129 and 353–77. 'German Plans V and VI'.

148 Campbell, p. 156.

149 Captain Dreyer, 'Brief Account': Commander (G) Blake, 'Notes made in the . . . Gun Control Tower': Commander Calvert, 'Notes made . . . in "B" Turret' and Lt. Shelley, 'Notes . . . on . . . Transmitting Station', all in ADM 137/302; expurgated versions in *OD*, pp. 52–61.

150 Campbell, pp. 156 and 187–93 attributes one of the direct hits to *Monarch* but that ship's 'Notes' (*OD*, p. 373) do not mention another ship firing at her target and suggest that her two salvoes at a *König* may have been fired (though without effect) at *Grosser Kurfürst*; *Markgraf*, also hit at this time, is another possibility. *König* was also hit by a ricochet.

151 'German Signals', Fifth Flotilla (received 6.25).

152 *Jellicoe Papers I* [80] p. 253.

153 *Jellicoe Papers, Volume II* [B] p. 432.

154 The time of the turn S is 6.55 in British 'Messages' and on 'Plan of Battle off Jutland (*OD*, Plate 1a submitted with Jellicoe's despatch – p. 5) but 6.51 and 6.52 on *Iron Duke*'s track charts (*OD*, Plates 2 and 6a).

155 'Track of BCF'. The salvoes fired by the battlecruisers at the 1SG between 6.17 and 6.31 (gunnery reports) made no hits.

156 'VABCF's Report', p. 331. 'SO3BCS Report'. *Inflexible*, 'Captain's Report' [125].

157 *FDSF III*, pp. 124 and 148–50. Roskill, p. 176. Gordon, pp. 457–8.

158 British 'Messages'. The 'Track of BCF' (which accompanied Beatty's report of 12 June) shows a course of SSE until 7.05, interrupted by a thirty-two-point turn at 7.00, and then a gradual turn to SW by 7.08. Chatfield's report of 4 June (*OD*, p. 145) states: 'The ship continued to circle to starboard. At 7.3 p.m. our course was altered to S.S.E. [the previously mentioned course change at 6.48 was also to SSE] and at 7.6 p.m. to South; at 7.9 p.m. to S.S.W. and at 7.11 p.m. to S.W. by S.'; VABCF's 'Narrative' says the same. 'VABCF's Report' (p.332) confirms that: 'Between 7 and 7.12 p.m. we hauled round gradually to S.W. by S.' The charts submitted with their reports by *Princess Royal*, *New Zealand* and *Indomitable* show the same general trend, as do Marder's Charts 9 and 10 in *FDSF III*.

159 'RA2LCS Report', *OD*, p. 186.

160 British 'Messages', by searchlight. *Falmouth*'s has time-of-despatch 6.40, time-of-origin 1845. Beatty's was received by *Iron Duke* at 7.00; its time-of-origin was 1755, presumably for 1855, which seems to rule out the possibility that it was sent after an early sighting of Scheer's second turn-about (Tarrant p. 153, who also on p. 145 remarks on Napier's failure to report).

161 'Track of BCF'. *FDSF III*, pp. 126–9.

162 Reports in *OD*, pp. 52–123 and pp. 355–77. Battlecruisers' gunnery records. Three plans of the battle, first drawn between 18 June and 29 August 1916 and published with the *Official Despatches* (Plates 1a and 4a from Jellicoe and Plate 8a from Beatty: for history, see *OD*, pp. 5, 51 and 143 and *Jellicoe Papers II* [153] pp. 428 and 478–9), place *Lion* some three to four miles closer to the enemy than *King George V*. These plans are inconsistent with the gunnery reports and the reports and charts submitted shortly after the battle.

163 'C.-in-C.'s Narrative', p. 18. *Thunderer*, 'Captain's Report', *OD*, p. 376.

164 Tarrant, pp. 157–65. 'German Plan V'. Campbell, Chapter 11. British 'Messages'. *OD* reports [162].

165 'VABCF's Report', p. 332; VABCF's 'Narrative' times the enemy sighting to NNW at 7.40. 'C.-in-C.'s Narrative', p. 20. Lt. Com. (G) *Indomitable*.

166 'German Plan V'. 'Track of BCF'. *FDSF III*, p. 140.

167 Battlecruisers' gunnery records. Lt. Com. (G) *Indomitable* and Captain Heaton Ellis. According to the British 'Messages', Beatty ordered 'Open fire' at 8.10. Campbell, Chapter 11.

168 Like *Tiger*, *New Zealand* lacked an Evershed installation. In the poor visibility, she may have had particular problems with keeping all instruments on the same target.

169 'German Plan V'. Tarrant, pp. 177–9 (also for a possible hit on *Pommern*).

170 'Summary of Reports from 2BS' in *OD*, p. 113. 'Track of BCF' for the turn S at 9.24.

171 *Jellicoe Papers I*, pp. 75 and 248.

172 *Grand Fleet Battle Orders*, 'Duties of Battle-cruisers . . .' in *Jellicoe Papers I*, p. 251. 'BCF Orders', pp. 254–5.

173 *Grand Fleet Gunnery & Torpedo Orders*, 167: 'Remarks on the action off Jutland on 31 May 1916', 17 July 1916 in ADM 137/293.

174 Jellicoe memoranda of 24 September and 23 October 1916 in BTY 6/6. Captains' reports in 'Jutland Despatches: Gunnery Notes', ADM 116/1487 and, with excisions, in *OD*, Appendix I.

175 *IDNS*, p. 308.

176 *FDSF III*, pp. 262–3. Chatfield, pp. 153–7.

177 BCF Gunnery Committee reports in *Beatty Papers I*, particularly pp. 347–50 and 363. Several passages from these reports were quoted verbatim in *GFG&TO*, 167 [173].

178 Admiralty, Gunnery Branch, *Spotting Rules 1916*, November 1916 in Ja 011, AL. For the development of these rules, see 'Battle Cruiser Force War Records: Volume VI, Miscellaneous', ADM 137/2134 and 'Committees formed to consider experience at Jutland, Part II', ADM 137/2028.

179 Admiralty, Technical History Section, *The Technical History and Index. A Serial History of Technical Problems dealt with by Admiralty Departments*, Part 23, 'Fire Control in H.M. Ships', December 1919, pp. 21–2, AL. Also William Schleihauf, 'A Concentrated Effort: Royal Navy Gunnery Exercises at the End of the First World War', *Warship International*, 35, 2 (1998), pp. 117–39.

180 'Notes on tactical exercises . . . 24 February 1917' and 'Grand Fleet Battle Instructions', 1 January 1918 in *Beatty Papers I*, pp. 403 and 457.

181 Admiralty, Naval Staff, Gunnery and Torpedo Division, *Progress in Naval Gunnery 1914 to 1918*, July 1919, pp. 50–1, ADM 186/238.

182 *GFG&TO*, 91: 'Full Calibre firings . . . in first quarter of 1918', 29 June 1918, para. 28 in ADM 137/293.

183 Enclosure with Admiralty to C.-in-C., 10 October 1916 in 'Committees formed to consider experience at Jutland, Part I', ADM 137/2027. *PNG 1914–18* [181] states that, in August 1917, there were 106 15-foot rangefinders in the fleet.

184 *GFG&TO*, 312: 'Rangefinder Errors', 29 December 1917.

185 *GFG&TO*, 105: 'Full Calibre firings with Main Armament . . . during second quarter, 1918', 10 September 1918, paras.31–2.

186 *GFG&TO*, 91 [182] paras. 13 and 31.

187 Quoted in William Schleihauf, 'The Dumaresq and the Dreyer', *Warship International*, 38, 1 (2001), p. 24.

188 *Technical History*, 1919 [179] pp. 28–30. Admiralty, Gunnery Branch, *Handbook on Gyro Director Training Gear (GDT) 1927*, ADM 186/279.

189 *Pace IDNS* , pp. 312–3.

190 'First and Second Interim Reports' in Admiralty, Gunnery Branch, *Reports of the Grand Fleet Dreyer Table Committee 1918–1919*, September 1919, pp. 4–5, ADM 186/241.

191 *GFG&TO*, 304: 'Full Calibre Firings . . . in third quarter, 1917', para. III/23.

192 *GFG&TO*, 91, para. 41.

193 'Third Interim Report', *Dreyer Table Committee* [190] pp. 5–13. For the date, see 'MR/DNO', January to June 1919, p. 1093, AL.

194 The imperfections of the gyrocompass itself explain why 'the arrangements for applying corrections for changes in course . . . were apparently highly unsatisfactory': *IDNS*, p. 313. For the introduction of the gyrocompass with mercury ballistic from 1919, see Fanning, *Steady As She Goes* [B] pp. 218–28.

195 'Third Interim Report' [193] p. 6.

196 *GFG&TO*, 123: 'Present position as regards Inclination . . .', 4 November 1918, para. 5 See also *PNG 1914–18*, pp. 32 and 42. *GFG&TO*, 105 [185] paras. 7 and 26. *Technical History*, 1919, p. 30.

197 *IDNS*, p. 314 for the American Ford Instrument Company.

198 'Final Report of the Committee. Future Development of Fire Control Tables', *Dreyer Table Committee*, pp. 14–19. For its date, see 'MR/DNO' January–June 1919, p. 1114.

199 *IDNS*, p. 331.

200 Admiralty, Gunnery Branch, *Handbook for Admiralty Fire Control Table Mark I (H.M. Ships 'NELSON' and 'RODNEY')*, September 1927, ADM 186/273–4. Hannibal C. Ford, *Range Keeper*, US Patent 1,370,204, filed 4 December 1917 and *Range and Bearing Keeper*, US Patent 1,450,585 filed 19 June 1918.

201 John Brooks, 'The Admiralty Fire Control Tables', in Antony Preston (ed.) *Warship 2002–2003* (London: Conway Maritime Press, 2003) pp. 69–93.

202 Beatty to the Secretary of the Admiralty, 7 February 1919, in *Dreyer Table Committee*, pp. 18–19.

203 Brooks, 'AFCTs' [201] p. 75.

204 *Sea Heritage*, pp. 236, 239, 261 and 276.

205 Dof GD's minute, 15 April 1921 in 'MR/DNO', 1921, pp. 2275–6.

206 ACNS's minute, 4 January 1926 in 'Fire Contol Table. New Design', in 'MR/DNO', July 1923 – June 1926, pp. 3180–8. See further Brooks, 'AFCTs', pp. 74–6 and 79.

207 *IDNS*, pp. 315–16.

208 *Sea Heritage*, p. 59.

209 Brooks, 'AFCTs', pp. 77, 79 and 82–3. Schleihauf, 'Dumaresq and Dreyer' [187] pp. 190–201 and pp. 221–4). The addition of clutch-brake motors (first developed for the AFCTs) enabled the range clocks to drive the elaborated range plots.

# 9

# AN EXCEPTIONAL CASE

Chapter 8 concluded that Beatty's gunnery defeat in the Run to the South was due primarily to the consequences of his tactics, compounded by the inefficiency of his battlecruisers' gunnery. However, to exonerate the British fire control from any significant part in the disaster, three further questions must be addressed. Did the fire control systems in Beatty's ships add to the difficulties already imposed by his tactics? Did the Argo Clock Mark IV contribute to *Queen Mary*'s supposedly better shooting? And might the British battlecruisers have been more successful if they had been fitted with the whole Argo system with its true-course plotter?

To begin with two general points. First, the rates were not too high, nor did the rates change too rapidly, for the German system; yet this was hardly more elaborate than the simple manual system that was probably still used in the 2BCS. Second, throughout the action, the courses were not greatly different. Consequently, the speed-across was always low and, while courses were steady, the range-rates and deflections were virtually constant. The sole causes of large changes in the rates were changes of course.

Prior to opening fire, *Lion* and the 1BCS held a steady course E before turning gradually to ESE. These conditions were suitable for range-rate plotting to determine, and the Dumaresqs and clocks to keep, the range and range-rate – as confirmed by *Princess Royal*'s accurate opening values after the initial approach. But, since only *Lion* is known to have made a bearing plot, it must be assumed that most opening deflections were based on estimates of enemy speed and course; however, this was not a serious handicap when speed-across was low. The 2BCS could not have plotted during their two large turns.[1] They must, therefore, have begun ranging and, presumably, plotting when the range-rate was at its highest – almost 800 yds/min. This would have made rangetaking even more difficult and further increased the scatter of plotted points, while the plotted ranges would have lagged behind the true range by 100 yards or so.[2] However, this lagging error was insignificant compared with *New Zealand*'s opening range error of about 2,000 yards.[3] Thus, in all the British ships, rate plotting was capable of recording the changing ranges with sufficient accuracy and, its particular strength, all the ranges that could be taken. The problem (except in *Princess Royal*) was that the ranges were too few and too inaccurate. And, in *Lion*, the dearth of ranges was made worse by adopting rates that were lower than the values implicit in the few ranges that were available to plot (the same mistake was made again during the approach to the second phase).

When firing began, *Princess Royal*'s Dreyer Table Mark III was probably set quite accurately for enemy range, course and speed. Her slowing rate of fire and lack of hits can be explained by the combined effects of *Derfflinger*'s unimpeded fire and smoke from *Lion*. But did her fire control table also fail to keep the range? And, more generally, if the other tables had after all been correctly set, could they have predicted ranges (and, in the 1BCS, bearings) accurately – even when rates were high or, during turns, changing rapidly?

At no time did the rates come anywhere near the maximum values for which the Dreyer Tables were designed (±2,000 yds/min.) or even the maximum rate of the earliest Vickers clocks (±1,300 yds/min.). Thus, while the rates were constant, all the British clocks were capable of predicting the range accurately. When Beatty's ships altered course, the gyrocompass connections to the Mark III and IV tables kept the rates, even if the enemy was obscured – as he was, by *Lion*'s smoke, in the case of *Princess Royal*. The operators of the Mark III tables had to transfer the changing rates to the clock in steps by hand. But the maximum rates of change were never too great for the smallest practicable steps (25 yds/min. and 2 knots); thus, as the leading ships turned from ESE to SbyE between 3.49 and 3.55, the estimated total range error due to stepwise, manual transfer is no more than 100 yards.[4] On *Tiger*'s Mark IV table, the changing rates were transferred automatically and continuously; hence no significant range errors were introduced. If *New Zealand* and *Indefatigable* had already received their Dreyer Mark I tables, they too would have transferred range-rate by follow-the-pointer, so the range errors would have been the same as for the Mark III. But, if they were still reliant on a separate Vickers clock and Mark VI Dumaresq, rate steps of 50 yds/min. – or, briefly, in rapid turns, 100 yds/min. – may have been necessary. While these larger steps may have resulted in range errors of some 200 yards, these are again barely significant when compared with the rangefinding errors, and no more than half the 400-yard spread of a 12-inch salvo.[5]

Until *Princess Royal*'s Argo Tower was knocked out at 3.56, her gun ranges were close to those of *Derfflinger*; thus the Dreyer Table Mark III had kept the range pretty well. The British ship fired her last two salvoes in this sequence at a constant range, which confirms that the table had allowed for her own turn-away. After the hit, there is a long gap in *Princess Royal*'s record,[6] which suggests that her plot was disrupted by the loss of the Argo rangefinder. But, if she had been able to keep plotting, could she have detected (even though she was not straddling her target) that the 1SG had actually turned away at about 3.54? Rangefinder ranges could be taken and plotted between salvoes, though both the frequency and accuracy of rangetaking must have deteriorated due to the concussion of firing, cordite smoke and enemy splashes; in such conditions, the ability to record the ranges from any rangefinder with a view of the target was particularly valuable. Even so, time would be needed before the rangefinder plot showed a clear deviation from the predicted (clock) range; then small step changes in range and rate could be made, just as when spotting, until the rate steadied enough to be measured. As the BCF committee concluded after Jutland, this rate-based method became impossible if the enemy continuously altered course – though they did not mention that, even then, the time-and-range plot was not entirely defeated. Rangefinder control remained as a final resort, though one that relied on the accuracy of the mean rangefinder range. However, during the whole Run to the South, Hipper made only six turns between 3.47 and 4.26, though *Moltke* and *Von der Tann* were forced to zigzag by the fire from the 5BS; in the main, the targets of the British battlecruisers altered course only infrequently.

All in all, Beatty's Dreyer Tables – even the Dreyer Tables Mark I if they had been supplied to the 2BCS – could achieve the standards of accuracy implied by the minimum spotting corrections – 100 yards for range, 100 yds/min. for range-rate. They could plot the ranges that were transmitted to them. If set correctly for enemy course and speed, they could keep the range and deflection (and, in the case of the Dreyer Tables Mark III and IV, bearing) on steady courses and under helm. Changes in enemy course could be detected from the range plot, though more time was needed to determine the new rate produced by the new enemy course. Only *Lion* made some use of the bearing plot. Except in *Princess Royal* up to 3.51 or so, all the battle-cruiser tables were handicapped by receiving ranges that were too few and, in some cases, grossly inaccurate. But they were well able to cope with the rates and changes of rate experienced during the Run to the South. To answer the first question: the Dreyer Tables did not add to the difficulties arising from Beatty's tactics.

Next, what of the claims for *Queen Mary*'s better shooting and the supposed superiority of her Argo Clock Mark IV? In all, she made four hits on *Seydlitz*, three in the first phase. But *Lion* made two hits on *Lützow* in the first phase and, probably, two more at the start of the second. Thus *Queen Mary*'s shooting was no better than would be expected from the Battle Cruiser Fleet's crack gunnery ship – and, of course, it was in no way remark-able compared with the ships of the 1SG. Furthermore, the functional superiority of her Argo clock must also be questioned. Without the help of signals, *Queen Mary* had to follow the lead of the two flagships ahead as they first made a succession of small turns away, after which 'we were . . . led by the Flagship on a snake-like course, to reduce the chance of being hit'.[7] Hence the operators of the Argo clock were faced with the constant dilemma of whether the control lever should be set to STEADY or

TURNING. It was probably left for most of the time at TURNING, in which case the clock bearing had to be continually adjusted by hand, just like the Dumaresqs in *New Zealand* and *Indefatigable*. Thus, in actual battle conditions, *Queen Mary* did not obtain much advantage from the fully automatic operation of the Argo clock, which applied only on a steady course. True, range-rate was always set automatically, but, in the Dreyer Table Mark III, the Dumaresq was adjusted automatically for all turns, whether temporary yaws or permanent changes of course. Thus the Argo Mark IV could not even claim an 'obvious superiority' over the two older Dreyer Tables, let alone over *Tiger*'s automatic, helm-free Dreyer Table Mark IV.

Lastly, could the completed Argo system have been more effective in the Run to the South than the fully developed Service system as fitted in (say) *Tiger* or *Barham*? The Argo system of 1914 comprised the Cooke-Pollen rangefinder on the new dual-observer mounting, the Argo Clock Mark V and the True Course Plotter Mark IV. Comparative tests made in *Royal Sovereign* in 1919 between 15-foot rangefinders confirmed that 'in coincidence adjustment there is nothing to choose between' the Cooke-Pollen and the Barr & Stroud FT, but that the Cooke-Pollen was 'superior . . in bad light conditions'.[8] Perhaps, therefore, in the worsening light and visibility of the second phase of the Run to the South, Cooke-Pollen rangefinders could have supplied more accurate ranges. But the 5BS also had to contend with these conditions, yet they obtained good enough ranges from their 15-foot FT24s to make up to seven hits at extreme range. This suggests that the light was not too bad for the battlecruisers' FQ rangefinders,[9] and that any contribution that these instruments made to the battlecruisers' poor ranging was due to their shorter, 9-foot length. Also, later in the battle, the good shooting of *Invincible* and *Iron Duke* was achieved with the same 9-foot rangefinders, after the light and visibility had deteriorated further, though the range was also lower. Though not conclusively, these pointers suggest that light conditions had to be even worse than those experienced in the Run to the South before a Cooke-Pollen rangefinder gave substantially more accurate results than a Barr & Stroud *of the same length*. Therefore, like for like, which is all that can be fairly compared, Cooke-Pollen rangefinders would have made little difference to the outcome of the Run to the South.

Since the Argo Clock Mark V could be coupled to a gyrocompass receiver, it had much the same automatic, helm-free functionality as the clocks and Electrical Dumaresqs of the Dreyer Tables Mark IV and IV*. So, with only slight differences between rangefinders and clocks, this last question becomes: could the Argo true-course plotter have provided better target data than rate plotting? As originally designed, the Mark IV plotter had a maximum range of 16,000 yards, so it would have been useless during the all-important approach. But, at the cost of reduced plotting accuracy, the gear ratios could have been changed to allow plotting up to (say) 20,000 yards. Argo's averaging range receiver did not progress beyond a cardboard model, so Pollen never demonstrated that it had any practical value. Hence the Mark IV plotter always relied on pairs of accurate, simultaneous ranges and bearings from a single Argo mounting. But, on the Run to the South, only *Princess Royal* (at the start) made a satisfactory range plot, and only *Lion* made a bearing plot. Its quality is unknown, but later reports suggest that, in part due to the rather coarse steps in which bearings were transmitted from the Argo mounting, satisfactory bearing plots were hardly ever made at wartime ranges. Thus, not a single ship at Jutland is known to have obtained the simultaneous, accurate pairs of ranges and bearings that were needed to make a true-course plot. Alternatively, if true-course plotting had been possible, clearly defined rate plots would have been possible too. However, the conditions of low speed-across prevalent throughout the Run to the South favoured Dreyer rate-plotters. Therefore rate-plotters, not true-course plotters, would have been quicker in first obtaining an opening range and rate, then in deducing enemy course and speed, and later in detecting any changes in enemy course and speed. Thus, by either argument, the third answer is clear: if Beatty's battlecruisers had been equipped with the complete Pollen system, including the Argo true-course plotter, they would have hit even later and even less often than was actually the case.

## THE ROYAL COMMISSION ON AWARDS TO INVENTORS

Before any attempt to draw some final conclusions, one more question must be asked: if the judgement on plagiarism in Chapter 6 is correct, why did the RCAI reach such an apparently different verdict after the hearing in 1925?

In reality, Pollen's dealings with the RCAI were a good deal more complex, and their verdict much more qualified, than described in *In Defence of Naval Supremacy*. Pollen first appeared before the RCAI in July 1920; the hearing concerned his claim that a course setting bomb sight invented by H. E. Wimperis had been suggested during a visit in January 1917 to Pollen, who was then working on a similar sight.

> Argo was awarded £500 for their 'suggestion' to Wimperis [who also received £500] as their patent was not novel if read broadly and there was no infringement if read narrowly.[10]

Thus encouraged, by December 1920 Pollen had returned to the RCAI with a preliminary submission founded on declarations:

> (A) that Mr. Pollen and his associates . . . invented and communicated to the Admiralty the method of finding a target's speed

and course which that Department adopted in the late Autumn of 1912.

(B) That the method of keeping the range under helm adopted by the Department some time after the Battle of Jutland was also invented by Mr. Pollen and his associates . . .

The Admiralty was able to counter that 'no new method of keeping the range under the helm was evolved after the Battle of Jutland', while Pollen had already undermined his own claim (A) in a letter written to the Admiralty in 1918; referring to his 1908 pamphlet *Reflections on an Error of the Day*, he admitted:

I dealt only with the fallacy of proceeding by time and range as the further fallacy of proceeding by both rates had not then been propounded.[11]

Despite the weakness of his claims, and the surprising omission of the Argo clocks, Pollen persisted and his claims were heard on 9–11 October 1923. He proved 'a voluble witness' and was advised by the chairman, Mr Justice Sargant, to 'answer the questions as shortly as you can, without making a speech each time'.[12] The outcome was that:

The Commission . . . are not prepared to recommend . . . that any remuneration should be allowed to The Argo Company and Mr. Arthur Hungerford Pollen . . .
   This Recommendation is made without prejudice to any claim . . . in respect of any alleged user [*sic*] by H.M. Government of the inventions embodied in the Argo Clock.[13]

When Pollen again appeared before the RCAI in 1925, he had applied for a rehearing of his original claim on the grounds that it was never heard in its entirety, since 'the Commission formed the erroneous view that the Claim related solely to a method of obtaining observations and plotting the results'.[14] The chairman of the Commission was now Mr Justice Tomlin, who permitted counsel and witnesses, including Pollen, to speak at length. The case dragged on from 22 June until 7 August, with hearings in all on fourteen days.[15] Yet, as before, the Commission rejected Pollen's claim to have invented rate-plotting, and came close to accusing him of misrepresentation.

After 1908 the Admiralty developed a system with another method of plotting, which Mr. Pollen then regarded we think rightly as something different from the method or system which he himself advocated. We do not think the view he now presents is consistent with his earlier view or can be supported.

Thus the award itself was only for the Argo clock.

> we are satisfied that Mr. Pollen and the Argo Co. Ltd. were the first
> to produce a mechanical integrator ... namely the Argo Clock, and
> that the clock mechanism of the Dreyer Tables Mark IV and V
> works substantially on the same principles though there are
> differences of mechanical detail.
>
> Further, we are satisfied ... that the principle and details of the
> Argo Clock were communicated to the Admiralty and to those at
> work on the Dreyer Table and directly contributed to the evolution
> of the clock mechanism of the Dreyer Tables Mark IV and V. The
> knowledge so acquired made plain the feasibility of converting the
> clock mechanism of the earlier types of Dreyer Table into a form
> which served the same function and was based upon the same
> principle as the Argo Clock and while we acquit all concerned of
> any intention or desire to copy ... (and any suggestion of the kind
> was disclaimed at the hearing) we think it impossible to question the
> influence of that work on the ultimate result.

The same hearing also considered a claim by Dreyer for a further award; the
Commission concluded that the Dreyer Table (specifically the Marks IV and V):

> has original features of considerable merit, the credit for which is
> due to Admiral Dreyer, even if in other respects it owes inspiration
> to other sources, or is the application of common knowledge.[16]

Dreyer's particular innovations were clearly identified in the course of the
hearings.

> THE CHAIRMAN: ... it is pretty plain that there are two features .
> .. in the Dreyer apparatus Mark IV and V which are not to be found
> anywhere else; one of those features is the clock plot, and the other .
> .. is the mechanism for moving the fore and aft bar to accord with
> the movements of the ship ... I do not think there is any dispute
> about it that they are novel features and the entire credit ... rests
> with Admiral Dreyer.[17]

However, in view of his position in the Navy and the award of £5,000 that he
had received in 1916, the Commission did 'not think it proper to recommend
any further award to him'.[18]

The 'Recommendation' of the Commission – signed by the chairman and
the secretary, P. Tindall Robertson – did not provide any further indication
of how, when and to what extent the details of 'the Argo Clock' (they did not
specify which mark) had exerted its influence on the Dreyer Table Mark IV

– presumably the Mark V was mentioned because its Electrical Dumaresq and clocks were the same as in the Mark IV and IV\*. However, at the hearings, the Commission had been at pains to establish what had been communicated to Henley at the Admiralty in May 1911.

> THE CHAIRMAN: . . . on the 15th. May the Mark II sketches . . . are communicated; the description contains a reference to the addition of a linkage . . . on the 27th. May sketches of that linkage are sent out.[19]

Yet, despite Mr Justice Tomlin's unwillingness to admit the fact,[20] no actual evidence was presented which proved that, in 1911, Henley had passed on details of the dividing linkage or other parts of the Argo Clock Mark II. In any case, the Commission's actual judgment does not refer to an Argo influence on the contemporary Seven Part Recorder or on the Dreyer Table Mark III of 1912,[21] but to '*converting* the clock mechanism of the *earlier types* of Dreyer Table . . . upon the same principle as the Argo Clock'. This seems closest to Dreyer's spurious proposal of December 1912 concerning '*additions* which if added to my fire control apparatus would make it more automatic than *at present*' (my emphases). Unfortunately, the voluminous minutes of the RCAI hearings have not revealed any more about exactly what knowledge was acquired that supposedly 'directly contributed to the evolution of the clock mechanism of the Dreyer Tables Mark IV and V'. I have been unable to find anything there on Dreyer's 1912 proposal, on the design of or patents relating to the Argo Clock Mark V of 1913, or on the similarities between its dividing mechanism and that in the Dreyer Table Mark IV of 1914.[22]

It seems that the Commission, perhaps swayed by Pollen's late insinuation that Elphinstone had seen the prototype Argo Clock Mark IV in 1911, concluded that, because certain principles and details could have been communicated, they had been. But which principles or details were meant? The Commission may have been alluding only to the general idea of a bearing clock – but that had appeared in the Dreyer Table Mark III. Perhaps it was referring to the actual design of the Argo Clock Mark IV with its two interconnected slipless drives for generating change-of-bearing; in December 1912 Dreyer had proposed something similar for converting the Dreyer-Elphinstone Mark III clock to more automatic working – but this scheme was not used in the Dreyer Table Mark IV. Or perhaps the Commission concluded that the dividing linkage, first proposed for the Argo Clock Mark II, had influenced the somewhat similar mechanism in the Dreyer Table Mark IV – except that the Electrical Dumaresq and C.D. gear constituted no conversion but a radical redesign of the earlier Mark III.

The method used by the RCAI secretary in recommending a value for Pollen's award to the chairman only obscures further how the Commission reached its conclusions. The main component of its £30,000 award was calculated on the basis of £200 per ship, including twenty-four battleships, fifty-nine cruisers and thirty-five new ships.[23] Even by 1930, only *Hawkins* had been fitted with a Dreyer Table Mark IV*. Seventeen modern cruisers (plus two aircraft carriers) also had Dreyer Tables, but these were of the Mark III* type, in which the bearing clocks were set manually for rate, using a graduated drum just like that introduced for the Mark III in 1912. All other cruiser tables were based on the Dreyer Turret Table, which had no bearing clock of any sort.[24]

Thus both the judgment and the sum awarded suggest that at least two key members of the Commission had not clearly grasped either the functional distinctions between the different marks of Argo Clock and Dreyer Table, or what knowledge may have been communicated, or how it influenced the designs of the Dreyer Tables. Nonetheless, even if its reasoning was faulty, the Commission was right to make an award to Pollen for his undoubted contributions to the development of fire control. On the other hand, especially in view of the liberal salary and other payments which Pollen received as governing director, the size of his award from the RCAI was not only miscalculated, but also unduly generous. And the Commission's judgment, which specifically acquitted all concerned of copying, provides no clear ground for accusations of plagiarism, particularly in 1911.

## THE REVISIONIST CASE

This book began with many questions about current interpretations of the Dreyer/Pollen controversy and the Admiralty's actions and decisions. All the answers that have now been arrived at point to the same conclusion, that there is a case for a thoroughgoing revision of the history of fire control in Britain in the early twentieth century. First, the charges of plagiarism against Dreyer and Elphinstone are unjustified and inappropriate. Argo's ideas for a bearing clock had some influence on the Dreyer Tables, but this must be set against the debt which Pollen's system owed to his long association with the Royal Navy. Second, the Admiralty was prepared, despite its difficult relationship with Pollen, to fund his developments and to order his instruments. Their eventual decision in favour of the integrated Dreyer Tables, made by Elliott Brothers, was justified both technically and commercially, while Pollen's own obduracy did much to provoke his final rejection. Third, wartime conditions confirmed that the Admiralty made the right choice. In the Run to the South, Beatty's gunnery defeat was due not to his fire control but to poor training, a badly handled approach and subsequent confusion in his line; the outcome would probably have been even worse had his battlecruisers depended on the Argo true-course plotter rather than Dreyer rate plots.

Although their debt to Service antecedents should be recognised, Pollen and Isherwood deserve full credit for many outstanding technical innovations; the idea of plotting own and enemy courses: the gyro-stabilised rangefinder mounting: the first electrically powered clock: Isherwood's beautiful slipless variable-speed drive and the automatic Argo clocks that used it so elegantly: and the true-course plotter, which, even if it did not work too well, was undoubtedly an outstanding piece of mechanical design. Pollen seems to have contributed fully to the conceptual ideas on which the Argo system was based. In contrast, many of the important features of the Original Dreyer Table were due to others – Norman, Peirse and W. W. Fisher, probably Gunner Newland – who were rarely given their proper recognition by Dreyer himself. Nevertheless, Frederic and John Dreyer had devised the rate plots, and Frederic alone had shown how the Dumaresq could keep the rates in a turn. And Frederic still deserves to be credited with the conception of the complete fire control table as an integrated system, combining connected elements for plotting, rate-determination, rate-keeping and range generation. Elphinstone then turned the initial concept into a working system. However, after the Original Table, the designs of the later tables were largely the work of Elphinstone and his designers at Elliott Brothers – in particular, the ingenious two-axis follower of the Electrical Dumaresq. Keith Elphinstone should now be recognised as an accomplished and original engineer: though he did not, I think, have quite the genius of Harold Isherwood.

The roles played by the DNOs who dealt with Pollen should also be reassessed. Barry was personally hostile. Jellicoe was at first sympathetic to Pollen's financial expectations, but later became impatient with the inventor's negotiating stance. Bacon was sceptical of the value of complex instruments in general and of the whole Argo system, but he came to favour a production order for the rangefinder mounting. This was placed by Moore on terms that covered Argo's costs both of production and of running the company for the next three years. Moore then sought to encourage competition between Pollen's system and the developing Dreyer system. However, by the time that Moore was promoted to Controller, he was determined that, in future, Argo must supply the Admiralty on normal, commercial terms. It was not until Pollen refused to accept such a change that Argo's long relationship with the Admiralty ended in acrimony.

The full revisionist case depends on the detailed, interlocking arguments that have been presented in this book. But there is a final issue that must be faced: why are my conclusions so different from those previously reached or accepted? When, around 1980, Pollen's case was once more taken up by Jon Sumida and Anthony Pollen, the latter attached particular significance to the interjections of one of the members of the Royal Commission, Mr A. M. Langdon KC, on the thirteenth (penultimate) day of the 1925 hearing. Without any justification that I have been able to find, Langdon inferred –

from the correspondence between Dreyer and Elphinstone about the Original Table (the last letter, from Elphinstone, was dated 4 July 1911) – that both men had been fully informed by Henley about the Argo proposal for the Mark II Clock. Anthony Pollen repeated this conclusion, though he also rearranged Langdon's several utterances, albeit without altering the sense, into a single, more coherent speech.[25] This whole passage from *The Great Gunnery Scandal* was then cited in *In Defence of Naval Supremacy* as an important part of the justification for claiming that 'Elphinstone . . . in October 1911 with Henley examined both the clock . . . and all the drawings'.[26] Anthony Pollen printed the whole of the RCAI's 'Recommendation' as an appendix to his book, though neither he nor Sumida attached any importance to the Commission's acquittal of 'all concerned of any intention or desire to copy'. Likewise, neither author raises any doubts about the other conclusions of the Commission, perhaps because the characteristics and history of the Dreyer Tables were not then clearly understood.

As well as drawing on Anthony's book, Professor Sumida also enjoyed complete access to Arthur's papers, including the private correspondence. With good reason, Sumida has placed his publications among the 'new model monographs', which are 'based on the use of a wide range of previously unexploited sources' and directed towards 'the integrated examination of the technical, personnel, economic, administrative, and financial factors in order to reinterpret the course of policy-making and its consequences in operations'.[27] Even so, he describes events and adopts assessments, both technical and personal, largely from Pollen's viewpoint, that of a struggling inventor battling to overcome the Admiralty's parsimony and technical conservatism and the opposition of the responsible officers, Bacon and Moore in particular.

This book has tried to show that the Admiralty's perspective was very different; the Admiralty saw a repeatedly over-optimistic promoter who often delivered late or not at all, regularly demanded large sums for his inventions, and threatened to take his (and, later, the Admiralty's) secrets abroad if he did not get his way. Extensive use has been made here of an important source that has not been cited in earlier works: the RCAI files in the Public Record Office relating to the claims of Pollen and Dreyer. They include the record of Pollen's first, unsuccessful appearance in October 1923, and Argo's own financial accounts. Further, as well as Pollen's official correspondence with the Admiralty (as cited by Sumida from the Pollen Papers), these RCAI files also contain many essential Admiralty documents, including those relating to the development of the Dreyer Tables. This book has also drawn on surviving technical documents (e.g. handbooks, reports, patents British and American) and on the Admiralty records (many of which were first identified by Sumida) that chronicle the development of long-range gunnery in the Royal Navy after 1900.

These sources have been invaluable in clarifying the relative chronologies for the development of the three British fire control systems and in comparing their technical characteristics. The first was the initial manually worked Service system which, although far from automatic, introduced many of the essential instruments. Their capabilities, and the different ways in which they were invented and procured, establish the technical and administrative context against which the rivalry between Pollen and Dreyer, Isherwood and Elphinstone, and Argo and Elliott Brothers, was played out. The second system is Pollen's A.C. The designs of the various clocks and plotters have been considered in sufficient technical detail to verify their actual functional characteristics and limitations. Also, the Admiralty's long and frequently stormy commercial relationship with Pollen has been contrasted with its generally easy and informal dealings with other supplier companies, including Elliott Brothers. Third, the chronological development of the Dreyer Tables, the principal characteristics of the different marks, and the inventions contributed by Dreyer himself, Elphinstone and others, have been described in more detail than previously, though some aspects unfortunately remain obscure, particularly the installation dates for the Mark I tables. It turns out that Pollen's unfavourable assessments of rival designs, and his overstated claims for his own, should be treated more sceptically than hitherto when making comparisons of the competing fire control systems.

Wherever possible, these comparisons have been extended beyond subjective, qualitative judgements to more objective quantitative analysis. In particular, the errors of the actual plotters and clocks have been related, on the one hand, to the inherent errors in the target and ballistic data on which they depended – especially inaccurate rangefinder ranges, and bearings imperfectly corrected for yaws or turns. And, on the other, to the errors that were acceptable in sight-setting – these last being determined by the minimum corrections that were practicable when applying the final spotting corrections that were necessary to hit, and to keep hitting. Thus, in practice, the errors inherent in the disc-and-roller mechanisms of the Vickers clock and the Dreyer/Elphinstone clocks were unimportant, and the stepwise, manual transfer of rates from the Dumaresqs to the clocks of the Dreyer Tables Mark I and III did not introduce significant errors. The quantitative approach has also been used wherever possible in discussing the consequences in the battles of the First World War of the Admiralty's choice of the Dreyer Tables. However, especially for Jutland, the necessary data could be found only by turning to many of the surviving primary sources, notably gunnery records, action reports and navigational and signal records. These sources were vital in understanding the gunnery problems inflicted on Beatty's ships by his tactics during the Run to the South. Furthermore, the same sources have provided important insights into Beatty's leadership of the Battle Cruiser Fleet during the subsequent phases of the battle.

## THE SIGNIFICANCE OF FIRE CONTROL

Although the influence and impact of fire control itself was not always exerted as has previously been supposed, nevertheless this reinterpretation of the Pollen/Dreyer controversy has proved relevant to questions of wider significance in naval history.

At no stage did fire control – whether developed by the Royal Navy or by Pollen – have any discernible influence on Fisher's dreadnought policy. Without doubt, all-big-gun ships, especially the lightly protected armoured cruisers, needed to be able to fire with good effect at long range. Yet, in early 1905 when the Committee on Designs was working out the details of *Dreadnought* and the *Invincibles*, the Royal Navy had remarkably little experience of firing heavy guns at long range (then regarded as about 8,000 yards), especially in salvoes. Also, the only available fire control instruments were the Mark I Dumaresq, Barr & Stroud 4½-foot rangefinders, and the same firm's early transmitters and receivers. All that was certain was that new and better instruments were in prospect – gunsights, the Scott/Vickers range clock, more accurate rangefinders and improved instruments for communicating data and orders. Perhaps Lord Kelvin mentioned Pollen's pamphlet of December 1904 to his committee colleagues.[28] But it was no more than the inventor's first credible proposal for a fire control system, of which only one part, the least difficult technically, yet existed. If Pollen had any influence at all, it can only have been by adding to the general optimism (mainly justified in the event, though no thanks to Pollen) that, by the time the new ships were ready, a satisfactory system would have been devised. The only time when Pollen's ideas might have had an impact on dreadnought policy came in mid-1906, at the time when Jellicoe was being persuaded that Pollen should be awarded a new and potentially lucrative contract. During discussions about possible designs for the 1907–8 programme, the DNO assumed that the newly proposed rangefinder mounting and automatic plotter would enable ships with 13.5-inch guns to out-range less heavily armed opponents.[29] But this decisive increase in calibre could not then be justified, and it was not made until the *Orion* and *Lion* classes were authorised in 1909. At the beginning of that year, Pollen had submitted the description of the complete A.C. system and had given the misleading impression, at least to some officers, that the clock was capable of keeping the range while its ship was manoeuvring. Perhaps this claim raised hopes that the new battlecruisers could hit while avoiding enemy fire,[30] but it is unlikely to have had any influence on Fisher. Quite apart from his animosity towards Pollen, in October 1909, after the *Lions* had been approved, Jackie was enthusing that 'the new system of Fire Control [which probably refers to that described in the 1909 fire control pamphlet] is quite excellent and knocks Pollen into smithereens'.[31]

This book has also concluded that the characteristics of the Dreyer Table do not, after all, explain away Beatty's decisive gunnery defeat during the Run to the South. Of the many actual causes, some were unavoidable disadvantages, like poorer light and deteriorating visibility. His windward position created a tactical problem, but not an insoluble one. But, before sighting the enemy, Beatty had not concentrated his squadrons, while both his approaches were too precipitate. Thus, in both phases, he failed to form an orderly line-of-bearing and some ships were hampered by their consorts' smoke. Mistakes in fire distribution were made by both sides, but only the Germans' concentration on *Queen Mary* was effective. With the exception of *Princess Royal* at the outset, British rangetaking was poor throughout. Faulty tactics, aggravated by inadequate training, deprived Beatty's fire control tables of the first essential of fire control, sufficient accurate ranges. The failures were not in technology, but in command.

It has also emerged that Beatty's own account in his despatch of the approach to the Run to the South is decidedly at variance with other sources, even the VABCF's own 'Narrative'. This realisation encouraged a more sceptical examination of his whole despatch and a comparison with other accounts, particularly the reports and charts in the *Official Despatches*. These sources have suggested some significant amendments to widely accepted navigational details of the Jutland battle. They also led back to four controversial issues that were first raised by Beatty soon after the battle; ever since, these issues have tended to obscure his real failings – though no direct evidence has been found that they were a deliberately laid smoke-screen. First, he blamed Evan-Thomas entirely for the delay in turning about to follow the battlecruisers to the SSE after 2.32, and, consequently, for the 5BS being too distant to support the battlecruisers during the first phase of the Run to the South. The real fault was that, between 2.40 and 3.30, Beatty did nothing to concentrate his squadrons in line, thus throwing away his great superiority in fire power and leaving too little time to form line. Second, Beatty's vehement denials that *Lion* turned through thirty-two points at about 7 o'clock may not have convinced many historians, but little notice has been taken of his failure to respond to *Falmouth*'s report some fifteen minutes earlier. Third, Beatty's criticisms of Jellicoe's turn away from the German torpedoes ensured that the BCF's negligible contribution to driving off the enemy attacks has been largely overlooked. Fourth, the complaints about lack of support from the 2BS obscured Beatty's own failure to keep his forces in contact with the enemy.

Thus what began as an investigation of fire control at Jutland has led to a critical reappraisal of Beatty's tactics and leadership in action. As the First World War ground on, the British people badly needed a naval hero, and Beatty, square-jawed, handsome and with cap rakishly atilt, certainly looked the part. But, among fighting admirals, he cannot be ranked highly. At the

Dogger Bank, *Lion* bravely bore the brunt of the action, mainly because Beatty had been unable to find a tactical solution that made effective use of his whole force; furthermore, the confusion that ended the chase was induced by Beatty himself when he already had no option but to relinquish command. At Jutland, in the Run to the South, Beatty twice handed the gunnery advantage to Hipper, with disastrous results. On the Run to the North, he left the 5BS unsupported to face the whole enemy battlefleet, while, for the remainder of the battle, the reality of his leadership fell far short of his carefully cultivated image. But this image was probably of considerable help in his two great achievements; as C.-in-C., he sustained the morale of the Grand Fleet for the remainder of the war, and, as First Sea Lord, he successfully defended the Royal Navy in the period of post-war disarmament.[32] Beatty must therefore still be regarded as a figure of some stature among British naval leaders.

## THE ROYAL NAVY AND TECHNOLOGY

As well as its importance to tactics and command, the history of British fire control also retains its relevance to the Royal Navy's response to technological innovation. But earlier studies have been unduly dominated by the one-sided accounts of two exceptional individuals, Percy Scott and Arthur Pollen, who, though for different reasons, came to detest the Admiralty. Thus Scott's memoirs have been taken as evidence of the Admiralty's 'usual opposition to all innovation'.[33] Yet the Admiralty fully supported the development of the production Director; it was not a case of too little, too late but of successful innovation against considerable technical obstacles. Also, it has been suggested that the decision to reject Pollen's system was made in ignorance by admirals unable to understand what was at issue, and that the supposed defects in the Dreyer Tables confirmed the scientific and technical backwardness of British industry. Whereas, in reality, the Admiralty was prepared to support Pollen over many years and to treat his case as exceptional. The final breech with Argo did not follow the perverse rejection of a technically superior fire control system; it was the result of reasoned choices between two systems offering distinct functionality, and between two suppliers with very different commercial relationships with the Admiralty.

Thus fire control was actually one more area of technology in which the Admiralty was open to innovation. However, the means to turn inventions into serviceable weapons or instruments remained much the same as they had been since the introduction of steam propulsion. In a few cases, the Royal Navy was prepared to support pioneering research, examples being Froude's on hydrodynamics and Jackson's on wireless.[34] Some development work was also done by the dockyards or the specialist establishments. But such work usually had to be accommodated in ad-hoc ways within the established organisational structures and budgets. In the main, the Royal Navy did not undertake the research and development demanded by unproven inventions. It remained a user, not a creator, of technology because it could rely on its industrial suppliers to meet its technological needs. Some examples from the start of the twentieth century: industry supplied the Navy with machinery of all types (notably engines, including the new Parsons turbines), turrets, heavy guns, armour, shell cases,[35] and rangefinders. The last came from Barr & Stroud, a firm that had developed its own technology and was able to make good profits in supplying not only the Royal Navy but many foreign navies too.[36] The Admiralty was also prepared to adopt technology that had originated abroad, at least if it was supplied through a British-based licensee or subsidiary; examples include the Anschütz and Sperry gyrocompasses, and the Curtis-Brown impulse turbine.[37] This was but one way of achieving what the Admiralty always preferred where possible: supply from more than one firm in order to promote effective competition, in both technology and price.[38]

The Navy could also rely for innovative ideas on its well-educated specialists, notably gunnery officers like Dreyer. However, attempts to develop these ideas within the Service, especially when the technology was unfamiliar, were often unsuccessful. The more effective policy was, if necessary, to protect the idea by secret patent, and then hand development to industry, as was done to good effect in the cases of Scott, Dumaresq and Dreyer himself. The Admiralty then had a strong say in the level of profit allowed on top of the firm's development and production costs.

There are interesting comparisons between the British and German approaches to innovation in fire control. Germany also adopted at least one invention by a gunnery officer, Paschen of the *Lützow*, and it would be surprising if there were not others. But rather than promoting competition between firms, *dirigiste* Germany assigned the development of her naval fire control system to one firm, Siemens & Halské – though, of course, Zeiss supplied the rangefinders and, probably, other optical components as well. The result was undoubtedly very effective. But, at Jutland, only British ships were provided with a full elevation-and-training Director and, as far as is known, no other navy had fire control plotters and predictors as sophisticated as the Dreyer Tables Mark IV. Once the United States entered the war, Admiral William S. Sims found:

a number of things . . . in the Grand Fleet in which we are very distinctly inferior. This includes such fundamentally important things as fire control, concentration and so forth . . . the British are very distinctly in advance of us in their application of electricity to fire control.[39]

Of course, the cooperation of Admiralty and British industry was not always successful. In gunnery, the most notable failure, which may have been complicated by the divided responsibility between the Admiralty and the Ordnance Board, was in the provision of armour-piercing shell. The full explanation is still elusive, though one factor appears to have been a lack of conviction within the NOD that the triple problems of shell case, burster and fuse could be solved.[40] In fire control itself, the 15-foot rangefinder might have been introduced more quickly, though Barr & Stroud was also slow in obtaining the hoped-for improvement in accuracy. Both failings occurred during Moore's time as DNO and Controller, and must be set against his successes, notably the introduction of the 15-inch gun and, I would aver, the Director and the Dreyer Tables. By relying principally on industry for design and development, and on *Excellent* and *Vernon* for evaluation and testing, the development of fire control, for most of the pre-war period, could be coordinated from the Admiralty by just one of the DNO's assistants. When appointed, each officer was a gunnery lieutenant showing particular promise, and a sufficient overlap was arranged with his predecessor (at least in the cases of Henley and Usborne) to give more continuity in experience and policy than has previously been supposed.[41] This minimal establishment achieved much, but it did depend on each officer in the chain of command to the Controller pursuing every initiative with sufficient vigour.[42] At times, the burden was too great.

But failures may also have been due, at least in part, to the flawed structure of the pre-war Admiralty. There was no part of the organisation responsible for representing the interests of users of weapons and instruments against those of the supplier departments reporting to the Controller. The user role was performed, though in no systematic way, by the Inspector of Target Practice (until the post was abolished in 1913),[43] and by the fleet Commanders-in-Chief. Their criticisms and demands sometimes stimulated improvements or the introduction of new instruments. However, until the creation of a proper naval staff, the Controller's departments had, as best they could, to identify requirements, procure the equipment and, with the assistance of Gunnery and Torpedo Schools, assess its performance. It is interesting, in view of his involvement (in several ways) on the supplier side, to find Frederic Dreyer as the first holder of the staff post of Director of Naval Artillery and Torpedoes, later Director of the Gunnery Division. While the Grand Fleet remained in being, Beatty and Chatfield were very reluctant to give up their prerogative to represent the gunnery user afloat,[44] but, after the war, the technical divisions which reported to the Assistant Chief of Naval Staff became fully responsible for requirements so that:

The material side of the Admiralty became, as it should be, not the master but the skilled servant of the Fleet itself.[45]

The small Admiralty organisation that was responsible for material procurement, and its reliance on industry for much research, design and development, was squarely in the tradition of British *laissez-faire*. As it had done in the Victorian era, in the period before the First World War the Royal Navy continued with these established and largely successful methods and used them in the development of its long-range fire control system. The Admiralty was prepared to treat Pollen as an exceptional case, but only until it was clear that more usual methods had produced different solutions that were fitter in meeting operational needs. In fire control, as in other naval technologies, the Royal Navy's record of innovation (though not perfect, an unreasonable expectation of any human institution) compares very well with the navies of other countries.

Without the distorting influence of the self-serving accounts of Pollen and Scott, (reminiscent of those by other disappointed engineers or disgruntled officers from the Victorian period) the true nature of this older British way of innovation can now, I hope, be more clearly perceived. During and after the First World War, Admiralty policy on research and development changed profoundly as it set up its own research establishments and even its own fire control design section.[46] Today, many of those establishments have been closed or privatised; research, as well as design and development, is subject to the rigours of the market, and, once again, the Royal Navy must often look to its suppliers for innovation. So perhaps there may even be some contemporary lessons in the story of how British dreadnoughts got their fire control.

## Notes

1  Especially if, as is probable, they were equipped with the earlier Argo mounting with the air-driven gyro, which stabilised only against yaw.
2  If it took between 5 and 10 seconds to read off and plot a range from a rangefinder receiver, the true range would have fallen meanwhile by some 70–140 yards,
3  The lagging error was mentioned but not quantified in *IDNS*, p. 300.
4  The enemy bearings recorded in *Lion*'s TS indicate a maximum rate of turn of 18°/min., which implies maximum rates of change of range-rate of 256 yds/min/min. and of speed-across of 1.65 knots/min. With the follow-the-pointer arrangements for range-rate, there should have been no problems in adjusting the range-rate in steps of 25 yds/min. at intervals of no less than 6 seconds. Thus the error-rate was 12½ yds/min. and the range error 75 yards after 6 minutes. Since more than a minute separated each 2-knot change of speed-across, there was plenty of time to convert each new speed-across to bearing rate. But a 25-yard contingency has been added to allow for any errors in range arising from small, uncorrected bearing errors. For the equations for rate of change of rates in turns, see 'FCBD', Appendix III.
5  Admiralty, Gunnery Branch, *Spotting Rules 1916*, p. 4 in Ja 011, AL.
6  Between 3.53 and 3.55, *Princess Royal* fired two salvoes at 12,800 yards: 'Record of Action' in *OD*, p. 388. From *Derfflinger*, the range fell to 11,300 metres

(12,350 yards) before, at 3.55, she fired at 11,500 metres (12,575 yards): von Hase, *Kiel and Jutland* [B] pp. 145, 147 and 152.

7 'Navigating Officer of H.M.S. *New Zealand*', in Fawcett and Hooper, *The Fighting at Jutland* [B] p. 39.

8 Admiralty, Gunnery Branch, *Progress in Gunnery Material 1922 and 1923*, p. 41, ADM 186/259.

9 The apertures of Barr & Stroud rangefinders was not increased until the FX models first ordered in 1917: Admiralty, Technical History Section, *The Technical History and Index . . . 1919*, 'Fire Control in H.M. Ships' (TH23) p. 33, AL.

10 John Bradley, 'The History and Development of Aircraft Instruments – 1909–1919' (Imperial College London: PhD thesis, 1994) pp. 196–9 (copies gratefully acknowledged). Pollen's first known patent on aircraft instruments (125,467 of 1916) was for ground-speed measuring apparatus, taken out (with a C. B. Chicken) on 17 August.

11 Wm Brookes & Son, Preliminary Statement, December 1920; V. W. Baddeley to RCAI Secretary, 28 April 1921; A. H. Pollen to Admiralty Secretary, 20 December 1918; all in T.173/91 Part II.

12 T.173/547 Part 2, pp. 2 and 11. The minutes of the 1923 hearings are in Parts 1–3, those for 1920 in Parts 4–5.

13 RCAI, 'Claim No. 1451, Recommendation', 17 October 1923, T.173/91 Part XI.

14 Wm Brookes & Son to RCAI Secretary, 5 December 1924, T.173/91 Part I.

15 Minutes of proceedings in T.173/547 Parts 6 to 19.

16 'Royal Commission on Awards to Inventors. Claims of Argo Company and A H Pollen, Rear Admiral Dreyer and Major Dumaresq. Recommendation', 30 October 1925 in DRYR 2/2. Reproduced in Anthony Pollen, *Great Gunnery Scandal* [B] pp. 252–5.

17 T.173/547, Part 18, p. 3; see also p. 11 and Part 17, pp. 89 and 111.

18 'RCAI Recommendation', 1925 [16].

19 T.173/547, Part 18, p. 11.

20 T.173/547, Parts 18 p. 59 and Part 19, p. 70.

21 For reasons that are unclear, the chairman was reluctant for counsel to discuss the Mark III table, stating 'it is not the Mark III that is the important thing but the Mark IV and Mark V': T.173/547 Part 18, pp. 57–8 and 81.

22 Only the 1912 proposal has been found in the evidence bundles.

23 Minute to chairman signed 'PTR 20.10.25' in T.173/91 Part VIII.

24 'Pamphlets on the Dreyer Tables Mark III* and IV* and the Turret Dreyer Table' in 'Guard Book for Pamphlets on Dreyer Tables', AL.

25 Compare *Great Gunnery Scandal* [16] pp. 136–7 with T.173/547 Part 18, p. 104. Arthur Pollen's belated claims about Elphinstone's alleged visits to York were made immediately after Langdon's intervention.

26 *IDNS*, pp. 219 and 275 (note 164).

27 J. T. Sumida and D. A. Rosenberg, 'Machines, Men, Manufacturing, Management and Money . . .', in John B. Hattendorf (ed.) *Doing Naval History, Essays towards Improvement* (Newport, RI: Naval War College Press, 1995) p. 30.

28 *IDNS*, p. 100.

29 DNO's minute, 21 June 1906 in Ships' Cover 223 (untitled), NMM.

30 As suggested in John Brooks, 'All-Big-Guns: Fire Control and Capital Ship Design 1903–1909', *War Studies Journal*, Vol. 1, Iss. 2 (1996), pp. 47–9.

31 *IDNS*, pp. 161–2 quoting Fisher to Hurd, 29 October 1909.

32 Roskill, *Beatty* [B] pp. 245–6 and 359–60.

33 *Ibid.* p. 63.

34 David Brown, *Warrior to Dreadnought* (London: Chatham, 1997) pp. 70–1. Hugh Lyon, 'The . . . Admiralty and private industry . . .', in B. Ranft (ed.) *Technical Change and British Naval Policy, 1860–1939* [B] pp. 44–5. Arthur Hezlett, *The Electron and Sea Power* (London: Peter Davies, 1975) pp. 27–37.

35 Lyon [34] pp. 46–52, though superseded in some details, provides a good summary.

36 By the outbreak of the war, the firm was on the verge of producing its own fire control table, which probably used a form of rate plotting. Subsequently, Barr & Stroud also supplied the Royal Navy with small numbers of its ROCORD (Rate of Change of Range and Deflection indicator), which combined the functions of the Dumaresq and a transmitting range clock. Michael Moss and Iain Russell, *Range and Vision* (Edinburgh, 1988) pp. 87–8. Admiralty, *Pollen Aim Correction System. General Grounds of Admiralty Policy and Historical Record of Business Negotiations*, February 1913, p. 19. Patent 1510/1911.

37 David Brown, *The Grand Fleet. Warship Design and Development 1906–1922* (London: Chatham, 1999) pp. 20–1.

38 For Admiralty encouragement of competition in boiler supply, see Roberts, *Battlecruisers* [B] p. 72. However, competition in gun mountings to Vickers and EOC from Coventry Ordnance Works did not have the desired effect on price: *DNOfS*, May 1912, p. 6.

39 Michael Simpson (ed.) *Anglo-American Naval Relations 1917–1919* (London: NRS, 1991) p. 330 (reference courtesy of the editor).

40 *FDSF III*, pp. 204–7. Iain McCallum, 'The Riddle of the Shells . . . 1882–1914', in Antony Preston (ed.) *Warship 2002–2003* (London: Conway Maritime Press, 2003) pp. 17–19 and *idem*, 'Achilles Heel? Propellants and High Explosives, 1880–1916', *War Studies Journal*, Vol. 4, Iss. 1 (1999), pp. 70–2.

41 *IDNS*, p. 334.

42 In addition to naval ordnance, the Controller was also responsible for torpedoes, mines, ship construction, naval engineering, etc. Chatfield, *Navy and Defence* [B] pp. 190–1.

43 *IDNS*, p. 246.

44 Brooks, 'Admiralty Fire Control Tables' [B] p. 69.

45 Chatfield [42] pp. 170–1 and 190–3.

46 Willem Hackmann, *Seek and Strike. Sonar, Anti-submarine Warfare and the Royal Navy* (London: HMSO, 1984) Chapters II and V. Brooks, 'AFCTs' [44] p. 75.

# APPENDIX

## THE FIRE CONTROL EQUATIONS

Resolve enemy speed and own-speed reversed along and across the line-of-sight (see Figure A.1). The speed-along *a* and the speed-across *x*, both in knots when *e* and *s* are in knots, are:

$$a = e \cos \iota - s \cos \beta$$
$$x = e \sin \iota + s \sin \beta$$

The range-rate is:

$$\frac{dR}{dt} = 33.78 \, a \text{ yds/min.}$$

Even if own ship is changing course, the rate of change of enemy compass-bearing is:

$$\frac{d\chi}{dt} = \frac{1935 \, x}{R} \, °/\text{min.}$$

When own course is steady:

$$\frac{d\beta}{dt} = \frac{d\chi}{dt}$$

and the rate of change of range-rate is:

$$\frac{d^2R}{dt^2} = \frac{1141 \, x^2}{R} \text{ yds/min/min.}$$

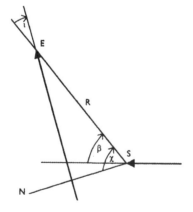

E is enemy ship, speed e knots.

S is own ship, speed s in knots.

ι is the inclination.

β is the enemy bearing relative to own course.

χ is the enemy compass bearing.

Angles are positive when measured clockwise, like compass bearings.

R is the enemy range in yards.

*Figure A.1* Courses, bearings and inclination.

# SELECTED BIBLIOGRAPHY

## ABBREVIATED SOURCES

### Unpublished

#### *Admiralty Historical Library* [AL]

DNOfS     *Paper prepared by the Director of Naval Ordnance and Torpedoes for the Information of his Successor.*
– January 1901, December 1903, February 1905, July 1907, November 1909 and May 1912.

'IQ/DNO'    Important Questions dealt with by D.N.O. Copies, Precis, etc.
– Vol. I – 1912, Vol. II – 1913, Vol. III – 1914.

'MR/DNO' Monthly Record of Principal/Important Questions dealt with by Director of Naval Ordnance
– volumes from 'January to June 1918' until 'July 1923 to June 1926'.

SPG        Admiralty, Gunnery Branch, *Half Yearly Summary of Progress in Gunnery, No. 7, July 1906* to *No. 14, January 1910* and *Annual Summary of Progess in Gunnery, 1910* and *1911*, Ja 238.

#### *Hampshire Record Office* [HRO]

ART       *Annual Reports of Torpedo School 1904–1914* (and other years, all in ART2).

PQ/DNO   *Principal Questions Dealt with by Director of Naval Ordnance, January to December 1905* (PQ16) and *January to December 1906* (PQ17).

#### *Public Record Office* [PRO]

T.173/91    Claims Files for Argo Co. Ltd., Arthur Hungerford Pollen and others, 1919–26 (T.173/91 Parts I to XII).

T.173/547   Minutes of Proceedings. Claims of Argo Co. Ltd., Arthur Hungerford Pollen and others, 1923–7 (T.173/547 Parts 1 to 19).

### Published

FDSF      Marder, Arthur, *From the Dreadnought to Scapa Flow. The Royal Navy in the Fisher Era, 1904–1919* (Oxford University Press)
– Volume I. *The Road to War, 1904–1914* (London, 1961)
– Volume II. *The War Years: to the Eve of Jutland* (London, 1966)

|   | – Volume III. *Jutland and After (May 1916–December 1916)* (Oxford, 1978). |
|---|---|
| *IDNS* | Sumida, Jon, *In Defence of Naval Supremacy. Finance, Technology and British Naval Policy 1889–1914* (London: Unwin Hyman, 1989). |
| 'MoT' | Sumida, Jon, 'A Matter of Timing: The Royal Navy and the Tactics of Decisive Battle, 1912–1916', *Journal of Military History*, 67 (January 2003) pp. 85–137. |
| *OD* | *Battle of Jutland 30th May to 1st June 1916. Official Despatches with Appendices*, Cmd 1068 (London: HMSO, 1920). |
| *PP* | Sumida, Jon (ed.) *The Pollen Papers. The Privately Circulated Printed Works of Arthur Hungerford Pollen, 1901–1916* (London: George Allen & Unwin for the Navy Records Society, 1984). |
| 'QfR' | Sumida, Jon, 'The Quest for Reach: the Development of Long-Range Gunnery in the Royal Navy, 1901–1912', in Chiabotti, Stephen (ed.) *Tooling for War. Military Transformation in the Industrial Age* (Chicago: Imprint Publications, 1996) pp. 49–96. |

### Thesis

| 'FCBD' | Brooks, John, 'Fire Control for British Dreadnoughts. Choices in Technology and Supply' (Kings College London: PhD thesis, 2001). |
|---|---|

## PRIMARY SOURCES

### Unpublished

#### *Churchill College, Cambridge* [CC]

| CLSN | Hugh Clausen |
|---|---|
| DRAX | Admiral Sir Reginald Plunkett-Ernle-Erle-Drax |
| DRYR | Admiral Sir Frederic Dreyer |
| FISR | Admiral Lord Fisher |
| MCKN | Reginald McKenna |
| PLLN | Arthur Pollen |

#### *National Maritime Museum* [NMM]

| BTY | Admiral Earl Beatty |
|---|---|
| CHT | Admiral Lord Chatfield |
| HTN | Admiral Sir Frederick Hamilton |
| THU | Rear-Admiral Henry Thursfield |

#### *Public Record Office* [PRO]

| ADM | Admiralty |
|---|---|
| CAB | Cabinet |
| T | Treasury |

# SELECTED BIBLIOGRAPHY

*Admiralty Historical Library* [AL]

*Imperial War Museum* [IWM]

## Published

Chatfield, Lord, *The Navy and Defence* (London: Heinemann, 1942).

Dreyer, Admiral Sir Frederic, *The Sea Heritage. A Study of Maritime Warfare* (London: Museum Press, 1955).

Fawcett, H. W. and Hooper, G. W. W., *The Fighting at Jutland* (London: Chatham, 2001, first published by Macmillan, 1921).

Von Hase, Commander Georg (trans. Arthur Chambers and F. A. Holt) *Kiel and Jutland* (London: Skeffington & Son, 1921).

Hyde, Viscount (ed.) *The Naval Annual 1913* (reprinted Newton Abbot: David and Charles, 1970).

Patterson, A. Temple (ed.) *The Jellicoe Papers. Volume I, 1893–1916* (London: Navy Records Society, 1966).

—— *The Jellicoe Papers. Volume II, 1916–1935* (London: Navy Records Society, 1968).

Ranft, Bryan (ed.) *The Beatty Papers, Volume I* (Aldershot: Scholar Press for the Navy Records Society, 1989).

Usborne, Vice-Admiral C. V., *Blast and Counterblast. A Naval Impression of the War* (London: John Murray, 1935).


## LATER WORKS

### Books

Beeler, John, *Birth of the Battleship. British Capital Ship Design, 1870–1881* (London: Chatham, 2001).

Brown, David K., *Warrior to Dreadnought. Warship Development 1860–1905* (London: Chatham, 1997).

—— *The Grand Fleet. Warship Design and Development 1906–1922* (London: Chatham, 1999).

Campbell, N. J. M., *Warship Special 1. Battlecruisers* (London: Conway Maritime Press, 1978).

—— *Jutland, an Analysis of the Fighting* (London: Conway Maritime Press, 1986).

Edgerton, David, *England and the Aeroplane. An Essay on a Militant and Technological Nation* (London: Macmillan, 1991).

—— *Science, Technology and the British Industrial 'Decline' 1870–1970* (Cambridge: Cambridge University Press, 1996).

Fanning, A. E., *Steady As She Goes* (London: HMSO, 1986).

Gordon, Andrew, *The Rules of the Game. Jutland and British Naval Command* (London: John Murray, 1996).

Halpern, Paul A., *Naval History of World War I* (London: UCL Press, 1994).

Hartcup, Guy, *The War of Invention. Scientific Developments, 1914–18* (London: Brassey's Defence, 1988).

Hodges, Peter, *The Big Gun* (London: Conway Maritime Press, 1981).

Lambert, Andrew (ed.) *Steam, Steel and Shellfire. The Steam Warship 1815–1905* (London: Conway Maritime Press, 1992).

Lambert, Nicholas, *Sir John Fisher's Naval Revolution* (Columbia, SC: University of South Carolina Press, 1999).

Mackay, Ruddock, *Fisher of Kilverstone* (Oxford: Clarendon Press, 1973).

McConnell, Anita, *Instrument Makers to the World. A History of Cooke, Troughton & Simms* (York: William Sessions, 1992).

McNeill, William. H., *The Pursuit of Power. Technology, Armed Force and Society since A.D. 1000* (Oxford: Blackwell, 1982).

Moss, Michael, and Russell, Iain, *Range and Vision. The First Hundred Years of Barr & Stroud* (Edinburgh: Mainstream, 1988).

Padfield, Peter, *Guns at Sea* (London: Hugh Evelyn, 1974).

Parkes, Oscar, *British Battleships* (London: Leo Cooper, reprinted 1990).

Pollen, Anthony, *The Great Gunnery Scandal. The Mystery of Jutland* (London: Collins, 1980).

Ranft, Bryan (ed.) *Technical Change and British Naval Policy, 1860–1939* (London: Hodder and Stoughton, 1977).

Roberts, John, *The Battleship Dreadnought* (London: Conway Maritime Press, 1992).

—— *Battlecruisers* (London: Chatham, 1997).

Roskill, Stephen, *Admiral of the Fleet Earl Beatty. The Last Naval Hero: An Intimate Biography* (New York: Atheneum, 1981).

Stevenson, David, *Armaments and the Coming of War. Europe, 1904–1914* (Oxford: Clarendon Press, 2000).

Tarrant, V. E., *Jutland. The German Perspective* (London: Arms and Armour Press, 1997).

### Articles and chapters

Brooks, John, 'The Mast and Funnel Question. Fire Control Positions in British Dreadnoughts, 1905–1915', in John Roberts (ed.) *Warship 1995* (London: Conway Maritime Press, 1995).

—— 'Percy Scott and the Director', in David McLean and Antony Preston (eds) *Warship 1996* (London: Conway Maritime Press, 1996).

—— 'The Admiralty Fire Control Tables', in Antony Preston (ed.) *Warship 2002–2003* (London: Conway Maritime Press, 2003).

—— 'The Midshipman and the Secret Gadget', in Peter Hore (ed.) *Patrick Blackett. Sailor, Scientist, Socialist* (London: Frank Cass, 2003).

Dreyer, Admiral Sir Desmond, 'Early Development of Naval Fire Control', *The Naval Review*, July 1986, pp. 238–41.

Lambert, Andrew, 'Responding to the Nineteenth Century: The Royal Navy and the Introduction of the Screw Propeller', in Graham Hollister (ed.) *History of Technology*, vol. 21, 1999 (London: Continuum, 2000).

Lautenschläger, Karl, 'The Dreadnought Revolution Reconsidered', in Daniel Masterson (ed.) *Naval History, The Sixth Symposium of the U.S. Naval Academy* (Wilmington, DE: Scholarly Resources, 1987).

Schleihauf, William, 'The Dumaresq and the Dreyer', *Warship International*, 38, 1–3 (2001).

Sumida, Jon, 'British Naval Administration and Policy in the Age of Fisher', *Journal of Military History*, 54 (January 1990) pp. 1–26.

## Theses

Bradley, John, 'The History and Development of Aircraft Instruments – 1909–1919' (Imperial College London: PhD thesis, 1994).

Clymer, A. B., 'Mechanical Integrators' (Ohio State University: Master of Science thesis, 1946).

# INDEX

*Sub-entries are ordered alphabetically unless a chronological listing appeared to be more appropriate. Ranks and all but a few titles are omitted.*

Lightning Source UK Ltd.
Milton Keynes UK
UKOW06f2325281215

265394UK00001B/19/P